1970

THE CHRISTIAN TRADITION IN
MODERN BRITISH VERSE DRAMA

The Christian
Tradition in
Modern British
Verse Drama:

The Poetics of
Sacramental Time

WILLIAM V. SPANOS

With a foreword by E. MARTIN BROWNE

RUTGERS UNIVERSITY PRESS
New Brunswick, New Jersey

Permission to quote has been kindly granted by the following:

Marie Auerbach—Erich Auerbach: "Figura," in *Scenes from the Drama of European Literature: Six Essays*, tr. Ralph Manheim (New York: Meridian Books, 1959).

Faber & Faber, Ltd., London—W. H. Auden: *For the Time Being: A Christmas Oratorio*, in *The Collected Poetry of W. H. Auden*, 1945. Ronald Duncan: *This Way to the Tomb*, 1946. T. S. Eliot: *The Cocktail Party, The Confidential Clerk, The Elder Statesman, The Family Reunion, Murder in the Cathedral*, Choruses from *The Rock*, in *Collected Plays; Four Quartets, The Hollow Men, The Waste Land*, in *Collected Poems*, 1909–1962. Norman Nicholson: *The Old Man of the Mountains*, 4th impression, 1955. Anne Ridler: *The Shadow Factory*, 1946.

Farrar, Straus & Giroux, Inc., New York—T. S. Eliot: *The Elder Statesman*, copyright © 1959 by T. S. Eliot, reprinted by permission of Farrar, Straus & Giroux, Inc.

Harcourt, Brace & World, Inc., New York—T. S. Eliot: *Collected Poems, 1909–1962, Murder in the Cathedral, The Family Reunion, The Cocktail Party, The Confidential Clerk*, and *The Rock*, copyright, 1935, 1936, by Harcourt, Brace & World, Inc.; copyright, 1939, 1943, 1950, 1954, 1963, 1964, by T. S. Eliot. Reprinted by permission of Harcourt, Brace & World, Inc.

William Heinemann, Ltd., London—Christopher Hassall: *Christ's Comet*, 2d ed., 1958.

David Higham Associates, Ltd., London—Dorothy Sayers: *The Devil to Pay* and *The Zeal of Thy House*, in *Four Sacred Plays* (2nd ed.; London: Victor Gollancz, Ltd., 1957). Charles Williams: *All Hallows' Eve* (London: Faber & Faber, Ltd., 1945), and *The Descent of the Dove* (London: Faber & Faber, Ltd., 1945).

The Macmillan Company, New York—John Masefield: *The Coming of Christ*, 1928. W. B. Yeats: *The Collected Poems of W. B. Yeats*, 1956, and *The Collected Plays of W. B. Yeats*, 1953.

Meridian Books, New York—Erich Auerbach: *Scenes from the Drama of European Literature: Six Essays*, tr. Ralph Manheim, 1959.

Oxford University Press, London—Christopher Fry: *A Sleep of Prisoners*, 1951. Charles Williams: *The Death of Good Fortune, Grab and Grace, The House by the Stable, The House of the Octopus, Judgement at Chelmsford, Seed of Adam, Thomas Cranmer of Canterbury*, in *Collected Plays*, 1963.

Princeton University Press, Princeton, New Jersey—Erich Auerbach: *Mimesis: The Representation of Reality in Western Literature*, tr. Willard Trask, 1953.

Random House, Inc., New York—W. H. Auden: *For the Time Being, A Christmas Oratorio*, copyright 1944 by W. H. Auden; reprinted from *The Collected Poetry of W. H. Auden*.

The Society of Authors, London—Gordon Bottomley: *The Acts of St. Peter: A Cathedral Festival Play* (London: Constable and Company, Ltd., 1933). John Masefield: *The Coming of Christ* (London, The Macmillan Company, 1928); Permission to reprint granted by the Society of Authors and Dr. John Masefield, O.M.

A. Watkins, Inc., New York—Dorothy Sayers: *The Devil to Pay* and *The Zeal of Thy House*, in *Four Sacred Plays* (2nd ed.; London: Victor Gollancz, Ltd., 1957). Charles Williams: *All Hallows' Eve* (London: Faber & Faber, Ltd., 1945); *The Descent of the Dove*, copyright 1939 by Charles Williams (New York: Meridian Books, 1956).

A. P. Watt & Son, London—W. B. Yeats: *The Collected Poems of W. B. Yeats*, 1956, and *The Collected Plays of W. B. Yeats*, 1933. Permission to reprint granted by Mr. M. B. Yeats and Macmillan & Company, Ltd.

To my mother, Mary,
who taught me the meaning of reverence by embodying it

FOREWORD

It is a strange experience to read an analytical account of a movement in which one has been closely concerned. From 1934, when my collaboration with T. S. Eliot began with the creation of *The Rock*, till my production of his *Elder Statesman* in 1958, I lived in the midst of the Christian verse dramatists, finding occasions for the creation of their plays and putting them on the stage. Now I read a book which makes a balanced assessment of the whole body of work, and find myself being carried to the sort of Olympian height from which one looks down upon a landscape in which one has lived.

Is the landscape then deserted? For the moment, yes, almost. More work, further development may well come from Christopher Fry and others of his generation; but for the present their voices are little regarded by a body of critics devoted to pessimist humanism or existentialism, who seem to have an unusual degree of control over a public which, though for the most part it expresses itself as disappointed with current plays, has not the confidence to demand the satisfaction it wants. There is an almost total absence of younger Christian dramatists; so that the succession to Eliot, Charles Williams, and their colleagues is left open, and the movement seems to have halted. If the march is resumed, it will be in a different rhythm.

But if it is, the new marchers will owe a debt to Mr. Spanos. No one has mapped so clearly the course so far taken, or defined the objective so succinctly. His phrase "the sacramental aesthetic," which pervades the book like a recurring leitmotif, and is explored to reveal the salient aspects of its relationship to the Incarnation, will stand, I believe, as a classic definition of the force motivating this group of dramatists. He shows, too, how inherently dramatic this force is, and how it provides the right touchstone for each of the writings he analyzes. I hazard a guess that this is one of the rare books about living authors which will strike most of them as positively just; and that the souls of Charles Williams and Dorothy Sayers will accept it as a step on the Affirmative Way.

For those who do not share its basic assumptions, the book may still have value; for one of the divisive factors in present-day criticism is the inability to do what every actor has to do in every part—agree to stand where his author stands in relation to the character he is playing. Mr. Spanos makes this stance easy for his fellow critics by the clarity with which he expounds his own convictions and relates them to the works he is studying. I hope that they will accept his invitation to try the experiment; and am grateful for the chance he gives me personally to see the work of the two generations of Christian dramatists, between whom it was my good fortune to be born, so that I shared the development of both, in so clear a perspective.

E. MARTIN BROWNE

London,
August 12, 1964

PREFACE

One of the most important ideological revolutions of this most revolutionary of times is that which Christianity has been undergoing in the twentieth century. At its center is the rediscovery and reaffirmation of the integrity as well as the significance of the temporal process. From the beginning of the century, Christian theologians as different from each other as the Anglican William Temple, the Catholic Gabriel Marcel, the Protestant Paul Tillich, and the Orthodox Nicolas Berdyaev have progressively minimized a traditional view of the Christian life which dichotomizes time and eternity and demands the rejection of the realm of the temporal as a means of achieving the real of the eternal. Instead they have increasingly affirmed the view of Christianity which apprehends time as the medium or, more accurately, the process of divine disclosure and thus demands radical commitment to its problematic concreteness.

This revolution in the direction of a new Christian humanism has had a significant influence on modern Christian writers, both poets and critics. What is discoverable as the ideological and aesthetic common ground in the work of Christian poets as different in inspiration and sensibility as Charles Williams, T. S. Eliot, W. H. Auden, David Jones, and Christopher Fry, and Christian literary critics as diverse as Allen Tate, Cleanth Brooks, Denis de Rougemont, William F. Lynch, Nathan A. Scott, Jr., and Walter J. Ong, is, to use Charles Williams' term, the Way of the Affirmation of Images: the ultimate assertion of the integrity and significance of the world, or, better perhaps, the affirmation of the world as a creation. This common thrust of the modern Christian theological and literary imaginations, however, has not yet emerged as a manifest cultural phenomenon. Thus Christian critical theory and art continue, unfortunately, to be viewed from the traditional humanistic perspective which interprets Christianity as positing an attitude *de contemptu mundi* and thus as a body of doctrines that is hostile to art, or, at any rate, the art that celebrates human life. As a result, Christian literary texts—the poems and plays of T. S. Eliot's late period are classic examples—are too often misread as embodiments of the poet's contemptuous rejection of the concrete life of man and are thus judged negatively.

There is a curious irony in this situation that is worth pointing out because of the light it sheds on the historical-cultural context of the Christian verse drama under discussion. In response to the conventional critique of the Christian attitude toward art, it can be said with equal certainty that it is not so much the modern Christian imagination, whether it manifests itself in the form of Paul Tillich's existential theology or T. S. Eliot's sacramental poetry and drama, that is inimical to temporality—the *haecceitas* of the things of this world—and thus to the art that imitates the life of man, as it is that species of the humanistic imagination which, during the time between Descartes and Wittgenstein, has become radically disillusioned in man's ability to achieve dialogue with the world (Sartre's *en soi*) and therefore has come more and more to concentrate its best energies on annihilating time and space (both in form and in content) for the purpose of immobilizing the dreadful process of change and dissolution and of attaining thereby the epiphany of pure timelessness. Confronted by the apparent absorption of physical frontiers into the positivistic urban waste land, this neo-Gnostic imagination, as Nathan A. Scott, Jr., has called it, activated the exploration and mapping of the uncertain boundaries of inner space and thus established the artistic tradition that begins with the exhilarating effort to reaffirm the validity of man's spiritual life and so to rescue art from the narrow confines of naturalism, and in the process develops an attitude that, despite assertions to the contrary, is perilously close to hatred of the phenomenal world and is objectified in a militant aesthetic of anti-art. I am referring, of course, to the tradition that in literature begins with some of the French symbolists (Lautréamont, Mallarmé, Jarry, Rimbaud, for example), extends through the post-symbolists (Proust, Woolf, and Joyce), the surrealists (Breton, Eluard, and Apollinaire), the absurdists (Ionesco, Beckett, and Pinter), to—most recently (and problematically)—the post-surrealist producers of Happenings and of "consciousness-expanding" psychedelic art. I point to this irony not to make qualitative distinctions as such. It would be absurd to minimize the artistic achievements of this tradition. My purpose rather is to suggest the revised perspective from which we must confront contemporary Christian art and criticism if we are to understand it fully and to assess its real worth.

This study of the modern British Christian verse drama movement, then, is not an essay in Christian apologetics. Although I must confess to having an ax to grind, it is not in behalf of one or another religious doctrine, but rather in behalf of the authentic critical enterprise. More specifically, I have tried to make this book a modest contribution to a small but growing body of contemporary criticism that is attempting to reorient an outmoded critical perspective on Christian art for the purpose of securing a just hearing for it. Thus my approach to the verse plays under consideration has been throughout to accept the *donnée* of the Christian poet-dramatist—the Incarnation as the agency of the redemption of time—and my purpose has been to define the strategies he has discovered in the effort to transcend the almost insurmountable problems he encounters when he decides to write verse drama in a fragmented world, and to evaluate the achievement in terms of the degree to which the *donnée* and the finished form of particular plays are organically integrated. I do not pretend that my judgments about particular plays and the movement in general are everywhere sound. I do hope, on the other hand, that I have suggested an avenue of approach that leads more directly than heretofore into the inner precincts of this drama (and incidentally of other modes of the contemporary Christian imagination) where its articulated figure is rooted.

This book owes much to recent scholarship and criticism in a number of fields. The bibliography will suggest the extent to which I have relied on other sources, but I feel that I should acknowledge my special indebtedness to Erich Auerbach's essay "Figura" and his great work *Mimesis,* both of which provided me with essential insights into the nature of the representation of reality, especially of Christian reality, in the Western world; to Francis Fergusson's *The Idea of a Theater,* which is still the best book on the drama written by a modern critic; and to the important work of Nathan A. Scott, Jr., which, by broadening the horizons of literary criticism to include the perilous religious frontiers reached by such theologians as Paul Tillich, Karl Barth, Rudolph Bultmann, and Dietrich Bonhoeffer, has illuminated the meaningful shape of the labyrinthine terrain of modern literature. All three played significant roles in the development of my understanding of the subject of this study. I do not wish to imply, however, that these critics are responsible for the way in which I have used their insights. I can only hope that my appropriations have not radically violated the thrust of their criticism and scholarship.

I cannot begin to acknowledge my personal indebtedness to those who, in one way or another, whether by providing me with necessary information or referring me to relevant scholarship or steering me away from faulty conclusions or warning me against excesses or simply lending a sympathetic ear, aided in the process of bringing this book to completion. However, I wish to offer my special thanks to Professor Paul Wiley of the University of Wisconsin, whose criticism of the manuscript in its early stages helped to clarify an extremely complex subject; to E. Martin Browne, who kindly imparted his immediate knowledge of the contemporary Christian verse drama to me whenever I asked; to the late Mrs. W. M. Thoseby, Steward of the Friends of Canterbury, who graciously provided me with a wealth of information about the history of the Canterbury Festival; to Dr. Hermann Muelder, Dean of Knox College, who obtained for me a generous grant to cover much of the cost of research and typing; to Linda Campbell, a student of mine at Knox College, who not only typed the final version of the manuscript but seems to have enjoyed doing it. I wish also to thank the editors of *The Christian Scholar, Drama Survey,* and *Modern Drama* for granting me permission to use in this book materials that originally appeared in somewhat different form in their journals: the studies of *Judgement at Chelmsford* in *The Christian Scholar*, XLV, 2 (Summer, 1962); of *Murder in the Cathedral* in *Drama Survey*, 3, 2 (Fall, 1963); of *Seed of Adam* in *The Christian Scholar* XLVIX, 2 (Summer, 1966); of *The Family Reunion* in *Drama Survey*, 4, 1 (Spring, 1965); and of *A Sleep of Prisoners* in *Modern Drama*, VIII, 1 (May, 1965).

In a more personal way, I wish to express my gratitude to Thomas Van Laan of Rutgers University, who, during our brief stay at the University of Kentucky, contributed greatly to my understanding of the sacramental imagination in our extended and often heated discussions of the subject; to Jerome Schiller of the Philosophy Department of Washington University in St. Louis and to Samuel Moon and Douglas Wilson of the English Department and Mikiso Hane of the History Department of Knox College, who, during my days at Knox, gave me the encouragement I needed as well as the gift of their friendship. Finally, and, I think, above all, I wish to express my profound gratitude to my wife Margaret, not only for her remarkable patience, which included keeping the children at a distance at the right times, but also for helping to shape my diffuse insights into what I hope is a tolerably articulated whole by vigorously insisting on critical clarity.

WILLIAM V. SPANOS

Harpur College
State University of New York at Binghamton
February, 1967

CONTENTS

What poetry should do in the theatre is
a kind of humble shadow or analogy of the
Incarnation, whereby the human is taken
up into the divine.

T. S. ELIOT,
The Aims of Poetic Drama

. . . if Christianity were not true, it
would have been necessary, for the sake of
letters, to invent it. It is the only safe
means by which poetry can compose the heavens,
without leaving earth entirely out of the
picture. The Incarnation, had it not been
necessary to man's redemption, would have
been necessary to his art. . . .

CHARLES WILLIAMS,
*Reason and Beauty
in the Poetic Mind*

I

MODERN LITERATURE
AND THE BOUNDARY
SITUATION

This is the dead land
This is cactus land
Here the stone images
Are raised, here they receive
The supplication of a dead man's hand
Under the twinkle of a fading star.

T. S. Eliot, "The Hollow Men"

Recent literary criticism has come to recognize that the serious modern writer, whether poet, novelist, or dramatist, confronts his task in complete awareness of the triumph of a secular world view over the traditional Judeo-Christian myth and of the consequent fragmentation of the common system of beliefs and symbols that in the past both unified Western culture and rendered the artistic enterprise a public function. Whatever the reaction to the collapse of Christian culture, whether it manifests itself as an exhilarating awareness of the liberation from form or as a debilitating awareness of imprisonment within the eternal rounds of Nothingness, this criticism has taught us to perceive the resulting literature of crisis, both in its subject matter and in its structure, as an encounter with the apparent meaninglessness of existence in a world in which, to use Nietzsche's phrase, God is dead or, at least, a *Deus absconditus.* The effect of this criticism has been salutary. Not only has it illuminated the difficult predicament of the modern writer but, perhaps more important, it has also revealed a hitherto shadowy dimension of contemporary literature: We are now beginning to perceive the work of art as a metaphor of the universe in which the writer lives—as a microcosm of the macrocosm.

It is remarkable, however, that modern criticism has, on the whole, failed to examine the Christian verse drama in the light of what I would call the existential diagnosis of the contemporary crisis. Whatever the reason for this, whether grounded in the assumption that Christianity is now an anachronism or that a literature which has its source in religious faith is categorically propaganda, the critics have largely ignored this drama or damned it with faint praise, as in the case of T. S. Eliot, whose stature as a poet demands attention. This neglect is unreasonable. For contrary to its alleged "medievalism," the verse drama of T. S. Eliot, Charles Williams, Dorothy Sayers, Christopher Fry, and the others who constitute this literary movement speaks uniquely to the modern predicament. Indeed, both its thematic and its formal sources lie in just as "existential" an awareness of the modern crisis as that of such writers as Jean-Paul Sartre, Albert Camus, Eugène Ionesco, and Samuel Beckett, who have been justly, if rather extravagantly, praised for their courageous confrontation of the contemporary Furies. If, therefore, we are to understand fully the dramatic strategies these poets evolved and to appreciate both their real achievements and their real failures, it becomes necessary, even at the risk of oversimplification, to survey the effects of a thoroughgoing secularism on the character of twentieth-century life, especially in England, and to isolate the basic aesthetic problems it generated.

There had been disillusionment in the promises of science and capitalistic liberalism prior to World War I. To Matthew Arnold, for example, whom Lionel Trilling has identified as "one of the first modern literary men," [1] the industrial city was the new Babel, a symbol of despiritualized man robbed of the means of measuring and articulating value. Although he proposed a return to the Hellenistic principle of order, to the best that had been thought and felt in the history of Western civilization, as an alternative to both the Christian and the scientific methods of confronting the new, it was his great antagonist, Thomas Henry Huxley, who eventually won the great debate in England. The reaction to the clamorous industrial city, in other words, took the form of social amelioration. It too operated on a secular and positivistic level.

Despite voices such as Arnold's, it was not until the outbreak of World War I in all its mechanized and brutally impersonal fury that the artistic and intellectual community in England was finally driven into the discovery of the spiritual waste land that the erosive belief in progress had left behind. The image of the modern desert drawn by the twentieth-century poet is familiar:

> What are the roots that clutch, what branches grow
> Out of this stony rubbish? Son of man,
> You cannot say, or guess, for you know only
> A heap of broken images, where the sun beats,
> And the dead tree gives no shelter, the cricket no relief,
> And the dry stone no sound of water.[2]

> Things fall apart; the centre cannot hold;
> Mere anarchy is loosed upon the world,
> The blood-dimmed tide is loosed, and everywhere
> The ceremony of innocence is drowned: . . .[3]

But the significance of this image of the modern waste land is given greater weight and a wider and deeper context when we recognize that it is essentially this image (in both its dimensions of aridity and of ruin) that existential philosophy has explicated in its important analysis of the contemporary predicament, whether its point of view is the atheism of the early Heidegger, the theism of Jaspers, or the Christianity of Berdyaev and Marcel. It would be as easy to find in passages from these writers a diagnosis of the modern technological world as a spiritual desert as it is to find images of the waste land in the literature of our time. But for the sake of brevity and succinctness I shall restrict such reference to Karl Mannheim's *Diagnosis of Our Time,* the content of which reveals in many respects the influence of existential thought, especially in its critical phase.[4] This choice is not as arbitrary as it may appear to be. For there is every reason to believe that Mannheim's book, indeed the chapter from which the following remarks are chiefly drawn, had a significant influence on T. S. Eliot's reflections on the problem of cultural disintegration precisely at the time he was moving away from a private toward a public art form, that is, the drama.[5]

In this important book Mannheim asserts that a society is organic and creative when its acts are directed by "paradigmatic experiences," those basic and essentially religious events "which carry more weight than others, . . . which are unforgettable in comparison with others that are merely passing sensations," and which are embodied in "primordial images or archetypes" such as "the Hero, the Sage, the Virgo, the Saint, the Repentant; or, dominating the realm of Christian imagination: Baptism, Absolution, Agape, the Eucharist, the Good Shepherd, the Cross, Redemption." Such images establish "an ontological hierarchy of value" that infuses all the concrete facets of life with immediate significance, each according to its degree. This value structure thus dramatizes existence, and in so doing generates the purposeful collective energy that characterizes the organic culture.

When the scientific method is applied to the moral sphere, the paradigmatic experiences are gradually undermined and the hierarchy of values is neutralized. There is justification, Mannheim observes, for examining the experiences of both a saint and a hysteric as examples of psychological mechanisms, but "deliberately to disregard the qualitative differences in these experiences becomes detrimental for society. . . . If there is no paradigmatic experience which induces us to lay different emphasis on the different phases of action, there is no climax towards which action will tend. This not only atomizes the life of the individual and replaces the idea of a character by a kaleidoscopic concept of life; it makes co-ordination of social action equally impossible."

In other words, by rendering all things equally important, moral positivism tends to negate the significance of all things. Our concept of life becomes "kaleidoscopic" and accordingly "our universe of discourse loses its articulation." This, according to Mannheim, is what is occurring in modern Western culture.[6] On the one hand, the ordinary person becomes dehumanized and falls into the hell of boredom (as he does in T. S. Eliot's *The Waste Land* and the novels of Evelyn Waugh). On the other, the sensitive man finds himself an alien in a desacralized and fragmented world, incapable of, in Martin Buber's term, "dialogue," the *I-Thou* relationship with others.[7] If he transcends the threat of dehumanization, he is still left to swim in fear and trembling in the high waters of the chaos of its shattered structures, his survival dependent solely on his limited private spiritual resources. The modern predicament, in other words, constitutes what Karl Jaspers has called "a boundary situation" (*Grenzsituation*), in which man, stripped of protective philosophical or theological systems, naked, unaccommodated, and alone, stands face to face with Nothingness.

This process has its analogy in the province of art. In denying transcendent significance to the things of this world, including human experience, in sundering concrete reality and value, and, ultimately, time and eternity, positivism first gave rise to a naturalistic aesthetic that pays respect to the concrete physical world at the expense of universal value. In reaction against this devaluation of art, the post-World War I poet was driven inward to search in the labyrinth of his consciousness for a personal value structure (and the symbols to express it) capable of interpreting and integrating, at least for himself, the anarchic experience of modern life. He became, as Nathan Scott puts it, "his own priest, his own guide, his own Virgil." [8]

The literature of the period of World War I, in other words, was not merely a reaction against nineteenth-century escapist romanticism, as most critics tend to assume. It was also, and perhaps primarily, a revolt against an emergent naturalism representing in some degree the literary equivalent of the scientific or positivist analysis of experience, as, for instance, Zola's *roman expérimental* and Ibsen's problem plays, and, proceeding from these, the novels of H. G. Wells, Arnold Bennett, and John Galsworthy and the plays of Henry Arthur Jones, Arthur Wing Pinero, Bernard Shaw, and Granville Barker. It was, in short, the result of an effort on the part of that species of perception called by Allen Tate (following Jacques Maritain) the "angelic imagination" to transcend the limitations of a mode of imitation which, based as it was on a positivistic interpretation of existence, was hard put to give the object or event it represented more than documentary status and therefore ephemeral social significance.

Put positively, the "angelic imagination" seeks to discover mean-ing and value in the Daedalian corridors of the individual psyche. It tries "to disintegrate or to circumvent the image in the illusory pursuit of essence. When human beings undertake this ambitious program, divine love becomes so rarefied that it loses its human paradigm, and is dissolved in the worship of intellectual power, the surrogate of divinity that worships itself. It professes to know na-ture as essence at the same time that it has become alienated from nature in the rejection of its material forms." [9] Actually, there are two species within the class of the angelic imagination: the angelic *per se*, which, on the analogy of the unfallen angels, attempts by "pure intelligence" to perceive *at once* the absolute or the essence of things (the imagination of Mallarmé, for example); and the diabolic, which, on the analogy of the fallen angels, perceives the realm of things to be an absolute chaos and concludes that nothing is real except the shaping consciousness of the private self (the imagination of Ionesco, for example).[10] This is a significant dis-tinction, but because it obscures the fact that both the angelic and diabolic imaginations affirm the self over against the concrete world of created things, it is not a useful one for our purposes. It is the solipsistic nature of so much contemporary literature with which we are primarily concerned.

The immediate literary antecedents of angelism lie in the pre-World War I period (though its philosophical roots, as Jacques

Maritain has shown, go back to Descartes [11]). It had its first re-markable flowering in France in the last years of the nineteenth century when the symbolists—Mallarmé, Baudelaire, Rimbaud, Verlaine, and others—turned inward against the scientific natural-ism of Zola and the realism of the Parnassian poets to create an incantatory poetry of sounds and suggestive nondiscursive images.[12] Unable to discover a continuity of meaning in the natural world, the French symbolist gathered the disintegrated and atomized fragments in nature into the alembic of the angelic imagination, which, in turn, transmuted their living substance into a magical formula of words according to his unique sensibility. Characterized by great technical—if often grotesquely manneristic—virtuosity, this poetry is usually capable of real emotional power but rarely of com-munal intellectual significance and thus widens the gulf between thought and feeling, a tendency that T. S. Eliot deplored.

Though much has been said of the influence of the symbolists on English and American poets,[13] the claim that it is the source of the mainstream of modern English poetry is not justifiable. The true, if rather volatile, heirs of the angelistic tradition in the post-war period were the surrealists and Dadaists, Guillaume Apolli-naire, Tristan Tzara, André Breton, Louis Aragon, Paul Eluard, and Philippe Soupault, among others, who transform the proud sym-bolist disdain for nature and conscious thought into arrogant and sometimes vulgar contempt.

In our time, the angelic tradition is manifested in much existen-tial literature, especially in the drama of the absurd of Eugène Ionesco, Arthur Adamov, Samuel Beckett, Harold Pinter, and others. In this drama the imitated action, including the personae and the language they use, bears little resemblance to the world perceived by the feeling–thinking man, the world of which the Aristotelian drama is a microcosm. (This drama is called anti-drama in reaction to the well-made naturalistic play, though ultimately to the Aristotelian definition of drama; this should not be obscured by one's equally strong antipathy toward the bourgeois *théâtre boulevard*.) Assuming the contingency of existence and the aliena-tion of the human consciousness from the objects of nature, including other men, the action is, rather, a projection of the individual playwright's psychic condition and takes the form of a series of logically unrelated images akin to those of the dream state. Like the world he perceives, the action the dramatist imitates is, in the Aristotelian sense of the word, plotless, that is, devoid of the narrative logic, the syntax of events, which is dependent on a commitment to time. If the total image of the imitated action has coherence, it is a coherence of blurred emotion.

The angelic imagination has unquestionably produced a body of great literature, especially of lyric poetry, in our time (though its insistence on the uniqueness and novelty of each work theoretically precludes the possibility of evaluation). But it has done so at a great cost. By destroying the traditional concept of plot and by transforming language into a vehicle for the expression of pure emotion, it has lost poetry its traditional public and rendered its very existence a precarious one. Most relevant to this discussion is its impact on the poetic theater. The drama is generically a preeminently public art form. In order to fulfill its inherent potential it must address an audience which represents a cross section of society through the mediation of recognizably human language and action. Since, however, the angelic imagination "tries to disintegrate or to circumvent the image in the illusory pursuit of essence," it must either abandon the drama as a viable art form or transform its essential nature. This explains, in part at least, why few serious contemporary writers have worked in these forms and why those who have came eventually (like Yeats) or at once (like the dramatists of the absurd) to see the drama as a means of private and timeless lyrical rather than public and time-bound dramatic expression, thus introducing a fundamental aesthetic contradiction into these forms. Further, this contradiction goes far to explain why the typical dramatic product of the angelic imagination from Yeats to the dramatists of the absurd is the short one-act play, and why the full-length work, such as the symbolist *Ubu Roi* of Jarry, the surrealistic *Les Mamelles de Tirésias* of Apollinaire, and the absurd *Amédée* of Ionesco, despite its shocking novelty and its achievement of an integral relationship between form and content, inevitably becomes tedious even to a sensitive and receptive audience. Indeed it is questionable, even if one sympathizes with Ionesco's satire of the fossilized language of the middle class and of its "rationalistic" world (and drama), as to whether or not our sensibilities can endure for the full length of even a short play like *La Cantatrice Chauve* (*The Bald Soprano*) the undifferentiated linguistic discontinuities of the Smiths and the Martins:

MRS. MARTIN   I can buy a pocketknife for my brother, but you can't buy Ireland for your grandfather.

MR. SMITH   One walks on his feet, but one heats with electricity or coal.

MR. MARTIN   He who sells an ox today, will have an egg tomorrow.

MRS. SMITH   In real life, one must look out of the window.

which disintegrates further into this unrelenting non-sense:

MRS. SMITH   Mice have lice, lice haven't mice.

MRS. MARTIN   Don't ruche my brooch!

MR. MARTIN   Don't smooch the brooch!

MR. SMITH   Groom the goose, don't goose the groom.

MRS. MARTIN   The goose grooms.

MRS. SMITH   Groom your tooth.[14]

No better case could be made for Karl Mannheim's cultural and (by implication) aesthetic thesis that the positivistic undermining of the ontological hierarchy of value established by the paradigmatic experiences of a community and of the images from the concrete world that objectify them neutralizes or, better, erodes the humanizing drama of the life of man and the art that imitates that life. If Ionesco's reversion to a more naturalistic form and language or, rather, to the Aristotelian concept of plot in *Tueur sans Gages* (*The Killer*) and *Rhinocéros* is any indication, even he seems to have discovered this truth about the life of man and the dramatic imitation of human events.

The problem confronting the post-World War I Christian dramatist was apparently insurmountable. He had to bridge the gap between the poet and a public that measured human progress and,
ultimately, the stature of man by the standard of a positivistic
analysis of human experience. He had to discover a principle of
imitation that was capable of employing the images of this public
world without reducing poetry to the level of prose, of transfiguring
secular contemporary life into a concrete-universal image and of
charging with new energy and freshness the worn-out traditional
symbols that in the past had objectified the great paradigmatic experiences of Western civilization. In short, his labor consisted of
reconciling angelism and naturalism and of reunifying the dissociated sensibility of modern man.

This task was not simply a matter of arbitrarily asserting the integral relationship of some areas of concrete reality and universal
significance and of leaving out what in the natural world seemed
alien to the Christian world view. What was necessary—and most
difficult—here within the boundary situation was a genuinely existential ontology that could potentially integrate the whole range
of human experience in all its diversity, including the accumulated
knowledge of three centuries of concentrated and accelerating scientific investigation, into a coherent and meaningful pattern. Only
then could a principle of dramatic imitation that pretended to represent contemporary human experience symbolically be justified.

It has been more or less the general tendency of modern criticism
to view the drama of T. S. Eliot, the outstanding theoretician and
playwright of the Christian verse drama movement, as an innovation in that genre, without antecedents. This view is misleading and
obscures the nature of the larger movement of which Eliot is a
part. Falling into that category of criticism that praises a poet
"upon those aspects of his work in which he least resembles anyone
else," it fails to recognize a fundamental principle of Eliot's literary
theory and practice, that the poet, if he is to avoid mere novelty,
must possess a sense of tradition, a perception, not only of the
pastness of the past but of its presence.[15] Such criticism thus tends

to minimize Eliot's real originality and to obscure his conception of the nature and function of poetic drama. There has been considerable commentary on his continuing interest in the Elizabethan dramatists and in the possibilities of a genuine contemporary verse drama. What it does not reveal, however, is that this interest, which is one shared by other dramatists of the Christian verse drama movement, manifests itself as a persistent quest for the essential principle of the popular English dramatic tradition. After tentative starts, this quest culminates in the discovery that this principle lay in what I call the sacramental realism of the medieval miracle plays; that it is grounded in the doctrine of the Incarnation, the Word made Flesh, which reconciles time and eternity and salvages the past from the refuse heap of history, thus allowing the dramatist to synthesize the diverse and transient world of concrete objects and events and the universal and permanent ideas into a multivocal poetic image; that after suffering a process of dissociation in the seventeenth century which gave rise to the naturalistic and angelic imaginations, it had more or less passed out of English drama; and that it had reemerged, albeit in a greatly altered and limited form, in the poetic drama of modern Ireland, particularly in that of W. B. Yeats, who both as a poet and as a dramatist insisted on the necessity of a sacramental view of life in which the things of the natural world are integrally related with a transcendent world order,[16] though in the end this view became a purely personal projection.[17]

What follows constitutes an effort to define the sacramental aesthetic that underlies the Christian verse drama movement and to examine both individually and as a developing movement the verse drama it nurtured. In the second chapter, the aesthetic implications of the doctrine of the Incarnation, particularly as these bear on the dramatist, are fully explored. In the following seven chapters, which are organized according to dramatic forms—the Historical Pageant, the History, the Nativity, and the Play of Contemporary Life—a number of works are analyzed in considerable detail to reveal how the sacramental aesthetic, as it develops from stage to stage—particularly from the representation of historical to contemporary events—affects their form and content. The concluding chapter attempts to evaluate the general achievement of this body of drama and to assess the potential of sacramentalism as a mode of dramatic imitation.

I have chosen to treat a relatively small number of plays individually and in detail rather than a large number in general for two reasons: first, because, with the exception of Eliot's, most of the plays of the Christian verse drama movement are not well enough known to generalize intelligibly about; and second, and more important, because the sacramental aesthetic, insisting as it does on the concrete, is most effectively revealed in the examination of the relationship between the particulars and the whole.

Though the sacramental aesthetic also operates in poetic drama written in prose such as Dorothy Sayers' cycle, *The Man Born to Be King* (1942), Christopher Hassall's Job play, *Out of the Whirlwind* (1953), and perhaps Graham Greene's *The Living Room* (1953), I have confined this study to verse plays. This restriction is not entirely arbitrary. Since the sacramental aesthetic reconciles the concrete and the universal, verse is in the last analysis its natural medium. For only verse is capable of reconciling the particular rhythm of the individual voice and the universal rhythm of the voice of Man.

2

THE INCARNATION: THE SACRAMENTAL AESTHETIC

That which hath been is now; and that which is to be hath already been; and God requireth that which is past.

Ecclesiastes III.15

During Whitsun Week in 1928, John Masefield's religious verse drama *The Coming of Christ*, written at the invitation of George Kennedy Bell, Dean of Canterbury and later Bishop of Chichester, was produced in the nave of Canterbury Cathedral. The production, designed by the noted artist Charles Ricketts and accompanied by the music of Gustav Holst, was a bold gesture on the part of Dean Bell. Not since the Middle Ages had the Church of England opened its doors to the artist. It was the beginning of a project which, by Dean Bell's subsequent founding of the Friends

of Canterbury Cathedral (1928) and the Canterbury Festival
(1929), was shortly to culminate in the Church's sponsorship of
the Christian poet and the development of a genuine Christian
verse drama movement.[1] Following his motion that the Church
continue to encourage the contemporary poet-dramatist, Bishop
Bell, speaking retrospectively before the Upper House of the Convocation of Canterbury in 1958, said that the event "aroused an
immense and nationwide interest, and it might fairly be called a
landmark because it was on the one hand the creation of a new
work of art by three contemporary artists of the front rank at the
invitation of the Church, and on the other hand its production set
the seal of the Mother Church of English Christianity on the
drama as dedicated to the service of God. At that Whitsuntide
1928, 30 years ago, the poet and the artist re-entered the Church." [2]

In the following years this alliance produced a body of verse
drama that, for popularity and genuine artistic merit, ranks as high
as any since the seventeenth century. At first the movement limited
itself to drama written expressly for church production: Pageants
such as T. S. Eliot's *The Rock* (1934), Gordon Bottomley's *The
Acts of Saint Peter* (1933), and Charles Williams' *Judgement at
Chelmsford* (1939); Histories such as T. S. Eliot's *Murder in the
Cathedral* (1935), Charles Williams' *Thomas Cranmer, Archbishop of Canterbury* (1936), and Dorothy Sayers' *The Zeal of
Thy House* (1937); and Moralities such as Williams' *Seed of Adam*
(1936), Christopher Hassall's *Christ's Comet* (1938), and Miss
Sayers' *The Devil to Pay* (1939). After World War II, however,
the movement went into a second phase, extending its boundaries
to include the professional theater. This period saw the development of a "secular" and contemporary Christian verse drama, exemplified by such diverse types as T. S. Eliot's *The Family Reunion*
(1939) and *The Cocktail Party* (1949); Anne Ridler's *The Shadow
Factory* (1945); Charles Williams' *The House of the Octopus*
(1945); Ronald Duncan's *This Way to the Tomb* (1946); Norman
Nicholson's *The Old Man of the Mountains* (1946); and Christopher Fry's *A Sleep of Prisoners* (1952).

The decision of the Church to open its doors to the drama had both a broad cultural and a specific aesthetic significance for the English poet confronting the problem of disintegration in the modern world: It gave him the opportunity to assume a creative cultural function somewhat similar to that enjoyed by the Irish dramatists Synge and Yeats; and it provided him with the grounds for an aesthetic capable of reconciling the dissociated sensibility of modern art without recourse to a private symbolism.

The activity of the Irish theater had clearly shown that the new drama, if it was to achieve public recognition, had to base itself on the central traditions of the people at large. The Georgian poets—John Masefield, Lascelles Abercrombie, Wilfred Gibson, John Drinkwater, and Gordon Bottomley—had found in the return of the Irish playwrights, particularly Synge, to nature and the peasant and to national legend for subject matter the poetry they believed would release the English imagination from its bondage to the commonplace. Unfortunately, they did not heed Synge's warning that unlike Ireland "the springtime of the local life" [3] of England was now but a memory, nor Yeats's remarkable suggestion that the roots of English culture lay in the King James Bible: ". . . it is precisely these stories of The Bible that have all to themselves, in the imagination of English people, especially of the English poor, the place they share in this country with the stories of Fion and of Oisin and of Patrick.

"Milton set the story of Sampson into the form of a Greek play, because he knew that Sampson was, in the English imagination, what Herakles was in the imagination of Greece; and I have never been able to see any other subject for an English dramatist who looked for some common ground between his own mind and simpler minds." [4] It was the Christian narrative that had formed and nourished the English imagination, and it was to this that the English poet would, in one way or another, have to appeal if he was to make contact with the popular imagination of the English people. When the Church endorsed the drama, it thus put at the poet's disposal cultural ground which, though not similar to that cultivated by Synge, was nevertheless analogous to it and certainly had more potential in England.

Both churchman and poet-dramatist were aware, of course, that the Christian sensibility in England had been thoroughly secularized; but they felt that the paradigmatic archetypes of the Christian experience were still alive and responsive to the stimulation of poetry and drama, particularly in those areas where the parish church was still the center of cultural life. And it was their hope that the parish and the drama would interact in such a way as to help recreate not only a vital Christian culture but also a public poetic sensibility that would free the poet from self-consciousness. As T. S. Eliot put it in an address delivered shortly after the production of *Murder in the Cathedral:*

> I like to think that at some time in the future every cathedral will have its own permanent company of amateurs and its own cycle of modern religious plays, and that they will rival each other in perfection of production. . . . Under present conditions, the universal craving for drama is imperfectly satisfied. The theatre—and consequently the standards of audiences everywhere —is excessively metropolitanized. Belated touring companies still carry to provincial centres, not necessarily what is best in London, but what has proved most successful and portable. Mechanization comes to kill local life. . . . Both as a symbol and as a force, what can better represent local life than the cathedral? Each cathedral has its own character and its own tradition, each is the central point of a district with its own character and tradition. A cathedral cannot be packed up and exported in tins; it cannot be communicated on either long or short waves. To experience it you must go to it, to know it you must live with it. This is why I hope that our cathedrals may become centres, each of its own characteristic dramatic activity.[5]

The Church's decision to incorporate theater into its cultural program coincided with the modern poet's growing awareness of the restrictions of a private and subjective mode of discourse and his desire to extend the boundaries of his poetry to include a broader public. In 1933, for example, Eliot, expressing the attitude of an increasing number of poets of the period, wrote: ". . . I believe that the poet naturally prefers to write for as large and miscellaneous an audience as possible. . . . The most useful poetry, socially, would be one which could cut across all the present strati- fications of public taste—stratifications which are perhaps a sign of social disintegration. The ideal medium for poetry, to my mind, and the most direct means of social 'usefulness' for poetry, is the theatre." [6] By the social usefulness of poetry Eliot did not mean, of course, its propagandistic potential. He meant, rather, its ability to address, quicken, and integrate the diverse public sensibility: "I do not mean that [the poet] should meddle with the task of the theologian, the preacher, the economist, the sociologist, or anybody else; that he should do anything but write poetry, poetry not de- fined in terms of something else." [7] Though the Church, by its very nature, conceived of the dramatic enterprise as an activity closer to evangelism than to art, it nevertheless provided the Chris- tian poet with a theater in which he could practice his art publicly.

Prior to the reconciliation of the arts and the Church, the re- lationship between poet and theater in England was more or less nonexistent. The enervated imagination of the general theatergoing public and the consequent grip that the prose drama had on the commercial stage had forced the serious poet either to restrict his creative efforts to private forms (including the closet drama) or, if his interest in the art of drama was insistent, to establish his own private theater, as John Masefield had done at Boar's Hill, Oxford. The latter alternative, which the Georgians finally adopted after their abortive effort to imitate the Irish drama of peasant life, could scarcely accomplish a renewal of verse drama. For the idea of a small private theater, with its necessarily select audience, was itself an admission of the futility of attempting to broaden the base of poetic drama to include the popular elements of discourse—pri- marily the concrete—without capitulating completely to its pres- sure; it was an acceptance, that is, of cultural disintegration as a *fait accompli*. "The theatre," Gordon Bottomley concluded, echo- ing the later Yeats, "is now a nexus of trades, an organism to sup- ply quite other (and often ephemeral) things: and I conceive that in future those who desire dramatic poetry will seek it in places set apart for it. . . ." [8] With the recognition of the drama by the

Church, however, the poet, as Eliot pointed out, was once again given the opportunity to write expressly for the theater and to learn his craft in the only way it can be learned: by the experience of live performance.[9] At the same time it delivered him both from an essentially coterie audience, which tends to demand poetry at the expense of entertainment, and from a strictly commercial audience, which demands entertainment at the expense of poetry. For the church is, in a very important sense, a public theater, the membership representing, to some degree at least, that "large and miscellaneous audience" for which poets, according to Eliot, prefer to write.

It was the hope of churchman and poet that the reconciliation of the Church and the drama would generate a revival of poetic drama not only on the amateur-local but also on the professional-national level. Indeed, Eliot insisted that one of the principle functions of the specifically church drama was to stimulate and to sustain an interest in significant religious subject matter that would eventually influence the professional drama: ". . . if we determine merely to preserve in ourselves two attitudes, one for cathedral drama and the other for West End, we should be dividing our minds unjustifiably and with bad results. We need to strive toward a kind of *reintegration* of both kinds of drama, just as we need to strive toward a reintegration of life." [10] For this reason the Christian verse drama movement at the outset placed considerable emphasis on the ability of religious drama to "amuse"; that is, "to hold the attention, to arouse the excitement, of people who are not religious as well as of those who are—or . . . of people who are not consciously and practically religious, as well as of those who are." [11] And this meant the avoidance of the mere nostalgic medievalism of the earlier church drama in favor of the treatment of religious themes in the light of contemporary knowledge and the use of a medium—form, diction, metric—whose contemporaneity would have a general appeal. The broad strategy of the movement pointed to the eventual reconciliation of poetry and entertainment, of the deep and permanent concerns of humanity and its ephemeral interests, of spiritual and physical reality. This strategy found its aesthetic counterpart in the sacramentalism of orthodox Christianity.

It is true that religious drama, both for commercial and for amateur church production, flourished in England throughout the first thirty years of the twentieth century. From Henry Arthur Jones's defense, "Religion and the Stage" [12] (which represents the beginning of a commercial interest in religion as dramatic subject matter) and William Poel's revival of *Everyman* in 1901 (which represents the beginning of an interest in specifically religious drama) to the production of Masefield's *The Coming of Christ*, literally hundreds of these plays were mounted on the stage. However brief their theatrical life, they no doubt had some influence on Anglican churchmen such as Dean Bell, and hastened the official reunion of the Church and the arts. On the whole, however, the types of drama they embody are fundamentally distinct from that which emerges out of the Canterbury Festival, for the religious assumptions of this drama are essentially sectarian, in line with the secularism that gave impetus to the disintegration of the traditional Christian world view (including its concept of history) and a truly Christian aesthetic, and hastened the decline of poetic drama.

It could not, therefore, employ a Christian scheme advantageously to recreate an authentic poetic drama. The secular religious drama of this period, such as Henry Arthur Jones's *Saints and Sinners* (1884), was reformist and based on a naturalistic aesthetic. In "Religion and the Stage," Jones insists that "In no case could it be profitable for the stage to become the backer or antagonist of any doctrine or creed. But inasmuch as religion is also a matter of conduct and practice and character, the drama has every right to take it for part of its subject-matter." [13] As his emphasis on naturalistic conduct and morality suggests, Jones's religion is primarily a matter of social amelioration. This becomes quite clear in his interpretation of Shakespeare's exemplary "religion," the naturalistic bias of which precludes recognition of the creative use that the Elizabethan makes of "creeds and doctrine": "How small a concern Shakespeare had for creeds and doctrines may best be gathered from the absence of any marked influence upon his plays of the religious struggle which England had passed through in the previous generation. And yet he is steeped in the language and spirit of the Bible. And it is just this attitude of his towards the English Scriptures that fits him to be the representative poet of England. With more care for dogma he might have sunk into the mere poetical figurehead of a sect or a creed; with less care for morality his work would have lacked the deep and permanent foundation that all great art instinctively chooses, of resting upon wide-reaching principles of justice and truth that all human hearts as instinctively recognize and accept." [14] The church drama, on the other hand, was "medieval": sentimental, moralistic, and nostalgic; in short, a vehicle for pious pageantry. Most of both kinds were written, not accidentally, in prose. In verse plays such as Laurence Housman's *Bethlehem* (1902) and A. M. Buckton's *Eager Heart* (1904) the verse, like the religious trappings, is ornamental, a device for impressing the stamp of piety on either a nostalgic backward look or an essentially moral or social message.[15]

What the English poetic drama had need of was an orderly (though not rigid) and public world view from which could be drawn an aesthetic capable of informing the imagery of poetry and the action of drama with transcendent meaning without denying their existential validity and of giving form to the chaotic experience of modern life. Guided by Yeats's example, T. S. Eliot had recognized the problem and had arrived at a partial solution in his early thinking about modern literature: "In using the myth, in manipulating a continuous parallel between contemporaneity and antiquity, Mr. Joyce is pursuing a method which others must pursue after him. . . . It is simply a way of controlling, of ordering, of giving a shape and a significance to the immense panorama of futility and anarchy which is contemporary history. It is a method already adumbrated by Mr. Yeats, and of the need for which I believe Mr. Yeats to have been the first contemporary to be conscious. It is a method for which the horoscope is auspicious. Psychology . . . ethnology, and *The Golden Bough* have concurred to make possible what was impossible even a few years ago. Instead of narrative method, we may now use the mythical method. It is, I seriously believe, a step toward making the modern world possible for art. . . . And only those who have won their own discipline in secret and without aid, in a world which offers very little assistance to that end, can be of any use in furthering this advance." [16] The solution to the problem of form given here is the private solution of Yeats. Later, however, Eliot, partially through Yeats's failure to create a public poetic drama, learned that the invention of a private system, however satisfactory for a particular poet, could not create a public poetry. Like Yeats (and unlike the Georgian verse dramatists), he insisted on the integral relationship between poetry and culture; but whereas Yeats capitulated in despair to the ideological confusion of his age, Eliot discovered in Christianity the inclusive system that he hoped would both order and give meaning to his art and also provide authentically concrete referents that would give it the wider public he was seeking.

The Church of England's reconciliation with the poet, coming as it did when a major poet was seeking for means of extending the boundaries of his art to achieve a wider public, was thus a propitious event for poetic drama in a second and even more important way. Besides providing him with a theater and an audience, it offered him the doctrine of the Incarnation (along with its concomitant system of referents), which, if it could not claim universal acceptance, could at least serve as the grounds of an aesthetic capable of appealing to those great and unforgettable paradigmatic experiences that, according to Karl Mannheim, had directed and inspired an organic and creative society in the past.

Historically, there have been two radically different interpretations of the significance of this crucial event (*kairos*) in the cosmic history of Christianity: the primitive Christian and the Greco-Christian or Gnostic. According to the latter, Christ "possessed only the semblance of a body but had no actually human body," and thus this view rejects "the judgment that redemptive history passes on the quite ordinary particular historical event that occurred in the incarnate Christ, and that includes the offensively ordinary fact of the death on the cross." [17] This antihistorical in-

terpretation ultimately led to the essentially Platonic Alexandrian
or Philonian method of Biblical exegesis, in which the events of
the Old Testament are denied their concrete reality to become no
more than allegorical or imperfect copies or shadows of spiritual
or eternal reality. In other words, it led, according to Oscar Cullman, one of the most radical contemporary spokesmen in behalf
of the historicity of Christ and the Christ process, to a view of history in which time (which is circular in motion, without a *telos*)
and eternity (timelessness) are dissociated and in which the former
is considered inferior to the latter.[18] In the primitive Christian or
Biblical view, however, Christ was perceived as the Word *actually*
made Flesh and, accordingly, time, far from being hostile to salvation, was perceived as the linear vehicle by which God's Providence (*oikonomia*) is fulfilled. This view ultimately led to what
has been called the fourfold method of Biblical exegesis, which
stresses the integrity of the literal level of the Old Testament narrative and, by extension, to a view of history in which time and
eternity are coterminous.

Despite the historical precedence of the primitive Christian view
and the condemnation of the Gnostic view as the Docetist heresy,[19]
it is the essentially Greek interpretation of Christ and time that
has had, until recently, the greatest impact on Christian theology.
In our time, however, the general thrust of Christian thought about
the Incarnation involves, as Nathan Scott has observed, "a profound discomfort with the kind of radical distinction between time
and eternity that has persistently figured in theological tradition,"
and constitutes a growing awareness that "the New Testament consistently proposes that that lambent point at which the meaning of
human existence is most fully disclosed is located not outside time
but within the historical continuum," and "therefore that . . .
time is not so much to be understood *sub specie aeternitatis* as
eternity is to be understood *sub specie temporalitatis*." [20]

It is known that this general view of the Incarnation and its implications for time constitutes the fulcrum of the crisis theology
of Christian existentialists such as Nicholas Berdyaev, Gabriel Marcel, Rudolph Bultmann, Paul Tillich, Dietrich Bonhoeffer, and

the later Karl Barth. It is less known, however, especially by the critics of Eliot's drama, that this view also, if less radically, constitutes the main thrust of modern Angelican theology from Charles Gore to William Temple.[21] Indeed, as early as 1934, the year T. S. Eliot wrote *The Rock*, William Temple, in his Gifford Lectures, was "already resisting the whole concept of time as a moving image of the static changelessness of eternity [the Platonistic view of time], as a realm ontologically inferior . . . to the absolute sufficiency of eternity." [22] Using the analogy of the creation of a poem, in which "the meaning, which is the ground of the poem's existence, only comes to actuality in the process of the poem's composition," [23] he writes that the "historical life is so intimately one with the eternal which it makes manifest, that if it could be annihilated, the eternal life would be different in quality. It is not incidental to God's eternity that . . . He lived and suffered and triumphed in the process of time. If that happened, then His eternal being is such as to necessitate its happening, so that its not happening would prove His eternal being to be other than Christianity believes. . . . The historical is evidence of the eternal, not only as a shadow is evidence of substance, but as a necessary self-expression of a Being whose essential activity is at once self-communication and self-discovery in that to which He communicates Himself." [24] There is, as Nathan Scott points out, a residual Hegelianism in Temple's interpretation of history, but the movement toward an incarnational view of time is apparent.[25] It was broadly within this theological environment that T. S. Eliot, Charles Williams, and Dorothy Sayers began to experiment in religious drama. The failure to consider this context has resulted in a distorted interpretation of the British Christian verse drama. For it is this incarnational bent of Anglican theology that goes far to illuminate the strategies that Eliot and the other dramatists of the movement evolved to confront and dramatize the discontinuities of contemporary history.

As Malcolm Mackenzie Ross has observed, the Incarnation, "respecting as it does both the divinity of the Word and the humanity of the flesh," [26] implies a sacramental aesthetic, an aesthetic that assumes the organic wholeness of the artistic imagination and of the orders of experience that are its objects. It is not difficult to understand, therefore, why it had a profound influence on the Christian verse dramatists, who were seeking to reintegrate the dissociated sensibility and the anarchy of the experience of modern life.

To recapitulate briefly, Christ's assumption of the body of man either redeems the things of this world (including the flesh), which had been corrupted by the Fall, or redeems man's spirit, thus allowing him once again to perceive the spirituality of time and temporal things.[27] In either case, at this point of intersection man and nature are reunited with the transcendent from which they had been separated, and their dignity, their importance, is therefore restored. Existence reassumes meaning. Every detail in the earthly scene becomes simultaneously uniquely real and universally significant. The Incarnation, in other words, in redeeming nature, in simultaneously giving intrinsic worth to and informing it with transcendent meaning, "makes possible, indeed demands, the sacramental vision of reality." [28] Considered in a historical context, this interpretation of the Incarnation had, as Erich Auerbach points out, a great impact on the European aesthetic, especially in the area of style, which in antiquity had been governed by the *Stiltrennung* (the separation of styles according to the social status of the subject). After the emergence of the Christian vision, "the age of separate realms of style [was] over." [29] The *Stiltrennung* dissolved and the polar styles, the high and the low, merged into one: "In antique theory, the sublime and elevated style was called *sermo gravis* or *sublimis;* the low style was *sermo remissus* or *humilis;* the two had to be kept strictly separated. In the world of Christianity, on the other hand, the two are merged, especially in Christ's Incarnation and Passion, which realize and combine *sublimitas* and *humilitas* in overwhelming measure." [30]

When translated in terms of its implications for poetic imagery, the fusion, through the agency of the Incarnation, of spirit and matter is of crucial importance to the Christian poet, especially to the modern Christian poet-dramatist; for it resolves the problem of imagery that confronts both the naturalistic and the idealistic or angelic imaginations. Whereas the naturalistic aesthetic compels the poet either to avoid imagery or to employ it ornamentally and the angelic aesthetic to deny the *existential* status of the image, the Christian aesthetic allows the poet to employ the objects of nature to express transcendent significance without sacrificing their identity, their particular reality. The image becomes, in other words, genuinely poetic, not a vehicle for conveying a truth derived from a merely rational discipline or emotional intuition. The Christian, according to Malcolm Ross, is

> compelled, under the fixed star of the Incarnation, to believe in existence. . . . He is compelled to believe in the particularity, the uniqueness, the *value*, of things. Therefore, the Christian artist may not, like the Platonist . . . oppose a shadow world of things to a real world of value. Rather, for the Christian artist, all things have their own separately structured, intrinsic actuality and value, while at the same time they participate proportionately in larger relationships and values which are moral and spiritual without ceasing to be actual, specific, concrete. The Word is made Flesh without ceasing to be the Word. Nor is the Flesh fleshless. Authentic Christianity does not seek to create reality by any factless copulation of imagination with value. Rather it discovers worlds beyond worlds even in a grain of sand—worlds that exist in a rising tier of being. Authentic Christian art celebrates the actual kinship that obtains between man and things, between subject and object.[31]

Moreover, the sacramental vision puts all of nature, even the most matter-of-fact object, at the poet's disposal for use as valid imagery.

In an analogous way, the doctrine of the Incarnation has even more significant implications for the Christian conception of time and history, and thus, for the imitation of human actions. Since the Incarnation occurs in time, in a moment of history, it absorbs the temporal into the eternal order, extending itself within history, "perpetually reordering it, reshaping its broken structures, never abandoning history, but redeeming it." [32] This theological concept of an eternal Presence requires a sacramental interpretation of history, in which time is viewed as an eternal present and events, no matter how distant from one another in time, are perpetually relevant symbolic actions. This sacramental interpretation of history, which manifested itself historically as the fourfold method of Biblical exegesis, is for our purposes best exemplified in Erich Auerbach's redefinition of the fourfold method:

> Figural interpretation establishes a connection between two events or persons, the first of which signifies not only itself but also the second, while the second encompasses or fulfills the first. The two poles of the figure are separate in time, but both, being real events or figures, are within time, within the stream of historical life. Only the understanding of the two persons or events is a spiritual act, but this spiritual act deals with concrete events whether past, present, or future, and not with concepts or abstractions; these are quite secondary, since promise and fulfillment are real historical events, which have either happened in the incarnation of the Word, or will happen in the second coming. Of course purely spiritual elements enter into the conceptions of the ultimate fulfillment, since "my kingdom is not of this world"; yet it will be a real kingdom, not an immaterial abstraction; only the *figura*, not the *natura* of this world will pass away . . . and the flesh will rise again. Since in figural interpretation one thing stands for another, since one thing represents and signifies the other, figural interpretation is "allegorical" in the widest sense. But it differs from most of the allegorical forms known to us by the historicity both of the sign and what it signifies.[33]

Thus, for example, in a *figura*, Noah's ark in the Old Testament is a prefiguration of the Christian Church, Isaac is a prefiguration of Christ, or—to go outside the Old Testament, which is the original object of figural interpretation, into history and literature—the historical Virgil is the type of the poet-prophet-guide of Dante's *Divine Comedy*, who at the behest of Beatrice undertakes to interpret for Dante the true earthly order and to guide him "toward its goal, the heavenly community of the blessed. . . ."[34] The second term of the *figura* fulfills the first. Yet both are seen and felt as historical events.

Further, since the ultimate fulfillment of God's eternal design has not yet worked itself out in time or history, these events and the events of the New Testament and, by extension, the events after the Incarnation are incomplete. They too point to some future event that will fulfill them. That is, history itself becomes a *figura*, concrete yet figurative; in short, symbolic. Thus, whereas an empirical interpretation of reality views history as a linear progression in which each event is univocal and self-sufficient and an angelic interpretation views history as an eternally circular and therefore meaningless motion from which one escapes by immobilizing or annihilating the moment, the sacramental or figural interpretation views time as dependent for meaning on eternity. This is not to say, however, that time loses its actuality, its existential validity, to become an allegory of eternity. The figures "point not only to the concrete future, but also to something that always has been and always will be; they point to something which is in need of interpretation, which will indeed be fulfilled in the concrete future, but which is at all times present, fulfilled in God's providence, which knows no difference of time. This eternal thing is already figured in them, and thus they are both tentative fragmentary reality, and veiled eternal reality." [35] History becomes an eternal present (both terms need emphasis), in which time and eternity, the many and the one, motion and stillness, perpetually inform each other. Every moment in history, every human action, is infused by a discoverable universal and permanent significance without loss of its unique actuality, its historicity.

The aesthetic implications of this sacramental concept of history for the modern artist, particularly for the poet-dramatist, are of the utmost importance in explaining the essential character of the Christian verse drama movement. First, by fully assuming it, he overcomes the artistic limitations of naturalism. The realist who views history merely as a linear progression (or recession) must imitate the surfaces of human experience. He achieves a faithful documentation of the actual, but to the extent that he is committed to the radical implications of naturalism, his representation of concrete reality will be devoid of spiritual significance or value, and, therefore, of authentic poetry. Furthermore, since human experience has no transcendent meaning, he must concentrate on the

social significance of experience and, in so doing, restrict his subject
matter to the contemporary scene. History tends to have little
genuinely relevant interest for the naturalistic imagination. As Hans
Meyerhoff observes: ". . . technology has greatly foreshortened
[modern] man's own perspective of time and, by enlarging his
mastery over *physical space,* has also confined him increasingly to
the *mental* and *emotional space* of the momentary present devoid
of continuity and significant relations with past and future. Thus
technology has expanded the dimension of physical space at the
expense of time, but has contracted the dimension of mental 'space'
to the fragmentary moment of the present." [36] The pastness of history, therefore, tends to destroy for the naturalist the dramatic
value of historical actions.

The Christian sacramental view of history, on the other hand,
validates both physical reality and value, unites the two. The historical event, like the object in nature, is itself but simultaneously
other than itself. Existence and essence, the concrete and universal,
interpenetrate, and human activity assumes poetic significance. Also,
since for the Christian artist history is an eternal present, in which
the past contains the present and the present contains the past,
both past and present are placed at the poet's disposal for poetic
treatment. This availability is not merely a matter of types of action
in the Christian narrative, such as the sacrifice of Isaac which prefigures the sacrifice of Christ, nor, for that matter, of types of great
historical actions, such as Thomas Becket's martyrdom, set in a
specifically Christian context; *all* human actions great or small, past
or present, are valid material for dramatic imitation. For in this
sacramental view, all human actions are figural, simultaneously
temporal and eternal, immediate and remote, concrete and universal, and therefore vital in the cosmic drama that is Christian history. The imaginative activity of the sacramental poet is, as it was
for Shakespeare and the Metaphysical poets, the process of discovering reconciling analogies in the concrete temporal disparates.

This aesthetic implication of Christian time, as Auerbach shows,
explains the lowly realism, the contemporaneous and everyday reality, of medieval miracle drama. Illustrating the thesis that the fig-

ural interpretation of history is also a dramatic principle by examining the French miracle play, *Mystère d'Adam* (most English mysteries would serve the same purpose), Auerbach writes that the play "is introduced by a liturgical reading of Scripture from Genesis. . . . Then come the dramatized events of the Fall. . . . The story is carried on to the murder of Abel. And the conclusion of the whole is a procession of the Old Testament prophets announcing the coming of Christ. The scenes which render everyday contemporary life . . . are, then, fitted into a Biblical and world-historical frame by whose spirit they are pervaded. And the spirit of the frame which encompasses them is the spirit of the figural interpretation of history. This implies that every occurrence, in all its everyday reality, is simultaneously a part in a world-historical context through which each part is related to every other, and thus is likewise to be regarded as being of all times or above all time." [37] It is also this principle that underlies the contemporaneity of historical and Biblical events in modern Christian verse plays such as T. S. Eliot's *Murder in the Cathedral*, Dorothy Sayers' *The Zeal of Thy House*, and Ronald Duncan's *This Way to the Tomb*; the realistic and contemporary actions (which most commentators have interpreted simply as a capitulation to the pressure of the modern prose theater) of the plays of the second phase of the Christian verse drama, Eliot's *The Cocktail Party* and Anne Ridler's *The Shadow Factory*, for example; and, by extension, the "secular themes" in plays such as Eliot's *The Family Reunion*, which is simultaneously about crime and punishment and sin and expiation.

Similarly, the Christian concept of history surmounts the limitations of that "mythic" art, prominent in our scientific age, which is the product of the time-ridden "angelic imagination." [38] The strategy of this type of creative mind is to inform human events with value by "mythologizing" that value. But in doing so, it tends to sacrifice what the naturalist achieves: the particularity, the reality of the vehicle. The poet who gives events psychological rather than ontological validity frees his imagination from the shackles of historical time that constricts the naturalist's vision to the surface of reality, but he also separates value and reality, subject and object, and makes the particular dependent on the abstract. This strategy denies the intrinsic validity of the action incorporated in the poetic vehicle (*das Ding an sich*), denies, that is, its existential status,[39] and results, too often, in a drama of the private mind, in which concrete reality disintegrates into vague, wavering symbols of psychic states, as in the case of the poetry of the French symbolists, the novels of Virginia Woolf, and the plays of Maeterlinck, of the early Yeats, and, more recently, of Ionesco and Pinter (which, paradoxically, have their source in an existential metaphysics).[40]

Francis Fergusson's "Myth and the Literary Scruple" is relevant here. In this essay he distinguishes (on the analogy of Malinowski's classification of the types found in primitive societies) three kinds of myth in literature: Historical Legends, "stories about the past which are believed to be true of the past, and which serve to give [a people] some significant conception of their history" (Dante's Christianized Virgilian Legend of Rome, for example); Folk or Fairy Tales, stories making "no claim to truth in itself" and told for fun or at most as pleasing illustrations of moral and political concepts (these range from Little Red Riding Hood to something as sophisticated as Paul Valéry's *Fragments du Narcisse*); and Religious Myths, stories believed to be true and which represent basic elements in the creeds, the morals, and the social structure of a people (the narrative of Christianity, for example).[41] It is, according to Fergusson, the second, the Fairy Tale type of myth, that is most at home in times, like the present, "of the most intransigent rationalism." [42] Yet in comparing Valéry's *Fragments*, which he considers an admirable example of the fairy tale conception of myth, with the episode of the Sirens (Purgatorio XIX) in Dante's *Divine Comedy*, which is the classic example of the religious myth, Fergusson recognizes the essential distinction between the two attitudes toward myth and the superior poetic potential of the latter: ". . . she [the Siren] seems to have more reality than Valéry's conventional figure: if not a metaphysical entity in her own right, she is at least an ineluctable trope, the embodiment of one eternally-recurrent human experience. That is because the Siren has her place in a vaster vision which includes the perspectives of ethics and faith. Valéry's Narcissus, on the other hand, is presented as 'pure' poetry." [43] The Christian narrative or myth is not for Dante an objectification of desire, a fairy tale fabricated to illustrate a psychological, a moral, or a political insight. It is conceived as a historical fact. Thus, not only the narrative itself but also history becomes an analogue, an incarnation "of the eternal engagement of God and man as it shapes itself in the startling sculptures of time," [44] in which human events as well as significance are validated. Furthermore, mythologies outside the scope of Christian history—that of the primitive fertility religions and of the ancient Greeks, for example—can be integrated into it. And if these are not considered historical, they can be, through the agency of the existential reality of the Christian narrative, visualized and placed as if they were. Taking his lead from Erich Auerbach, Fergusson writes: "If Dante can handle the figures of myth with such subtle and flexible realism—that is, with respect both for the reality of the imagination in which they appear, and for the different reality of the figures themselves—it is because he understands them, not in conceptual terms, but by analogy with the Incarnation. The process whereby a myth is brought to life in a human imagination corresponds to that by which Christ lives again in the spirits of the faithful, through belief, concentration, love, and an imitative movement of spirit. . . . It is because Dante believes so completely in the reality of this basic Analogue that he can both share in the lives of many kinds of myths, and yet also pass beyond them, to consider their meaning in other terms, and in relation to each other. His belief in the 'primeval, greater and more relevant reality' of the Christian Narrative gives him a key to the heritage of myth, makes him a master . . . of the mythic modes of understanding." [45] It is also, I submit, the belief in "the reality of this basic Analogue" that, in a more general way, lies behind the easy commerce between pagan and Christian imagery in much of the poetry and drama of the Elizabethans.

The sacramental view of history, then, puts pressure on the Christian artist, particularly the dramatist, to respect both everyday reality and, as in the case of Dante's use of the Siren or of Eliot's use of the *Oresteia* in *The Family Reunion*, the "reality" of mythic figures in Fergusson's second sense. In so doing, it rescues not only value from naturalism but also concrete reality from the mythologizer. And this is achieved without resort to a private system of values.

I do not wish to give the impression that the Anglican churchmen were completely conscious of the aesthetic implications of Christian dogma. Bishop Bell's statements on the relation of religion and drama, for example, were few, brief, and general. His importance, as Gerald Weales notes, lay not in formulating principles but rather in initiating activity in the drama within the Church and lending authority to it.[46] At the outset of the movement he appears to have considered the function of religious drama in terms of its broad aesthetic appeal, his own taste inclining toward a Georgian simplicity and pre-Raphaelite religious aestheticism, as his choice of Masefield, Holst, and Ricketts as collaborators in the 1928 Canterbury project suggests.

On the other hand, it has gradually become clear that the Christian verse drama movement was part of a serious revival of Anglican theological-aesthetic criticism of modern English culture which diagnoses its fragmentation, its division of experience, in terms of a radical dissociation of sensibility, and grounds its criticism of much contemporary theology on the tendency to bypass nature and to escape from the knowledge about it accumulated by scientific investigators instead of committing itself to nature and time and making the effort to integrate scientific knowledge into the Christian world view. This general alliance, which is reflected in the Anglican-oriented cultural and literary criticism of both churchmen such as V. A. Demant, George Every, and Martin Jarett-Kerr, and literary critics and scholars such as Basil Willey, C. S. Lewis, S. L. Bethell, Charles Williams, Dorothy Sayers, Norman Nicholson, E. Martin Browne, Robert Speaight, and T. S. Eliot, suggests that the churchmen who early advocated the reunion of Christianity and drama had at least a broad awareness of the aesthetic implications of the theology of the Incarnation. If that awareness was at first oriented in the direction of pious aestheticism, it soon fell under the influence of the larger cultural movement and became integrated with it. This development is clearly revealed by Karl Mannheim in the introductory footnote to the section of *Diagnosis of Our Time* (1943) which speaks to the question of the function of Christianity in the culturally fragmented contemporary world: His argument, he observes, "was written for a group of British friends, Christian thinkers. . . . The Group [called the Moot], consisting of theologians, clergymen, academic teachers, Civil Servants, writers [including T. S. Eliot], etc., used to meet four times a year for a week-end with the avowed purpose of understanding recent changes in society in their relevance for Christianity. Several years ago, the author was invited to join the group as a sociologist, and in this capacity he wrote the present statement." [47]

After this, it was not surprising for an Anglican theologian to relate Christianity and the arts in the light of the crisis of culture. Thus, for example, Bishop Bell (echoing T. S. Eliot) says in 1953 that "the Church needs [the poets and artists]. And they need the Church. The Church needs their vision in drawing men to worship God and in teaching men the Truth about life. And they need the help of the Faith of the Church for their creative work." [48] And later he asserts that the "crisis of culture," and by extension the separation of the Church and the drama in England can be attributed to "the continuing Puritanism of English culture," under which term he includes (as previous references to the materialism and secularism of that culture imply) both a religious and a secular attitude.[49] Implicit in these statements is a specific awareness of the integral relation of poetry and culture and at least a general recognition of its corollary: that if the drama is to fulfill both its long-range cultural function, the regeneration of the public imagination, and its artistic potential, the creation of a genuinely poetic drama, it must found its aesthetic on the cardinal doctrines of Christianity.

At any rate, there is no question that the poet-dramatists of Canterbury were from the beginning conscious of the sacramental aesthetic implicit in the doctrine of the Incarnation, though complete awareness manifested itself gradually; the development fell into roughly two stages, the first devoted to the exploration of the implications of sacramentalism for poetic imagery and historical events, and the second to the exploration of its implications for naturalistic and contemporary action.

As early as his famous essay "Tradition and the Individual Talent" (1917), we find T. S. Eliot articulating the radical importance of a sacramental view of history for poetry. Indispensable to the modern poet, he says, is the historical sense, which "involves a perception, not only of the pastness of the past, but of its presence; the historical sense compels a man to write not merely with his own generation in his bones, but with a feeling that the whole of the literature of Europe from Homer and within it the whole of the literature of his own country has a simultaneous existence and composes a simultaneous order. *This historical sense, which is a sense of the timeless as well as of the temporal together, is what makes a writer traditional. And it is at the same time what makes a writer most acutely conscious of his place in time, of his own contemporaneity.*" [50] Although Eliot's point of view in this passage is not one that can be labeled as specifically Christian, the definition obviously prefigures his discovery of the tradition in the Christianity of the Incarnation, his conversion, and the Christian poetry of his late period. To fulfill the demands of his view of tradition, Eliot at first had to create out of the available fragments of philosophy, religion, and myth an eclectic world order (it informs *The Waste Land*) somewhat in the manner of Yeats. In so doing he chose for himself the condition of alienation and for his poetry the mode of private utterance. For a poet who attached so much importance to the cultural function of poetry, however, such a resolution of his dilemma could not be final. The step from the private "classicism" of his early period (by which he meant the process of discovering form in the anarchy of experience through the agency of an ordered system of referents or beliefs that has the sanction of time) to orthodox Christianity was not a betrayal of his early views of life and art as some—F. R. Leavis, for example—conclude, but a fulfillment; [51] and it is paralleled in his artistic development by the abandonment of a private for a public vehicle, which his conversion and the reconciliation of Church and art made possible.

Thus in *Four Quartets* (which, significantly, contains not only the focal themes but also the seeds of various formal characteristics of the plays) there is a poetic exploration of time which, after rejection of the naturalist and secular existential interpretations of history, finally arrives at a Christian interpretation that turns out to be Eliot's theological counterpart of the definition of tradition presented in the early essay quoted above:

> Home is where one starts from. As we grow older
> The world becomes stranger, the pattern more complicated
> Of dead and living. Not the intense moment
> Isolated, with no before and after,
> But a lifetime burning in every moment
> And not the lifetime of one man only
> But of old stones that cannot be deciphered.[52]

And this eternal present which informs all orders of being is, as the Chorus in Eliot's *The Rock* reveals, grounded in the Incarnation:

> Then came, at a predetermined moment, a moment in time
> and of time,
> A moment not out of time, but in time, in what we call history:
> transecting, bisecting the world of time, a moment in time
> but not like a moment of time,
> A moment in time but time was made through that moment: for
> without the meaning there is no time, and that moment of
> time gave the meaning.[53]

The point of intersection that gives meaning to time and makes time the agent through which meaning is revealed is, on one level, a redemption of time and, therefore, of nature, a reordering of the universe and reestablishment of integral harmony among all created things. Though the perception of redeemed time occurs infrequently, it nevertheless enables Eliot the poet to conceive experience analogically, to see, without denying their identity, the objects of the various levels of nature as correspondences and conveyors of transcendent meaning. Thus in his poetry he reaffirms not only the integrity and dignity of the image but also the analogical relationship between images, which were forfeited after the Cartesian *cogito* had alienated subject from object and reduced the function of metaphor to that of ornament:

> Garlic and sapphires in the mud
> Clot the bedded axle-tree.
> The trilling wire in the blood
> Sings below inveterate scars
> And reconciles forgotten wars.
> The dance along the artery
> The circulation of the lymph
> Are figured in the drift of stars
> Ascend to summer in the tree
> We move above the moving tree
> In light upon the figured leaf
> And hear upon the sodden floor
> Below, the boarhound and the boar
> Pursue their pattern as before
> But reconciled among the stars.[54]

Correspondingly, the Christian interpretation of history allowed Eliot to treat time in a similar, that is, sacramental way. Thus, for example, in "East Coker," we find him suddenly fusing present and past: a particular moment in the present when the poet, meditating on his relation to the ravages of circular time ("In succession / Houses rise and fall, crumble, are extended, / Are removed, destroyed, restored. . . .") as he approaches the village of his sixteenth-century ancestors, looks into an open field across which the light of the sun falls

> . . . leaving the deep lane
> Shuttered with branches, dark in the afternoon,
> Where you lean against a bank while a van passes,
> And the deep lane insists on the direction
> Into the village, in the electric heat
> Hypnotised. . . .

with a particular moment in the field's past when, to the music of pipe and drum, its sixteenth-century inhabitants are dancing

> . . . around the bonfire
> The association of man and woman
> In daunsinge, signifying matrimonie—
> A dignified and commodious sacrament.
> Two and two, necessarye coniunction,
> Holding eche other by the hand or the arm
> Whiche betokeneth concorde. Round and round the fire
> Leaping through the flames, or joined in circles,
> Rustically solemn or in rustic laughter
> Lifting heavy feet in clumsy shoes,[55]

Both become startlingly coexistent in time and place, thus momentarily negating the circular motion of time and redeeming its neutrality and joylessness. On the basis of the principle of an eternal present the events are contained within but are not confined to each other. The past endows the present with all its associations without, however, losing its particular historical identity. It becomes not an illustrative example but a symbolic action, a myth that illuminates and integrates the present, the decayed houses and the poet's meditation on them, but not, as the visualized scene indicates, at the expense of the past's historicity. This myth, though fragmentary, carries with it the significance of the Christian scheme. It is this poetic use of Christian time that throws light on scenes in the Christian verse drama such as the one in Eliot's *Murder in the Cathedral* in which the knights, after participating in the murder of Becket, turn suddenly to the audience and, in a contemporary idiom, implicate them in the recent crime.

At the time of *Murder in the Cathedral* and *Four Quartets*, Eliot's translation of the theology of the Incarnation into the sacramental aesthetic does not go much beyond the validation of the poetic image and the past. The "naturalization" of poetry—the adoption, that is, of a low style (*sermo humilis*)—and of the action, which is inherent in that theology, occurs later, simultaneously with his decision to write verse drama for the commercial theater. The premium he placed at the time of *Murder in the Cathedral* on the principle of order and his emphasis on the Way of Negation in his exploration of the spiritual life appear, in part at any rate, to have inhibited his extension of the implications of the Christian aesthetic to incorporate a full-bodied realism. Since these two phases of Eliot's development mark, in a general way, of course, the two phases of the Christian verse drama movement, it should be noted that the second, more realistic, phase is emergent in the contemporary rhythms and diction, in the occasional relaxation of the normal tension of the verse, and in the realism of one or two episodes of these works that is so very different from the dusty piety of the archaic "thee's" and "thou's" and the unearthly nostalgia of the ornamental decor of earlier church drama.

For Charles Williams, as for Eliot, the Incarnation is of primary importance to his poetry and drama. However, his interpretation has a different emphasis. Whereas Eliot stresses the redemptive function of the Incarnation, Williams, reacting against the modern tendency to interpret the Redemption as a redemption only of spirit rather than of both spirit and matter, places emphasis on its creational function. More specifically, Williams believes, as Anne Ridler points out, in the Scotist principle "that Christ would have become incarnate, even if there had been no Fall, for 'In His union and conjunction with Body, God finds His final perfection and felicity.' " [56] The Redemption, that is, is incorporated in the Creation and is not different from it. It was "on the principles and to the principles of our first unfallen nature. Man could not longer be innocent; he was corrupt, and his best efforts were, but for the new grace, doomed to death. But his best efforts were, and are, of no other kind than had been decreed. His blood might be tainted, but the source from which it sprang was still the same. His natural life was still, and is now, a disordered pattern of the only pattern, a confused type of the one original. . . . The most extreme goodness may be found in it and asserted of it—so long as the absolute invalidity of it apart from the new life is also declared. The most absolute domination of the new life may be asserted, so long as the accidental goodness of the old is never denied." [57] The Redemption, in other words, was a redemption, not only of man's spirit, as the Church, under the influence of Docetism, often implies, but also of man's body, which was originally good.

The difference determines Williams' choice of the Affirmative Way and Eliot's choice of the Negative Way, but it does not lead to a radical difference in their poetics. Both remain sacramental. According to Williams, God's primal decision to be born into the world "was the decree that brought mankind into being. It was His will to make creatures of such a kind that they should share in that particular joy of His existence in flesh. He bade for Himself a mother and all her companions. . . . It was the great and single act of active love, consonant with nothing but His nature. . . . Our flesh was to hold, to its degree, the secrets of His own." [58] Through the Incarnation, the body of man became an Image of God, but not, as the Platonist would have it, one which merely *reflects*, but one which *contains* the spirit: "But the *Anthropos* in Christ was not 'like' the *Theos*: it was like nothing but itself. So the body is not 'like' the soul; it is like nothing but itself. The principle of our sensuality is unique and divine. It is . . . rooted in substance. 'Soul is form and doth the body make' is a fine Platonist line. But the soul ought not be allowed to reduce the body to its own shadow—at any rate, in the Christian Church." [59] And, though Williams is primarily concerned with the human body, what applies to the body of man applies, of course, each in its own degree, to the various orders of the natural world.

When Williams translates his definition of nature into poetic theory, the image, as in Eliot, assumes a sacramental character. The symbol (his generic term for the sacramental image), he writes, "has its own being, as well as being a part of some other greater being, and representing the whole of that greater being in its own part." [60] It is different from allegory (and, correspondingly, from the fairy tale conception of myth) in precisely the same way that the Christian interpretation of nature is different from the Platonic. Allegory is a narrative that speaks of a subject in terms of another that is "suggestively similar." The two groups of terms are not identical; thus the vehicle becomes a *means* of illustrating an abstract idea and the integrity of the object in nature it uses is violated. For example, "there is not, in Spenser, the *identity* of Despair. All his caves and cliffs and owls and corpses, thorn-stitched garments and hollow eyne, will not make that poetic identity sure." [61] The symbol, in other words, is not a means and does not distort the thing in nature it represents; it rather unifies the natural and supernatural or the physical reality of the object and its value into a single unique experience. Such, for example, is Dante's Beatrice, who is one with theology,[62] Milton's Satan, who is one with despair, and Shakespeare's Macbeth, who is one with murder: "For identities of that kind we have to start with figures as intensely themselves as can be managed; the less themselves they are, the less identical with facts of another category they become. But the more themselves they are, the less 'suggestively similar' of another kind of fact can they be. This is the law of symbolism—that the symbol must be utterly itself before it can properly be a symbol. But the more himself a man is the less he is likely to be *similar* to anything, even a virtue; for virtue and vice are to us only known by men." [63] That Williams' definition of the symbol does derive from his interpretation of the Incarnation is made clear in his reaction to the conclusion of Spenser's *An Hymne to Heavenly Beautie*, where the poet apostrophizes his soul to renounce all the things of this world: ". . . though perhaps sanctity must sometimes endure such a state for a season, it must not, for poetry, nor indeed finally for sanctity, be the conclusion. It was said of the God whom Spenser was there hymning that He loved the world, and certainly, whether the doctrine of the Resurrection be true or not, it seems only by some such resurrection of the earth in their reconciled minds that the poets can justly find union." [64]

Nor are the objects of nature in this aesthetic isolated and self-sufficient. On the analogy of the hierarchical yet coequal and co-eternal character of the three Persons of the Trinity, the creatures of nature are seen to be ordered organically and hierarchically yet equally and are integrated with the supernatural order in a vast web of "co-inherence," each class in nature imaging forth sacramentally, in its own degree, its supernatural counterpart. Thus, for example, the structure of the body, for Williams, is in some degree an index to the structure of the supernatural world,[65] an analogy he makes much of in his Arthurian poems, where the Empire is projected as a human body.[66] Correspondingly, man in society (whether the family, nation, Christendom, etc.)—the city of man —images the archetypal order of heaven—the Heavenly City—which is at once hierarchical and republican.

This system of correspondences is, if not identical with, at least strikingly akin to that traditional microcosm-macrocosm relationship that according to S. L. Bethell and others nourished the poetic genius of the Elizabethan Age.[67] Though Williams allows that the idea that man is a small replica of the universe "led . . . to many absurdities and (if you choose—like any other idea) to some evils," [68] such as many of the formulations of astrology and other occult schools, he believes that the epistemological principle behind it—that of analogy—is utterly true and necessary for poetry and poetic drama. Thus, with Eliot, Williams' rendering of the Incarnation into poetic theory reunites the dissociated sensibility, the divided imagination, that has more or less characterized the poetic mind since the seventeenth century.

Williams' interpretation of the Incarnation, like Eliot's, affects not only his vision of the things of this world but also his vision of time, of history, and of human action. Since God's decree to become incarnate creates the condition in which His Providence will be fulfilled, history becomes the process of fulfillment. Like the natural object, the historical moment or the human event in time is absorbed into the eternal and the moments of time become "co-inherent." This is clearly indicated in Williams' discussion of Augustine's conception of original sin and its relation to the Redemption:

> "*Fuimus ille unus,*" he said; "we were in the one when we were the one." Whatever ages of time lay between us and Adam, yet we were in him and we were he; more, we sinned in him and his guilt is in us. And if indeed all mankind is held together by its web of existence, then ages cannot separate one from another. Exchange, substitution, co-inherence are a natural fact as well as a supernatural truth. "Another is in me," said Felicitas [a refer-

ence to the Redemption]; "we were in another," said Augustine. The co-inherence reaches back to the beginning as it stretches on to the end, and the *anthropos* is present everywhere. "As in Adam all die, even so in Christ shall all be made alive"; co-inherence did not begin with Christianity; all that happened then was that co-inherence itself was redeemed and revealed by that very redemption as a supernatural principle as well as a natural. . . . To refuse the ancient heritage of guilt is to cut ourselves off from mankind as certainly as to refuse the new principle. It is necessary to submit to the one as freely as to the other.[69]

Thus Williams, like Eliot, views history sacramentally, as an eternal present in which the human act, both individual and social, is simultaneously an act in and out of time and in which the acts in time, past, present, and future, are co-inherent. His translation of this vision of time into an aesthetic principle results in one of the central characteristics of his art. In his early verse play *Seed of Adam,* for example, he presents Adam (the Natural Man) as a *figura* of Caesar Augustus, and in the progress of the play fuses the two into a single character. The principle is perhaps most clearly illustrated by the vision of London in his last novel, *All Hallows' Eve* (1945), which closely parallels in technique, if not in artistic merit, the lines already referred to from Eliot's "East Coker," where past and present are represented as coexistent:

Not only space but time spread out around her as she went. She saw a glowing and glimmering City, of which the life was visible as a roseal wonder within. The streets of it were first the streets of to-day, full of the business of to-day—shops, transport, men and women. . . . Then, gently opening, she saw among those streets other streets . . . other Londons into which her own London opened or with which it was intermingled. No thought of confusion crossed her mind; it was all very greatly ordered, and when down a long street she saw, beyond the affairs of to-day, the movement of sedan chairs and ancient dresses, and beyond them again, right in the distance and yet very close to her, the sun shining on armour, and sometimes a high battlemented gate, it was no phantasmagoria of a dream but precise actuality. . . . Once or twice she thought she saw other streets, unrecognizable, with odd buildings and men and women in strange clothes. But these were rare glimpses and less clear, as if the future of that City only occasionally showed. Beyond all these streets, or sometimes for a moment seen in their midst, was forest and the gleam of marshland, and here and there a river, and once across one such river a rude bridge, and once again a village of huts and men in skins. As she came down towards what was to her day the centre of the City, there was indeed a moment when all houses and streets vanished, and the forests rose all around her, and she was going down a rough causeway among the trees, for this was the place of London before London had begun to be, or perhaps after its long and noble history had ceased to be, and the trees grew over it, and a few late tribes still trod what remained of the old roads. . . .

In this City lay all—London and New York, Athens and Chicago, Paris and Rome and Jerusalem; it was that to which they led in the lives of their citizens.[70]

On the surface Williams' treatment of time in this passage appears to be similar to Virginia Woolf's in *Mrs. Dalloway* or *Orlando*, for example. But there is a crucial difference. To define this difference here would be to anticipate the subsequent discussion of T. S. Eliot's *The Family Reunion*. Suffice it to say that it has its source in the difference between incarnational time and the Bergsonian *durée réelle*.

Within the sameness of T. S. Eliot's and Charles Williams' interpretation of the Incarnation there is a difference of considerable importance, a difference that determines, in part, the variety within unity of the Christian verse drama movement. It lies in the *Way* each asserts as the means by which the human soul may achieve the vision of the redeemed creation or come to God: in the terms of the fifth-century Greek mystic Dionysus the Areopagite, who first used them, the Way of the Affirmation of Images and the Way of the Rejection of Images. These are defined by Thomas Aquinas in his commentary on *The Book of the Blessed Dionysus Concerning the Divine Names*:

> . . . By means of the ordering of all things, which has been as it were projected out of Him and which bears certain images and likenesses of its divine patterning, we ascend in ordered degrees

so far as we are able to that which is above all things, by the
ways of negation and transcendence, and the conception of a
universal cause.

Thus God is known in all things and yet apart from all things;
and He is known through knowledge and through ignorance. On
the one hand, He is apprehended by intuition, reason, understanding, touch, sense, opinion, imagination, name, and so on;
while on the other hand He cannot be grasped by intuition nor
can He be uttered or named, and He is not anything in the world,
nor is He known in any existent thing.[71]

The *via negativa*, the greatest exponent of which is St. John of the
Cross, defines God negatively and, correspondingly, achieves union
with ultimate reality through the rejection of created things, the
images of this world. It is, generally, the Way of Eliot. The *via
positiva*, on the other hand, defines God positively and achieves
union through the affirmation of the created world. It is the Way
of Williams.

This distinction, which is embodied in Williams' ubiquitous
formula "This also is Thou; neither is this Thou," suggests that
Williams is closer than Eliot to the interpretation of the Incarnation outlined above. Actually this is not the case. For the two ways
are ultimately related. Eliot tacitly acknowledges this when he
introduces *Four Quartets* with an epigraph taken from Heraclitus'
Fragments: hodos ano kato mia kai hoüte ("The way up and the
way down are one and the same").[72] Williams too recognizes the
relationship: "Rejection was [according to the formal doctrine of
the Church] to be rejection but not denial, as reception was to be
reception but not subservience. Both methods, the Affirmative
Way and the Negative Way, were to co-exist; one might almost
say, to co-inhere, since each was to be the key of the other. . . .
'Your life and your death are with your neighbour.' No Affirmation
could be so complete as not to need definition, discipline, and refusal; no Rejection so absolute as not to leave necessary (literally
and metaphorically) beans and a wild beast's skin and a little water.
Those who most rejected material things might cling the more
closely to verbal formulae; those who looked most askance at the

formulae might apprehend most easily the divine imagery of matter. The Communion of the Eucharist, at once an image and a
Presence, was common and necessary to both." [73]

Seen from another perspective, both ways assume that nature
(including the flesh) and time have been redeemed by the Incarnation, but that Man in his weakness since the Fall is subject to sin
and therefore must, in his capacity as individual, achieve *awareness*
of redeemed nature and time by a perpetual analogical reenactment, as it were, of the crucifixion, a dying to the self in order to
give life to the self and to the creation and time:

> At the moment which is not of action or inaction
> You can receive this: "on whatever sphere of being
> The mind of a man may be intent
> At the time of death"—that is the one action
> (And the time of death is every moment)
> Which shall fructify in the lives of others: [74]

The way of negation does not distrust nature and time; it distrusts
what the self may make of these and therefore rejects their aid. It
is this distrust of self based on the Fall that leads Eliot to conclude
that

>   . . . to apprehend
> The point of intersection of the timeless
> With time, is an occupation for the saint—
> . . . .
> For most of us, there is only the unattended
> Moment, the moment in and out of time,
> The distraction fit, lost in a shaft of sunlight,
> The wild thyme unseen, or the winter lightning
> Or the waterfall, or music heard so deeply
> That it is not heard at all, but you are the music
> While the music lasts. These are only hints and guesses,
> Hints followed by guesses; and the rest
> Is prayer, observance, discipline, thought and action.
> The hint half guessed, the gift half understood, is Incarnation.[75]

The Way of Affirmation, on the other hand, has faith in the self
and therefore accepts, in a process of "exchange" (Williams' term),
the gifts of nature and time, which, in turn, receive the gift of self.

The alternative ways correspondingly affect the themes and the imagery of each poet. In Eliot the *via negativa* results in themes that explore the potential of the ascetic life and, after *Murder in the Cathedral*, imagery that rarely calls attention to itself; and in Williams, the *via positiva* results in themes that celebrate the creation and imagery that suggests if rather austerely its plenitude. But the two ways do not in themselves affect the essential definition and quality of the poetry and dramatic action. Both poets, that is, ground their art in a sacramental aesthetic. This point is worth stressing, for the obvious differences in the poetry and verse drama of Eliot and Williams have hitherto hidden the more important similarities and obscured the fact that both poets derive from the same tradition.

Neither T. S. Eliot nor Charles Williams has formulated a systematic aesthetic or theory of poetic drama from his theology. Eliot's dramatic criticism focuses on the nature and function of dramatic verse. What he says about other aspects of poetic drama is couched in traditional critical terminology. Williams has written very little about aesthetics and even less about verse drama. One must, on the whole, infer the relationship between aesthetic and theology from the body of their writing. That their work as Christians is, however, available for translation into a Christian aesthetic is clearly revealed by Dorothy Sayers, another poet-dramatist of the Canterbury Festival. Under the influence of both poets, though primarily of Williams, she outlines the first principles of a sacramental aesthetic based on the analogy of Trinitarian theology whereby the artistic process "is seen to be threefold—a trinity— experience, expression, and recognition; the unknowable reality in the experience; the image of that reality known in it expression; and the power in the recognition," [76] and thus is analogous to the respective activity of the Three Persons—God, Christ, and the Holy Ghost—of the Deity. Since it is concerned with art—the embodiment of unknowable reality—Miss Sayers' aesthetic has, for all practical purposes, as its central principle the Incarnation (though, of course, it is theoretically coequal with the other creative activities).

The core of Miss Sayers' aesthetic is embodied in the distinction she draws between the classical and Christian modes of representing reality. For the Greek, who "did not look on history as the continual act of God fulfilling itself in creation," [77] art is mimetic, representational, imitative. For the Christian it is something quite different:

> . . . let us take note of a new word that has crept into the argument by way of Christian theology—the word *Image*. Suppose, having rejected the words "copy," "imitation," and "representation" as inadequate, we substitute the word "image" and say that what the artist is doing is *to image forth* something or the other, and connect that with St. Paul's phrase: "God . . . hath spoken to us by His Son, the brightness of this glory and express *image* of His person."—Something which, by being an image, *expresses* that which it images. . . . There is something which is, in the deepest sense of the words, *unimaginable*, known to Itself (and still more, to us) only by the image in which it expresses Itself through creation; and, says Christian theology very emphatically, the Son, who is the express image, is not the copy, or imitation, or representation of the Father, nor yet inferior or subsequent to the Father in any way—in the last resort, in the depths of their mysterious being, the Unimaginable and the Image are *one and the same*.[78]

This passage, which clearly recalls William Temple's poem-Creation analogy, though too dogmatically exclusive, summarizes all that has been said about the influence of the sacramental principle on the image of poetry and the action of drama, and no elucidation is necessary. Less apparent, perhaps, but not less present in the passage is the recurrent objection of the Christian dramatist not only to naturalism, which univocalizes the imaged object, but also, and more important, to the "angelic imagination," which in viewing the object as nothing more than a copy of an Idea or the objectification of a state of mind damages its reality, its existential identity. This becomes explicit when Miss Sayers goes on to express the proposition that the art deriving from both the naturalistic and idealistic aesthetic is to sacramental art what the idol is to the

Image in Christianity (her actual terms are "Spellbinding art," which she defines, perhaps unfairly, as propagandistic, and "Entertaining art," that is, the art of wish-fulfillment or escape).[79]

To summarize, the reconciliation of the Church and art had a profound significance for the modern poet seeking means of both revitalizing poetic drama as a serious art form and regaining a broad public for it. Not only did the Church put at his disposal a public theater in which he could practice the art of poetic drama as a public mode of discourse; it also provided him with the grounds of an aesthetic that lent itself to the solution of the fundamental problems of the modern poetic drama. Sacramental vision reconciles the concrete reality and value that the empirical world view dichotomizes; and, in so doing, it rescues value from naturalistic and reality from idealistic art. By means of it, all objects in space (nature) and all events in time (history) are placed according to a universal scheme and given transcendent significance. Thus the analogical mode of knowledge and the poetic image are rehabilitated and human events (or actions), no matter when they occur in time, are given symbolic dimension and contemporaneity. Further, because of the inclusiveness and "truth" of the Christian narrative, all myths outside its proper limits can be interpreted by it and thus become, along with the events of the Christian past, available to the poet as means of controlling, of ordering, of giving form to what Eliot has called "the immense panorama of futility and anarchy which is contemporary history." The pressure of the sacramental aesthetic is, in other words, toward a "naturalization" of value—both in the verse and in the action of drama—within a form that gives order to the multiplicity of experience.

I do not wish to give the impression that acceptance of the theology of the Incarnation by the modern poet automatically established the reconciliation of reality and value within a satisfactory form in the modern Christian verse drama. The movement toward this goal has been gradual and its full achievement is as yet far from complete. Nor did it automatically guarantee a high order of poetic drama. Fulfillment of the sacramental vision has thus far been vitiated by the self-consciousness of the poet's theology. But that the movement is in the direction of a reconciliation which does not sacrifice form and that this has produced a number of verse plays which are of a high poetic order and which are also available to a public audience the examination of this drama will clearly reveal.

3

THE HISTORICAL PAGEANT:
THE RHETORIC OF
ACTION

> *All who are in her [the Diocese of Chelmsford],*
> *past, present, and to come, unite themselves to*
> *her in the great exchange of mortal and divine*
> *love through the Incarnation and Atonement.*
>
> Charles Williams, "Synopsis,"
> *Judgement at Chelmsford*

Long after his first efforts in the poetic drama, T. S. Eliot observed that because his early Histories, *The Rock* and *Murder in the Cathedral*, were written under special circumstances, his solution of the problems they posed had little relation to those he encountered in the commercial theater. About *Murder in the Cathedral*, for example, he wrote: "It was only when I put my mind to thinking what sort of play I wanted to do next, that I realized that in *Murder in the Cathedral* I had not solved any general problem; but that from my point of view the play was a dead end." [1]

Taking their lead from these retrospective remarks on his early church plays, the critics have tended to minimize their relationship to his later commercial plays and their contribution to a revival of genuine public poetic drama. One must not, however, be misled by Eliot into dividing too sharply the religious verse drama of the 1930's, written for the Church or for Christian audiences, and that of the postwar period, written for the commercial stage. The matter of Eliot's late essays pertains to his subsequent concern with the exigencies of verse in the drama of contemporary life. But the problem of verse represents only a special and advanced aspect of the broader though more pressing problem to which he addressed himself from the beginning of his career as a dramatist, that is, the general problem, posed by the disintegration of modern culture and the consequent bifurcation of the dramatic sensibility, of the levels of vocality in the action (and imagery) of drama. To solve this problem, Eliot and the other Christian dramatists resorted to the sacramentalism implicit in Christian doctrine. And it is, on the whole, this aesthetic that gives continuity to the prewar church plays produced at Canterbury (and elsewhere) and the later "secular" Christian drama, and that clarifies the developments in and the achievements of the latter body of verse plays. The difference lies not in any radical departure in theory but in the degree to which the implications of the sacramental aesthetic are worked out.

In the beginning the Christian verse dramatist is satisfied to employ the sacramental aesthetic for the achievement of overt and broad poetic effects, a "rhetoric" of action, by projecting past and present events in visual counterpoint. This approach has its roots not only in his reaction to the flatness of the naturalistic prose drama but also, as T. S. Eliot indicates, in his fear that the shock of the sacramental integration of the Christian past into a secular present, as in the medieval "history" play, would be too great for a modern audience inured to the discontinuity of the religious and secular life: "It was permissible for shepherds to joke and play pranks in the fifteenth century, or for Noah's wife to bawle and drink ale, but levity—and perhaps unusual seriousness as well—are unsuitable to the twentieth century. Nothing in the nature of a shock is tolerable. . . ." [2] Only later, when the commercial theater has been prepared by these early experiments for poetic drama with religious themes, does the effort to reconcile realism (including contemporary action) and religious significance, in verse, plot, and content, take on a greater emphasis. Yet even in the early plays, which, in deference to the prevailing view that remoteness renders verse more acceptable to a modern audience, draw their subject matter from the past, the pressure of the sacramental aesthetic toward this reconciliation gradually manifests itself with greater explicitness.

This chapter will examine in some detail the first phase of the historical church drama, in which the dramatist experiments with the aesthetic implications of Christian time in an effort to overcome the remoteness of past action. For this purpose, I have chosen three Historical Pageants, Gordon Bottomley's *The Acts of Saint Peter* (1933) T. S. Eliot's *The Rock* (1934); and Charles Williams' *Judgement at Chelmsford* (1939). Although these are minor plays, the achievement they represent is greater than their occasional nature and their conventional form would suggest; moreover, they are crucial to an understanding of the Christian verse drama movement. By revealing a means of rescuing the past, of rendering it contemporaneous, these episodic pageants prepare the way for the later imitation of a single extended historical action that is at once itself and other than itself and, beyond that, for the imitation of a contemporary action in which concrete reality and value are ultimately reconciled and rhetoric becomes poetry.

The naturalistic or objective concept of time puts severe limits on the range of relevant human actions available to the dramatist. Since such a concept views time quantitatively and linearly, without organic continuity, the dramatist must resort to the present, the contemporary scene, in order to achieve the social relevance that is naturalism's proper domain. But this results in a kind of drama that does not fulfill our subjective or imaginative needs, though it may appeal to our sense of social justice. To address these, the modern playwright, as Theodore Spencer has pointed out, has been compelled to project his action into a historical or cultural past.[3] This in itself, however, does not solve the problem of "poetry" in drama conceived from an essentially naturalistic point of view. For to the extent that the dramatist is faithful to the objective concept of time, he must project himself into the historical period to recreate the action in all its documentary detail, and thereby deny it real contemporary relevance.

The alternatives of the dramatist who accepts naturalistic time yet wishes to create "significant" historical drama are at least two-fold. In the first place he can "enrich" the past action with a poetic aura without negating its essential reality as, for example, Stephen Phillips and Gordon Bottomley do in their historical verse plays. In this case, however, the drama will suffer from remoteness and the lack of a clear and hard symbolism. Though Bottomley gives the pagan British action of *Gruach* (which presents the meeting of the heroine and her future husband, Macbeth, and reveals her uncanny psychic power over his will) a vivid psychological and even historical reality, he fails to engage the contemporary consciousness. For the archaic and romantic texture of imagery (including the lyrical literary echoes and the grand gestures), rather than placing the realistic action in a wider, more universal, context as it is intended to do, renders it historically distant and emotionally remote; in other words, decorative and essentially irrelevant.

Though it is necessary to experience the whole play to get the full sense of this colorful pastness of the past, it is clearly suggested by Gruach's bitter speech after her grand entrance (carrying "a great tangle of Spring wild flowers in the lap of her green gown") and scornful desecration of the white and gold wedding dress (she spills the flowers on it) that Fern is embroidering for her:

> I hate all yellow things,
> And most the yellowness of Springtide life—
> Yellow and yellow, cowslip, crocus and primrose;
> Daffodil and jasmine, yellow and yellow.
> These commoners of Spring put me in mind

> That now the darker flower which matches me
> In loneliness, a purple hellebore,
> Should also have returned to Glen of Shadows.[4]

In the second place, the dramatist can disregard naturalistic time entirely and deliberately recreate the past action in terms of psychological or subjective value, as, for example, the early Yeats does. In this case, however, the action tends to suffer from a too personal interpretation and/or a rarefication of the reality of the event. Thus in *The Shadowy Waters*, which ostensibly treats the conflict between the two worlds of time and eternity, Yeats's preference for the Higher Reality is so great that the world of time is refined out of existence. This is clearly indicated by the vague image of the natural world evoked by the play. To Dectora, for example, Forgael, the protagonist, is hardly a human creature:

> Bend lower, O king, that I may crown you with it.
> O flower of the branch, O bird among the leaves,
> O silver fish that my two hands have taken
> Out of the running stream, O morning star,
> Trembling in the blue heavens like a white fawn
> Upon the misty border of the wood,
> Bend lower, that I may cover you with my hair,
> For we will gaze upon this world no longer.[5]

Both these alternatives prove in the last analysis to be unsatisfactory for the poet-dramatist seeking to engage a modern audience without sacrificing poetic significance. On the one hand, the past remains intractably the past despite the poetic decoration, and, on the other, the past loses its identity or, at any rate, the texture of particularity that suggests its temporal reality.

For the Christian dramatist, however, there is a third alternative: the imitation of a historical action in terms of the sacramental concept of time. According to this view, the temporal order is absorbed into the eternal design and history is made co-terminous. The events of the past, no matter how distant from any particular present, are rendered figural or symbolic, significant without loss of identity, and, accordingly, relevant to the contemporary consciousness. And because the sacramental view of history points toward ultimate fulfillment, the pressure of the corresponding aesthetic is toward the future. In other words, the sacramental imitation of a past action tends to favor the terms of the contemporary scene and sensibility. This is clearly seen in the medieval mysteries, where "historical," that is, Biblical actions, are conceived figurally within a larger context and universally represented in terms of the everyday reality of the present, that is, the time of composition; as Malcolm Ross points out, it also characterizes, if less definitely, the drama of Shakespeare.[6] In *The Second Trial before Pilate*, one of the plays of the great York cycle, the Biblical episode is not only an event from the narrative of the sublime drama of redemption, it is also an image of ordinary fifteenth-century English feudal life.[7] The characters are conceived as contemporary figures: Pilate as a powerful and boastful though easily swayed Duke; Annas and Caiaphas as flattering and scheming bishops of the church, relentless in their efforts to bring Christ low (they are referred to as "prelates of peace"); Pilate's retainers as sadistic knights (also called "chevaliers") who take delight in scourging Christ and joking about his "kingship"; and Christ, "descendant of Duke Jacob's kin," as a silent man of great though simple dignity, who refuses to defend himself with flowery words against the gross charges of "witchcraft" (to Annas and Caiaphas he is a "warlock"). The setting—as it emerges from the frequent references to Pilate's feudal domain, the castle's halls, the ceremonial banners—and the popular diction and speech rhythms also contribute to the image of medieval life. The contemporary and realistic tenor of the play is suggested in Pilate's first speech, though the heavy alliteration (which is typical of the late medieval mysteries) may indicate an effort to recapture at least a suggestion of the high style:

> Lordlings, that are limited to the law of my alliance,
> Ye shapely soldiers all shining to show,
> I charge you as your chieftain that ye chat for no chance,
> But look to your lord here and learn at my law.
> As a duke I may condemn you and draw;

Many bold bairns are about me;
And what knight or knave I may know,
That lists not as a lord for to lout me, I shall learn him
In the devil's name, that dastard, to fear me.
. . . .
Therefore, my lusty lads within this land lapped,
Stint now stepping softly and stoutly be bearing.
. . . .
What brat over broadly is brawling,
Or unsoftly will say in these halls,
That caitiff thus crying and calling,
As a boy shall be brought into bales.
                    Therefore,
Talk not nor treat not of tales.
That fellow that grins here or yells,
I myself shall hurt him full sore.[8]

Nor is the visual image created by the verbal texture of the play
mere decoration. For the sharp contrast between the resplendent
setting (one also imagines Pilate and the two bishops dressed in
ceremonial garb) and the plain figure of Jesus ("his weeds are
worn") is a metaphor of the contrast between the magniloquent
boasting of Pilate and flattery of the prelates and the significant
silence of Jesus, which itself is an enactment of the theme expressed
in Jesus' only speech.

The play, then, is simultaneously a representation of an episode
in Biblical and in English history. And because past and present
are fused, the action also signifies a meaningful constant in the
irregular motion of the cosmic drama. It is this public multivocality, which depends on the continuity, the eternal presentness of
history, that the early experiments with the concept of sacramental
time were seeking to achieve.

Like the post-Romantic poetic Histories, the pre-Canterbury Pageant drama sought to infuse poetry into Biblical events by locating
the action, through verbal and visual decor, in a remote past. It
achieved instead a "charming medievalism" and a pious senti-

mentality. Charles Clay's famous *The Joyous Pageant of the Holy Nativity*, written in the early twenties, is a notable example.[9]

Gordon Bottomley's pageant, *The Acts of Saint Peter*, written for the octocentenary celebrations of the consecration of the Cathedral Church of St. Peter at Exeter a decade later (1933), represents a significant advance over these and, in some respects, over his own earlier efforts. There is in the sequence of action a symbolic significance and in the verse a contemporaneity traceable to the pressure of an embryonic conception of sacramental time that is utterly foreign to the great majority of earlier religious plays. Yet insofar as the concept of sacramental time is imperfectly conceived, Bottomley's pageant fails to achieve the special dramatic rhetoric that depends on a sense of the continuity of past and present actions. It provides therefore an instructive example of a transitional Christian verse play.

Conceived in epic terms, the pageant is divided into twelve loosely connected episodes in the life of the Apostle. More important, however, is the broader structural division into two equal parts: the first culminating in the Crucifixion (Episode VI), following Peter's denial of Christ; and the second, in Peter's final acceptance of Christ's burden and his own crucifixion in Rome (Episode XII). Preceding each episode a Chorus representing the modern church (though it is not clearly projected) comments omnisciently on the action directly to the audience.

This outline immediately suggests that Bottomley conceives the double action figurally. Peter's crucifixion is analogous to Christ's, and both establish a recurrent redemptive pattern that, with the interpretive commentary of the Chorus, is to engage the imagination of a contemporary audience. The suggestion of the recurrent pattern is further emphasized by the fact that during each crucifixion the Chorus modulates into a funereal chant employing the same three-stress rhythm and the same opening line. Thus after John expresses his desperate hope that Rome's wisdom, in the person of Pilate, will save Christ, the Chorus introduces the moving Crucifixion scene:

Rome's wisdom failed
Cold, secure, blind.
The spent night paled;
Earth's heavy mind

With dawn woke in gloom
And dark fierce flame.
With whips, cross, tomb
His Kingdom came.[10]

And following the Roman soldiers' binding of Peter to a cross, the
Chorus again breaks out:

Rome's wisdom failed,
Hard, secure, blind.
Although not assailed;
Heedlessly, undesigned.

An old, unknown man
Out of obscurity
In innocence began
A state no eye could see.

[p. 81]

The significance of these choruses becomes more clear when it is
seen that this striking verse pattern is used only for these scenes.

To enhance further the sense of historical continuity, the several
episodes are given at least a modicum of psychological realism. Episode I, for example, depicting Andrew's and Peter's departure from
home to follow Jesus, is projected as a relatively realistic family
situation in which both mother and wife (Peter's), each in her
own way, obstinately and bitterly refuse to understand the brothers'
call. On occasion, however—Episode XI for example, which presents the conversion of the gay Roman prostitutes—the narrow
bounds of the scene inhibit the full development of characters and
result in a violation of probability.

Finally the verse represents a movement in the direction urged
by the concept of sacramental time. Though on the whole it fails
to achieve distinction, it does have at least the negative value of
avoiding the archaisms of diction and rhythm that give so many of

the pre-Canterbury religious and secular history plays the hothouse aura that alienates a contemporary audience. At its best, as in the moving Crucifixion scene, the dialogue achieves a restrained and poignant dramatic power. This scene, because of Bottomley's adroit management of point of view, has been called "the best, as well as the most economical dramatization" of this phase of the Christian narrative "in our time." [11] As the light begins to fail and Christ's voice and the derisive shouts of the mob assail the remorseful Peter, who has just denied Jesus for the third time, the guilt-ridden Judas enters to demand his company as a right:

JUDAS   Peter. . . Peter. . .

PETER   *as though awakening:* Who is it?

JUDAS   I. . . Judas. . .

> (PETER *returns to his concentration of anguish.*)

JUDAS   You will have to speak to me.
          I shall wait until you do: it is my right.
          You denied Him: you cannot reject my company.

PETER   My punishment begins.
          It is true. What then? Do you dare
          To come where He is dying, as I dare?

JUDAS   You and I have only each other now.
          We dare not go to the others, or even go home.
          We have each forsaken Jesus: He is dying yonder:
          It is uniting us for ever, Peter
          I cannot let you go.

                                                      [pp. 37–38]

The great difference in the diction between this and the pseudo-Shakespearean echoes of, say, Laurence Housman's *Little Plays of St. Francis* ("Sweet night, how we have fouled thee! Into thy fold / Have come like wolves, and all the flocks of peace / Into a howling wilderness have scattered!" [12]) or even of Bottomley's earliest work, is obvious. It only remains to point out that the traditional blank verse line becomes in *The Acts* a freer structure, modulating according to the dramatic situation between a primary 5-stress and a secondary 3-stress pattern (each containing an indefinite number of syllables) that, in its suggestion of contemporary speech rhythms, points toward the later experiments in dramatic verse of T. S. Eliot and other post-World War I Christian dramatists, particularly Ronald Duncan and Anne Ridler.

And yet, in the last analysis, because he does not follow through the implications of sacramental time, Bottomley fails to absorb the temporal into the eternal, the concrete into the universal, and thus to give a genuine poetic significance to the Biblical action he is imitating. A fundamental contradiction exists between the two actions that should be analogical. In the first part, the drama centers around the irony of Peter's own denial of Christ after his censure of others (his mother, his wife, and Judas) for not believing. In the second part, however, though the action ends in his own martyrdom, Peter's unwillingness to seek safety from the Romans suggests his failure to fulfill the commitment to the burden of the Cross which he undertook in repenting his apostasy. Rather, he gives himself up to the Romans' persecution out of a kind of world-weariness—"I cannot stay with you always. It would not be long, / And I desire the end of this endless living. / Let it come now. . . . Here. . . . Alone . . ." (p. 78). This, like the "angelic" attitude toward the ravages of the temporal of Bottomley's drama of the pagan British past, runs counter to the sacramental view of time. His crucifixion, therefore, does not convey a sense of redemptive force. Indeed, the general emotional tone of the play works against nature. It suggests not only that the world is a sad, even terrible, place but also that life is a futile ordeal better avoided. This is the theme, for example, of the episode of Lazarus and the daughter of Jairus (Episode II), both of whom have been resurrected from the dead. Lazarus recognizes that they have been revivified by

> The still indifference that denies
> All that it looks on in vain
> Desire to see again—again—
> Places, presences, lights, all strange
> By beauty never due to change.

[p. 15]

The implication, of course, is that one comes to heaven by rejecting nature rather than through nature.

Furthermore, though the function of the Chorus is apparently to engage a modern audience in the contemporaneous significance of the action, to relate the past action and the present audience in an act of communion celebrating the continuity of history, it does so only on occasion. The choric commentary following Peter's departure from home, where it excuses modern man for his failure to affirm because "Dark powers have interfered" (p. 10), is one of these occasions, but on the whole the choric commentary focuses too consistently on the specific past action instead of enlarging its sphere of significance. The lack of modern references, in itself a negative attribute, is symptomatic of this basic failure.

Despite its innovations, *The Acts of Saint Peter* is thus a play about a weak man who, too weary to continue the temporal struggle of Christendom, commits a kind of suicide in order to get to heaven, where he can find the rest he ardently desires. As such, the play fails to fulfill the poetic potential implicit in the sacramental aesthetic.

Whereas Bottomley's use of the sacramental concept of time is uncertain, T. S. Eliot's use of it in *The Rock*, written in collaboration with E. Martin Browne[13] on behalf of the Forty-Five Churches Fund of the Diocese of London (1934), is decisive. Yet no one has recognized its importance as an aesthetic principle in the play. In a letter to *The Spectator*, June 8, 1934, written to correct the impression given by a reviewer that *The Rock* represented a serious effort in the drama,[14] Eliot wrote: "The 'play' makes no pretence of being a 'contribution to English dramatic literature.' . . . My only seriously dramatic aim was to show that there is a possible *rôle* for the Chorus. . . ."[15] On the basis of these remarks, most commentators on Eliot's drama have not taken *The Rock* very seriously, and those who have treat it in terms of its contribution to choric verse in the theater.[16] Although it is true that the choruses represent, from an artistic point of view, the best features of the play, it does not necessarily follow that they are most important in regard to the future of Eliot's verse drama. If poetic drama includes the poetry of action as well as the poetry of language, if, that is, action as well as verse can achieve poetic stature, we must examine the dramatic action as an aspect of the imagery of a play, even though Eliot has chosen to focus his critical attention on the problem of verse, to discover wherein lies the poetry it achieves. Such an examination of *The Rock* reveals that what really looks forward to Eliot's later work is the experimentation with sacramental time for the purpose of achieving a rhetoric of action.

The form of *The Rock*, in keeping with Eliot's early suggestion that the modern poetic drama might profit by recourse to the popular contemporary modes of entertainment,[17] is that of the musical revue. Though this is symptomatic of the sacramental pressure, it is primarily in the structure that the aesthetic of sacramental time manifests itself. The structure is conceived as a series of actions operating on two time levels, one in the present, the other in the past. The contemporary actions, presenting the building of a church in modern London by a group of Cockney workmen, take us from the laying of its foundations, through the several difficulties encountered (bad foundation, lack of money, political agitation, and adverse criticism), to its completion and anticipated dedication. Opening out from each of the contemporary episodes are complementary archetypal scenes from the history of the Church that magnify the contemporary episodes. Interspersed through the pageant is a Chorus, representing the Church Militant, whose function it is to introduce the actions and/or comment to the audience on them. Behind the Chorus is The Rock, a figure that represents the Church Triumphant and therefore addresses the Chorus (and the audience) from the perspective of eternity, or the fulfilled design of Providence.

That the dramatic action of *The Rock* is represented in terms of the aesthetic of sacramental time is clearly revealed in the first episode, which establishes the structural pattern of the pageant. In this episode, the workmen, Alfred, Edwin, and Ethelbert, or as they prefer to call each other, Fred, Ed, and Bert, discuss the modern concept of progress while building, not too enthusiastically, the foundations of a new church at the top of a rocky hill in London (the associations of these names with past and present suggest, of course, the historical continuity of their activity).[18] To Alfred's suggestion that science and education have rendered the need for churches obsolete ("Well, in those times there was a lot to be said for buildin' churches. But ain't all that past and done with?"[19]), Ethelbert, who is alive to the significance of building churches, replies:

> There's some new notion about time, what says that the past—what's be'ind you—is what's goin' to 'appen in the future, bein' as the future 'as already 'appened. I 'aven't 'ad time to get the 'ang of it yet; but when I read about all those old blokes they seems much like us. . . .[20]
>
> [pp. 15–16]

Before he finishes, the lights suddenly change and, in a figural scene reminiscent of the one in "Burnt Norton" in which the poet encounters his seventeenth-century ancestors, the workmen witness the doubts of a group of Anglo-Saxons about the new Christianity, the conversion of their king, Sabert, and his vow to build a church "on my hill to the west of London" (p. 18) in honor of St. Paul. Though the two scenes cannot be said to be fused, they are at least juxtaposed analogically. The present is placed in the perspective of a past action of great significance, the laying of the foundations of the English Church, to suggest the organic continuity of history, the co-presence of time.

This figural pattern is completed in the last episode of the pageant. It begins with the workmen now proudly admiring the completed church and anticipating its dedication and ends with a kaleidoscopic vision of several dedications of English churches in the past, the last of which is the dedication, in the reign of Queen Anne, of Wren's St. Paul's, arisen out of the ashes of London and "Enthroned on the hill of King Sabert" (p. 81). Thus the actions on both time levels are visually joined to fulfill artistically the theme that the building of a particular modern church is not only a unique and isolated act but also a part of the larger process: the building of the temporal Church. The completed modern church, therefore, stands as a *figura* of the Church completed in eternity.

But the significance (and the artistic complexity) of the action lies deeper than that which is implied by the idea of a beginning and an end suggested by the frame episodes. In between these are scenes depicting the difficulties that the modern church-builders undergo and complementary archetypal scenes from the past. The latter are not presented chronologically, nor do they depict consistently the vicissitudes of the English Church. Rather, ranging back and forth in time and place, they suggest a pattern of recurrence. They objectify, therefore, the theme expressed by the Chorus at the beginning of the play that the temporal Church "must be forever building, for it is forever decaying within and attacked from without; / For this is the law of life" (p. 21). The structure of *The Rock*, then, is not merely progressive, but cyclically progressive, the end being a new beginning which incorporates all the past. Thus we see the contemporary action of the building of a church not only as a process moving toward completion that implies rest for the builders—that is, as a *figura* of an action to be fulfilled at the end of time—but also, and more important in terms of the emphasis of the pageant, as a recurrent historical process related to the perpetual struggle of Good and Evil that requires, as The Rock says, perpetual commitment and labor on the part of the earthly builders:

> All men are ready to invest their money
> But most expect dividends.
> I say to you: *Make perfect your will.*
> I say: take no thought of the harvest,
> But only of the proper sowing.

> [p. 9]

In other words, we see the contemporary action multivocally, from the perspective of both history and eternity, and therefore as one having permanent significance.

When we see the structure in this light, it becomes clear that the choruses of *The Rock* derive their function from the sacramental concept of time. There are two principal choruses in the pageant, the Chorus proper, consisting of seven men and ten women, and the single figure of The Rock. The former, which addresses the audience, speaks as the voice of the temporal Church (thus incorporating, in part, the audience). Though not dramatic in any real sense, its speeches vary from doubt of its efficacy in the modern world, through satire of and mourning over the contemporary predicament, to rejoicing in the understanding of God's divine economy, thus reflecting the development and significance of the action. The Rock, on the other hand, which addresses the Chorus, represents, as Giorgio Melchiori points out, "a figure and type of Christ" [21] and therefore the eternal Church on whose permanent foundation the temporal Church is built ("and upon this rock will I build my church"). His speeches, accordingly, are characterized by an eloquence that suggests dignity and certainty and mirrors the eternal Church's "resistance to dissolution." [22] Thus the choric commentary helps clarify the significance of the structure. The Chorus draws the contemporary religious consciousness into the historical focus, thereby establishing a means of measuring it historically. The Rock draws the historical religious consciousness into the eternal focus, thereby establishing a means of measuring it from the point of view of eternity. The choruses, in other words, explicitly integrate past and present and time and eternity.

Accordingly, Eliot, unlike Bottomley, casts the choric verse of *The Rock* into a definitely modern mold. Open to the pressure of sacramental time toward the concrete and the present, he incorporates in the speeches of the choruses, particularly those of the Chorus, not only the contemporary speech rhythms that break with the blank verse tradition, but also a contemporary idiom and tone, including images from and references to modern knowledge and problems:

> I journeyed to London, to the timekept City,
> Where the River flows, with foreign flotations.
> There I was told: we have too many churches,
> And too few chop-houses. There I was told:

Let the vicars retire. Men do not need the Church
In the place where they work, but where they spend their Sun-
    days.
In the City we need no bells:
Let them waken the suburbs.
I journeyed to the suburbs, and there I was told:
We toil for six days, on the seventh we must motor
To Hindhead, or Maidenhead.
If the weather is foul we stay at home and read the papers.
In industrial districts, there I was told
Of economic laws.
In the pleasant countryside, there it seemed
That the country now is only fit for picnics.
And the Church does not seem to be wanted
In country or in suburb; and in the town
Only for important weddings.[23]

[pp. 7–8]

This bold verse has come a long way from Bottomley's tentative
modernity. But it is, as E. Martin Browne has observed, a verse
that also looks back to the distant past in its reminiscences of the
realistic verse of the medieval poets.[24] In other words, Eliot sacramentally integrates past and present into the structure of the verse
(as he was also to do in *Murder in the Cathedral*) and thus enhances the concrete-universal image that the action suggests. The
verse is not yet dramatic, but the development is immanent in the
aesthetic on which it rests.

The influence of *The Rock* is clearly seen in Charles Williams'
remarkable Pageant play *Judgement at Chelmsford*, written in
1939 (under the pseudonym of Peter Stanhope) to celebrate the
twenty-fifth anniversary of the Diocese of Chelmsford.[25] Like Eliot,
Williams casts his matter in the form of an "ecclesiastical revue,"
employing such devices as song, dance, and dumb show to provide
variety and spectacle. As E. Martin Browne has noted, however,
the greater unity of conception renders the work "more ecclesiastical and less of a revue" [26] than *The Rock*. It is Williams' more
complex use of the aesthetic of sacramental time in the execution
of the theme of *Judgement at Chelmsford*, the quest for the mean-

ing of the Cross and its discovery in the doctrine of "exchange" (which has its origins in Christ's substitution of Himself for man), that gives the conception this greater unity and the work a more organic structure.

As in *The Rock*, the action of *Judgement at Chelmsford* is worked out on two time planes, present and past, that are united rhetorically by the idea of an eternal present, thus raising the play above the conventional Pageant, whose episodic structure is its basic limitation. On the level of the present, Chelmsford approaches the Gate of Heaven seeking entrance into the community of Christian Sees—that is, the Heavenly City. She is intercepted by the Accuser, who insists that first she must see herself as she really is, must confront "Her history, her ways of living." [27] He calls the five Sees, who, to the sound of bombers and the *Dies Irae*, enter to sit in judgment of her defense. The remainder of the action on this level presents Chelmsford's gradual and painful awakening to knowledge of herself, her discovery of and commitment to the truth of Christianity, her reconciliation with the terrible Accuser, and her redemption.

Interspersed throughout the direct action, and representing (on one level) her "defense," are eight archetypal episodes, varying in form, from Chelmsford's "life" that proceed chronologically into her historical and legendary past. Episode I ("Modern Times") depicts the feeble state of the Diocese of Chelmsford in the modern period through a priest who can offer little more than self-denial to a young girl who is eager for life. Episode II ("The Chelmsford Witches") then projects the denunciation of the witches (1645) by the witch-hunter Matthew Hopkins, an unsuccessful lawyer of Manningtree, who under cover of the love of God "bought himself comfort by hunting the covetousness of others" and thus "ran with the witches through the ditches of the soul" (p. 84). Episode III ("The Reformation") presents the violent and hate-filled conflict between Catholic and Protestant over the identity of Christ and the consequent martyrdoms of Thomas Becke, Benedictine Abbot of St. John Baptist at Colchester, and the Protestant Rose Allen of Essex. Episode IV ("Barking Abbey") depicts the gay and exuberant proceedings of the girls in a medieval convent when, at the Christmas feast of the Triduum (a period of misrule during which a girl abbess was elected to rule as she wished), they perform a morality play by Nicholas Udall. Episode V ("John Ball and the Peasants' Rising") presents the peasants' revolt of 1431 in Essex, their petition to King Richard that the Church fulfill its duty to satisfy the people's earthly needs, and their repulse by the state, presumably with the approval of the bishops. Episode VI ("Martyrdom of St. Osyth") shows the barbarous martyrdom at the hands of the Danes of the nun Osyth of Essex, who, in the face of death by the axe, can, through faith, see

> . . . the City where Love loves and is loved.
> It was striking out of earth; all the liking
> of man for man, woman for woman, man for woman
> opened outward into a glory; it ran
> out of the hidden points of the flesh and the soul
> into the whole pattern of exchange of beauty,
> and Fate free, and all luck good.
>
> [p. 126]

Episode VII ("Old King Cole") then presents the legend of the visit of Constantius, the Western Caesar, to the court of the legendary King Cole of Colchester, his meeting with the king's daughter, Helena, whose sacramentalism—"God has made flesh / part of his infinite and adorable redemption" (p. 135)—reveals to him the vision that Rome lacked—Love, "the only untired god that is left" (p. 134)—and his figural prophecy that their son (who became the first Christian Roman Emperor) would "draw a new doctrine into the heart of Rome" (p. 136) and breathe new life into the Pagan City.[28] Finally, Episode VIII ("St. Helena and the Invention of the Cross") depicts Thomas Ken of Little Easton preaching on the significance of St. Helena's finding of the true Cross, which itself is presented in pantomime during the sermon.

In a note to the published play, Williams writes in his typically enigmatic way that "*Judgement at Chelmsford,* unlike most pageants, combines all its Episodes into a complete whole. Each, therefore, must be understood not as a separate incident, but as an incident related to all the others and to the final climax" (p. 63). The aesthetic means of accomplishing this difficult integration involves the relationship between Chelmsford's present and past, her contemporary and historical self. At the beginning of the pageant, we see that her quest is characterized by an unwarranted certainty of her righteousness, which is, in fact, an evasion of the reality of the world and time—her nature and history. This failure of her understanding, this self-deception, is the burden of the Accuser's satiric censure:

THE ACCUSER   Halt there, sweet!

CHELMSFORD   Whose feet here
    interpose between me and those who await me?

THE ACCUSER   Child of the Apostles, do you hope to come
    quite so easily into heaven? think again.
    The Apostolic Sees will have something to say
    to that; and I too, whether they do or not.

CHELMSFORD   Who are you? where do you come from?

THE ACCUSER   I come
    from going with time up and down the earth,
    testing the worth of the confessors. . . .
  . . . .

CHELMSFORD   But why
    to me now, to-day, at the gate of heaven?

THE ACCUSER   Sweet, your world is become perilous to you.
    This is no age with long peaceful hours
    fastidiously changing young things into old;
    families, cities, churches gradually thriving
    through the happy quiet virtues, as the corn grows.
    The air is dangerous with flames other than Pentecost
    and a host other than angelic rides—hark!

        (The noise of aeroplanes at a distance)

    Dark and dark alike carry the things
    that strike bitterly and awfully at bed and board

leaving the dead in the shelters and in the streets.
Hark!

> (*The distant sound of bombs; a faint scream or
> two. Aeroplanes*)

If you were called to-night to be judged, how
could you answer? . . .   [pp. 72–73]

Chelmsford's evasion of reality reveals her lack of understanding
of the principal truth of Christianity, the redemption of nature
and time by Christ's love, embodied in the Incarnation. Unable
to perceive her history sacramentally, in terms of an eternal present,
she must, when called upon to examine it, see it with eyes that
cannot penetrate beyond the surface of experience. Thus her past
(the episodes that constitute her defense) opens out "naturalistically," beginning in the evil-ridden present, in which, as the priest's
(the Church's) inability to recognize the young girl's claims on life
reveals, the doctrine of exchange is almost buried by the debris of
time and change, and proceeding backward stage by stage into her
past until she witnesses the discovery of the Cross.

John Heath-Stubbs, one of the few critics to note the formal
beauty of *Judgement at Chelmsford*, interprets the historical episodes in terms of the structure of Dante's *Divine Comedy:* "The
series of historical scenes is . . . unfolded, moving backwards in
time but in a logical progression probably suggested by Dante's
Commedia. First is shown the limbo of modern life, then the inferno of Matthew Hopkins . . . and the Essex witches. We move
to a purgatorio, whose climax is the martyrdom of the Abbess
Osyth by the Danes, and hence to a paradiso represented by the
legendary marriage of St. Helena of Colchester to Constantius
Chlorus . . . which symbolizes the ideal union of Church and
City." [29] This interpretation is broadly justifiable, but it does not
do justice to the internal harmony achieved by the aesthetic of
sacramental time. The process is actually a quest into her being
which peels off layer upon layer of time and consequently brings
Chelmsford increasingly stronger intimations (underscored by the
Accuser and the Sees in their commentary on each episode) of

her true identity and of the significance of the Incarnation until she identifies herself with St. Helena and finally with Christ and discovers the meaning of the exchange on the Cross.

Though the episode of the martyrdom of Osyth (VI) is the turning point of Chelmsford's understanding, it is not until Episodes VII and VIII, which present first the love of Constantius and Helena and their vision of the City, the new Rome grounded in Christian love, and then Helena's finding of the Cross, that she comes to understand fully the sacramental nature of Christ's redemptive mission, to acknowledge her history, and finally to perceive the eternal design being fulfilled in it.

Commenting on Constantius' intuitive affirmation of the world, the goodness even of evil, the Accuser says to Constantinople: "This man died at York: his son was Constantine, and a Christian —no one knows why" (p. 136). Constantinople's reply, which is based on the analogy of Constantius' love for Helena and Christ's love for man, confirms the holiness of the redeemed body and, by extension, of nature and time:

> Indeed no one knows why.
> But in some exchange between the Omnipotence
> and man, in some such ravishing hour as this,[30]
> when our incarnate and most courteous lord
> exhibits the actual unveiled beauty of flesh
> to eyes of love; making the love and the loving,
> the lover and the beloved, the beloved and the lover,
> into a glorious mystery of himself—
> might that not be an obscure reason in God?
> Brother, our lord is incarnate; you forget—
> and not a mirage in a desert of piety.
> The infidel has walled up Holy Wisdom,
> which this man's son first built, but a million lovers
> circulate Holy Wisdom through the world,
> to be spiritual sees of Christendom. There is
> an apostolic tradition in the blood
> when the flood of the spirit takes it, as the water
> mingles with the precious and original blood.
>
> [pp. 136–137]

At this point Chelmsford, having gained a partial insight into the redemptive function of the Incarnation, affirms her history, both its good and evil. She bears witness on the one hand to the rumors that Paradise shoots through man's flesh,[31] and, on the other, to "the insolent and inflamed horror" that "sweeps / over man's Christendom of flesh, and leaps / teeth and claws on his heart" (p. 138). Her affirmation, which is both an act of repentance, a passage from pride to humility, and a change in her mode of perception—a passage from escapist idealism to existential knowledge of the world and thus to the verge of sacramental realism—is underscored by the Accuser's climactic exclamation: "Ha, sweet, have I driven you to *ground* at last?" (p. 138).[32] Now she is free to command Christ to fulfill his promise never to fail those who call upon Him:

> . . . I bid my Christ to his bond.
> Could he, if he wanted, rid himself of me for ever?
> Never; it is mine to command and his to obey.
> Pray, shall I? this I say when I pray:
> *Be quick, be quick; it is I; you love me; come.*
>
> [p. 138]

thus preparing the way for the final episode, Thomas Ken's sermon on the Invention of the Cross.

In this episode which, somewhat like Thomas Becket's sermon in *Murder in the Cathedral,* draws the theme of the play into focus, the vicar of Little Easton tells how St. Helena found the true Cross in Jerusalem (the journey and discovery are presented in dumb show as he speaks), interpreting the action as the archetypal journey and discovery that each Christian soul can and must make to renew Christendom:

> . . . and this is in all of you to be found as surely, O much
> more surely, than the Empress of Rome found the wood of the
> beams in Jerusalem. And it is this which saves, justifies, sancti-
> fies the Church of God—all of you, and I, and that fortunate
> Helena, and her son, and her husband, and any and all men in
> all districts and dioceses; and the Church and all mankind has

good cheer by this. And we in this land that was of the East Saxons and is now Essex, and belonged once to old Rome under Caesar and now to new Jerusalem in Christ; and especially you, my own people of Little Easton, rejoice we all to-day for the great and wonderful Invention of the Holy Cross, that Christ found for all us and we in him, and all souls that be by his most sweet manhood and foundation bound fast to him. . . .

[pp. 143–144]

Discovering her identity in St. Helena, Chelmsford recognizes the pilgrimage into her past as a search for and discovery in Jerusalem of the significance of Christianity. In an act of exchange analogous to Christ's she accepts the burden of the Cross, which frees her to perceive her history sacramentally—as an eternal present in which, through Christ's Incarnation, what at first she thought, in her fallen state, was evil is actually the reverse side of good [33]— and finally to enter into the community of Christendom and, in Williams' term, the "co-inherence" (the organic and sacramental order created by the reconciliation of the things of time and eternity):

CHELMSFORD   O Grief, I take the Joy your grief brings;
  Joy, what is Grief while that Joy lives?

THE ACCUSER   Sweet lady, this is the answer to all.

JERUSALEM   Fair daughter, this the truth of all.

CHELMSFORD   Blessed master, now I can love you right.

    (*To the* ACCUSER)

Blessed father, now I can see you right.

    (*To* JERUSALEM)

Call them, all those that are I.
Call them, to be one pattern here with me.

THE CHORUS   Adeste, fideles, laetantes, triumphantes.

    (*All the persons enter.*)

CHELMSFORD   Are you all here?

ALL THE PERSONS   All; all.

CHELMSFORD Answer then, I for you and you for me—
     all you my past, all you my present, all
     you invisible powers that shall be yet my future.
     Say, shall I name the glory, in you and for you?

ALL Lady, we name the glory, in you and for you.

CHELMSFORD Say, shall I take the Cross, in you and for you?

ALL Lady, we take the Cross, in you and for you.

CHELMSFORD Say, shall I melt to the Love, in you and for you?

ALL Lady, we melt to the Love, in you and for you.

JERUSALEM Brother, finish your work.

                                        [pp. 146–147]

At this point the Accuser takes Chelmsford from the Cross, out of history, embraces her passionately, and leads her up the steps to the Five Sees, the Heavenly City of God, whom she embraces as the whole company sing the *Te Deum* (the play, we remember, begins with the *Dies Irae* accompanied by the sounds of war). She is brought to the fulfillment figured in her discovery of the Cross, and the final tableau becomes a dramatic and visual image of the sacramental concept of time. "All who are in her, past, present and to come," writes Williams, "unite themselves to her in the great exchange of mortal and divine love through the Incarnation and Atonement" (pp. 68–69).

In his synopsis to *Judgement at Chelmsford,* Williams writes:

> Each episode . . . has . . . two sides: the historical and the spiritual. Thus the complete pageant offers a representation not only of the history of the diocese, but of the movement of the soul of man in his journey from the things of this world to the heavenly city of Almighty God.
>
>   [p. 63]

In other words, the history of Chelmsford (which, more particularly than Williams expresses it, simultaneously represents the individual man, the diocese, the English Church, and, ultimately, Christendom) and the journey of the soul in the present are one and the same thing. What we discover by critical analysis of the double action of the pageant is that Williams achieves this unification of past and present into a multivocal whole by means of the aesthetic of sacramental time. He presents the individual experience of the present in the context of historical events that are at the same time archetypal or paradigmatic, thus rendering the present and the past actions analogous and continuous.

Judgement at Chelmsford, therefore, falls into the same category as Eliot's *The Rock*. But it reveals a greater subtlety of design and possesses a greater dramatic power, though it should be remembered that Williams had the benefit not only of Eliot's experiments in the latter but also of *Murder in the Cathedral*. Williams conceives his protagonist as a symbolic *individual* who encounters a particular antagonist in an agon the operation of which wrings changes in both, whereas Eliot makes his protagonist the Chorus—which is, more or less, the voice of the poet and therefore omniscient—and his antagonist the audience, thus externalizing the conflict, a limitation that Eliot came to recognize later, as his remarks on *The Rock* in his essay "The Three Voices of Poetry" clearly indicates: ". . . it was the second voice, that of myself addressing—indeed haranguing—an audience, that was most distinctly audible. . . . This chorus of *The Rock* was not a dramatic voice; though many lines were distributed, the personages were unindividuated. Its members were speaking *for me*, not uttering words that really represented any supposed character of their own." [34]

This brings us to the matter of Williams' use of the Chorus in *Judgement at Chelmsford*. In one of his few statements on the drama, he reveals impatience with this convention, declaring that "commentators in a play ought only to be there if there is the very strongest need for them. . . . But commentators are otherwise dangerously weakening; they are turned from the play to the audience. . . ." [35] Thus from the beginning of his career as a dramatist, he sought to integrate the Chorus into the action without, however, sacrificing its function as commentator: "An alternative—which I have been trying—is to make the Chorus—after the protagonist—the most important character. This has not often been done, and I think it holds possibilities, both in dramatic opposition (and union) on the stage, and as a method of analysis of the elements of a single 'body,' and of synthesis. It is the chief actor confronted not by a mass but by another individual which I have in mind. . . ." [36]

The Accuser is such a figure. On one level he represents the fallen world of time which Chelmsford is trying to circumvent in her pilgrimage to the Gate of Heaven. Thus at the beginning of the action, his harsh accusations against her, his satirical reduction of her pretensions, and his inexorable demand that she see herself as she really is, that she witness the truth of her history, render him in her eyes a terrible figure, at worst a Satanic mocker of spiritual aspiration, at best a pitiless prosecutor of a perverted justice. This is because her perception of the created world of time as evil is unauthentic and her attempt to reject it, a form of self-deception. At the end of the action, however, having driven Chelmsford to ground at last, he becomes her lover because she has come, through her discovery of the significance of the Cross, to perceive evil itself as an agent of good—to perceive, that is, the world of time sacramentally. Ultimately, then, the Accuser is more than an image of the fallen world that Chelmsford sought to reject, more than an antagonist. He is an image of the sacramental world of time, or as he puts it, of "God's *true* knowledge of all things made" (p. 147).[37] This is suggested at the outset of the play when the Accuser introduces himself in the words that Satan uses to introduce himself in the Book of Job:

> I come
> from going with time up and down the earth,
> testing the worth of the confessors. David and Job,
> Peter and Paul, Becket and Wesley knew me;
> there are few who do not. The Creator of all,
> Primal Wisdom, Primal Justice, Primal Love,
> made me and bade me to my work. . . .[38]

[p. 72]

And it becomes clear when Chelmsford, at the moment she recognizes the redemptive nature of the Incarnation, declares to the

Accuser: "Blessed master, now I can love you right." As such, his function has also been that of omniscient, though covert, commentator.

The Accuser, who reappears in various guises in Williams' plays —as Satan in *Rite of Passion* (1931), the Skeleton or *Figura Rerum* in *Thomas Cranmer of Canterbury* (1936), the Third King and his wife-mother in *Seed of Adam* (1936), and the Flame or *Lingua Coeli* in *The House of the Octopus* (1945)—constitutes a governing convention in Williams' dramaturgy, indeed of the dramaturgy of several playwrights of the Christian verse drama movement, and his symbolic significance is deeper than I have suggested here. For the moment, however, it will suffice to say that in the Accuser, Williams discovers at once a means of presenting in the action of *Judgement at Chelmsford* a dramatic rhythm, in Francis Fergusson's terms, of *Poiema*, *Pathema*, and *Mathema* (or Purpose, Passion, and Perception [39]) and of analyzing the motives of Chelmsford and revealing to her the direction of reintegration, in other words, of reconciling the function of individual actor and unindividuated choric commentator.[40] He is not only Chelmsford's antagonist, who somewhat like the vice in the medieval morality engages his adversary in external and spiritual conflict, but also the omniscient and loving observer, who through a verbal counterpoint to Chelmsford's statements hints at and gradually clarifies the distinction between Chelmsford's unauthentic dualistic view of time and eternity and authentic sacramentalism, thus both driving and guiding her into God's true knowledge of all things made, in which the contradictions that afflict her soul are resolved.

By achieving this "difficult poise," [41] which depends on the Accuser's paradoxical nature as sacramental principle, Williams makes the crucial distinction for his audience without resorting to his own voice as Eliot does in *The Rock*, and also transforms Chelmsford's history into a symbolic or archetypal action, at once itself and other than itself, the history of the Diocese of Chelmsford and a symbol like Job himself of the Christian progress through the world. In his use of the aesthetic of sacramental time, that is, he has transmuted an unlikely subject matter and an even more unlikely form into a drama of considerable beauty and power that transcends its religious occasion.[42]

In the foregoing analyses, I have deliberately avoided calling the artistic relationship between past and present "poetic." What is central to the form of these pageants is the juxtaposition of images of action in which that of the past receives a primary aesthetic emphasis at the expense of the contemporary image, and therefore nearly assumes an illustrative function. Thus each episode from the past comes dangerously close to Romantic historical drama or pre-Canterbury "medieval" drama that paints the past in a poetic or sentimental twilight. What saves these plays from this category of drama is the analogical relationship between past and present, which establishes the continuity of the two events in time, and the choruses, which make this continuity explicit. An intermediate descriptive term, between decorative and poetic, is necessary. For, if a poetic action is defined as a fusion of past and present, in which the permanent and ephemeral, the eternal and temporal, are reconciled into a single dramatic image, and a decorative action as one in which the past is artificially and only remotely related to the present, the action of *The Rock* and *Judgement at Chelmsford* may appropriately be called "rhetorical." Seen from this point of view, the general development of the Christian drama moves toward the fusion of the images of past and present actions and the achievement of a poetic rather than merely a rhetorical effect.

The first group of History plays, beginning with T. S. Eliot's *Murder in the Cathedral*, written for production at the Canterbury Festival, represent in a general way an intermediate stage in this development.

4

THE CANTERBURY HISTORY:
FIGURAL IMITATION

. . . the image of the Trinity was made in man,
that in this way man should be the image of the
one true God.

St. Augustine, *On the Trinity*

In 1935, T. S. Eliot's *Murder in the Cathedral* was produced at the annual Canterbury Festival under the auspices of the Friends of Canterbury. This was the first of a series of Christian Histories commissioned for production at Canterbury and dealing with some aspect of the cathedral's past. In 1936 Charles Williams' *Thomas Cranmer of Canterbury* was produced, and in 1937, Dorothy Sayers' *The Zeal of Thy House*. These verse plays represent as a group a significant development in the art of the Christian verse drama. In them the sacramental concept of time is seen to operate as a genuine aesthetic. Whereas the Historical Pageant, despite its contemporary relevance, constitutes a series of actions lacking dramatic development, the Canterbury History embodies a multi-vocal action that is also fully developed, single and unified. The limitations of the technique of juxtaposition are transcended by the integration of past and future within the particular moment in history that is being dramatized. The emphasis is still on the past, but a sense of the contemporaneity of the past is achieved implicitly rather than explicitly. As a result the rhetoric of action is transmuted into something as close to poetic action as the imitation of history will allow.

Most recent commentators on Eliot's *Murder in the Cathedral* see the play as an atavism or at best a special achievement, rather than as a work of positive merit that points toward the reconciliation of value and reality and the renewal of poetic drama in the contemporary theater. Denis Donoghue, for example, asserts that Eliot's history suffers from "structural flaws . . . similar to those of certain late nineteenth-century verse plays." [1] D. E. Jones, although finding greater merit in the play, concludes similarly concerning the usefulness of *Murder in the Cathedral:* "But when he came to [portray a part of the contemporary scene in a religious play within the theater] he had to face the fact that *Murder in the Cathedral,* although it may be said to herald the revival of true poetic drama in England, was very much a special case and did not supply a generally applicable formula." [2]

This criticism is misleading. Based on the examination of the verse, with which Eliot was primarily concerned in his late dramatic criticism, or of the theme in isolation, it fails to consider the play as dramatic action and thus to perceive the sacramental aesthetic that gives it a poetic dimension and prepares for the later development in the verse.

Though the art of *Murder in the Cathedral* is our primary concern, it is essential to understand aright the temptations of Becket and the pattern of development of the Chorus, and, consequently, Eliot's interpretation of martyrdom, if we are to arrive at a real understanding and just evaluation of the play's formal character and its relevance to the later commercial plays. For it is the sacramental vision—the perception of Providence fulfilling itself in time —achieved by Thomas and the Chorus through the temptations and the murder that governs the sacramental dramatic design and makes the play an organic whole.

The conventional interpretation of the first three tempters regards them as existing on the level of worldly satisfactions—the first representing sensual pleasure, and the second and third political power. Francis Fergusson, for example, writes: "The First Tempter, a courtier, offers pleasure, 'kissing-time below the stairs.' The Second, a Royalist politician, offers secular power, 'rule for the good of the better cause.' The Third, a baron, offers the snobbish comfort of acceptance by the best people, the security of the homogeneous class or tribe." [3] D. E. Jones says that the tempters represent "the appeal to the senses which he [Thomas] partly indulged in his days of worldly prosperity, the lure of temporal power such as he has wielded during his Chancellorship, the prospect of beating Henry at his political game by accepting the proffered alliance with the discontented barons. . . ." [4] Denis Donoghue sees them as "(a) 'the good time.' . . . (b) 'Power.' . . . (c) 'Treachery.' . . ." [5] It can be seen from these interpretations, taken more or less at random, that the Third Tempter presents a significant problem of duplication. This is a special difficulty for those, like Fergusson and Donoghue, who stress the allegorical nature of the form of *Murder in the Cathedral.*

The interpretation that views the first three tempters as existing on the level of worldly satisfaction focuses on a level that in terms of the play as a whole is peripheral and therefore misleading. Examined in their dramatic contexts, the speeches of the three tempters are seen to orient Thomas' vision in the direction of the past, the present, and the future, that is, on the level of time. Seen in this light, the first three tempters prepare us to read the Fourth as an embodiment not only of Becket's pride but also, and more accurately, of his "angelic" vision—his desire to circumvent the time world in the pursuit of essence—and therefore to discover the sacramental nature of his conversion.

The First Tempter advocates not merely the life of pleasure, but a return to the "good time past," to self-indulgent youth. That it is the temporal orientation, the past, which is important in the temptation is revealed by the whole tenor of Thomas' reaction: "You talk of seasons that are past. I remember / Not worth forgetting." [6] The Second Tempter urges Thomas not merely to seize temporal power but to seize it now, in the present moment, while the king is away. He warns him against two kinds of "deceitful shadows," against "Mirth merrymaking" and "godlovers' longing" (the past and timelessness) and insists repeatedly, "Power is present. Holiness hereafter" (p. 186). Finally, the Third Tempter counsels Thomas not merely to ally himself with the barons against the king in a struggle for power but to join "in the fight for liberty," to live, in other words, for the future: "time past is time forgotten. / We expect the rise of a new constellation" (p. 189). That Thomas takes the "new constellation" to mean democracy and therefore sees it as emphasizing future possibilities is clearly revealed in his climactic rejection:

> It is not better to be thrown
> To a thousand hungry appetites than to one.
> At a future time this may be shown.

> [p. 189]

The first three tempters, then, represent, above all, historical time or the world in its three temporal manifestations. Ultimately they represent a mode of perception that gives the human will the authority, limited only by its mortality, to control events and makes man the measure of all temporal things.

Becket's repudiation of the first three tempters is motivated by his awareness of his election to martyrdom. This is ostensibly grounded in a mode of perception which is the opposite of the tempters' naturalistic vision, one, he thinks, which is in accord with the will of God. Actually, however, his agons with the three tempters reveal his unwillingness to descend to earthly considerations (the imagery representing Thomas as an eagle soaring high above the lower orders is pervasive), an overweening pride based on an angelic and not a temporal perspective. There is, in other words, something radically wrong with his vision.

In the initial encounter, the First Tempter asserts, "Your Lordship is too proud!" (p. 184) and, following the Archbishop's curt and final dismissal, concludes enigmatically:

> Then I leave you to your fate.
> I leave you to the pleasures of your higher vices,
> Which will have to be paid for at higher prices.
>
> [p. 184]

In the second encounter the reference to Thomas' angelism is even more emphatic. Against the tempter's advocacy of present power, Thomas opposes "Holiness":

> . . . shall I, who keep the keys
> Of heaven and hell, supreme alone in England,
> Who bind and loose, with power from the Pope,
> Descend to desire a punier power?
>
> [p. 187]

But it is obviously a tainted holiness, which the Second Tempter, like the First, recognizes when he too concludes:

> Then I leave you to your fate.
> Your sin soars sunward, covering kings' falcons.
>
> [p. 187]

In the third encounter Becket's angelic perspective is less explicit though no less present:

> Shall I who ruled like an eagle over doves
> Now take the shape of a wolf among wolves?
>
> [p. 189]

Thus when Thomas has dismissed his "temporal tempters" (p. 193) and is confronted by the Fourth Tempter, it is with surprise and reluctance that he receives the unexpected visitor. But the tempter is aware that the Archbishop is prepared for him:

> As you do not know me, I do not need a name,
> And, as you know me, that is why I come.
> You know me, but have never seen my face.
> To meet before was never time or place.
>
> [p. 190]

The Fourth Tempter's explanation in the last line implies his nature. Appearing only when Thomas' rejection of time is complete, he represents a spiritual rather than a secular attitude. He advocates perception from the perspective of the fourth dimension of time, eternity, and thus is the embodiment of the vision Thomas opposes to the temporal point of view of the first three tempters. This is clearly indicated by his ironic repetition of the metaphor of the keys of heaven and hell that Thomas has used against the Second Tempter:

> Fare forward to the end.
> All other ways are closed to you
> Except the way already chosen.
> . . . .
> You hold the keys of heaven and hell.
> Power to bind and loose: bind, Thomas, bind,
> King and bishop under your heel.
> . . . .
> To be master or servant within an hour,
> This is the course of temporal power.
> . . . .
> You hold the skein: wind, Thomas, wind
> The thread of eternal life and death.
>
> [p. 191]

In other words, Becket's last temptation represents the egocentric Satanic vision: the desire to perceive as God, to be outside time, thus avoiding the limitations of mortality, yet to control it, to keep it on its knees perpetually:

> King is forgotten, when another shall come:
> Saint and Martyr rule from the tomb.
> Think, Thomas, think of enemies dismayed,
> Creeping in penance, frightened of a shade;

> Think of pilgrims, standing in line
> Before the glittering jewelled shrine,
> From generation to generation
> Bending the knee in supplication.
>
> [pp. 191–192]

And that, of course, is why the fourth temptation is "the greatest treason" (p. 196).

What, then, is the authentic vision, the alternative to the naturalism of the first three tempters, if angelic perception leads to "The right deed for the wrong reason"? Taking advantage of Becket's agonized recognition and acknowledgment of his "soul's sickness" (p. 193), the Fourth Tempter, in one of the great ironies of the play, repeats the words the Archbishop had spoken without complete awareness of their meaning, we now realize, to the Women of Canterbury at the beginning of the action:

> You know and do not know, what it is to act or suffer.
> You know and do not know, that acting is suffering,
> And suffering action. Neither does the actor suffer
> Nor the patient act. But both are fixed
> In an eternal action, an eternal patience
> To which all must consent that it may be willed
> And which all must suffer that they may will it,
> That the pattern may subsist, that the wheel may turn and still
> Be forever still.
>
> [p. 193]

Until this point in the action, Thomas has seen Being as a wheel of which the center and circumference, eternity and time, God and the creation, are dissociated and opposite entities, the center, as active agent, arbitrarily moving the circumference. Accordingly, Thomas has unwittingly but actively sought to escape from the circumference into the center from which point he can control the movement of the circumference. This interpretation is enforced by two references to the wheel which pertain directly to Thomas' mode of perception. The first occurs in his encounter with the First Tempter. To the latter's suggestion that he make the winter of his age a spring, Thomas replies:

Only
The fool, fixed in his folly, may think
He can turn the wheel on which he turns.

[p. 184]

Here Thomas sees himself on the circumference, but the discontinuity of eternity and time is implied dramatically in the disdain he reveals for the life in time. The second reference occurs significantly in his encounter with the Fourth Tempter. This time it is the tempter who employs the image:

You have also thought, sometimes at your prayers,
. . . .
That nothing lasts, but the wheel turns,
. . . .
When miracles cease, and the faithful desert you,
. . . .
And later is worse, when men will not hate you
. . . .
But pondering the qualities that you lacked
Will only try to find the historical fact.

[p. 192]

What was ambiguous in Thomas' reference to the wheel is made explicit in the Fourth Tempter's projection of Thomas' thoughts. Martyrdom for him is at once a means of escape from the circumference, where, according to his discontinuous view of Being, "nothing lasts," and of achieving the center, from which he can move the circumference.

What Thomas realizes when the Fourth Tempter reverts to his earlier speech is that the center and the circumference are not discontinuous. He sees rather that the center represents a reconciliation of eternity and time, God and the creation, action and suffering, and that this pattern is figured, however grossly, on the circumference. The role, therefore, of those in the perpetually changing world of time is not to escape it but to achieve within and in behalf of time an analogous reconciliation of action (the will seeking the permanence of eternity) and suffering (the will consenting to the operation of eternity), a patient activeness (the martyr), or an active patience (the community), "That the pattern may subsist, that the wheel may turn and still / Be forever still" (p. 193).

In apprehending the eternal design in the flux of time, Thomas bears witness to the Incarnation, which Eliot defines in "The Dry Salvages" as "The point of intersection of the timeless / With time," where "the past and future / Are conquered and reconciled." [7] He bears witness, that is, to the act of Love that redeems and thus infuses time with sacramental significance. He accepts what William Lynch, in a discussion of the temptation in the desert, calls "the great qualitative leap into the human way . . . found in the New Law with Christ the second Adam as its athlete in the confrontation of the finite." [8] Accordingly, he now perceives his martyrdom as an integral part of God's design initiated by the Incarnation, and he submits his will to it. On the analogy of Christ's decisive assumption of flesh, he descends in Love into time and thus achieves the reconciliation of action and suffering that brings him the peace he defines in his sermon, the "still point" in his own life, and prepares him for true martyrdom. This is conclusively established by his last words in Part I: "I shall no longer act or suffer, to the sword's end" (p. 197). In the words of his Christmas morning sermon, which expresses his achieved epiphany, his recognition of the integral relationship between sacramental vision and the Incarnation, he becomes the paradoxical free "instrument of God" (p. 199) in time, and his martyrdom, "a smaller figure" (p. 199) of the sacrifice of Christ that extends the Redemption through time. [9]

Becket's sermon, as Louis Martz points out, is a nodus that binds the two parts of the action together. [10] In it, Thomas explains that the martyr is made not only for the glory of God but also for the salvation of men. For the martyrdom to be efficacious, the community must, like the martyr, undergo a process of enlightenment. The sermon defines not only the figural relation between Thomas and Christ, but also, though implicitly, that between the Women of Canterbury and the Christian community contemporary with

Christ in their roles as witnesses of the sacrifice, as sharers "of the eternal burden" (p. 208). It is this second analogy that receives primary emphasis in Part II of *Murder in the Cathedral.*

In "The Dry Salvages" Eliot says that

>   . . . to apprehend
> The point of intersection of the timeless
> With time, is an occupation for the saint—

For the mass of mankind there are only "hints and guesses." [11] Thus, whereas the divinely elected Thomas is an active witness, the earthbound Chorus is essentially a passive witness. But just as Thomas must "descend," bringing the eternal design into time, and *submit* to a passive activeness in fulfillment of his purpose, the Women must "ascend," bringing time into the eternal design, and *consent* to an active patience. They must willingly lay themselves open to the operation of Providence.

In Part I of the play, we see the Chorus immersed in the flux of naturalistic time. They have a dark foreboding of the cataclysmic and absurd action that is about to break into and reverberate through the world they inhabit. Although they unconsciously identify the coming of Thomas with the coming of Christ and with the seasonal cycle, they are nevertheless reluctant to acknowledge this figure of the Incarnation and the part they must play in its realization. Fearing the communal engagement demanded by life in sacramental time, they desire to avoid contact with the center that turns the circumference. They prefer the "quiet seasons" and seek "to pass unobserved" (p. 176), to preserve their inert existence, its irresponsible privacy, and its inconsequential and boring regularity:

>   We do not wish anything to happen.
> Seven years we have lived quietly,
> Succeeded in avoiding notice,
> Living and partly living.
> . . . .
> We have kept the feasts, heard the masses,
> We have brewed beer and cyder,

Gathered wood against the winter,

. . . .

We have seen births, deaths and marriages,

. . . .

We have all had our private terrors,
Our particular shadows, our secret fears.

But now a great fear is upon us, a fear not of one but of many,
A fear like birth and death, when we see birth and death alone
In a void apart.

[pp. 180–181]

Although the Women recognize their passive role on the circumference of Being—"For us, the poor, there is no action, / But
only to wait and to witness" (p. 177)—their passivity is that of the
semiconscious animal. Thus, in order to bear witness truly (there
is, of course, irony in their use of the term), to activate their passivity, they must come to perceive communally the eternal design
operating in time.

The Chorus develops from the beginning of the play, but the
first decisive step in the agonizing process toward bearing their
"share of the eternal burden" is taken when the Women witness
Thomas' first encounter with the four knights and understand the
inevitability of his murder. Prior to this point, their anxiety is
essentially unconscious. Now they perceive the evil in the world in
a vision of a chaotic universe where the orders of time and of
creatures are abolished,[12] become conscious of their involvement
in the universal disorder, and paradoxically recognize that what
they had persuaded themselves were merely the natural and inconsequential accidents of otherwise orderly lives in time are actually manifestations of the pattern of radical sin inherent in created
things. The impending murder of Thomas, they admit,

. . . was here, in the kitchen, in the passage,
In the mews in the barn in the byre in the market place
In our veins our bowels our skulls as well
As well as in the plottings of potentates

[p. 208]

acknowledging their collective guilt.

In their next utterance, shortly before the murder, the Women perceive with horror that the ultimate result of their sin is total separation from God, entry into the Void, the abyss of Nothingness,

> Where the soul is no longer deceived, for there are no objects,
>   no tones,
> No colours, no forms to distract, to divert the soul
> From seeing itself, foully united forever, nothing with nothing,
>
> [p. 210]

and in their hour of need are driven to call out for an intercessor. Their acceptance of responsibility for the imminent death of Thomas, of their "[consent] to the last humiliation" (p. 208), has become the positive or active consent to the operation of the eternal design in their lives.

With the murder of Thomas, the terrible action is consummated; it has come full circle. The Women of Canterbury can no longer "pass unobserved" on the circumference of the wheel of Being: "How how can I ever return, to the soft quiet seasons?" (p. 214). Here for the last time the Women revert to the three-stress line which catalogues the dehumanized life on the circumference, but now it is presented in the past tense to reveal the end of the cycle:

> We did not wish anything to happen.
> We understood the private catastrophe,
> . . . .
> Living and partly living;
>
> [p. 214]

Through the murder, the intrusion of the absurd, as it were, they too, in their own way, have borne witness to the awful reality of the eternal pattern. They have been shaken into an authentic collective consciousness of their integral relation to the still point, the center of the wheel. Their witness, it is true, is a negative one. All their diffuse intimations of evil operating in time have coalesced in the moment of martyrdom into a vision of a pattern which is the absolute antithesis of the Incarnation: "An *instant eternity* of evil and wrong" (p. 214).[13] But the recognition of the one, which is the Fall, leads simultaneously to the awareness and acceptance of the other, which is the Redemption. Echoing Job and looking forward to the affirmations of Barth, Tillich, Berdyaev, Marcel, and other Christian existentialists, the Women assert in the end, "the darkness declares the glory of light" (p. 220). Thus, in their final chorus, they express their new vision of the universe. Now, through the sacrifice of Christ renewed in the martyrdom of Thomas, through the ultimate reconciliation of time and eternity, all the irreconcilables of life in naturalistic time—nature and spirit, man and beast, the pattern of man's life and the pattern of the seasons, and past, present, and future—are reconciled and reintegrated into a great sacramental image of the eternal design. This new vision completes what Thomas has called "the figure of God's purpose" (p. 208).

In *Murder in the Cathedral*, Eliot employs the term "figure" on two crucial occasions to characterize the historical event he is dramatizing. This is no mere synonym for "metaphor." The term has close affinity with typology, or, more precisely, the Christian interpretation of history embodied in the concept of the *figura*, the analysis of which we owe to Erich Auerbach.[14] In a *figura*, we recall, two persons or events of different times—the sacrifice of Isaac and the sacrifice of Christ, for example—are related in such a way that the first signifies not only itself but also the second, while the second encloses or fulfills the first; yet both point to a third, no less real, image in the future which will be the ultimate fulfillment of the first two events. Neither of the two events in time, then, has the factual self-sufficiency, the sense of finality, that the naturalistic or scientific interpretation of time accords to events. Nor, on the other hand, are they merely abstract, ahistorical mirrors or copies of a complete Idea, as the Platonic interpretation of time would have it. Both remain real but incomplete, subordinated to the real future event which will fulfill them. Accordingly, they are integrally, that is, analogically, related, not horizontally in the temporal dimension, but by their vertical relationship to an eternal design that has always existed, yet is to be fulfilled in the historical future.

This is exactly how the murder of Thomas Becket is interpreted by Eliot. Thomas and, through Thomas, the Women of Canterbury are shown coming to perceive the Incarnation of Christ not only as a moment in the historical past but also as a moment that extends through time, as an eternally present act; accordingly, they perceive the action in which they are participating not as an inconsequential accident in English history but as a significant event simultaneously in and beyond English history. Eliot thus interprets the murder as a *figura Christi*, a sacramental action, itself and other than itself, that confirms or fulfills in a moment of time the redemptive function of the real and archetypal sacrifice of Christ and that prefigures at the same time the final fulfillment of the eternal pattern.

Thus, though the *figura* is essentially a Christian method of historical interpretation, it is also an aesthetic principle. The figural imitation of a historical event such as the murder of Becket results in a dramatic action which transcends without negating its historical pastness: Through the event's analogical relationships with a previous event (in the case of Becket, the Sacrifice of Christ) and with the eternal pattern which is figured in both, the image of the historical action assumes a symbolic significance for all time. Figural imitation, then, is a genuinely poetic mode of representing reality. It renders actions at once concrete and significant, particular and universal, and thus rescues value, including the value of the past, from naturalism and concrete reality from "angelism."

In order to give his historical action a symbolic dimension and, accordingly, contemporary relevance without sacrificing its historicity, Eliot resorts to the strategy of figural imitation. He projects Thomas' murder, the present action, as an analogy of the archetypal *figura*, the Sacrifice, or rather the Incarnation, of Christ, which prefigures the action, clarifies its significance, and extends its effect beyond itself. Though Thomas' Christmas morning sermon contains a direct definition of the analogy, Eliot's primary means of achieving the figural relationship between past and present, Thomas and Christ, is both subtler and more organic. He shapes the action of Thomas' murder within a matrix of various kinds of verbal and visual references and allusions which evoke the pattern of the Incarnation: The Coming, The Temptation, The Passion, and The Redemption.

The first phase of the Christic pattern is established by references to "the Coming," which reverberate like musical phrases throughout Part I. Though they usually refer to the coming of Thomas to Canterbury after his seven years of exile, the simultaneous association with the coming of the new year and the Coming of Christ is insistent, thus suggesting the end of a figural cycle and the beginning of another, which in turn suggests the eternal presentness of the Incarnation. (The reiteration of the sacred number seven gives it a symbolic dimension: it becomes a part of the "coming" complex, signifying the end and the new beginning.) At the beginning of the action, the Women intuitively recognize Thomas' return from France as inextricably one with the coming of the terrible spring and of Christ:

> The New Year waits, destiny waits for the coming.
> Who has stretched out his hand to the fire and remembered the
>   Saints at All Hallows,
> Remembered the martyrs and saints who wait? and who shall
> Stretch out his hand to the fire, and deny his master? who shall
>   be warm
> By the fire, and deny his master? [15]
>
> . . . .
> Winter shall come bringing death from the sea,
> Ruinous spring shall beat at our doors,
>
> . . . .
> Some malady is coming upon us. We wait, we wait,
> And the saints and martyrs wait, for those who shall be martyrs
>   and saints.
>
> . . . .
> Come, happy December, who shall observe you, who shall pre-
>   serve you?
> Shall the Son of Man be born again in the litter of scorn?

[pp. 175–177]

The references are then picked up by the Priests of Canterbury, but now they are in ironic counterpoint to the dignity which the prophetic Women give them. The First Priest, echoing the Women, begins the movement:

> Seven years and the summer is over.
> Seven years since the Archbishop left us.
>
> [p. 177]

Shortly thereafter, a Herald enters to give them "notice of his coming" (p. 177), and to describe Thomas' reception in terms evoking Christ's entry into Jerusalem:

> He comes in pride and sorrow, affirming all his claims,
> Assured, beyond doubt, of the devotion of the people,
> Who receive him with scenes of frenzied enthusiasm,
> Lining the road and throwing down their capes,
> Strewing the way with leaves and late flowers of the season.[16]
>
> [p. 178]

The recital reaches its climax with the Second Priest's attempt to allay the worldly fears of his colleagues: "Yet our lord is returned. Our lord has come back to his own again" (p. 179). In his summarizing speech, the Third Priest gathers the references to the coming into a partial expression of the central symbol of the Incarnation—the still and turning wheel—thus preparing for its full revelation:

> For good or ill, let the wheel turn.
> The wheel has been still, these seven years, and no good.
> For ill or good, let the wheel turn.
>
> [p. 179]

In the final movement of this section, the Women, with Thomas' arrival imminent, return to the theme of the coming. They identify it now with the coming of a cosmic death—"You come with applause, you come with rejoicing, but you come bringing death into Canterbury" (p. 180)—and by incantatory repetition of the reverse of the image seek, in their dread, to prevent the coming:

O Thomas, return, Archbishop; return, return to France.

. . . .

O Thomas, Archbishop, leave us, leave us, leave sullen Dover, and set sail for France.

[pp. 180–181]

With Thomas' arrival, the references to the coming are finally resolved in the central wheel symbol. Rebuking the Second Priest for chiding the Women, the Archbishop reveals that "they know and do not know" that the coming they fear is the coming of the still point, a figure of the Incarnation, into the round of their lives. But since Thomas also knows and does not know, the end of this movement is a new beginning, which through the second phase of the Christic action, the Temptation analyzed above, will lead to a full understanding of the sacramental import of his coming.

Thus, without sacrificing dramatic effects such as irony and the tension of unresolved action, Eliot not only succeeds in establishing the image of Christ, the first pole of the *figura*, in the historical action, but also goes far in revealing the sacramental significance of the Incarnation. It is this creative use of references that characterizes Eliot's treatment of the subsequent phases of the figural action.

Figural or sacramental interpretation is not restricted to establishing analogical relationships between events in the Christian era. Although, as Auerbach shows, the method arose out of the need of the Christian Fathers to bring the events of the Old Testament into harmony with those described in the New Testament without negating their historicity, it was not long before other historical lacunae in the Christian narrative, pagan and profane, came to be interpreted in the light of the New Testament: [17] The universal Roman monarchy, for example, became for Dante a *figura* of the Kingdom of God.[18] The point is that the seed of wider application is inherent in the method. The ultimate function of figural interpretation is, as Malcolm Mackenzie Ross notes, to integrate *all* history, including *all* human knowledge, early and late, into the universal design of Christianity: "A fully sacramental Christianity must be able to penetrate again the whole world of knowledge. It must penetrate and reinfuse the historical order—not as it was, not as it might have been . . . but the historical order as it is, as it has actually become.

"If knowledge is indeed to be reordered again by Christianity . . . no scrap or particle of knowledge can be ignored or dismissed. For sacramentalism must seek to take into itself its very opposite. It can exclude nothing." [19]

Whether or not such a synthesis is possible in our time is outside the bounds of this discussion, but that the figural method is salutary for art, and particularly for drama, is clearly indicated in *Murder in the Cathedral* by the figural use to which Eliot puts not only specifically Christian events but also modern anthropological knowledge. Thus besides the figure of Christ, he integrates a second figural level, pre-Christian, though drawn from the realm of modern knowledge: the dying corn god of the pagan fertility religions, whose sacrificial death renews the land and the community.

The figural relationship between the Waste Land–dying god complex and the Women of Canterbury–Thomas–Christ complex is established in the first chorus and sustained and developed throughout the action. It reaches a climax in the chorus following the murder, when the Women, overwhelmed by their corporate guilt, see the blood of the hero as the ultimate defilement of nature: "The land is foul, the water is foul, our beasts and ourselves defiled with blood" (p. 214). It culminates in the final chorus, when the Women, having perceived that the blood of Thomas "forever renews the earth" (p. 221), express their vision of the fructification of their lives and the life of nature. The renewal, of course, is not merely a matter of fertility. It is also "a matter of securing the divinely ordained order of Nature." [20]

The parallel in the play between the seasonal death and renewal and Christian martyrdom has often been noted. What has not, however—and it is a crucial omission in the criticism of *Murder in the Cathedral* and of Eliot's plays in general—is the operative aesthetic principle that unites the three levels organically, that, in the phrase Eliot uses in reference to the Metaphysical poets, "is constantly amalgamating disparate experience": [21] the principle of figural or sacramental interpretation which is grounded in the Incarnation, where the

> impossible union. [sic]
> Of spheres of existence is actual,[22]

Failure to perceive this principle results in an embarrassing inability to account for the integral relation of the various levels of references that permeate the play. Even as perceptive a commentator as Miss Patricia Adair obscures rather than clarifies the art of *Murder in the Cathedral* when she writes: "To express [the theme of life coming through death] Mr. Eliot sometimes uses the Christian symbolism of the Cross, blood, redemption; but his more frequently used and far more powerful image is much older than Christianity. It is the image of the Seasons, the death and renewal of the earth, which has been woven into the rhythms of man's life from primeval times." [23] Although it is not untrue, this criticism lacks focus. The implied qualitative distinction between the Christian symbolism and the seasonal imagery suggests that the relationship between the two is mechanical, that the levels are "yoked by violence together." Recognition of the figural principle clearly reveals them to be "amalgamated," a single image.

Through the figural aesthetic, Eliot creates an experience that is valid both within and beyond the bounds of the conventional conception of the Christian era. What is necessary for the understanding and appreciation of the play, even though it is about Christian martyrdom and its deepest level of meaning lies in this theme, is not so much formal belief in Christianity as sacramental vision, which is an aesthetic as well as a theological principle.

But Eliot cannot count on an audience, even a Christian audience, whose imagination is oriented sacramentally. The aesthetic sensibility he must address is that which perceives according to the dictates of the modern naturalistic view of time, that interprets past events as irrevocably past and interesting only for their sensational violence, or, at best, their rational-historical cause. Eliot's dramatic problem is therefore double: he has to create both a viable dramatic action and, simultaneously, a dramatic form capable of animating, at least for the period of the play, the dormant sacramental imagination of his audience. He has to dissolve its naturalistic time consciousness so that it may perceive the action, not as a murder or a suicide or an interesting case history, but as a martyrdom, or sacrifice, that has communal and lasting significance.

Here again the figural aesthetic provides Eliot with a solution. Since the *figura* not only relates past events and absorbs them into the universal design but also and primarily looks to the future, to the ultimate concrete fulfillment, it tends to impose on the dramatic form conventions that relate the figural action and the contemporary audience. Thus the formal framework that Eliot adopts to contain the action is, as Ronald Peacock points out, broadly liturgical, consisting of a series of "direct links at various points with [the] audience"—the choruses, portions of Becket's speeches preceding and following the temptations, the sermon, the four knights' defense. But the function of these is not only to make the work "a continuous invitation to celebrate in religious fellowship the spiritual triumph of a saint." [24] They also serve to reorient the time mind of the twentieth-century audience and to focus it on the figural nature of Thomas' murder without resorting to the "harangue" that mars *The Rock*. As in the thematic development, the distinction which these links exploit is, on the level of perception, that between naturalistic and sacramental time, and, on the corollary level of moral significance, that between murder or suicide (the moral import of the act seen from the point of view of naturalistic time) and martyrdom (its moral import seen from the perspective of sacramental time). At first, the audience is identified with the naturalistic time mind. As the action develops, however, and the audience begins to realize its sacramental significance, the links, both directly and indirectly, give impetus to the reorientation.

The function of the Chorus in this respect has already been suggested. As "the type of the common man" (p. 221), it mediates between the audience and the action, its development guiding that

of the audience which it represents. It is therefore the least direct
link. More overt and perhaps bolder, though no less justified by
the figural method, are the other links involving direct appeal to
the audience.

After he has apprehended the sacramental significance of his
election to martyrdom, Thomas turns to the modern audience,
which is by now uneasy about the "historical" event, the "murder
in the cathedral" it is witnessing, and identifies its superficial, its
prosaic, historical consciousness:

> What yet remains to show you of my history
> Will seem to most of you at best futility,
> Senseless self-slaughter of a lunatic,
> Arrogant passion of a fanatic.
> I know that history at all times draws
> The strangest consequence from remotest cause.[25]
>
> [p. 197]

This serves to shock the audience out of its habitual refuge in
naturalistic time. In the sermon which follows, Thomas again addresses the audience. Here he not only distinguishes between naturalistic and sacramental vision—"as the World sees, this [the
simultaneous celebration of the Birth and Death of Christ] is to
behave in a strange fashion" (p. 198)—but also clarifies the nature
of sacramental vision and thus prepares the audience to apprehend
the murder sacramentally.

After the murder, when the four knights step forward to defend
their act before the audience, it is from the point of view of the
modern time mind, the point of view that Thomas had attributed
earlier to the audience, that the defense is carried out. They assume
the cause-effect approach of the courtroom or of the naturalistic
drama (along with its "commonsense" prose idiom), and present
the murder of Thomas as "a problem," "a case," which one of the
knights entitles, after Agatha Christie, "*Who killed the Archbishop?*" They identify their "reasonable" secular motives with
the desires of the audience—"We have served your interests . . ."
(p. 218)—and after summing up "the facts" of Becket's irrational

behavior, ask, in words that echo those the Archbishop had spoken to the audience, that they "unhesitatingly render a verdict of Suicide while of Unsound Mind" (p. 219). But now the audience cannot but see the shallowness of, and be repelled by, the knights' (which has been their own) "reasonable" point of view. Hugh Kenner describes Eliot's strategy aptly:

> [His] great dramatic problem is that the distinctions he wishes to dramatize do not terminate in distinct actions, but in the same action. In this dilemma he has recourse to the unexploited contrast lurking in every detective story, the contrast between actions as they were performed . . . and the same actions as the Sleuth glibly recounts them in his context of omniscience. A detective story is a twice-told tale; it is the second telling that we think we understand. The second telling—the one in the last chapter—establishes this illusion by reducing person to purpose and behavior to design. Eliot's ingenious stratagem was to give the first telling the substantiality of dramatic exhibition, and produce the glib summing up as a fatuous anticlimax.[26]

It has to be added, however, that it is through the formal conventions inhering in the figural method—the links that make the audience participants in the action—that Eliot not only clarifies the distinctions that terminate in a single action but also traps (in Denis de Rougemont's sense of the word [27]) his audience into perceiving it sacramentally without recourse to palpable design.

In *Murder in the Cathedral*, then, T. S. Eliot, by means of the figural aesthetic, transcends the univocal realism of naturalistic drama without resorting to the strategy that altogether bypasses or dissolves concrete reality and thus destroys the essential form of drama and negates its public function. It is true that Eliot fails to "naturalize" the action to the extent demanded by the figural aesthetic, which suggests that his respect for history and human events is at this point a grudging one. But the commonly held pejorative conclusion that the play is an allegory, "a demonstration of a particular theological idea," as Francis Fergusson puts it,[28] is an unsatisfactory one. For *Murder in the Cathedral* is more "naturalistic" than most critics are willing to admit. This can be seen not only in the unconscious pride that Thomas reveals throughout Part One, but also, as D. E. S. Maxwell shows, in the ironic humor he manifests in his encounters with the first three tempters and especially in the considerable internal conflict mirrored in his confrontation with the Fourth Tempter.[29] But it is in Part Two that the primary evidence lies. Here Eliot patently represents the murder of Thomas in the naturalistic mode. This has been remarked by some critics, but it is usually judged as a serious flaw in the allegorical structure: "The first [of three things that tend to obscure the changed orientation of Becket's will] is the effectiveness of the second act, which so impresses us with Becket's human force, his energetic fortitude before death, that the interchange with the Fourth Tempter is obliterated from memory, and thus rendered inaccessible to the Fourth Knight's suicide verdict which ought to have recalled it and brought it viably into salience at the climax of the play." [30] When, however, the naturalism of Part Two is seen in the light of Thomas' achievement (at the end of Part One) of sacramental vision and his consequent descent into time, the humanity of Thomas becomes an integral part of an action that is conceived and at least partially executed by Eliot not as an illustration of a theological principle but as a sacramental image or figure that is at once itself and other than itself, historical and eternal, transitory and permanent, real and significant.

The recognition of the sacramental, or more precisely the figural, aesthetic as the operative principle of *Murder in the Cathedral* is a necessary condition of perceiving the continuity of Eliot's efforts in the poetic drama. For it is the figural aesthetic that governs the formal nature of the action and of the language—the verse—of all Eliot's plays, and influences, in a general way, the commercial verse drama of the Christian poets of the post-World War II period. It is the means by which Eliot integrates Greek and Christian myth into the action and achieves the ironic distinctions between the action seen naturalistically and sacramentally in his late plays. (In *The Family Reunion*, to mention the most obvious example, the distinction between crime–punishment and sin–expiation is analogous to that between murder and martyrdom in *Murder in the*

Cathedral.) Finally, since the figural aesthetic exacts respect for concrete reality and points insistently to the future, it lies behind Eliot's acknowledgment of the claims of the present, the contemporary scene, and his progressive efforts to achieve a more "naturalistic" action and verse.

Following the practice of dramatizing events connected with the history of Canterbury Cathedral, Charles Williams' *Thomas Cranmer of Canterbury* was produced at the Festival of 1936, the year following the production of *Murder in the Cathedral*. Like Eliot's play, though less surely, the sacramental aesthetic lies behind the form and infuses a symbolic dimension into the historical action. However, it is not so much the sacramental concept of time, although that is implicitly suggested, as the impulse of sacramentalism, seen in the development of the Chorus of *Murder in the Cathedral*, toward reconciling and integrating within the divine economy the disparates that come under the conventional categories of good and evil in the world that constitutes the theme and imposes the particular form of Williams' play.

The action of *Cranmer* encompasses, in a series of brief though integral episodes, the life of the protagonist from his peaceful scholarly days at Cambridge (1528) to his recantation, retraction, and martyrdom in 1556, shortly after the accession to the throne of the Catholic Queen Mary. Though the drama is projected within the larger historical context—the conflict between Roman Catholicism and the English Reformation, which Cranmer had a large part in shaping—Williams focuses primarily on the historically elusive Archbishop. His purpose is to probe the very depths of Cranmer's complex being to reveal the weakness below the surface of his actions that led him to moral compromise at every step of the way. But Williams is not writing a character study in the nineteenth-century tradition of historical drama. He presents Cranmer's life, like that of Chelmsford, as a progress, reluctant though it may be, to the paradoxical truth of the Incarnation that organizes the strife-torn world he helped bring about into a pattern figuring the eternal design, thus establishing the action in a universal context.

The means by which Cranmer comes to perceive the truth about himself and consequently to achieve the peace he seeks throughout is the Skeleton or *Figura Rerum*, a character similar to the Accuser in *Judgement at Chelmsford*. Throughout the first part of the play, Cranmer tries desperately to avoid contact with the darkly hostile figure, to lock him out of his consciousness, to deny his existence. But despite Cranmer's efforts, the Skeleton, pursuing him relentlessly, counterpoints the protagonist's actions and words by seemingly derisive comments that reveal the truth behind them and eventually bring him to self-knowledge. He is, on one level, the "bare bone of fact eternally behind all the ideas and words of men, the fact which is both life and death, the fact, to face which is the only way to the Love of God." [31] His ultimate identity and his dramatic function are, however, best postponed until the action of this difficult play has been examined more closely.

Cranmer's unauthentic perspective is suggested at the outset of the action. On entering, he commends the life of peaceful Cambridge, the humanist delights of body and mind, and reveals at the same time a certain unconscious pride in both his physical and intellectual parts:

> From riding to reading sweetly the days go.
> I praise God for his space of Cambridge air,
> where steeds and studies abound, that my thighs,
> body and mind, have exercise,
> each o'erstriding his kind, in beast or word.
> Steed and speech go reined and spurred. . . .
>
> . . . .
>
> Coming in from the gallop, I vault on language, halt
> often but speed sometimes, and always heed
> the blessèd beauty of the shaped syllables. I would let go
> a heresy or so for love of a lordly style
>
> . . . .
>
>   . . . Blessed Lord,
> thou hast given me horses, books, Cambridge, and peace:
> foolish the man, having these, who seeks increase.[32]

The dramatic irony in the speech, especially in the last line, is signaled in the first lines of the play, in which the Singers pray that

"God . . . without whom nothing is strong, nothing is holy; In-crease and multiply upon us thy mercy; that . . . we may so pass through things temporal, that we finally lose not the things eternal" (p. 3). Thomas praises aesthetic delights and implies a desire to rest in this state. The Singers' prayer, on the other hand, insists on the necessity of movement through "things temporal" and an increase of knowledge achieved thereby. Interrupted by a violent doctrinal quarrel between a priest and a preacher, who establish the contextual conflict in which he will henceforth move, Cranmer laments the religious wars that disturb his Cambridge peace but acknowledges his "soul's duty" to participate. Even this, however, is a mental exercise:

> . . . here too must we wring
> souls duty out of that beauty: *verba verbera—*
> even sluggards as I. . . .

[p. 4]

Thus when he goes on to assert, on the basis of his three years of Biblical study, the truth of Protestant "communion" with Christ against the Catholic "adoration" of Christ, the tone suggests a doctrinaire certitude that belies wholehearted commitment. At this point the Skeleton, ambiguously announced by the Singers— "Blessed is he that cometh in the name of the Lord" (p. 5)—sud-denly appears to suggest in his enigmatic way what Cranmer is not aware of:

> Fast runs the mind,
> and the soul a pace behind:
> without haste or sloth
> come I between both.
>
> . . . .
> till on the hangman's day,
> and along the hangman's way,
> we all three run level,
> mind, soul, and God or the Devil.

[pp. 5–6]

There is, in other words, a radical division between soul and mind in the depths of Cranmer's being, with the latter the predominant force in his life, so that both the nature of the peace he desires (which is of the soul) and the duty or good he conceives (which is of the mind) are partial. The one tends to evade the conflicts of the Christian life, the other, to be doctrinaire, lacking the substance, the flesh, of existential commitment. Both are ultimately egocentric and thus un-Christian. Coming in between soul and mind, the Skeleton is to reveal along the way of Cranmer's life the reality he avoids, the reality that will unify mind and soul, make him a wholly conscious man. What this reality will be—God or Devil—will depend on the choice that Thomas makes.

Cranmer, however, pays no conscious attention to the Skeleton. Rather he prays in his unconscious pride that the king, God's minister, "smite / his people with might of doctrine" (p. 6), that is, enforce the Protestant image of the right way, "that the King's law might run savingly through the land," and promises, "so might I, if God please, outcast from my brethren stand" (p. 6). Returning to the theme of Cranmer's self-deception in terms of the inverted image of the chase, in which the pursuer becomes the pursued, that will reverberate through the action, the Skeleton comments ironically on this merely verbal gesture of sacrifice:

> We of heaven are compassionate-kind;
> we give men all their mind;
> asking, at once, before they seek, they find.
>
> We are efficacious and full of care;
> why do the poor wretches shriek in despair?
> They run; after each, entreating him, runs his prayer.
>
> Populous with prayers is the plain of Paradise,
> skirring after the men who prayed, whose cries
> beseech heaven to refrain; heaven hears not twice.

and concludes with apparent malice:

> We see our servant Thomas; we see
> how pure his desire—Amen; let his desire be.

[p. 6]

The Skeleton thus presages the events that bring Cranmer's version of Christianity into legal being in England and, later, those that betray his inability to pay the price (martyrdom) of his intellectual convictions.

Subsequently, the drama proceeds in a contrapuntal movement, the main line focusing on Cranmer's actions, the subordinate line on the reaction of the lords and commons to them. On the one hand we see Cranmer's unwittingly proud and therefore unauthentic efforts to establish his image of Christianity at the expense of Christian values. When King Henry VIII offers him the archbishopric, Cranmer accepts it, despite his knowledge of the king's dubious motives (his desire to marry Anne Boleyn "legally"). On the surface the acceptance is based on the desire "to serve God and its [the land's] friends and peace" (p. 9), but, as the Skeleton ironically notes, this motive is tainted by Cranmer's desire to force his image of the Christian way on English life:

> Besides, even your thoughts must consider your world,
> and a little hurry to be of use to your world.
> . . . .
> Has not much adoration quenched communion?
> Must not Christ intend to restore communion?
> Now is your chance, Thomas, to serve Christ!
>
> [p. 9]

Again, when King Henry, having become disillusioned in Anne, asks him to procure a confession from her, Cranmer acts ostensibly on the grounds of justice to Anne and to the king. But, as he begins to suspect after the king has ordered Anne's execution, behind his "justice" is the fear of offending Henry, thus jeopardizing his ambition:

> . . . I have searched my heart often to know
> if I went too friendly; she and the Nun of Kent,
> poor creatures, shut in prison, and I went,
> speaking them softly; did I speak too soft?
> I cannot shout, but what they said I told.
> If I deceived—did I deceive? . . .
>
> [p. 17]

What is only a vague uneasiness in Cranmer's mind is made explicit by the Skeleton. At the bottom of his actions, he says, lies "the grand hydroptic desire of humane learning" [33] which Christ spurned but which Cranmer thinks "good and better than Anne!" (p. 17). The Skeleton, putting Cranmer's exclusive concern for words in the same category as Anne's false image of the crown and the king's false image of Anne, warns Cranmer that words as such are no wiser nor safer than these, and goes on to hint darkly at the unauthentic nature of an image of the Christian life grounded in the love of verbal systems rather than in the terrible ambiguities of concrete life:

> . . . will you hierarchize the glancings
> of everywhere the translucent golden-tinctured wafer
> on men's eyes, the webbed light of the glory
> wherein is the angle of creation? along those lines,
> up and down my sides, communion and adoration
> flow and ebb and flow. . . .[34]
>
> [p. 18]

On the other hand, the contrapuntal action reveals the growth of the antagonistic forces set in motion by Cranmer's efforts to "enfranchize Christ into English speech" (p. 20) that, as the Skeleton has predicted, threaten his security, alienate him from the lords and commons, and bring him closer to a trial of his convictions. The lords feel he is a threat to their power and accuse him before the king of infecting the "realm with heresy" (p. 21) and instigating rebellion. And the commons, aware now that the abbey lands have passed into the unscrupulous hands of the nobility, demand a return to the old rites and mysteries.

Thus, when Henry dies, Cranmer is left without political protection and he begins to falter. This is revealed not only by his capitulation to the lords' use of force against the rebellious commons but also by the hardening of his image of Christianity. While Cranmer angrily declares its absolute validity before the commons, the Skeleton comments satirically:

How absolute we are! . . .

. . . .
You were less certain in old days at Cambridge.
This is the ruinous nonsense of the mind,
that men come mightily to believe their causes,
because of their mere rage of controversy,
and without morality to believe in morality.

[p. 28]

The end of Part One brings to a climactic union the two movements when Cranmer, seeking refuge in the composition of the
Book of Common Prayer, acknowledges for the first time the existence of the Skeleton. His fear finally manifest, he asks the intruder
who he is. The Skeleton replies enigmatically that he is "the
delator of all things to their truth" (p. 34) and asks in turn, "Do
you run to me or do I run to you?" (p. 35). Cranmer now perceives
that he is being called to the genuine Christian commitment he
is inwardly still incapable of undergoing (an irony underscored by
the fact that the scene begins with his recital of the communion
prayer he has just written, which reads in part, ". . . here we offer
and present unto thee, O Lord, ourselves, our souls and bodies, to
be a reasonable, holy, and lively sacrifice unto thee . . . ," and
ends with the choric singers' repetition of these same words).
Echoing the alternative presented by the Skeleton earlier in the
action, Cranmer cries out ambiguously, "Christ or devil, leave me
to lie in peace." The Skeleton, however, continues to gnaw at
Cranmer's consciousness and in the process suggests his paradoxically benign nature:

Stop me loving, would you? stop me proving
the perfect end in the diagram of bones?
You believe in God; believe also in me;
I am the Judas who betrays men to God.
Friend, friend!

[p. 35]

But Cranmer, invoking his work, refuses to listen and flees from his
tormentor. As the Skeleton observes, Cranmer has not as yet been
driven to ground: "I must run then after you" (p. 35).

Though Cranmer has momentarily escaped the face-to-face encounter with his pursuer, the Skeleton has activated his consciousness of the disparity between his mind and soul, his outward assertions and his internal desires, or in existential terms, of his bad faith and self-estrangement. At the beginning of the episode, Cranmer, commenting on his intention to write the *Book of Common Prayer*, had said:

> O but this—that words be as muscles and veins
> to Christ's Spirit bringing communion, the shape
> of his advent, nor none there to escape
> into the unformed shadow of mystery mere,
> but find a strong order, a diagram clear,
> a ladder runged and tongued; now my hand,
> my unworthy hand, shall set itself to that end.
> Be for the need of the land the ritual penned.
>
> [p. 31]

The episode concludes with the Skeleton predicting that he will bring Cranmer to climb "the rungs of my ladder, where the redeemed / walk," the ladder which Cranmer falsely "dreamed / . . . was set from his English hand in the English land" (p. 36), thought, that is, was a matter of words.

Part Two of *Cranmer* depicts the accession of Mary to the throne of England and, as his remaining supports disintegrate, the protagonist's "unheroic" progress to martyrdom. Acutely aware now of the imminence of the trial of his commitments, he shrinks in terror from an unknown singer (the Skeleton) in the street:

> A voice but now cracked from the street like a thong
> high to the sky, stinging all ears with *Wait,*
> *wait,* singing *the day of the hangman's way.*
> I sit in my study; a fit of fear takes my heart
> while in my mouth the grand art
> fails, speech fails; the thong cracks to the sky;
> . . . .
> Tyndale was burned; Forrest was cruelly burned—
>
> [p. 37]

Despite the temptation to flee, he is determined to stand to what he has done.

In his confrontation with Queen Mary, Cranmer again catches
a momentary glimpse of his sin, his unauthentic reliance on learning, which has, he admits, transformed him into a puppet of the
Devil:

> I live askance in a jest, the puppet of the prince
> of the air, long since damned, I damned long since.
>
> [p. 46]

Though he calls on Christ to help him, Cranmer is still unwilling
to capitulate to the Catholic opposition. He reasserts his image of
Christianity and demands that he be shown where he erred. Again
the Skeleton points up Cranmer's intellectual pride

> In thinking, though it was important for you to be right,
> it mattered at all in the end whether you were right.
>
> [p. 47]

With his degradation, Cranmer is bereft of a further prop, the
Church. And then, confronted by his earlier argument that the
king is head of the Church and asked if he intends to deny his own
principle, he acknowledges finally the essential emptiness of words
and is thus stripped of his last material support. The Skeleton comments:

> There is an hour—this, Thomas, is the hour—
> when the pure intellectual jurisdiction
> commits direct suicide: the minds and the world
> die, and the life shivers between their bones.
>
> [p. 51]

And Cranmer recants, denies God, or rather his image of God, to
save his life. Realizing that he has become alienated from God,
he acknowledges his essential weakness as a human being, abandons
his abstract approach to Christianity, and, standing naked and unaccommodated before the absurdity of his predicament, finally
opens himself to the operation of Grace. At this point, the Skeleton
fulfills his earlier paradoxical prophecy that "When you have lost

him [God] at last you shall come into God" (p. 52), and reveals
to Cranmer the true nature of the Christian life:

> Thomas, all your life you have sought Christ
> in images, through deflections; how else can men see?
> Plastic, you sought integrity, and timid, courage.
> Most men, being dishonest, seek dishonesty;
> you, among few, honesty, such as you knew,
> in corners of sin, round curves of deception;
> honesty, the point where only the blessed live,
> where only saints settle, the point of conformity.
> Mine is the diagram; I twirl it to a point,
> the point of conformity, of Christ. You shall see Christ,
> see his back first—I am his back.
>
> [PP. 53–54]

When Cranmer asks,

> Can life itself be redemption? all grace but grace?
> all this terror the agonizing glory of grace?

the Skeleton explains:

> I am Christ's back; I without face or breath,
> life in death, death in life,
> each a strife with, each a socket for, each,
> in the twisted rear of good will, backward-running speech,
> the derision that issues from doctrines of grace
> through the division man makes between him and his place.
> . . . .
> I am the thing that lives in the midst of the bones,
> that (seems it) thrives upon moans, the thing with no face
> that spins through the brain on the edge of a spectral voice.
> Rejoice, son of man, rejoice:
> this is the body of Christ which is given for you;
> feed on it in your heart by faith with thanksgiving.
>
> [P. 54]

Subjected by his intellectual self-sufficiency, Cranmer has throughout his life divided existence—spirit and matter, eternity and time,
life and death: the whole range of antinomies included in the

basic antinomy of good and evil—which, in turn, has bred a similar abstract opposition against him. But Cranmer's weakness, which has been manifested as a desire for the peace of Cambridge and a fear of the violence of concrete life, has precluded the possibility of an existential enactment of his intellectual ideals. His recantation, then, his denial of his image of God, is an acknowledgment of human weakness, of radical sin, which in turn leads him, as it does the Women of Canterbury in *Murder in the Cathedral,* to an authentic understanding of the true meaning of the Incarnation: that it reconciles the opposition between good and evil and the other divisions introduced into the world when man sought to perceive as God, thus redeeming existence, rendering it a "point of conformity" where the meaning of the old terms are transformed.

Williams' analysis of the Fall and the Incarnation (which he sees sacramentally as one) in *He Came Down from Heaven* provides an informative gloss to this climactic moment in *Cranmer.* Following Thomas Aquinas, he holds that it was in the nature of God to know both good and evil, since he "would not know good things perfectly, unless he also knew evil things." But in heaven evil can be known by "simple intelligence." Thus it is part of God's knowledge to "understand good in its deprivation, the identity of heaven in its opposite identity of hell, but without 'approbation,' without calling it into being at all." This kind of knowledge, however, is not possible for man. The Fall was the desire to know as God, that is, to know *both* good and evil. But, being human, he cannot know evil, as God can, by simple intelligence. His act of disobedience, thus, transforms his original knowledge of good into the knowledge of good as evil and accordingly introduces schism (alienation) into the universe, initiates the process of division within what Williams calls the web of co-inherence.[35] The only remedy for "man's determination to know good as evil," then, was to know it now "through an increased knowledge," "to know the evil of the past itself as good and to be free . . . to know all things as occasions of love." This was the function of the Incarnation: "It is the name now given to the heavenly knowledge of the evil of earth; evil is known as an occasion of good, that is, of love. It has been always so known on the side of heaven, but now it can be so known on the side of earth also." Pardon, or reconciliation, could not be achieved by mankind for it "could not endure the results of its choice, the total deprivation of good, and yet recover joyous awareness of good. What mankind could not do, manhood did, and a manhood which was at the disposal of all men and women. It was therefore possible now for mankind itself *to know evil as an occasion of heavenly love.*" The condition, repentance, "is no more than a passionate intention to know all things after the mode of heaven." [36] In short, the remedy involves the discovery of good in the existential experience of evil, that is, the fallen world of death.

Cranmer comes to see, in other words, that existence, the truth of the things in this world, is not, as a merely intellectual (or moral) interpretation of Christianity would have it, divided between good and evil but rather that it is, through the Incarnation, all good, the apparent evil being the good seen perversely as evil from the point of view of the fallen state. "I am," says the *Figura Rerum,*

> the thing that lives in the midst of the bones,
> that (seems it) thrives upon moans, the thing with no face
> that spins through the brain on the edge of a spectral voice.

He comes to see that it is "Christ's back," the earthly manifestation of the divine knowledge of good or love.

After this revelation, that is, after Cranmer is finally caught by the Skeleton—who as the truth of things is now seen as an agent of heaven—and his divided soul and mind have become unified ("I have made equilibrium," the Skeleton says; "I have drawn him level" [p. 56]), Cranmer, now a whole man, becomes free and achieves peace, though it is very different from the peace which he had previously desired. Thus, when he discovers that despite his recantation he must burn, he can enact existentially the Christian sacrifice, which throughout his life has been merely a verbal beauty for him. Strengthened by his sacramental vision, he is no longer the pursued:

> Into thee [Christ] now do I run, into thy love,
> that which is all the cause thou wert man for us,
> and we are nothing but that for which thou wert man,
> these horrible sins the cause of thy being man,
>
> [p. 57]

He retracts his recantation, plunging the hand that offended into
the fire, a gesture that fulfills the Skeleton's sardonic response to
Cranmer's earlier doubts about the Real Presence ("how can the
flesh absorb spirituality?"):

> Ah, you do not quite know, incredulous Thomas,
> what the flesh can do when it is put to it.
> You shall do a thing one day with the flesh of that hand
> to astonish men as God may astonish you.
>
> [p. 41]

Thus does he symbolize his new commitment to sacramental
Christianity.

Cranmer's final strength, however, is human. On the way to his
martyrdom, he is addressed for the last time by the Skeleton: "let
us say all: / if the Pope had bid you live, you would have served
him." Cranmer replies: "If the Pope had bid me live, I should
have served him" (p. 59). In this exchange, Williams underscores
the central theme of the play. In reiterating, apparently unheroi-
cally, the essential weakness that has turned him from God, Cranmer reveals his new awareness of the Love of Christ that is manifested in his assumption of flesh in behalf of fallen man, of the
sacramental nature of human life, in which man's very weakness
through the Incarnation is transformed and made into the "occasion of good." He reveals, in other words, his awareness of the
paradox of the Fortunate Fall, wherein Adam's sin is seen as a cause
for rejoicing, since it brings about the Incarnation and indirectly
the salvation of man.

Thus Cranmer's anguished flight from the Skeleton, which is
actually a progress toward him, is roughly analogous to the archetypal "progress" from the aesthetic to the moral and finally to the
religious phase of the existential Christian described by Sören
Kierkegaard.[37] Prior to the opening of the play and briefly at the

beginning, we see Cranmer as the humane scholar of peaceful and cloistered Cambridge, enjoying the aesthetic pleasures of body and mind, the riding and particularly the reading for which he "would let go / a heresy or so." He is in a state of innocence, or, as David Roberts defines the aesthetic phase, of "immediate continuity with nature and feeling before any moral distinctions are attempted." [38] Thus he is detached from the concrete, living present, where ethical decisions must be made, preferring to contemplate the orchestrations of an unreal though delightful past:

> I am everywhere out of place but among books
> where past voices make canticles of peace.
>
> [p. 18]

The intrusion of the violent events of the present (the theological conflict) brings Cranmer's aesthetic phase to an end by forcing him to make a responsible decision about his doctrinal commitment. Henceforth, though in each case (as in Kierkegaard) the stages overlap, we see Cranmer in the ethical phase, in which he seeks to attain moral self-sufficiency, to become arbiter of his own and others' fate through the distinctions he makes between the right and the wrong Way. This effort activates the conflict in him between his allegiance to abstract doctrine (his legalistic image of Christianity) and his individual inclinations. And this, in turn, drives him to the edge of despair, where he must choose between the apparently real void and the absurd "New Life." In choosing martyrdom, to believe, in other words, that the Skeleton is indeed "Christ's back" or, as the Skeleton puts it on another occasion, "the Judas that betrays men to God," Cranmer takes the "leap" that brings him into the religious stage, where he discovers that the Incarnation resolves time and eternity and therefore evil and good and the other antinomies produced by the divisive ethical mind. Here he achieves the momentary peace of Kierkegaard's knight of faith, the "peace of continuity (community) on the other side of moral conflict, and . . . reaches the fruition of personal responsibility within the context of collective guilt and salvation." [39]

Seen in the light of this movement, the Skeleton, whose surface function, as we have seen, is to bring Cranmer to self-knowledge by mirroring his inmost desires, assumes a deeper significance. On one level, he represents the fallen world, the realm of death, from which the self-deceived Cranmer, like Heidegger's unauthentic man,[40] is a fugitive. Thus at the beginning of the action, his stinging denunciation of Cranmer, his satirical reduction of the latter's certainty and his inexorable demand that he see himself as he really is, renders him a terrible and threatening figure. This is because Cranmer perceives the concrete time world, the violent world of the Reformation, as categorically evil and attempts to reject it. At the end of the action, however, after the Skeleton has driven Cranmer into "the precincts of his last evasions," [41] he undergoes a transfiguration in the eyes of the protagonist. Like the Furies in the Greek myth or Satan in the Book of Job (that other ancient work appropriated by existentialists as a mythical construct of the human predicament)—to which we will return in our discussion of T. S. Eliot's *The Family Reunion*—he becomes a Kindly One. This is because Cranmer has come, through his leap of faith, to perceive evil as an agent of good, to perceive, that is, the world of time sacramentally.

Ultimately, then, the Skeleton is more than an image of the fallen world that Cranmer is seeking to flee. He is, like the Accuser in *Judgement at Chelmsford*, the omnipresent, omniactive sacramental principle, the point of intersection between time and eternity, God and man, good and evil: He is the Hound of Heaven who relentlessly pursues the protagonist, who generates the anxiety or dread (*Angst*) which undermines, first, man's aesthetic and then his ethical posture and finally brings him, through increased knowledge, the recognition of the goodness of all life; that is, of the sacramental nature of existence (*Figura Rerum*) and then to an I-Thou relation with God. He is "the delator of all things to their truth" (p. 34), and the truth he ultimately represents is that of the Incarnation. From the point of view of the aesthetic or the ethical he is diabolic because life in these phases is full of contradiction and pain, full of evil. But he does not allow Cranmer to rest in either phase. Indeed, it is through the existential confrontation with the contradictions, the evil, in life that he brings the protagonist to authentic vision. This is why he calls himself the "Judas who betrays men to God" and later "Christ's back." [42]

The full meaning of the Skeleton suggests Williams' dramatic strategy. As in the case of Eliot, the problem that he confronts is that of infusing a symbolic dimension into the historical action he is presenting. More specifically, it is that of distinguishing within the framework of a single action its naturalistic or pragmatic and its sacramental significance, of revealing, that is, Cranmer's ultimate strength in the presentation of his apparent weakness and, through the image of Cranmer, the universal validity of the paradox of the strength of human weakness, the mysterious goodness of evil. To solve this problem, Williams resorts to the figure of the Skeleton, whose dramatic function is somewhat similar to the liturgical links in *Murder in the Cathedral* which both define the distinctions that Eliot is dramatizing and render the action immediate to the contemporary audience.

At once a symbol of Cranmer's unconscious temporal orientation and of the sacramental principle operating in the world, the Skeleton, like the Accuser in *Judgement at Chelmsford*, functions, therefore, as Cranmer's antagonist and as the omniscient observer, whose ironic commentary (directed at times to Cranmer and at times to the audience) eventually leads Cranmer into the religious phase, which resolves the contradictions in his soul, and the audience into the sacramental meaning of the action. Through the figure of the Skeleton, Williams is able to transform the historical Cranmer into an archetype of the Christian pilgrim and his history, his journey through the world of time, into a *figura* of the falling and rising Christic action.

The archetypal figure who acts as an agent of reconciliation appears, it should be noted, in various forms in the later work of other Christian verse dramatists. He is, for example, the prototype, both in theme and function, of Mephistopheles in Dorothy Sayers' reinterpretation of the Faust legend, *The Devil to Pay*, which was produced at Canterbury in 1939:

FAUSTUS   Who made thee?

MEPHISTOPHELES   God, as the light makes the shadow.

FAUSTUS   Is God, then, evil?

MEPHISTOPHELES   God is only light,
      And in the heart of the light, no shadow standeth,
      Nor can I dwell within the light of Heaven
      Where God is all.

FAUSTUS   What art thou, Mephistopheles?

MEPHISTOPHELES   I am the price that all things pay for being,
      The shadow on the world, thrown by the world
      Standing in its own light, which light is God.
      So first, when matter was, I was called Change,
      And next, when life began, I was called Pain,
      And last, when knowledge was, I was called Evil;
      Nothing myself, except to give a name
      To these three values, Permanence, Pleasure, Good,
      The Godward side of matter, life, and knowledge.[43]

The figure is recognizable in the character of Satan in Ronald Duncan's *The Death of Satan* (1955), in which the atrophy of a sense of sin, of belief in the reality of Satan, in the world of time is attended not only by the death of Satan but also for man by the death of God, that is, by negation of meaning in the universe; and in the Verger of Anne Ridler's *The Missing Bridegroom*. He also appears in T. S. Eliot's plays of contemporary life.

   Williams, it is true, does not achieve in *Cranmer* a fully sacramental action. Though he is faithful to the historical circumstances of Cranmer's life, the action of the play is, on the whole, verbalized rather than projected dramatically. It is a unified whole, but the unity, unlike *Murder in the Cathedral,* is essentially conceptual. Williams extends his plot over too long a period of the protagonist's life, and it is necessary therefore that he merely *refer* to important events rather than present them on the stage. There is, as Janet Adam Smith observes, "simply a succession of things happening to Cranmer, and Cranmer's way of meeting each situation." [44] Thus, as profound as the conception may be and as poetically as it may be conceived, the play lacks the tension, the sense of crisis, that only engagement in immediate action conveys. As a result the action tends to exist for the conception, to function, that is, as illustration. Yet to conclude, as most critics do, that *Cranmer of Canterbury* is merely a "drama of words" which cannot succeed on the ordinary stage [45] is to neglect the complex psychological realism of Cranmer's character, the deep split in his psyche that in manifesting itself in startling ambiguities of behavior generates a genuine dramatic energy.

Williams, Anne Ridler has said, did not "consciously acquire dramatic technique, for he was preoccupied with ideas rather than with form. But drama was natural to him because ideas existed in a state of tension in his mind. Surely the dialectical method is a dramatic method . . . as no one was better able to assess the value, the essential point, of a contrary opinion, so his own opinions often seemed to be reached through the clash of opposites, and to have in them the elements of both." [46] In other words, the dialectical method, more appropriately the sacramental aesthetic, which resolves opposites and integrates or synthesizes them into a concrete pattern where the old terms lose their original identity, demands that psychological reality be given its due. Thus Williams' play, though it is essentially a drama of ideas rather than of action, tends toward a psychologically realistic treatment of the ideas. It projects a protagonist who is more a real human being than a vehicle for the author's ideology (though the sacramental aesthetic makes him this also), a man whose views are held as ambiguities that are realistically resolved in his agonized progress rather than as blacks and whites, one of which will triumph in the end, as is the case in didactic or propagandistic drama. It is this humanization of the ideas that energizes *Cranmer*, that makes the historical action more than mere illustration and saves it from closet drama.

The poetry of *Cranmer* represents a difficulty similar to that revealed in the action. As dramatic verse, it does not wholly succeed. In general the language that expresses the argument is extremely complex and makes extraordinary demands on the attention of an audience.[47] More particularly, the speeches of the various characters tend to be undifferentiated, each revealing the same verbal idiosyncrasies (a defect also of the verse of Williams' disciple, Christopher Fry). Though charged with energy, the syntax is often crabbed, and the diction is too consistently "poetic" and occasionally, like much of Gerard Manley Hopkins', excessive in the sense that the sounds and associations of words go beyond the demands of the occasion, thus both distorting its meaning and orienting attention from the action to Williams' striving wit:

> since the secession and embroilment of the sons of Noah,
> to certain chosen spermatozoa is revealed,
> semper, ubique, the propriety of proprietorship,
> the rite and religion of themselves;
> see how they fight for their Vincentian canon,
>
> [p. 30]

This failure, as Anne Ridler observes, constitutes a defect of what Helen Gardner has called the auditory imagination, that " 'special feeling for the connection of words in sound and meaning,' that 'power to compel words to serve [the poet's] particular purposes while respecting their general meaning.' " [48] Williams' dramatic verse, in other words, is often overwrought, too deliberately labored, and, therefore, like the action of *Cranmer*, tends to lack the spontaneity of the dramatic voice. "It has to be pondered," Bonamy Dobrée says, "and therefore can never make an immediate mass appeal." [49]

And yet the verse as such is often magnificent, possessing the sinewy energy, reminiscent of the poetry of the Metaphysicals and the best of Hopkins,[50] that derives from the integration of thought and feeling:

> But now is man's new fall: now the fresh creature,
> his second nature, nurtured by grace from the old,
> lusts to withdraw itself and withhold
> from the lawful food of God's favour; it lies
> on the sea-broad floor of the Church, and its eyes
> shut themselves on the steep sacramental way,
> for it beats its heart in a half-sleep,

> blindly covered by that panoply's art it was bid
> rid itself of; multiple show and song
> throng in its dreams the bare step of the Lord
> and are adored in comfortable fearful respect.
> It rises to genuflect where ceremony and rite
> compose a moon-bright image. O in Paradise—
> cries the tale—when Adam saw
> himself in Euphrates, false awe and false delight
> threw him in a plight of self-circling adoration,
> where salvation's way was lost, which Christ restored
> in means of communion; now are means of communion adored
> yet dyked from approach; untrod, unexplored,
> is the road; . . .

> [pp. 4–5]

The imagery has an extremely wide area of reference, ranging from Biblical to mathematical and scientific figures, and is, as the imagery of pursuit or that embodying the paradoxical sacramental principle reveals, integrated into the action, becoming one with it. The metric, which avoids the outworn regularity of Georgian blank verse, is characterized by a variety of line lengths in free rhythms (though the ground line is a loose five-stress structure), an abundance of alliteration, and an internal rhyme scheme that charges directly or ironically the crucial terms. Supported by the fresh and vigorous, often incisive diction, it thus broadly enacts the shifting moods of Cranmer and the volatile ironic wit of the Skeleton, if not their particular emotions.

The verse of *Cranmer*, despite its excessive diction and its labored syntax, is thus not merely verbalism as is so much of the verse of the post-Shakespearean English historical drama from Dryden to Tennyson. Williams' verse is rhetorical, but it is neither bombastic nor sentimental. Grounded in and controlled by a sacramental vision of reality, it is, rather, at its best, the intensified utterance of men placed squarely in a significant universe and therefore to a certain extent justifiably "poetic."

Thus, though Williams' play does not achieve the kind of realism that the sacramental aesthetic ultimately demands, it does possess a dramatic energy deriving from at least the partial union of reality and value in the action and verse that renders it a real if minor achievement in poetic drama, one that has not been fully appreciated.

Like T. S. Eliot's and Charles Williams' Histories, Dorothy Sayers' *The Zeal of Thy House* was commissioned by the Friends of Canterbury Cathedral and was produced in the Chapter House at the Festival of 1937. Drawing her material from the contemporary chronicle of Gervase of Canterbury, Miss Sayers dramatizes the rebuilding of the cathedral choir by the architect William of Sens, after it had burned down in 1174.[51] But *The Zeal of Thy House* is not merely history or psychological drama. Though a play of lesser poetic stature, it is, like *Murder in the Cathedral* and *Thomas Cranmer of Canterbury*, grounded in the sacramental aesthetic and accordingly achieves in the action the multivocality and the contemporary relevance that characterize the drama under analysis.

The general dramatic idea of Miss Sayers' play has its origin, perhaps, both in Eliot's *The Rock*, which also treats of the building of a structure that is at once a particular church and a symbol of the earthly City of God or Christendom, and in Gervase's chronicle, in which the monk draws an analogy between Canterbury Cathedral and the earthly City of God, Jerusalem: "Bethink thee now what mighty grief oppressed the hearts of the sons of the Church . . . I verily believe the afflictions of Canterbury were no less than those of Jerusalem of old, and their wailings were as the lamentations of Jeremiah." [52] More particularly, it is based on Miss Sayers' sacramental aesthetic sketched out by the archangel Michael at the end of the play and fully elaborated in *The Mind of the Maker* (1941), in which the three Persons of the Trinity provide an analogy for the triple nature of the artistic enterprise: the unknowable reality in the experience (God), the image of that reality in the experience (the Incarnate Christ), and the power of the recognition (the Holy Ghost).[53]

Miss Sayers' dramatic problem in *The Zeal of Thy House* is "to supply a supernatural interpretation of a piece of human history"; [54] in other words, to give the action a symbolic dimension without negating the historical event she is dramatizing. To achieve this, her overt strategy is to project the action on two levels: the human and the divine. The first, which presents the drama of William of Sens, is worked out in naturalistic terms. The second, which reveals the role of the choric archangels, Michael, Gabriel, Raphael, and the Recording Angel Cassiel, in the rebuilding of the burned choir, places the action in the context of the eternal design, thus establishing (though perhaps a little clumsily when compared to Eliot's strategy) the necessary distinctions between its naturalistic and sacramental import.

On the human level, Miss Sayers presents the events in the career of William of Sens that culminate in his fall from the scaffolding of the structure he is building. Arrogant and aggressive, though vital and dedicated to his work, the architect is elected over two rivals by the Cathedral Chapter to rebuild the burned choir of Canterbury.[55] Taking up with the Lady Ursula, a young and wealthy widow whose devotion to the church becomes adoration for him, William flaunts his pagan sensuality and excessive pride in his masterpiece before the astonished churchmen and delighted artisans. The result is disaster. Distracted from their tasks by the architect's brazen flirting with his mistress—the youthful worker Simon to eager interest in the sexual overtones of the affair and the puritanical priest Theodatus to self-righteous prayer—his helpers fail to detect the flaw in the rope of the windlass that will carry William to the great arch where he is triumphantly to set the keystone. The rope breaks, and William plunges to the ground. Unwilling to leave his masterpiece before it is completed, he continues to direct his workers from a couch, until, in a dream, he acknowledges his sin of pride, repents, and leaves the work to be finished by others.

On the supernatural plane, the four invisible archangels, participating in and commenting chorically on each crucial event, transform the apparent accidents into events of universal significance. In Part One, for example, the choice of William as architect is, on the human level, decided by the senile Father Ernulphus, who, when called upon to cast his deadlock-breaking vote, wakes from a doze and repeats the last name spoken. On the supernatural plane, however, William's election is decided when Gabriel whispers the architect's name into the old man's ear. Thus accident is transmuted into divine election. Again, in Part Three, Michael cuts the rope with the "sword of judgement" that has been "in the making," [56] thus charging William's physical fall, which no doubt is intended to recall Solness' fall in Ibsen's *The Master Builder*, with spiritual significance. Finally, Gabriel appears to William in his agonized dream and thus transforms the psychological intimations of guilt into a divine revelation of the architect's overweening pride in his art.

But it is not so much the active angelic intervention in the human action as the commentary on it that defines the symbolic significance of the play and gives it its genuine poetic dimension. As in *Murder in the Cathedral*, though less surely, this commentary, by integrating verbal references and allusions into the action, establishes the drama of William of Sens as an analogue of the Christic action interpreted from the point of view of Miss Sayers' Trinitarian theology of the Creation, as a *figura* of Christ or God in His role of Creative Energy or Activity, of incarnate deity, fulfilling in time the divine economy or design.[57]

Miss Sayers works out the analogy in terms of references to Adam and Christ, the second Adam, in their capacities as makers, which establish the two significant divisions in the play. In the first part William and Ursula are represented as figures of Adam and Eve. Though they do not clearly *enact* the Fall—and this is one of the serious flaws in the figural structure—they do recapitulate it in their first encounter. Responding to Ursula's desire to hear about and participate in his "dreams," William eulogizes masculine creativity and asserts its superiority over its feminine counterpart:

> . . . What does a woman know
> Of the love of knowledge, passing the love of women?
> The passion of making, beside which love's little passion
> Shows brittle as a bubble?—To raise up beauty from ashes
> Like the splendour of resurrection; to see the stone

Knit unto stone and growing, as in the womb
Bone grows to bone; to build a world out of nothing—
That is my dream; that is the craftsman's dream,
The power and the glory, the kingdom of God and man—
Of man, never of woman. Women create
Passively, borne on a wind of lust, for a whim,
At the caprice of a man, in a smile, in a spasm
Of the flesh; we, with the will, with the blood, with the brain,
All the desire of the soul, the intent of the mind.

[p. 50]

Aware of his overreaching, Ursula picks up William's equation of the "love of knowledge" with "the passion of making" and reminds him of Eve's primary role in the drama of the Garden. Acknowledging that knowledge and creative work are given to man and not to woman, she goes on:

. . . But by whom
Came either work or knowledge into the world?
Not by the man. God said, "Ye shall not know;
Knowledge is death." And Adam was afraid.
But Eve, careless of peril, careless of death,
Hearing the promise, "Ye shall be as gods,"
Seized knowledge for herself, and for the man,
And all the sons of men; knowledge, like God;
Power to create, like God; and, unlike God,
Courage to die. . . .
. . . .
. . . My simple Adam,
It is too late to scare woman with risks
And perils—woman, that for one splendid risk
Changed the security of Paradise,
Broke up the loom and pattern of creation,
Let in man's dream on the world, and snatched the torch
Of knowledge from the jealous hand of God
So that fire runs in man's blood for ever.[58]

[p. 51]

Carried away by the urgency of Ursula's dynamic argument, William acknowledges her part in his humanistic creative vision and, like Adam, falls definitively into sin, thus jeopardizing, on one level, the work he is building and, on another, Christendom itself. After this proud affirmation of his powers until his fall from the scaffolding, William blasphemously represents his creative mind and works in terms of his rivalry with God the Creator:

> We are the master-craftsmen, God and I—
> We understand one another. None, as I can,
> Can creep under the ribs of God, and feel
> His heart beat through those Six Days of Creation;
> . . . .
>   . . . He made His masterpiece,
> Man, that like God can call beauty from dust,
> Order from chaos, and create new worlds
> To praise their maker. Oh, but in making man
> God over-reached Himself and gave away
> His Godhead. He must now depend on man
> For what man's brain, creative and divine
> Can give Him. Man stands equal with Him now,
> Partner and rival. Say God needs a church,
> As here in Canterbury—and say He calls together
> By miracle stone, wood and metal, builds
> A church of sorts; *my* church He cannot make—
> Another, but not that. This church is mine
> And none but I, not even God, can build it.
> . . . .
>   . . . God's crown of matchless works
> Is not complete without my stone, my jewel,
> Creation's nonpareil.
>
> [pp. 69–70]

As the archangels reveal in their choric commentary on Ursula's and William's colloquy, however, the Fall of the first Adam is the occasion of the coming of the second Adam to continue the broken work of God. To Gabriel's interpretation—

> Thus Eve cast down the gauntlet in God's face:
> "My will for Thine; man's purpose against God's;
> Slay me and slay the man, slay all my seed,
> But let man's knowledge and man's work go on."—

Michael responds antiphonally,

> Thus God took up the gauntlet in Eve's face.
> Having, like man, courage to look on death:
> "My son for thy sons, and God's blood for man's;
> Crucify God, but let the work go on."

And Raphael concludes:

> O felix culpa, quae
> Talis et tanti meruit Redemptoris!"

[pp. 51–52]

thus preparing for William's rebirth as the second Adam in Part Four.

After his plunge from the scaffolding of the great arch, which is a fortunate fall, both a judgment of his egocentric creative vision and the means of bringing him into the New Life, William's progress is represented in terms of his analogical relation to Christ, the second Adam, as master craftsman. Despite his crippled condition, William refuses to relinquish his work. Since he cannot accept its completion by other hands, he reveals that his pride in his creative imagination is yet intact. Thus, though he confesses his fleshly sins before the Prior, there is no release from the guilt that torments him. At this point the archangel Michael appears in a dream to reveal to William his real sin and in the ensuing antiphonal duet establishes by degrees the analogy with Christ. At first it works ironically against William, who sees his fall as the judgment of a God jealous of his prestige as a creator and thus refuses to abandon his work:

MICHAEL   No; thou shalt lay it down of thine own will.

WILLIAM   Never. Let Him heap on more torments yet—

MICHAEL   He can heap none on thee, He hath not borne—

WILLIAM   Let Him strike helpless hands as well as feet—

MICHAEL   Whose Feet and Hands were helpless striken through—

WILLIAM   Scourge me and smite me and make blind mine eyes—

MICHAEL   As He was blindfolded and scourged and smitten—

. . . .

WILLIAM   Wring out my blood and sweat—

MICHAEL   Whose sweat, like blood,
    Watered the garden in Gethsamene—

WILLIAM   For all that He can do I will not yield,
    Nor leave to other men that which is mine,
    To botch—to alter—turn to something else,
    Not mine.

MICHAEL   Thou wilt not? Yet God bore this too,
    The last, the bitterest, worst humiliation,
    Bowing His neck under the galling yoke
    Frustrate, defeated, half His life unlived,
    Nothing achieved.

                                        [pp. 102–103]

Having shaken William, Michael goes on to explain that even though God, in confronting the "test of mortal time" as man, was prevented from completing his work, his faith—his truly artistic or sacramental vision that perceives the eternal design in time—enabled him to cry out exultantly on the Cross, "It is finished," and leave the work to his disciples. At the end of his speech, Michael draws the analogy to completion:

    Thus shalt thou know the Master Architect,
    Who plans so well, He may depart and leave
    The work to others. Art thou more than God?
    Not God Himself was indispensable,
    For lo! God died—and still His work goes on.

                                        [p. 104]

Acknowledging his sin of pride, William recognizes at last that the church he has been building is part of a creative act that transcends his private purposes. Thus, as Michael puts it,

        . . . broken on the self-same rack
    That broke the richest Prince of all the world,
    The Master-man. . . .

                                        [p. 107]

William, in an act of humility analogous to Christ's, returns to France, leaving the cathedral to be finished by others.

It is therefore the aesthetic of sacramental time, which views history as an eternal now—Adam and Christ and William of Sens as co-present—that allows Miss Sayers to dramatize a particular architect as Everyman and the Cathedral of Canterbury as the Church or Christendom without dissolving their historical identity and thus to achieve a multivocal image of an action. Although she lacks the control over her analogies and the range of references, particularly in the category of modern knowledge, that distinguish the dramatic art of T. S. Eliot and Charles Williams, it is, as the above analysis indicates, not quite true to say, as Gerald Weales does, that her problem "as a playwright is that she seems incapable of moving from the experience to the expression of her own trinitarian aesthetic." [59] Nor is it true that "Her religious plays, for all the supernatural framework of some of them and the dogmatic theology that informs all of them, are concerned as, say, those of Laurence Housman with the human aspects of the religious experience." [60] *The Zeal of Thy House* is certainly concerned with "the human aspects of the religious experience," but not in the same naturalistic sense that Housman is concerned with them. And this is a crucial distinction, for Miss Sayers' aesthetic is sacramental and *The Zeal of Thy House* multivocal, a dramatization at once of the human and divine. In fact, it is her acknowledgment of "the human aspects," the concrete world of man, that renders the image of the action, if not the play as a whole, more truly sacramental than Williams' *Cranmer of Canterbury* and even Eliot's *Murder in the Cathedral*. It is a similar point about Miss Sayers' art in *The Zeal of Thy House* that George Kernodle makes when he writes in an early essay: "If she lacks Eliot's ear and his marvelous gift of poetic imagery, she has a surer visual sense. In this play her theme is worked out completely in dramatic action, while Eliot depends more on the rich fabric of his words." [61]

Miss Sayers' real limitation, which applies also to her other Canterbury verse play, *The Devil to Pay*, lies in her circumscribed poetic talent. Desiring to achieve the kind of dynamic rhetoric that characterizes the dramatic verse of Thomas Lovell Beddoes, whose poetry she admired,[62] Miss Sayers often falls into an excessive and nostalgic rhetoric that cuts across and vitiates the realism and the "presentness" of the sacramental action. This can be seen, for example, in the speech in which William finally acknowledges his sin:

> O, I have sinned. The eldest sin of all,
> Pride, that struck down the morning star from Heaven
> Hath struck down me from where I sat and shone
> Smiling on my new world. All other sins
> God will forgive but that. I am damned, damned,
> Justly. Yet, O most just and merciful God,
> Hear me but once, Thou that didst make the world
> And wilt not let one thing that Thou hast made,
> No, not one sparrow, perish without Thy Will
> (Since what we make, we love)—for that love's sake
> Smite only me and spare my handiwork.
> Jesu, the carpenter's Son, the Master-builder,
> Architect, poet, maker—by those hands
> That Thine own nails have wounded—by the wood
> Whence Thou didst carve Thy Cross—let not the Church
> Be lost through me. Let me lie deep in hell,
> Death gnaw upon me, purge my bones with fire,
> But let my work, all that was good in me,
> All that was God, stand up and live and grow.

> [pp. 105–106]

The general awkwardness of the blank verse, the archaisms, and the imprecision of the diction, the overformal syntactic constructions and the prosaic imagery: all these not only hark back to older poetic modes but, more important, disperse rather than heighten the emotion of the dramatic situation and thus undermine its intended realism.

The prose of the play is more surely colloquial and modern. But although its references are consonant with those of the verse, it too suffers from a lack of the flexibility and sharpness that prose in a verse play must have. This is especially noticeable at the points of transition such as the one in Part Two where the flat prose dialogue between William and Ursula suddenly leaps into the high rhetoric of the scene recapitulating the drama in the Garden from which I have quoted above:

WILLIAM   I do not think you came here to see architectural drawings.

URSULA   I came—to see the architect. (*Pause.*) Did you realise that this was not the first time we had met?

WILLIAM   I realised it perfectly. I had the honour to pick up your glove yesterday in the market-place.

URSULA   I was much indebted to you for the courtesy.

WILLIAM   I was much indebted to you for the opportunity. I am an opportunist. So, I fancy, are you. We have that much in common.

URSULA   Is that an impertinence, I wonder?

WILLIAM   Yes.

URSULA   I ought to be offended with you.

WILLIAM   If you are wise, you will be. Let us be plain.
The first time our eyes met, we knew one another
As fire knows tinder. You have seen what havoc
Fire works. Let be.

URSULA   I do not fear the fire.

[p. 49]

The usual result is an unintentional discontinuity between the prose and verse sections which, as Eliot says in speaking about his own plays, "makes the auditor aware, with a jolt, of the medium at the expense of the action." [63] Closely related to this is the sharp division in the language of the archangels. Wisely intending to humanize them, as Williams does Gabriel and Grace in his moralities, by giving them a sense of humor and a homely wisdom, Miss Sayers unfortunately produces an excessive cuteness:

THE YOUNG CHERUB (*suddenly*)   Why did God create mankind in two different sorts, if it makes so much trouble?

(*The Angels are inexpressibly shocked.*)

RAPHAEL   Hush! You mustn't ask Why.

MICHAEL   Angels never ask Why.

GABRIEL   Only men ask Why.

CASSIEL   And you see what happened to them, just for asking Why.

MICHAEL   Do you want to eat of the Tree of Knowledge, like Adam and Eve?

GABRIEL   And find Michael there, with his big sword?

RAPHAEL   And put our Master to the trouble and pain of another crucifixion?

CASSIEL   Or start another war, like that lost brother whom we must not name?

ALL   Criticising God's creation! I never heard of such a thing!

[PP. 53–54]

And this creates an unbridgeable gap between their comic and serious utterances.

Miss Sayers' weakness, which in her own terms might be called a deficiency of Energy or Sonship (the principle of Incarnation), however, is instructive. When the worst is said about the infelicities of her language, there still remains the multivocal drama of the image of the action which rivals that of *Murder in the Cathedral* and *Cranmer of Canterbury*. And this achievement by a dramatist of lesser poetic gifts speaks more eloquently than Eliot's and Williams' genius in behalf of the potential for drama of the aesthetic of sacramental time.

5

THE NATIVITY:
THE HUMANIZATION OF
THE MORALITY

> Thomas   *Beloved, as the World sees, this is to*
> *behave in a strange fashion. For who in*
> *the World will both mourn and rejoice*
> *at once and for the same reason?*
>
> T. S. Eliot, Murder in the Cathedral

Lacking a true sense of the sacramental significance of the Incarnation, the religious dramatists of the pre-Canterbury period wrote Nativity plays, which, like their Histories, suffer from medievalism. They failed to achieve a symbolic dimension and accordingly a sense of contemporaneity, because they did not interpret the event in terms of a permanent system of referents. Reading the birth of Christ, consciously or unconsciously, as an event irrevocably past or as an instructive fairy tale, they created, rather, a dramatic image —with all the flamboyant trappings of "poetry" and romance—that served the function of illustration or ornamentation, one which lacked either the sense of historical continuity or the concreteness of reality. The verse dramatists of the Canterbury period, on the other hand, have created a body of Nativity drama that represents a significant advance in the art of this genre. Though lesser in stature than the best of the Histories, these plays have at least the negative merit of avoiding the cloying sentimentality and the antiquated prosody of such plays as A. M. Buckton's famous *Eager Heart* and even of Laurence Housman's *Bethlehem*, and the positive merit, however imperfectly realized, of achieving a multivocality that rescues the dramatized action from the past. As in the Histories, the operative principle in this drama is the sacramental aesthetic.

Though difficult to generalize about, the Canterbury dramatists' approach to the Nativity is somewhat different from their approach to the Christian History play. In the History, they achieve multivocality primarily by relating the historical event figurally with the archetypal Christic action. By revealing its analogical relation with a past event, they establish its analogical relation to the future and thus, implicitly, its permanent significance. In the Nativity play, however, the dramatists are imitating the Incarnation itself. They are compelled, then, to employ other though not radically different means to extend the significance of the action through time. The tendency is to project the action in terms of man's archetypal or paradigmatic response to the crucial event in the cosmic drama of redemption. These plays tend, in other words, to assume the Morality form. But the Nativity-Moralities with which this chapter will deal are different also from the conventional medieval Morality, particularly that of the academicians, who treat the action primarily as a logical illustration of an abstract code of behavior. They stress at first the sacramental effect of the birth of Christ on history, and later, because the dramatist is relieved of the burden of explicitly establishing the analogical relation between events in history, the immediate, the human reality of the action, though, paradoxically, no identifiable historical time is represented. In both cases the resulting dramatization becomes, in varying degrees, something more than mere allegory as it is conventionally defined.

This chapter will examine three Nativities essentially of the first type, John Masefield's *The Coming of Christ* (1928), Charles Williams' *Seed of Adam* (1936), and Christopher Hassall's *Christ's Comet* (1938), and three essentially of the second type, Charles Williams' *The Death of Good Fortune* (1939), *The House by the Stable* (1939), and, more briefly, *Grab and Grace* (1941), to show the means by which the Canterbury dramatists achieve a symbolic dimension that transcends without negating time. Further, it will suggest that the chronologically later plays look forward in a general way to the verse drama of contemporary and everyday reality that emerges after World War II as the dominant form of the Christian verse drama.

John Masefield's *The Coming of Christ*, written at the invitation of Bishop Bell and produced in the nave of Canterbury Cathedral during Whitsun Week in 1928, is by no means a great verse play, but it is superior to the pre-Canterbury Nativities (and to Masefield's earlier religious drama) in that it is infused with a sense of presentness and, accordingly, freshness and energy that the earlier plays lack. This is traceable to an embryonic sacramentalism. Like Bottomley's pageant *The Acts of Saint Peter*, it provides an instructive insight into the tactics the Canterbury dramatists were to develop into a full-scale strategy in the effort to revive the verse drama and more specifically to reclaim the Nativity as a living form.

Though the simple action of *The Coming of Christ* is presented without intervals, it falls structurally into four distinct parts. In the first, which takes place in Heaven, the *Anima Christi*, about to assume the flesh of Man, is confronted by four angels, The Power, The Sword, The Mercy, and The Light, who put the facts of man's brutality to Him, prophesy His crucifixion, and attempt to persuade Him to abandon His purpose. Though He trembles at the prospect, He nevertheless reasserts His decision. In the second, the three kings, Baltasar, Gaspar, Melchior—representing respectively totalitarian power ("I rule the weak, for their own good" [1]) capitalistic wealth ("I plan, and my money finds means, and the concept is done, / Done well, that it profit mankind and beget me a gain," pp. 29–30), and humanistic knowledge ("I seek for truth in things and dreams," p. 31)—express the futility of their chaotic and ephemeral pursuits and the desire to discover order, beauty and permanence in human life:

> That men may see God making fair
> Each daily thing; God helping man;
> And Death a wisdom in the plan. . .
> Think of it, brothers.
>
> [p. 33]

In the third part, the three shepherds, Earthy, Sandy, and Rocky, who, in the tradition of the medieval mysteries, provide the comedy and topicality, voice a postwar economic and political discontent until the Power appears to bring them tidings of the birth of Christ. Finally, in the fourth part, the three kings and the shepherds, the high and the low, gather to bear witness with the angels to the Nativity and to offer their appropriate gifts.

Erich Auerbach, in his analysis of Adam's reference to the Redemption in the twelfth-century *Mystère d'Adam*—"Ne me ferat ja nul aïe, / For le filz qu'istra de Marie" ("No one will help me now except the Son who will come forth from Mary")—writes:

> . . . it is clear that Adam has advance knowledge of all of Christian world history, or at least of Christ's coming and the redemption from original sin which he, Adam, has just committed. In the very depth of his despair he already knows of the grace which will be fulfilled in its time. That grace—albeit a thing of the future, and even of a specific historically identifiable part of the future—is nevertheless included in the present knowledge of any and all times. For in God there is no distinction of times since for him everything is a simultaneous present. . . . One must, then, be very much on one's guard against taking such violating of chronology, where the future seems to reach back into the present, as nothing more than evidence of a kind of medieval naïveté . . . this simultaneous over-all view is at the same time the expression of a unique, exalted, and hidden

truth, the very truth of the figural structure of universal history. Everything in the dramatic play which grew out of the liturgy during the Middle Ages is part of one . . . context: of one great drama whose beginning is God's creation of the world, whose climax is Christ's Incarnation and Passion, and whose expected conclusion will be Christ's second coming and the Last Judgment.[2]

Considering the outline of Masefield's play, it can be seen immediately that the structure is grounded in a point of view similar to the one behind the medieval Christian drama that conceives of the Nativity and the Crucifixion as a single event, the Incarnation, which, therefore, is an integral part of the eternal design, the cosmic drama of Christianity that ends with the Second Coming and the Last Judgment. Thus the birth at the end of the play, which in isolation, as it is represented in most pre-Canterbury Nativities, would have only a univocal significance, becomes on the theological level—conceptually at least—an image of the redemptive function of the Incarnation and on the artistic level a sacramental or figural action that, in pointing toward the future, transcends without destroying its pastness.

Since the structure is conceived as a part of the cosmic drama, it puts pressure on the playwright to imitate the Nativity in terms of the historical future, that is, in terms of the contemporary world in which he lives. Thus Masefield, in a way analogous to the medieval dramatists, depicts through appropriate references the three kings and the three shepherds as representatives, if not individuals, of the twentieth century, more specifically, of the post-World War I period. The Magi are not only the rulers of modern life, the totalitarian, the capitalist, and the humanistic man of knowledge, they also suffer from the peculiarly postwar diseases of futility, despair, guilt, and alienation. Baltasar, whose "sergeants press each mother's son / Throughout my realm into my ranks" (p. 26), is conscious of the awakening of the weak, foresees the dissolution of his temporal power, and mortally fears an impending judgment. The imagery he employs to express his guilt is that of the war poetry of the twenties:

And Death is coming soon, and I
Dread all the men I made to die;
They come about me in the night,
I see their skull-bones bleaching white
And feet-bones sticking from the grave.

[p. 27]

Gaspar, for whom wealth is fulfillment, who usures

my gold to all Kings,
Command all the men on the sea, of the mind, of the field,
Set thinkers to conquer disease, or to fashion men wings,
And wealth is the weapon I wield

[p. 29]

also acknowledges the futility of his frantic pursuit of pleasure and
comfort in terms that place him in the disillusioned postwar world:

I must die, leaving all I possess, losing all of my schemes,
. . . .
All the glory of bringing to market the things of my dreams,
All the roars of my mills on the streams:

[p. 30]

Melchior, having taken all human knowledge for his province in
his search for a meaning that justifies existence and finding it un-
availing, expresses his anguish, like the others, in one of the characteristic postwar moods:

Then, in the dark, in bitter pain,
Wisdom that is not of the brain
Will whisper and be dumb again.

[p. 31]

Collectively they reveal, as one reviewer aptly puts it, "how little
joy [man's] almost immeasurable gains and discoveries have
brought to the God-hungry man of the first half of the twentieth
century." [3]

Masefield depicts the shepherds with even greater historical particularity. They are not only modern workingmen. They are ex-

soldiers still bearing the scars of the late war. Two of them, embittered by the tyranny of the militaristic State and yearning for the fulfillment of their basic needs, reject religion and put their faith in the Marxist class war:

SANDY   What we want is a good revolution. . .

EARTHY   That's it. . . till a man has his due.
Let the many be served by the few.

SANDY   Let us have a turn at the fire, the rich have a turn at the fold.

EARTHY   It's time they did, the rich and great,
To pay for what they did to me:
They said that I must serve the State
And fight poor heathen over-sea.
And there I stayed among the mud
In beds of lice and deeds of blood,
Until they chose to let it be.
Four years they kept me, "serving," so they said;
Ordered like dogs, and Death to all who disobeyed.

[p. 36]

The kind of dramatic vitality that this sacramental contemporaneity gives to *The Coming of Christ* is underscored by comparison with an earlier Nativity such as *Eager Heart* in which the sacramental aesthetic plays no operative role. Like Masefield, Miss Buckton conceptualizes the Nativity as an event in the twentieth century—

Out on the plains the shepherds watch! and we,
Dwelling in cities, keep our doors ajar!
Lest He should come this way, the royal child,
Two thousand years our King! [4]

But this chronological projection, being arbitrary, contradicts the dramatic image shaped by the texture of the verse. In contrast to the medieval mystery dramatist and to Masefield, Miss Buckton makes no effort to imitate the action in terms of contemporary life. The pious heroine, Eager Heart, the Magi, the shepherds, Joseph and Mary, are not even remotely representative of modern life.

They are, rather, as the archaic and "poetic" rhetoric clearly reveals, the embodiments of a distant and vague past; they are, that is, figments of the tender-hearted and pietistic Victorian imagination. Some indication of this grotesquely sentimental sensibility is given by the colloquy before Eager Heart's "lowly" dwelling, back to which the star has led her and the Magi and shepherds:

E. Heart   (*distressed*) O sirs, this is a little house and mean!
           A poor maid dwelleth here, of no great name.
           The star points other-where, methinks, not here!

1st King   Nay, gentle child! We go not from this place
           Till we have seen the owner of these doors,
           And bid her open!

E. Heart   Then, O gracious King,
           Must I confess! These humble doors are mine!
           And nothing there-within is worth your glance!
           . . . .
           Then must I tell you all: Therein doth sit
           A Stranger, with a Mother and her Child.
           Three souls, upon this bitter night they stood
           Begging of me, for the sake of Him who lay
           In a manger-stall in far-off Bethlehem,
           A little food and shelter! All my feast
           Lay ready for the King! O spurn me not,
           That even I prepared a little place,
           Hoping to house Him! But these needy ones
           I could not leave unfed.
           . . . .
                           I took them in.[5]

Like Bottomley's, however, Masefield's sacramentalism suffers from an uncertainty that thwarts the achievement of an organic unity of theme and form in *The Coming of Christ* (an uncertainty, incidentally, that is more markedly at the heart of the failure of his other major religious verse plays, the incomplete *Good Friday*, ca. 1914; *The Trial of Jesus*, 1925; and *Easter*, 1929). His view of Christ's mission lacks consistency; it vacillates between a moralistic and sacramental interpretation. Though his characters acknowledge the redemptive function of the Incarnation, an un-Christian pessimism, which has its source in his underlying naturalism, vitiates the drama of the action and undermines the sacramentally conceived structure. This divisive pessimism, as Gerald Weales notes,[6] is clearly seen in the overly urgent dramatic emphasis Masefield places on Christ's imminent failure on earth in the first scene of the play, which tends to overwhelm the redemptive significance of the Nativity in the last part. Though in the closing hymn of the kings and shepherds the paradox of the Redemption is posited —"On God relying, / And Death defying, / He puts on dying / That Life have birth" (p. 56)—its commonplace expression cannot poetically obliterate or redeem the dark futility generated at the outset by the four angels:

> The insect made of clay whom worms devour,
> Whose sole imaginings are how to steal
> His brother's bread and how to shed his blood,
> Whose apathy is as evil as his energy.
> Man will not change for one voice crying truth,
> And dying, beautiful as fire, for wisdom.
> Like a stone falling in a stagnant pond,
> You will but make a ripple swiftly stilled
> By the green weed.
>
> [p. 11]

Similarly, the conversion of the shepherds is too easy, suggesting a token acknowledgment of the redemptive function of the Incarnation.

Nevertheless, to evaluate the structure in the partial light of Masefield's predominantly moral interpretation of Christ is to do an injustice to Masefield's art. There is some truth in Weales' conclusion that Masefield's vacillation in his plays "between a conventional celebration of a Christian occasion . . . and his own insistence that the world has rejected Christ . . . gives the plays their interest" but "should not be confused with dramatic virtues." [7] Such a comment, however, reveals a failure to recognize the conceptual singleness of the Crucifixion and the Nativity and thus renders the embryonic sacramental structure utterly meaning-less.

The uncertain sacramentalism of the structure is also mirrored in the representation of the characters of the drama and the verse they speak. Indeed, the pressure of Masefield's moralism is so great that he fails to give reality nearly the due that the sacramental aesthetic demands. The angels, for example, are purely allegorical figures, splendid illustrations of abstract ideas; and the Magi, though they are given something of a sense of chronological iden-tity, lack completely the particularity of human beings. Only in his treatment of the shepherds does Masefield achieve an element of realism that is consistent with sacramentalism. But because their reality is isolated, one suspects that it is more the result of a me-chanical imitation of the medieval *Second Shepherds' Play* than of sacramental imitation.[8]

In the poetry the sacramentalism is hinted at by the recurrent and centrally located images that relate the coming of Christ with the coming of spring:

> Awake and sing: for in the stable-cave,
> Man's heart, the sun has risen, Spring is here,
> The withered bones are laughing in the grave,
> Darkness and winter perish, Death and Fear;
> A new Life enters Earth, who will make clear
> The Beauty, within touch, of God the King; [9]

[pp. 23–24]

But this imagery never rises far above the conventional, nor is it sustained. The analogy therefore lacks the poetic force that the sacramental fusion of vehicle and tenor gives to the same analogy in Eliot's *Murder in the Cathedral* or even in R. H. Ward's liturgi-cal Nativity, *The Holy Family.* Occasionally the simplicity and restraint of the diction and rhythm, as in the speeches of the shep-herds quoted above, give a forceful and lyric dignity to the verse, placing it in the realm of real human emotion. In general, however, the verse is characterized by the disembodied eloquence of orna-mental rhetoric that harks back to pre-Canterbury dramatic verse.

Here, for example, is Melchior's speech to the Christ Child in the Nativity scene:

> I who have sought in unknown things to where their hidden
> wisdoms are,
> And weigh the changing moon and tell the coming of the rov-
> ing star,
> And know the Spring's wild secret heart which sets all blood
> and sap astir;
> Yet seeing you, I know how wise,
> Beyond my wit All-Wisdom lies,
> The near thing, life, is still the far,
> I am but the vain minister
> Still offering myrrh.

[pp. 51–52]

To a certain extent, no doubt, the stately and decorative verse was imposed on Masefield by the acoustics of the cathedral for which his play was written.[10] But the primary impulse behind it is the angelic or allegorical imagination, that, in opposition to the sacramental imagination, tends to *use* rather than to express reality.

On the whole, then, *The Coming of Christ* lacks a sense of the dramatic. It is, as the reviewer of the *London Times* says, "a memorable pictorial and decorative achievement," but it is precisely this emphasis on the decorative that undermines the actual, the human order, and neutralizes the drama of the action. In the terms of this study, the weakness of the play lies in Masefield's failure to fulfill the implications of his sacramental structure. Nevertheless, *The Coming of Christ* represents a real advance over the "medievalism" of the pre-Canterbury religious verse drama. It is certainly, as Gerald Weales says, "the culmination of the scattered activity of the religious theater during the teens and twenties and the beginning of the new professionalism that marked the later development of the movement." [11] More important, however, its embryonic sacramentalism revealed, if it did not fulfill, the latent poetry inherent in what was apparently a moribund dramatic form.

The poetic potential of the Nativity is more fully realized by Christopher Hassall in *Christ's Comet*, produced in the Chapter House of Canterbury Cathedral during the festival of 1938.[12] Breaking with the tradition of presenting plays related to the history of the cathedral, Hassall returns to the theme of the first Canterbury production. He conceives and projects the Nativity sacramentally, as a crucial act in the Christian world drama. The operative aesthetic of the play, he writes, was designed to show the spectator—"from the unfamiliar angle of the pre-Christian world"—" 'God's ancient promise visibly fulfilled' " and to enable him "to regard it . . . as at once a timeless and an historical event." [13] He takes as his text the theme that Thomas Becket expresses in his Christmas sermon in *Murder in the Cathedral*: that "at this time of all the year . . . we celebrate at once the Birth of Our Lord and His Passion and Death upon the Cross" (p. 198). Echoing Becket, Hassall writes that *Christ's Comet* "is a Nativity play with a difference, so big a difference that it is also a Passion Play. It is about Death and Birth, Good Friday and Christmas" (p. viii).

Deriving his plot from Henry Van Dyke's story of a fourth Magus, *The Other Wise Man*,[14] Hassall divides the action into a loose two-part structure, the first, set in the year of the Nativity, depicting Artaban's journey from Trebizond to Jerusalem in search of the child who, according to prophecy, is to become the Messiah of the Jews, and the second, set in the year of the Crucifixion, depicting Artaban's ascent of Golgotha and his discovery of the Cross. Thus Hassall establishes the Nativity in the context of the Crucifixion and the whole in the context of Christian history.

The first act presents Artaban's quest in the light of his pagan interpretation of the prophecy. On learning of the advent in the skies above Trebizond of the star (Christ's Comet) which will "signify the birthplace of a second / More glorious Alexander" (p. 7), he and the other three pagan kings set out on a journey which takes them to the court of Herod in Jerusalem. They conceive of the new king as a worldly hero, a political deliverer, who will destroy the power of Rome and give new vitality to the tired temporal world:

> . . . Many priests
> Gifted with dreams, Barok especially,
> Have written of this star, and of a queen
> Whose first-born shall uncrown the Roman eagle.
>
> [p. 7]

On perceiving the comet, Artaban cries: "Now Rome's in ashes, and the world reborn!" (p. 14).

Artaban's vision and accordingly his purpose is transformed at the worldly and decadent court of Herod. He catches a glimpse of the real identity of the new king as Achiabas relates an impossible tale he has heard in the market place of a divine birth, including "a great host of goddesses in air, / Angels to use their term" (p. 32). To Herod and his court it is a ludicrous story, the subject of mockery,

> . . . They mentioned the Messiah,
> Something about good-will and peace on earth
> But *what* they sang is neither here nor there,
> Since it is plain they never sang at all,
> But were imagined by a crack-brained sot,
> Either in sleep, or in his cups. . .
>
> [p. 32]

But for Artaban, it strikes an archetypal response:

> But this rumour,
> Starts an insistent echo, as it were,
> Struggling to tell the soul it is not false.
> A new, compelling sort of beauty.
>
> [p. 33]

And after Herod's affirmation of the beauty of temporal power, Artaban's intuition of the identity of the new king and the nature of the new Power and the new City becomes at least partial understanding:

I thought at first our guide of moving fire
Would bring us to the cradle of a soldier
Born to discomfort Rome, but now a voice
Summons my erring heart. . . .
. . . .
By heaven, I'll break no more Italian bones,
But to my own rebellious heart lay siege
And starve the pride out, that my Captain
May enter by the scarlet gate to find
A city scoured, and humble to his law.
I tell you this same child, this Prince of Peace,
Shall found an empire and a capital town
That, in comparison, shall make your Rome
A bandits' bivouac. . . .

[p. 35]

Artaban's rejection of his temporal understanding of the new king marks the end of his first journey. Though Bethlehem lies "Beyond that hill . . . / Not half an hour away" (p. 42), he relinquishes his purpose in order to set out instead on a new journey, on a new quest for the true identity of the child. He has found that the distance to Bethlehem is longer, the "hill" he must climb higher than he had imagined. To the three kings he says:

Over the crest
And down again, there ends your journey; mine
Begins at dawn, but I shall meet you there
After a lifetime, which is very soon,
Considering the hugeness of that hill.

[p. 42]

At this point he conceives the hill he must climb as the life of humility and suffering that brings man into sympathy with the ethical Christ.[15] He is not aware that his climb will bring him face to face with the crucified Christ on the crest of Golgotha.

The second act presents the termination of Artaban's quest in his discovery, through his acknowledgment of the Sacrifice, of the sacramental nature of the Nativity. The act begins darkly. After having wandered through the world for thirty years in search of the ultimate truth of the Nativity, Artaban returns to Jerusalem, from which he had set out. Now old and almost blind, he encounters a robber, one Jesus Barabbas, who tells him of his miraculous escape from the cross that afternoon when the mob, asked by Pilate to choose between him and another Jesus, unexpectedly chose the Nazarene to be crucified. As Barabbas relates the fantastic story, Artaban recognizes the crucified Jesus as the princeling of the Nativity and his waning hope becomes despair:

> . . . Have I outlived the child
> Whose comet we have followed through the world?
> I do not understand nor wish to live.
>
> [p. 55]

But the next stage brings Artaban to the edge of illumination. Leading him to the foot of Golgotha and indicating that his "path lies up the hill" (p. 56), Barabbas insists on quitting the scene. Questioned, he reiterates insistently "This is the hill" (p. 56), as if the phrase signified the ultimate horror, and reveals that the source of his fear lies in feeling

> Like one who visits his own tomb, walking
> Beneath this hill, where by the laws of logic
> I should be hanging by my arms.
>
> [p. 56]

He thus points to the redemptive function of the Sacrifice, the substitution of Christ for Man, and accordingly to the truth for which Artaban has been searching.

The last scene resolves the paradox of the Nativity and the Crucifixion. The action, which represents Artaban's ascent of Golgotha, recapitulates the whole circular spatial and temporal journey from Jerusalem to Jerusalem, and from Christ's Birth to His Death. To the tolerant but uncomprehending sentry who guards the Cross, Artaban says "I have taken years / To climb this hill, more years than you have lived, Young Roman" (p. 60). Thus on achieving the crest, he addresses the crucified Jesus as if he were the child of the Nativity:

> . . . Here ends
> The doubt, the watching, and the weary road.
> . . . .
> I never knew such happiness as seems
> To shine out of this firmament of sorrow.
> The hill was even loftier than I dreamed.
> Sweet child, I bring a humble heart, just as
> Was promised. Have the others gone away,
> The camel-riding princes? Am I so far
> Behind? You were so difficult to reach,
> O steep, and stony, and bewildering hill!
>
> [p. 60]

When his companion tells him that this place is not Bethlehem but "Golgotha, / A place of skulls, there's no nativity here," Artaban replies, "Oh there'll be Birth enough from this day forth / To cancel an eternity of dying" (p. 60). At this point, the Angel of the Tree appears to him and draws into focus the pattern that Artaban's physical-spiritual, that is, sacramental journey has traced:

> Good man, the Lord hath seen your suffering.
> Open your eyes, and look upon your King.
> His name is the Beginning and the End,
> The victim that did nothing to offend.
> Here finishes the gospel of His pain,
> Here God and man are reconciled again;
> Here also is your haven, justly earned,
> With time to your first setting-out returned;
> For those who find truth, truth is born in them,
> And they are witnesses at Bethlehem.
> Thus by your witnessing the End, and winning
> Faith in your heart, you witness the Beginning.
> This is the cave beyond the difficult hill
> Where Christ yet sleeps, the kings are kneeling still,
> And where the mother of eternal Day
> Will show her Child to all who find the way.
>
> [p. 61]

The play ends following the death of Artaban with a tableau that projects the Angel's words into a vision of the Nativity in which Artaban partakes with the other three kings in the Adoration.

We see, then, that unlike Masefield's Nativity, Hassall's *Christ's Comet* achieves an integration of content and structure. The theme of the Incarnation, of the oneness of the birth and death of Christ, is worked out in terms of Artaban's journey-quest which takes him through the stages of the Christic action, from birth (in the sense of sloughing off the old pagan man) through the life of suffering, to death and rebirth, or, in terms of the central image of the play, from the foot to the summit of Golgotha. The drama of Artaban's life, in other words, is projected as a *figura Christi*, which, without negating its actuality, without becoming sheer allegory, takes on a symbolic dimension that transcends it, becomes multivocal, and so justifies Hassall's subtitle, *The Story of a Thirty Years' Journey Which Began and Ended on the Same Day.*

The remaining question concerns the extent to which the pressure of the poet's sacramentalism exerts itself on the verse of the play to give the image of the action the realistic sense that appeals to the contemporary sensibility and renders the multivocality authentic. That Hassall is aware of the necessity of achieving a reconciliation of concrete reality and poetry in the verse is clearly revealed by his remarks in the preface to the 1958 edition that he wanted *Christ's Comet* "to be tough in texture and secular in feeling until the last few pages which . . . would transform the whole" (p. vii). He seeks to create this sense of reality primarily by filtering the events of the Nativity-Crucifixion through pagan eyes, primarily those of Achiabas, Barabbas, and the Roman Sentry, but also by infusing a contemporary note into the linguistic texture of the play. This effect can be seen in the contemporary idiom and rhythms of much of the prose:

> Well, it's a way of seeing the world, and I never ate so much in my life. Rations—good; pay—moderate; future prospects—dubious; present objective—well, since you ask me, Captain—an enigma. Funny thing, though, that comet, while it lasted. It's what they call a "celestial body," you know. There's a joke there somewhere, if only it would crystallise.
>
> [p. 16]

Occasionally, though more effectively fulfilled, it can also be seen in the verse, particularly of the latter part of the play, as in the colloquy between the sentry and Artaban on the crest of Golgotha:

SOLDIER   Are you related to one of these bodies?

ARTABAN   No.

SOLDIER   Then you must hurry home. Those are my orders.
    Maybe, you are disciples of this teacher;
    If so, you're both unnaturally daring.
    Your friends have scuttled off like rabbits.

ARTABAN   Soldier,
    How near is He, the teacher, as you call Him?
. . . .

SOLDIER   You'll find the centre cross
    Is his, the one with the comic inscription
    "Jesus Nazarinus Rex Judaeorum."
    Don't hang about too long. You are not supposed
    To come as close as this, but get your breath,
    Indulge your superstition, then be off.

[p. 59]

But in the last analysis Hassall fails to achieve a dramatic verse that satisfies the demands of the sacramental aesthetic. In his effort to avoid the flatness of the language of most naturalistic drama, he overemphasizes its ornamental possibilities both in theory and in practice, thus cutting across the toughness of texture he desires.

The decline of verse drama, Hassall says in "Notes on the Verse Drama," began when the theater was transformed from an open-air (The Globe) to a roofed structured (Blackfriars), for this necessitated "the development of the theatre-goer's love of ready-made, as opposed to imagined, spectacle." [16] As a result, "Today, . . . the mind's eye need never be open and alert, and our scripts are impoverished because the pictorial function of dialogue has been usurped by the designer." [17] Thus despite Eliot's warning, he returns deliberately to the Elizabethan model, or at least to that much "of the old practice as is not a relic but still lives," [18] namely, to the view that the function of dramatic verse is to give the audience a concrete and vital image of the world in which the action transpires and to the corollary principle of the "big vocal gesture," [19] the bold and colorful rhetoric that distinguishes dramatic verse from the prose of naturalism.[20] He is aware that the Elizabethan model cannot command attention by conspicuous innovation "but it may hope to succeed by a judicious blending of modern language and outlook" (p. 9, 1st ed.) with rhetoric. But the choice as his model for *Christ's Comet* of the dramatic blank verse of Thomas Lovell Beddoes, which he dubiously affirms to be a perfect example of the adaptation of Elizabethan dramatic verse "to the exigencies of contemporary speech" (p. 9, 1st ed.), betrays the prominence his theory gives to decorative rhetoric. Thus, despite Hassall's claim that the blank verse of his play "is often little more than present-day prose conversation, coaxed, almost imperceptibly into iambics, but elevated into rhetoric, or something more than rhetoric, as occasion demands" (p. 9, 1st ed.), the general effect is essentially ornamental. This is the case not only of the set speeches that are designed to provide the visual imagination with a concrete image of an offstage scene, as in that of Strabo, Artaban's astronomer, when he announces the advent of the comet to the wandering kings:

> There is a fountain underneath my tower
> That sleeps by night, like men, and so reflects
> In miniature the stooping atmosphere.
> Sometimes I lean over the parapet
> To verify my chart, or watch a tortoise
> Slip from the brim into its element
> And shake the universe. Tonight being clear,
> I rested from my compasses more often
> To examine that unsteady sky, and thus
> Inclined toward earth, I spied upon the water
> What seemed at first a mirrored flame, and then
> A living fish of phosphorescent gold
> Newly arisen from its bed of slime.
> Fearing the turret overhead had caught
> Alight, I raised my eyes and saw a star,

[pp. 11–12]

It is also the case, though to a lesser extent, of the dramatic speeches, as in the response of the four kings on first perceiving the comet in the skies:

ARTABAN
and
MELCHIOR   The Comet!

BALTHAZAR   Now must they kneel who put our faith to scorn.

ARTABAN   Now Rome's in ashes and the world reborn!

> KASPER, *a dark-skinned and exotic figure, stands at the entrance with the light behind him, as if he had stepped out of the glow, or had been created by it.*

Kaspar! Your darkness brings with it strange brightness,
Like waking to a sudden hope at midnight!

BALTHAZAR   O Kaspar, we were never so well met.

MELCHIOR   Concurrence marvellous of dusk and daybreak!

ARTABAN   The gods are prodigal.
Their favours grow more numerous than raindrops:
Rich vessels block the quay, our cultured vines
Drag on the ground, unable to support
Their weight of purple daring. . . .
. . . .
We must delay no longer. Open the gates.

[p. 14]

This is, to be sure, a fairly high order of rhetoric, easily more vital than Laurence Housman's nostalgic verse in *Bethlehem:*

> Kings from far countries have ye come to see
> A king whose reign shall make all kingdoms free.
> Low at His feet your crowns ye cast to ground;
> From this day forward ye shall go more crowned.[21]

But it is, after all, rhetoric, and as such it transgresses against the tough realism that emerges on occasion and tends to undermine the contemporaneous tone that the image of the action establishes and that the sacramental aesthetic demands. In this, Hassall's dramatic poetry suffers from the limitation that characterizes in some degree most of the earliest plays of the Canterbury movement.

If the action of *Christ's Comet* represents a thirty years' journey that begins and ends on the same day, Charles Williams' *Seed of Adam*, commissioned in 1936 by the Chelmsford Diocesan Religious Drama Guild, is a drama which represents a single event, a quest, that incorporates the "four thousand" years between the Fall and the Nativity. Unlike Masefield's and Hassall's, Williams' play achieves the sense of the eternal presentness of time and thus its multivocality, not by integrating the Birth and Death of Christ, but rather by stressing, primarily through the character of the Third King, whose function is similar to that of the Skeleton in *Cranmer* and the Accuser in *Judgement at Chelmsford*, the incarnational function of the coming of Christ. *Seed of Adam* is different from *Cranmer* in that it "is not so much a presentation of the historic facts as of their spiritual value," [22] yet it follows the basic dramatic pattern of Williams' Canterbury play: It constitutes a movement away which is actually a movement toward a mode of authenticity. Alienated from God since the Fall into the world of generation and death, Adam is seeking vainly the Way of Return to Paradise, which, ironically, is an obsessive flight from death and Nothingness. In his darkest moment, he encounters the threatening figure whom, as his repeated references to the coming of "the thing that was threatened" (p. 163) suggest, he and his children have been anticipating in terror. Upon the face-to-face confrontation, Adam discovers the terrible figure to be the agent of renewal.

Though conceived as a single, continuous act, the play's action is divided structurally into two parts. The first delineates the image of the fallen Old Testament man or, on the human level, of the man who, to paraphrase Heidegger, renders death and nothingness public to escape its personal finality. The second presents the achievement of the New Testament man, or, on the human level, the man who confronts death authentically and is spiritually renewed by the encounter, which reconciles both images.

The opening movement of the play reveals the futility of Adam's

or Everyman's quest for the Way of Return. His children, represented by the Chorus, have allied themselves, one faction with
Gaspar, the Tsar of Caucasia (the King of Gold), who offers them
the objective way of external things, the way of hedonistic pleasure
and economic progress, and the other, with Melchior, the Sultan
of Bagdad (the King of Frankincense), who offers them the subjective way of inner things, the way of aesthetic delight and abstract
system-making.[23] When Adam rebukes them for having abandoned
their proper concern, their sardonic response reveals their defection
to be a desperate effort to escape the burden of mortality, "the bitterness of having nothing" (p. 152), to which they have become
heirs through Adam's Fall. Having lost hope of finding the Way—

<blockquote>
Where
shall we go? climb invisible cords into the air?
for road, river, and lane
are searched; it is not to be found.
</blockquote>

[p. 153]

—they have taken the ways that minimize the vague but real and
persistent threat that stalks them in the fallen world:

<blockquote>
Father Adam, if we go looking and snooping around corners,
we see terrible shapes trooping,
things eagle-beaked, giants with scimitars.
In Eden you found them friendly; here
what should we do but hide while they stride and deride
the bitterness of our having nothing?
Have you seen us slinking from those neighbourly taunts?
Better to go drinking the rhythms of the Sultan.
</blockquote>

[p. 153]

But this kind of inebriation fails to provide comfort, and thus they
sound collectively the note of despair, of the terrible boredom of
nothingness (an allusion to Macbeth's speech on the futility of
the round of time in the fallen world), that will reverberate
through the play: "And to-morrow everything begins again!" (p.
153).

The two camps fall into a conflict that resembles a battle between monkeys; and Adam realizes that it is he who is responsible for both the anguished futility and the disorder of their self-sufficient lives, the suicidal divisiveness inherent in their notion of the private and collective Paradises. Though he is vaguely aware that the Way resides somehow in the Fall or rather the world of death—"They cannot find the centre, the core of the fruit / where the root of return is. I dropped it; it is gone" (p. 154)—he does not know in what sense this is true. Thus he decides that he must at least "set my law upon them" (p. 154), bring the order and peace of civilization into their lives. But this way of the rational Caesar, of the Grand Inquisitor, as it were, is itself a mode of escape.

The nature of Adam's limited vision is partially clarified by his inability to understand the absurd affirmation or commitment to all the things of this world of his youngest born, Mary, whom he calls a "zany of goodwill" (p. 155). Eve tells him that Mary has gone to the fair, where she is

> Watching mountebanks, laughing at clowns,
> applauding jugglers and tightrope walkers,
> listening to talkers, admiring lovers,
> riding with children on the roundabout,
> everywhere in the middle of the rout,
> being, by her nature, all things to all men.
>
> [pp. 154–155]

Adam replies with exasperation,

> Will she never discover any preference: any partial
> liking for this where or that when?
>
> [p. 155]

Like Chelmsford and Cranmer, he manifests the tendency of the rational or, in Kierkegaard's term, the ethical, man to compartmentalize the world of objects into good and evil. To Adam, for whom the world is inexorably fallen, Eve's significant suggestion that "Paradise perhaps is hers and here" (p. 156), is a ludicrous contradiction. Thus he has decided to marry his daughter to the warlike and dutiful Joseph (whom Williams projects, after an old Mohammedan tradition, as a young Islamite cavalry officer in the Sultan's guard) in order to save her from the persecution of her brothers and sisters while he is fulfilling his task of "conquering yonder apes" and bringing the "peace" of law into the world. Again it is in terms of the legalistic ethics of the natural man that Adam conceives the marriage: "A heart of purity and a mind of justice / to be integrity" (p. 156).

Following Adam's departure, the Incarnation is announced to Mary by the Archangel Gabriel; and in her subsequent colloquy with Joseph on the subject of love (which unfortunately is dramatically disastrous), her vision becomes manifest, prefiguring that of the New Testament. When Joseph awakens from the sleep Gabriel has cast upon him, he becomes aware of a change that Mary has undergone. He perceives that she is in love and asks with whom. But Mary refuses to distinguish:

> Dearest, to be in love is to be in love,
> no more, no less. Love is only itself,
> everywhere, at all times, and to all objects.
>
> [p. 159]

Like Adam's, Joseph's ethical emphasis on preference in love is divisive. To show preference is not only "to begin to separate the 'image' from the reality of which it is only a partial and sacramental manifestation," [24] but also to make judgments on and thus distinctions concerning the worth of the objects or images of this world. It initiates the process of division, or in Williams' terms, of rendering "incoherent" the "co-inherent" universe, in which the natural and supernatural, time and eternity, are integral. Mary knows that all the things of the finite world of time and place image forth the "glory," or God, and that she is but one of them:

> The glory is eternal, and not I,
> and I am only one diagram of the glory:
> will you believe in me or in the glory?
>
> [p. 160]

To be granted this knowledge is to take a crucial step toward the perception of all things as occasions of love or good. This is the meaning of Joseph's reply to Mary: "It is the vision of the Mercy" (p. 160).[25]

Joseph's vision in Mary, which is given to him, as to Dante, by Grace, thus leads Mary to the discovery of the significance of the Annunciation, the deeper meaning of the Mercy: that God, in an act of love or "substitution," will become an image of this world, that the Word will become Flesh, to redeem all of Adam's children. Love

> shall make his flesh as one in time and place.
> It shall come in the time of Augustus Caesar,
> in the place of Bethlehem of the Holy Ghost,
> in the coast of Judaea; not quite Jerusalem,
> but not far from Jerusalem, not far but not quite.
> O Thou Mercy, is this the secret of Thy might?
> When Thou showest Thyself, that Thou art not there
> to be found? we find Thee where Thou art not shown.
> Thou art flown all ways from Thyself to Thyself,
> and Thy ways are our days, and the moment is Thou.
> O Thou Mercy, is this the thing to know?
>
> [p. 160]

Thus the difference between Adam's and Mary's vision is the difference between that of the Old and that of the New Testament, between the preference and division of law and the commitment to life in time, which, because of its terrors, leads to anguish but also, and through anguish, to the discovery of love and the unity of a sacramental world. The Way of Return is not virtually lost, as Adam supposes because his sin has defiled history. Indeed, it lies in, and is disclosed by, encounter with the world of place and time, that is, history:

> Joseph, come, take me to Bethlehem;
> there the apparition and the presence are one,
> and Adam's children are one in them;
> there is the way of Paradise begun.
>
> [p. 160]

The second part of *Seed of Adam* begins with a transitional chorus (reminiscent of the early speeches of the Women of Canterbury in Eliot's *Murder in the Cathedral*) that harks back to Mary's sacramental vision and anticipates the coming of the Third King. The children of Adam have found no satisfaction in the pursuit of the pleasures of either the inner or the outer life. Though they are aware of the maxim of the prophets *"this also is Thou; neither is this Thou"* (p. 160) that formulates Mary's sacramental vision, they are incapable of affirming its senselessness. For them there is only the dread of Nothingness: the "fear," as Williams puts it in the "Synopsis" of the play, "of the coming of some terror upon them out of the ends of time and space" (p. 173):

> The Chorus What did you see on the banks of the body's stream,
>   in Thule, in Britain, in Gaul, in Rome,
>   under Bagdad's dome, by the mounds of Caucasia?
>
> Solo One came walking over the sand,
>   one and a shadow from a desert land;
>   I saw a knife flash in a black hand.
>
> [p. 161]

Again, though this time with greater force, they sound the note of consuming despair over the meaninglessness of their mortality:

> From bone, from brain, from breasts, from hands,
> from the mind's pillars and the body's mounds,
> the skies rise and roll in black shadows
> inward over the imperial soul:
> over our sighs in the moon of dusty sorrow—
> *O, O, could everything begin before to-morrow;*
> over the creak of rusty grief—
> *to-morrow will be soon enough for belief;*
> over the kitchens of a pot neither cold nor hot,
> and the thin broth, and the forming of the clot—
> *not quite Thou and not quite not.*
>
> [p. 161]

And they call on Adam to save them from oblivion.

At this point, Adam, in one of the boldest strokes of the play, reenters as Augustus Caesar to proclaim his victory over the world and the *pax Romana*, which is the equivalent of the Utopian state:

> I was Julius, and I am Octavianus,
> Augustus, Adam, the first citizen,
> the power in the world, from brow to anus,
> in commerce of the bones and bowels of men;
> sinews' pull, blood's circulation,
> Britain to Bagdad. I in brawn and brain
> set knot by knot and station by station.
> I drive on the morrow all things to begin again.
> Look, children, I bring you peace;
> I bring you good luck; I am the State; I am Caesar.
>
> [p. 162]

Though his transcendent function is that of preparing the world for the coming of Christ, Adam-Augustus is not aware of it. What he does know is that he has not found the Way of Return in the concept of the State and that the "thing that was threatened comes" (p. 163). In desperation he orders his soldiers to take a census of the whole world, of the living and the dead, "to find whether anywhere it has been said / what place or person Paradise lies behind" (p. 162).

At the moment when the soldiers are about to report their futile effort, the mysterious Third King and his companion appear. They have come to destroy and devour Adam's children, thus fulfilling the dark premonitions of the Chorus and Adam-Augustus. For these pursuers are dramatic symbols of death and hell or, rather, the view of death held by man in a world in which God is absent. Echoing Adam's earlier allusion to the fruit he had eaten in the Garden, the Third King traces his origin to the Fall:

>   . . . did you know
> I was the core of the fruit you ate?
> Did you remember, ungrateful that you are,
> how you threw me away, with such a swing
> I flew over Eden wall, dropped,
> and stuck between two stones?
> You did not see; you did not look after me!

Smell and taste for you; let the core go to hell.
But God looks after the sparrows.
Presently the sun split the core,
and out grew I, the King of the core.
I have travelled to get back to you ever since.

[p. 165]

As Williams says elsewhere, Adam's eating of the fruit is motivated by the desire to know as God, that is, to know *both* good and evil, but being human, he cannot know evil, as God, by pure intelligence; he can only know it in experience, that is, existentially. His act of disobedience transforms his original knowledge of good into the knowledge of good as evil and accordingly introduces schism in the universe, initiates the process of division within the web of co-inherence. Thus the remedy involves an increase of knowledge: the discovery of good in the experience of evil.[26] But Adam has thrown the core of the fruit away. In his act of self-sufficiency, he sows the seed of despair, for he has rejected and then has attempted to flee from the experience of evil in which lies the Way of Return to Paradise.[27]

On one level, then, the Third King is the despair generated by the encounter with Nothingness or, as Williams put it, "the experience of man when man thinks he has gone beyond all hope of restoration to joy" ("Synopsis," p. 174). And his cannibalistic consort, Mother Myrrh,[28] whom the Third King identifies as the "small worm" in the "heart of the core" (p. 165), is his agent, that is, the consuming anguish of despair that renders the natural man's life a living death or Hell. But as in *Cranmer* and *Judgement*, the dark antagonist is also a figure of reconciliation. For, paradoxically, despair and Hell, the very opposites of joy and Paradise, not only reveal the futility of self-sufficiency and evoke remembrance of Heaven, which material (the Tsar) and intellectual (the Sultan) accomplishments tend to obscure, but also are the occasion of the Incarnation. As Adam has unconsciously suggested, the Way of Return is to be found in the core of the eaten fruit, in the experience of the fallen world. Thus it is Mother Myrrh who, in the very act of attacking Mary (which takes the startling form of a ritualized dance), brings on the labor that transforms her hatred into a bless-ing ("and holy is his Name," p. 169). Like death in Tolstoy's "Ivan Ilych," she becomes precisely a midwife to the birth of the New Adam. And it is the Third King who announces the New Life in Christ to Adam: "You desired twice—me and not me, / the turn and the Return; the Return is here" (p. 169) and defines the sac-ramental nature of the Incarnation: "Flesh is become that firma-ment of terrible crystal / your prophet saw" (p. 170).[29] Upon Adam's acknowledgment and affirmation of the here and now, which includes the Third King and his consort, Christ is born; that is, Adam and his children discover meaningful order in the apparent chaos of temporality—in T. S. Eliot's phrase, the still point in the turning world. And the despairing refrain of the chorus becomes, in the words of Joseph and Mary, "To-day everything begins again," and "see how to-morrow is also now" (p. 171). In defining the quest for the eternal or for the ground of Being as a paradoxical penetration downward into temporality and the mo-ment of illumination as the discovery of the eternal presentness of time, Williams is virtually expressing the nature of the authentic life of Christian existentialism.[30]

It can be seen now that the seed of Adam in Williams' title is not only fallen man in despair and Hell. It is also Christ, the seed which, according to the prophecy in Genesis, was to bruise the head of the serpent in the fullness of time, or, on the personal level, the New Man who has discovered that "whosoever will save his life shall lose it: and whosoever will lose his life for my sake shall find it." [31] The theme of Williams' play, writes Alice M. Hadfield, "is the double seed of Adam, which is the incurable deterioration and death of all men, and the new life in the son of man, Jesus Christ. The everlasting perishing which preys on man's best dreams and efforts grows from the seed of the fruit which Adam ate. It desires to feed on the source of life itself, the child Jesus, but its attack is wholly defeated and even turned into an assistance at the birth of the child. The new life lives from the energy of de-struction." [32] We are, in other words, back to the concept that plays such an important role in the drama of the Canterbury movement: the Fortunate Fall, which calls forth the Incarnation or, on the personal level, locates the way of return in the fallen world and defines the authentic quest for salvation, not as "angelic" flight—a circumventing of existence "in the illusory pursuit of essence"—but as "an increase of knowledge," that is, an existential encounter with the agonizing alternatives of life in time.

Williams' Nativity represents a remarkable transformation of the conventional product of the genre into a symbolic drama of dynamic energy, one that transcends the pastness of the "history" it dramatizes and the religious occasion for which it was written. His strategy is clearly that which he employs in *Cranmer of Canterbury:* the projection of the sacramental principle itself as a symbolic figure which transforms the original terms of the conflict and resolves them into a sacramental pattern. But in *Seed of Adam,* Williams achieves a sense of temporal and spatial inclusiveness, and thus a universality, that *Cranmer* does not possess; and he does this without sacrificing too seriously, as he does in *Judgement at Chelmsford,* the unified singleness of the action.

The source of this inclusive unity lies implicitly in the theme of the Fortunate Fall, which views the Fall of man and the Incarnation, like the Birth and Sacrifice, as a single event, which sees, that is, the Incarnation as an eternally present act in which the events of the Old Testament and Christian history are figurally related. That Williams was thinking in terms of the aesthetic implications of figural interpretation is clearly revealed in his notes to the play, where he deals with the problem of the protagonist. "I was prepared," he writes, "to bring in anyone. After all, the Nativity was a local event, besides being universal" (p. 175). Conceiving Adam and Augustus as the two poles of a *figura,* both "historical" yet symbolizing the ethical man, who brings law into the world in preparation for the New Life, Williams' next step is virtually an inevitable conclusion. He fuses the characters of Adam and Augustus and accordingly achieves at once historical extension and dramatic unity; universality and, to a lesser extent, particularity. As Anne Ridler observes, the fusion has the "remarkable effect of compression—the audience feels the whole sweep of time from the creation of man down to the civilized organization of the Roman Empire, concentrated in this one moment before the Incarnation, and preparing for it." [33]

Williams' use of the *figura* as a principle of imitation is, however, dramatically less effective than Eliot's in *Murder in the Cathedral*. Whereas Eliot establishes the two poles of the *figura* by analogical reference to one of them, Williams' method is that of historical inclusiveness. Though he achieves a sense of universality he must, to a greater extent than Eliot, sacrifice the historicity of the action he is dramatizing, thus cutting across the ultimate demands of the sacramental aesthetic.

Williams attempts to counter this tendency by integrally relating the characters of the play in terms of the metaphor of the family and especially by particularizing them, by giving Adam, for example, an impatience and petulance that comically reduce his tragic severity, and Mary a youthful gaiety and assertiveness that energize her innocence and purity. But in the last analysis *Seed of Adam* fails to achieve a complete integration of universal and particular. Despite the figural compression of time that tends to localize historic scope, the play is ultimately a drama of ideas, the emphasis falling too heavily on the universal. It is, much more than *Murder in the Cathedral* or even *Cranmer*, a dramatization of the concept of sacramentalism than it is a sacramental drama. The dramatic success of Mother Myrrh's conversion, for example, depends not on dramatic inevitability but on intellectual analysis, the grasping of the idea that Hell is the midwife of the New Life. Similarly the verse of *Seed of Adam* as in *Cranmer*, which is of the same period, is not dramatic, even though it is genuinely poetic. Though Williams employs contemporary idiomatic devices as Eliot does to render the action contemporary and in this sense "real" ("have you nothing better to do / in our world but play hide and seek with oblivion?" p. 152),[34] the verse, even in the dramatic passages, lacks differentiation. Its function, as in the scene depicting the doubts of Joseph, is on the whole to convey ideas rather than the emotional-ideational complex of the committed human voice.

Nevertheless it is a mistake to conclude, as do most critics who have written on Williams, that he is purely a cerebral dramatist, though intelligence certainly informs his drama, and that his plays are allegorical in the conventional univocal sense of that word. This does injustice to the broad sympathy he has for the actual, the concrete history of man, and for the particular human predicament. Adam is above all Everyman, but he is also recognizable, however faintly, as a particular Adam. This particularity is to manifest itself more strongly, first in some of the historical scenes of *Judgement at Chelmsford* (the delightfully human Barking Abbey episode, for example) and then in the one-act Moralities of the war period, and finally in the full length *House of the Octopus*, which represents the height of Williams' achievement in the drama.

After the outbreak of World War II, Charles Williams moved from London to Oxford, where the Oxford University Press, for which he worked as an editor, established its wartime offices. There he made the acquaintance of Ruth Spalding, who headed the Oxford Branch of the Pilgrim Players (later to become the Rock Theatre Company [35]) and as a result wrote three one-act verse plays, *The Death of Good Fortune, The House by the Stable*, and *Grab and Grace*, the first two of which are Nativity-Moralities and the third (a sequel to *The House by the Stable*) a Passion-Morality. These works represent a significant development of Williams' dramatic method. They reflect his effort to naturalize, to humanize his actions, and to transform the rhetoric of his previous dramatic verse into the poetry of the spoken word, the high into the low style. Partly owing, no doubt, to the wartime need of the Pilgrim Players for plays with public appeal and partly to his growing awareness of the pressure of sacramental time toward greater everyday realism and contemporaneity, Williams achieved a closer fusion of the archetypal and individual antinomies, a greater sense of actual presentness and, accordingly, a more truly sacramental drama than he had heretofore written.[36]

The first of these plays, *The Death of Good Fortune*, is the least successful of the group. Though much of its verse reveals a reduced complexity and a somewhat tempered poetic diction that suggests the "realistic" direction it is taking, the action itself is projected too rigidly in ideological terms and thus is lacking in the dynamics of encounter.

The theme of the play, that "all chance is heavenly, all luck is good," [37] is, like the themes of Williams' earlier works, grounded in the theology of the Fortunate Fall, in the idea that the Fall of man occasions the Incarnation and thus the redemption of the world. The action, then, involves a movement that distinguishes between Good Fortune (the central personification of the play) seen from a fallen and naturalistic point of view and from a Christian and sacramental point of view. But in this play Williams does not employ a figure that is capable of making the distinction dramatically. He resorts rather to an omniscient presenter (who is also chorus), the Virgin Mary, who arbitrarily establishes the figure as the sacramental principle by guiding the pagan god Good Fortune through a visionary experience of the Incarnation, thus transforming his nature. To the audience Mary says:

> I have determined that in this town this very day
> this gay popular lord shall come to his change
> and a strange new vision of himself; for now
> my lord my Son has made this clear—
> That all luck is good luck.
> . . . .
> Let us see Good Fortune come now to his trance.

[p. 179]

Thus though Good Fortune's devotees (an old woman, a young man, a king, a magician, and a lover, who constitute a cross section of mankind) are left in the end to make the difficult decision about the validity of the transformation, the choices they do make lack dramatic force. For the situation they are confronted by, one cannot help feel, has been contrived; they have not arrived there through dramatic necessity.

The action presents, first, the "coming" of Good Fortune (the recurrent references to him as "a star" establish an ironic relationship with Christ) and his deification by mankind. He represents, as he says, "the action of the heart / when all goes well" (pp. 181–182), that is, the fallen or naturalistic attitude toward the experience of this world. However, as Mary has pointed out in her presentation speech, he is actually other than he thinks:

> . . . his nature is heavenly,
> but when men fell, he was half-blinded;
> he does not know himself nor do men know him.
>
> [p. 179]

Only a girl, the daughter of the magician, questions his divinity and recognizes his boast, "I am not of earth; I am aerial" (p. 183), as a manifestation of his illusory nature and his gifts as man's unwillingness to face the full reality of existence, as the "twist of man's heart to defend itself" (p. 183). But she is easily silenced by the others, who, in their eagerness for comfort and gain, address themselves to him in a ritual of adoration. At this point Mary again interrupts the action to define further for the audience the identity of Good Fortune and to inform them of her decision to bring him to his revelatory death:

> . . . I saw a star sliding,
> shining, guiding their god-divining caravan.
> Its name was called *TYXH*, its flame was fortune,
> its messenger and shape on earth was this lord here,
> whose sphere above attended my Son's birth;
> but he, being blinded by cloud, is half-minded
> to glorify himself for only half his worth;
> I must teach him all: it is time that he should die.
>
> [p. 184]

With the death of Good Fortune, the affairs of his devotees take a bad turn and they succumb to despair. The king offers stoic resignation as an alternative. But the lover, partially true to his vocation as Williams sees it, is unwilling to capitulate, asserting rather that "love must live," that man must affirm the images of this world, though he does not know how. The two turn to the magician for a judgment between the lover's "living in death" and the king's "dying in life," between romantic "rage" and stoic "resignation" (p. 189). When the magician conjures a vision to discover the answer, he perceives a moving star descending to earth, whirls suddenly to follow its course, and for the first time becomes aware of Mary, into whom the star has passed. The point of this rather labored and imperfectly realized sequence is that both attitudes rest ultimately in despair at the accidental nature of existence, which in turn evokes the need of an intercessor and prepares for conversion: "when all fails," asks the magician, "what is the right thing to be?" (p. 190).

Mary thus artificially enters into the action of the play to distinguish for despairing man the true from the false, the natural from the sacramental, identity of Good Fortune. Her reply to the magician's question is simply "When your god Good Fortune dies, the only thing / is to bid your god Good Fortune rise again" (p. 191). The three men (now apparently transformed into the Magi) entreat her to perform the miracle. She raises the body of Good Fortune into a state of trance, and, in a paradoxical order that recalls the movement of Artaban in Hassall's *Christ's Comet*, directs him "forward" through a vision (which he reports as he progresses) of the Crucifixion to the discovery of the Christ child, who bids him live: for "all luck is good." Thus on returning to life he identifies himself with the Star of the East, defines his new nature, and asks which of his former devotees will acknowledge him now:

> I found myself riding through the heavens; below,
> on earth, wise men were riding to a Birth,
> to a lonely, difficult, universal gospel
> of the nature, its nature and all things' nature.
> . . . .
> I became other than I was and a new creature;
> I was the master of all chances; all chances
> made the multiple star in which I rode.
> . . . .
> I will be called Blessed Luck for ever;
> . . . .
> Who among you all has professed me now?
> Who moves with me to welcome all chances that may come?

[p. 193]

Typical of Williams' Kierkegaardian integrity, the denouement of *The Death of Good Fortune* is no sentimental reduction of the problem of belief. It gives the skeptical demands of morality their due. Confronted with the difficult decision, the old woman and the king cannot surmount their private calamities to commit themselves to the "wild" vision of the new Good Fortune. Even the magician, the lover, and the girl, all of whom have had some insight into the power of love, cannot fully acknowledge this absurdity as a fact. The magician knows but does not believe; the lover and the girl believe but do not know. They can only accept the difficult task of a moment by moment choice of believing that God is at work in the world or that He is not. As Mary says:

> . . . you must always make your choice,
> or always, at least, know that the choice exists—
> all luck is good—or not; even when the ninth
> step is nine times as difficult as the first.

[p. 194]

Despite, however, the dramatic tension of this conclusion and the reduced rhetoric of the verse, it can be seen from the analysis of the whole action that the play does not achieve the stature of drama. Williams' emphasis on Mary's deterministic choric function is too heavy and his portrayal of the characters who represent mankind too abstract and puppetlike. The action therefore is reduced to illustration, and the play becomes too patently a dramatic explication of doctrine.

The final effect of *The House by the Stable* and its sequel *Grab and Grace* is entirely another matter. In his early plays Williams' effort to avoid the sentimentality and nostalgia of the pre-Canterbury imitations of the medieval mystery play resulted in the overemphasis of idea. Even though a sense of the reality of history is conveyed, the eternal significance tends to overwhelm the concrete and human. In these plays, however, he achieves, both in the action and the verse, a truer reconciliation of the human and supernatural, the concrete and abstract, the everyday and the remote, in short, of reality and value—a reconciliation that places them squarely in the medieval dramatic tradition of figural or sacramental realism. All time is caught up in the concrete moment of the action. Thus value is revealed, as is the design of God, not *by* but *in* the concrete. The imitated action, in other words, becomes more truly a sacramental image.

In *The House by the Stable* (an analysis of which is applicable to *Grab and Grace* as well) the ideological development is basically, though less intricately, the same as that of *Seed of Adam*: Man in his fallen state succumbs to pride, to self-sufficiency, forgets his original place in the co-inherent web of the universe, that is, Paradise, and accordingly imperils his soul and exposes himself to Hell. At this point in the argument the unconscious intimations of his previous state, the force of which is in inverse proportion to the degree of separation from Paradise, emerge and, with the help of the Grace implicit in the Incarnation, save him from damnation. Again the theme that the action defines is that of the Fortunate Fall. Echoing the formula that underlies *The Death of Good Fortune*, Gabriel (Heavenly Knowledge) tells Hell as they dice for man's soul:

> . . . all luck is good.
> Toil and spoil as you will, still in the end
> the flick of every chance must fall right.[38]

What is different from *Seed of Adam* and the earlier plays in general is that the literal level is projected in terms of a clearly particular, however simple, human action. This involves the effort of a very clever whore (Pride) and her pimp (Hell) to cheat the protagonist, a simpleton susceptible to physical beauty and flattery, of a precious jewel (his soul) that he is supposed to own by feigning love for him, plying him with drink, and luring him into a dice game in which the dice are loaded against him.[39] The characters are not, however, personifications of abstract ideas; they are highly individualized without loss of their generic attributes. And the setting too is particularized, though its concreteness is that of everyday reality rather than that of place. Thus, despite the conventional abstract names and the internal logic of the relationships seen, for example, in the externalized *Psychomachia* (Gabriel versus Pride and Hell), the action is not allegory in the conventional sense; it is not, that is, merely a *means* of conveying an ideology. It exists, rather, for its own sake, has its own identity.

Because the parts of the literal level are integrally related to the whole movement, it is difficult to convey the sense of its dramatic autonomy. However, the realism can be suggested by drawing attention in exemplary scenes to the psychological integrity with which the characters are portrayed and the consequent sense of dramatic engagement they generate.

Such a scene is the first agon in the conventional *Psychomachia*, involving Gabriel, Pride, Hell, and Man. Following Pride's carefully wrought and successful stratagem to get Man to wager his jewel against Hell's house in a dice game, the episode opens when Man's servant, Gabriel, whose slightly domineering protectiveness occasionally asserts itself as comic self-righteousness, interrupts the proceedings to announce that a poor couple, "a youngish working man" and his wife, "a fair-faced girl" who is "near her time," are outside seeking shelter from the harsh night. Before Man can answer, Pride interposes in words that betray the brutal snobbery of the "respectable" female:

> Man, this servant of yours clacks his tongue
> more freely than mine should do; must you keep
> rooms where any riff-raff tramps may sleep—
> and have supper too, I suppose? you, sir,
> I am speaking to you.
>
> [pp. 201–202]

Gabriel parodies her biting question and when her companion, Hell, indignantly threatens the servant, Man makes a feeble attempt to assume the role of conciliator, succeeding only in revealing his weakness of character and his pathetic uncertainty and dependence, which continually undercut and reduce the assertiveness and self-sufficiency he is trying to cultivate:

> Rest quiet, Hell:
> I have had this fellow for servant a long time,
> ever since before I came hither, wherever
> I was before I came hither; he suits.
> He is neat and quick and keeps out of the way,
> and looks after my accounts—at least someone does,
> and it isn't I; let him alone.
>
> [p. 202]

But instead of proceeding to address himself to the issue that confronts him, he resorts to the wine he has been drinking.

Not to be deflected from his purpose, Gabriel, returning to the attack, makes it impossible for Man to avoid a decision. In a hesitating manner that looks at once toward Pride and the issue and suggests therefore his simultaneous fear of the shrewish tongue of his lover and desire to help the travelers, Man replies:

> Why. . . it were wrong to turn a mother away
> and pity to turn a woman, on a hard night,
> in a plight of that kind; but tramps in my rooms . . . yet
> one should be tender when one is comfortable, sweet,
> tender to the poor, yes?
>
> [p. 202]

But Pride, who knows Man far better than he knows her, does not fulfill his expectations. Instead she appeals in a low, worldly key to his need for identity:

> I confess, dear Man,
> I cannot see why; one cannot do what one would—
> no, not you even, my bountiful god—
> and (as things go) they are only encouraged to expect
> more than anyone can do. My darling, have a care.
>
> [p. 202]

When Man's indecisive agreement ("Well, there is that. . .") is interrupted by Gabriel's impatient and forceful lead ("I think, sir, / you should see them now"), Man jumps at the new opportunity to fulfill the promptings of his essential humanity, though he is not forgetful of his commitment to Pride:

> Do you? Well. . . well,
> just for a moment then; let them come in.
> You are always ready to beguile me. And as for you,
> Hell and my sweet Pride, be merry the while.
>
> [p. 202]

His eagerness betrays the timidity that lies below the condescending tone he assumes to mollify his lover.

Nor is the drama of *The House by the Stable* static. In the ironic scene following the Nativity, which depicts Man dicing with Hell, the sense of concrete dramatic encounter is revealed through characters who have undergone changes determined by the preceding action. Man is now very drunk and thus less disposed to take his lead from Pride. He is far more assertive, almost brutal, though the very force of his assurance suggests his weakness and his growing sense of guilt. Pride, on the other hand, aware of Man's new voice, is more accommodating, more tolerant of his private inclinations, yet, because she suspects the identity of his servant, is more impatient to finish the dice game, which Man keeps abandoning:

PRIDE   How slow you are! Man, your Pride is waiting.

MAN   (*he is now rather drunk*) Waiting, is she? let her wait then.
Why, you hussy, you are a part of me.
I am not to be called in as if I were Gabriel
to be scolded at pleasure.

PRIDE   No; it was but that leisure
of ours, at Hell's house, I was wanting. . . but so,
just as you say.

MAN   Ha, yes: again.
To it again.   [p. 208]

In the Adoration scene, following Gabriel's victory over Hell in the dice game (which is symbolic of the transformation of bad luck into good fortune, evil into good), his expulsion of Pride and Hell from Man's house, and his recalling of Man to awareness of his guests, it is the human situation as it has accumulated through the action that carries the theological significance. When Gabriel calls Man to the stable, the truant, still feeling the effects of the wine he has been drinking, "stumbles" into the presence of the Holy Family. His first clumsy words of justification betray his anxiety and guilt:

> It is almost too bright here to see. Where
> is the lady? I did give her a hunch of bread
> and a place to lie; she might else have been dead.
>
> [p. 214]

Fearing that Man's all too human foolishness will make a farce of the "great scene," Joseph tells him, "Do not talk nonsense," and Gabriel, even less indulgent, adds, "Do not talk at all." They forget that the scene exists for Man's need and not for their sense of propriety. But Man is not to be silenced. He is confused and wants to come to terms with his guilt:

> No, but I am trying to understand: why
> should I who had one house, and another beyond
> promised, have been so fond as to offer straw
> in a stable? and yet. . .
>
> [p. 214]

Following another effort by Gabriel to silence Man, Mary, who is more tolerant of his absurdities, takes him by the hand and reveals her Son to him.[40] This act releases in Man a torrent of emotion which, unlike the usual sentimentalism of such scenes, is a confusion of self-justification, penitence, kindness, guilt, wonder, and humility:

> I did not quite refuse you, did I? or did I?
> I cannot tell; Hell has made me stupid.
> Did I deny you all or did I not?
> Look now, he must have something to please him.
> The house is full of things, and none right.
> Stop; I remember something out of sight,
> out of thought, but always I have had round my neck.
>
>   *(He fumbles at his breast and pulls out a jewel.)*
>
> There; it was once bright; it might serve.
> I do not know what it is at all.

But if you should want a bed for the rest of the night,
there is my room the best.

[pp. 214–215]

The psychological ambiguities in this speech epitomize the truly
dramatic quality of the character of Man in *The House by the
Stable*. Similar ambiguities also characterize Man in *Grab and
Grace*, which retells from the perspective of the Passion the archetypal action of his fall into Pride and regeneration through Faith
and Grace. At the end of this play, for example, Man's decision
to exile Pride to the "malignant lands," that is, to acknowledge his
mortality, "the province of death," has by no means been an easy
one; nor is the denouement, in which Man cannot, because of his
former love of Pride ("I loved her; God knows how I loved her,"
p. 243), bring himself to accept Faith, a sentimental violation of
the weak and irresolute character that Williams has drawn.

It is obvious that Williams' dramatic verse has also undergone
a change in these plays, a simplification and humanization analogous to that of the action. It is no longer the tough, often overwrought rhetoric of *Cranmer* and *Seed of Adam*, with its poetic
diction, its profuse and difficult imagery, its eccentric rhythms, and
its incantatory internal rhyming that despite its poetic power tends
to assert its autonomy over the dramatic action. In *The House by
the Stable* and *Grab and Grace*, Williams achieves a "low" style
that is more tractable to the exigencies of dramatic encounter
without abandoning the strengths of his earlier style. Though, as
Anne Ridler notes, the poet's "language never becomes a colloquial
language," [41] the verse in these plays does, on the whole, give the
illusion of dramatic speech. This is evident in the more simple and
ordinary diction:

Think:
is there no shed near where these could be stored
for a night in reasonable comfort? I can't afford
to have them inside; my Pride will not stomach it,

[*The House by the Stable*, p. 204]

. . . I

and you too were so beshouted and bevenomed
by that slug-slimy Gabriel that we lost our heads
and ran too soon. . . .

[*Grab and Grace*, p. 219]

But it is primarily in the free yet controlled rhythms of the verse line, the indefinite number of syllables contained within a varying four- and five-beat structure, that the illusion of the spoken word is most clearly suggested. There are, to be sure, still signs of the old crabbed rhythms and syntax, but these are rarely prominent enough to impede or obscure the modulations of the human voice. In *Grab and Grace*, for example, when Pride, having returned after the Crucifixion in the guise of Self-Respect, sees Man's new companion and asks caustically, "This / is another friend of yours?" Man replies:

Her name is Faith.

She was a friend of Immanuel, the child born
the night you went. . . O well, Pride—
I beg your pardon; it is old habit in me—
we need not go into all that now.
There was a misunderstanding of what he meant
and a tussle—you, my dear, will understand
there was something to be said on my side;
but anyhow—it was all rather unfortunate—he died.

[pp. 226–227]

The dramatic sense of this passage is achieved not only by means of the naïve point of view that sees the Passion of Christ in the everyday terms of a "tussle." Integral with this point of view is the carefully wrought metric that conveys the emotional modulations of the naïve and undisciplined mind. In the third line of the speech, for instance, Man's embarrassed and confused recollection of Pride's earlier humiliation is enacted in the strong caesural pause that comes between the assuredness of the two iambic feet and the awkwardness of the trochee and imperfect foot that follow, and in the reduction of the number of syllables and stresses in the whole line. But this free movement is not that of prose. For the metric also underscores the key terms and thus transforms the speech. In the sixth line, for example (the rhythm of which in tumbling over itself stresses Man's guilty compulsion to go on with the story of Jesus despite his conscious desire to suppress it), the emphasis placed on "what" and in the seventh, on the first syllable of "tussle," first by the breathing pause following "misunderstanding" and then by the shift from two iambic feet to an anapest, charges the lines with a powerful ironic significance. In other words, Williams' metric simultaneously expresses the waywardness of the human response and contains it within the larger ideological context.

Charles Williams' *The House by the Stable* and *Grab and Grace*, are not, then, mere allegories. They do not reveal the angelic univocalism, the one-to-one relationships of that genre, in which the dramatic image exists for the ideological significance. They reveal rather the multivocality, the fusion of vehicle and tenor, of sacramental drama, in which particular and universal, the real and the significant, are simultaneously enacted. Man is generic Man, Pride is the sin of Pride, Gabriel is Heavenly Knowledge; but these characters are also and simultaneously particular and concrete individuals who between them work out not only an abstract *Psychomachia* but also a human drama that has an identity of its own.

If the actions of these plays are "allegorical," they are so only in the sense that they correspond to the definition of allegory implicit in the medieval fourfold method of Biblical exegesis, in which the literal or historical, the allegorical or doctrinal, the tropological or moral, and the anagogical or eschatological levels are simultaneously present, in which, for example, Jerusalem is *at once* "(a) the historical city of the Jews, (b) the Church, (c) the Christian soul, and (d) the heavenly Jerusalem, the Church triumphant." [42] It would be rash indeed to interpret Williams' action as fourfold (though this can be done for several plays of the Canterbury movement, including Eliot's *Murder in the Cathedral* and Williams' *Judgement at Chelmsford*). But the determining factor in the predominant medieval conception of allegory is not whether or not the action achieves four levels of meaning, but rather that secondary levels are contained *within* the first, the literal level. In other words, the fourfold method of Biblical exegesis is more or less synonymous with figural interpretation, which is the source of sacramental art. Both are grounded in the Incarnation, which gives history a multivocal identity. Since the conventional definition of allegory tends to deny the validity of the vehicle, the literal level, it seems to me that "sacramental" is a preferable term to characterize the multivocality of plays like *The House by the Stable* and *Grab and Grace*.

In the final scene of *The House by the Stable*, when Man remembers the jewel that has hung all this while around his neck and offers it to the Christ child, the archangel Gabriel is astonished by his casual discovery: "But this is your soul / I have searched for all this time!" Laughing at his angelic ignorance of the human way, Mary replies:

> Great Hierarch, even
> the angels desire to understand these things,
> and a mortal hand does more than the Domination.
> Leave Man and my Son and me our mystery;
> let us think our own way and not yours.
>
> [p. 215]

In these lines she expresses the paradoxical theme of both plays, that since the Fall man's way to heaven leads not away from but through the increased knowledge of the world redeemed by the Incarnation. But the lines do more than that: They express the mimetic principle that governs these plays. Just as "the mortal hand does more than the Domination" in this world, so also the sacramental imagination, which discovers and projects essence *in* existence, the Word *in* the flesh, is more genuine, more creative, than the angelic imagination, which tries to circumvent or at best to *use* material forms in the pursuit of essence. Like Mary and Christ and Man, the dramatist, too, according to Williams, must think in mortal, not angelic terms.

By transforming the historical protagonist into a concrete Everyman or Adam, Charles Williams definitively establishes the tend-

ency perceptible in the earlier pageants and histories of giving the
illusion of perpetual contemporaneity to the dramatized action
and suggests the dramatic possibilities of a more thorough realism
in the modern Christian drama. Thus, for example, Dorothy Sayers'
prose nativity, *He That Should Come* (1939) represents, like
Williams' realistic moralities (though on an inferior artistic level),
the intermediate stage between the Christian history, which dramatizes the traditional "great events," and the drama of contemporary
reality, which presents Everyman in an everyday modern setting.
In this play, which projects the birth of Christ in a highly realistic
context, her purpose is to "show the miracle that was to change
the whole course of human life enacted in a world casual, . . .
absorbed in its own affairs and completely unaware of what was
happening . . . to illustrate, in fact, the tremendous irony of history." [43] Indeed, the realism of the play is so prominent that she is
forced to defend her sacramental strategy in order to counter criticism that the play lacks a religious tone:

> I feel sure that it is in the interests of a true reverence towards
> the Incarnate Godhead to show that His Manhood was a real
> manhood, subject to the common realities of daily life; that the
> men and women surrounding Him were living human beings,
> not just characters in a story; that, in short, He was born, not
> into "the Bible," but into the world.[44]

Even in the ritualized Nativity which is deliberately antirealistic
in form, the Christian poet dramatist no longer hesitates to give
the protagonist at least a contemporary identity, if not a particular
personality. This, for example, is the case in R. H. Ward's interesting plays, *Holy Family* (1941), *The Destiny of Man* (1943),
and *The Figure on the Cross* (1944), in which the choric protagonists are projected in the liturgical mode, the characters emerging
from the choric mass at dramatic moments in the narrative somewhat in the manner of a seventeenth-century religious oratorio such
as the *St. Matthew Passion* of Heinrich Schütz.[45] Like that of the
verse dramatists of the Canterbury movement, Ward's aesthetic
has its source in the Incarnation.[46] Each of these plays presents
Man enacting analogically some aspect of the archetypal Christian

action in the light of the contemporary predicament. In his Nativity *Holy Family*, for example, Ward projects (in a way that is perhaps too reminiscent of Eliot's development of the Women of Canterbury) Man's response to the birth of Christ as a gradual movement from despair of life in naturalistic time to the joy of life in sacramental time. Unfortunately his emphasis is too heavily on the eternal pattern, on the timelessness of the Christic drama rather than on the concrete human event in time, an emphasis suggested in his preface to *Holy Family*, where, in describing the setting, he writes: "Just as the place the chorus lives in is nowhere and everywhere, so the time it lives in is both never and always." [47] Thus his characters are invariably abstractions with whom it is difficult to become engaged. Nevertheless, his imagery and diction, in keeping with the tendency established by Charles Williams' Moralities, clearly create the image of time-ridden modern man:

> O Lord, forgive us our blindness, forgive us.
> We are too heavily bowed under burdens.
> The washing on Mondays, the daily cooking,
> The scrubbing, the sewing, the sweeping of floors.
> We are too much oppressed by tyrannies,
> The tyranny of the clock by the hearth,
> The clock in the office, the workshop, the station,
> The tyranny of the insistent moment of time.
> There is no time, no room, no will
> For anything but the daily burden.[48]

It is also the case in W. H. Auden's remarkable Christmas oratorio *For the Time Being* (1945), which is more a philosophical poem than a play about the Nativity. The birth of Christ is projected in rhythms, images, and tones that identify the context even more concretely and fully than Ward's as the postwar world, the "in-coherent" City,[49] in which man suffers the estrangement and anxiety of the existential predicament:

> . . . I mean
> That the world of space where events re-occur is still there,
> Only now it's no longer real; the real one is nowhere
> Where time never moves and nothing can ever happen:

> I mean that although there's a person we know all about
> Still bearing our name and loving himself as before,
> That person has become a fiction; our true existence
> Is decided by no one and has no importance to love.
>   That is why we despair; that is why we would welcome
> The nursery bogey or the winecellar ghost, why even
> The violent howling of winter and war has become
> Like a juke-box tune that we dare not stop. We are afraid
> Of pain but more afraid of silence; for no nightmare
> Of hostile objects could be as terrible as this Void.
> This is the Abomination. This is the wrath of God.[50]

As Amos Wilder observes, Auden's integration of the fragmentary secular and religious options of modern thought and symbol from Freud to Kierkegaardian Protestantism into a Christian framework in this as well as in later works has its source in the doctrine of the Incarnation and accordingly the sacramental vision.[51] This is made quite clear in the central section of the oratorio, "The Meditation of Simeon," where Auden explores its implications:

> Because in Him the Word is united to the Flesh without loss
> of perfection, Reason is redeemed from incestuous fixation on
> her own Logic, for the One and the Many are simultaneously
> revealed as real. So that we may no longer, with the Barbarians,
> deny the Unity, asserting that there are as many gods as there
> are creatures, nor, with the philosophers, deny the Multiplicity,
> asserting that God is One who has no need of friends and is in-
> different to a World of Time and Quantity and Horror which
> He did not create, nor, with Israel, may we limit the co-inher-
> ence of the One and the Many to a special case. . . .
>   For the Truth is indeed One, without which is no salvation,
> but the possibilities of real knowledge are as many as are the
> creatures in the very real and most exciting universe that God
> creates with and for His love. . . .[52]

It is this synthesis of the diversity of contemporary images and the eternal significance that renders the language of *For the Time Being* superior to the apparently similar though actually very different language of Auden's and Isherwood's earlier plays, *The Ascent of F-6, The Dog Beneath the Skin,* and *On the Frontier.*

The Morality-Nativities that culminate in Charles Williams' diptych, then, appear, as much as it is possible to tell from the short time span of the movement, to constitute a transitional phase between the historical and the contemporary "secular" Christian drama of Eliot and the Mercury Theatre poets, Anne Ridler, Ronald Duncan, and Norman Nicholson, that emerges in the postwar period. Although Pageants (Dorothy Sayers' *The Just Vengeance*, 1946), Christian Histories (Laurie Lee's *Peasants' Priest*, 1947; Christopher Fry's *Thor with Angels*, 1949; Robert Gittings' *The Makers of Violence*, 1951; and Anne Ridler's *The Trial of Cranmer*, 1956 [53]), and Mysteries dealing with the life of Christ continued to be written through World War II and after, they no longer constitute the main stream of the Christian verse drama movement. It is interesting to note that this pattern of development is, in a general way, analogous to the pattern that characterizes the development of the English medieval poetic drama. Behind both movements is the pressure of a sacramental aesthetic.

6

T. S. ELIOT'S *The Family Reunion:*
THE STRATEGY OF
SACRAMENTAL
TRANSFIGURATION

*True beings are lived in the present, the life of
objects is in the past.*

Martin Buber, *I and Thou*

T. S. Eliot's progress from historical to contemporary subject matter, the high to the low style, the second (authorial) to the third
(dramatic) voice of poetry, from, that is to say, a "poetic" to a
realistic medium, in his late verse drama is generally interpreted
as a strategy to overcome the resistance of the secular bias of the
general playgoing public. This is no doubt partially true, but that
the change represents, as this interpretation holds, a sharp break
with his previous aesthetic principles is less tenable. The development is not arbitrary. Seen in the context of the Christian verse

drama movement at large, it represents, rather, a logical transition toward the fulfillment of the demands implicit in the sacramental view of time.

It is worth reviewing at this point some of the implications that the doctrine of the Incarnation has for time. Christ's assumption of the flesh absorbs the temporal into the eternal order, "amalgamates" the most extreme disparates, and thus sacramentalizes history—reorders it into a significant pattern without denying its identity. It becomes an eternal present, in which the particular historical act not only signifies a past action but also and primarily prefigures an ultimate concrete fulfillment. In other words, the pressure of sacramentalism is, on the historical level, futural. The ideal attitude toward history thus involves an existential commitment to a present (the closest one can come to the actual future in temporal life) which contains the past and points ahead. Though the past is valid, its validity rests in its figural or symbolic relevance to the present. According to this view, then, it is really un-Christian to attempt to live wholly in the past, since such an effort is a tacit betrayal of a lack of faith in the redemptive function of the Incarnation, or, in historical terms, in the meaningfulness of the temporal process. As Eliot says in *Four Quartets*:

> . . . A people without history
> Is not redeemed from time, for history is a pattern
> Of timeless moments. So, while the light fails
> On a winter's afternoon, in a secluded chapel
> History is now and England.[1]

But the Incarnation redeems more than merely an abstract process called history; it also redeems the real, the concrete world of human events, the small as well as the great, the everyday as well as the extraordinary. Sacramental vision thus demands commitment not only to the contemporary scene but also to the ordinary reality of modern life. The Incarnation, then, has radically important implications for the Christian dramatist, who must project human events on the stage. In rendering the concrete present significant, a crucial moment laden with the import of the past in

the process of fulfilling the eternal design, it opens to poetic imitation a domain hitherto dominated by the naturalistic dramatist.
It thus resolves, for the Christian poet-dramatist at least, the problem posed by critics such as Joseph Wood Krutch of the unavaila-
bility to the poet of the mean and ignoble modern world.[2] As
W. H. Auden puts the Christian alternative to angelic or narcis-
sistic solipsism in *For the Time Being:*

> Because in Him the Flesh is united to the Word without
> magical transformation, Imagination is redeemed from promis-
> cuous fornication with her own images. The tragic conflict of
> Virtue with Necessity is no longer confined to the Exceptional
> Hero; for disaster is not the impact of a curse upon a few great
> families, but issues continually from the hubris of every tainted
> will. Every invalid is Roland defending the narrow pass against
> hopeless odds, . . .
>
> Nor is the Ridiculous a species any longer of the Ugly; for
> since of themselves all men are without merit, all are ironically
> assisted to their comic bewilderment by the Grace of God. . . .
>
> Nor is there any situation which is essentially more or less in-
> teresting than another. Every tea-table is a battlefield littered
> with old catastrophes and haunted by the vague ghosts of vast
> issues, every martyrdom an occasion for flip cracks and senten-
> tious oratory.
>
> Because in Him all passions find a logical In-Order-That, by
> Him is the perpetual recurrence of Art assured.[3]

On the level of style, the pressure of the doctrine of the Incarnation is in the direction of an adjustment analogous to that of
subject matter and thus demands that the dramatist employ the
language and rhythms of ordinary modern speech, and by extension, the third, the dramatic voice of poetry. The pressure is not
toward a capitulation to the commonplace, but rather, through
the agency of the Incarnation, a transfiguration of the everyday
event.

This Christian "low" style, which, as Auerbach has convincingly
shown, has its historical source in the dissolution of the classical
Stiltrennung and the accompanying merger of the polar styles into
one characterized by a sublime *Humilitas*,[4] constitutes the central,

the native, tradition of English dramatic verse from the medieval mysteries through the Elizabethan drama.[5] Since the reassertion of the *Stiltrennung* in the neoclassical Restoration Period, however, it has become more or less axiomatic that the language and rhythms of eloquence are the appropriate media of poetic drama and that the language and rhythms of ordinary speech are the appropriate media of the prose drama. Thus with the passing of a dynamic view of man, the high style of modern poetic drama has, by increasing the remoteness of the extraordinary events it imitates, rendered this genre artificial and alien to the life of the times. As the nineteenth-century and Georgian verse drama clearly reveal, the high style encourages the disengagement of the audience from the action and its significance and ultimately the repudiation of the traditional public function of poetic drama. By reclaiming the idiom and rhythms of modern speech and the dramatic voice without seriously damaging, as naturalistic prose tends to do, their ability to convey value, the sacramental aesthetic thus opens up the possibilities of bringing dramatic verse back into the tradition and of achieving a reunion of modern man and poetry.

In *Murder in the Cathedral* T. S. Eliot transforms a historical into a sacramental, a particular into a concrete-universal, action by establishing it in the context of a recurrent Christian archetype into which a pre-Christian archetype has been figurally integrated. Though he thus transcends the fundamental limitation of the historical or mythical action of Romantic and Georgian drama—its patent remoteness from contemporary life—Eliot's solution is an incomplete one. As he notes in "Poetry and Drama," he relied too heavily on overt Christian doctrine (Becket's sermon and the liturgical links) at the expense of the dramatic encounter of character to convey to his audience the universality of the past action he is imitating. Furthermore, the verse he employs, despite its theoretical neutrality, its commitment "neither to the present nor to the past," [6] is, because of its elevated tone, too closely associated with the historical past, while the prose, particularly in the last scene, is too insistently contemporary. The sharp division of styles tends to cut across the theme of the integral presentness of the past. Eliot, in other words, is at this time still somewhat under the influence of the classical *Stiltrennung,* which in modern poetic drama betrays a lack of faith in the poetic potential of the ordinary and leads to the separation of audience and action. It is this realization, I think, that lies behind his just, though too harsh, self-criticism in "Poetry and Drama" for adhering in *Murder in the Cathedral* to the generally held view that "Verse plays . . . should either take their subject matter from some mythology, or else should be about some remote historical period, far enough away from the present for the characters not to need to be recognizable as human beings, and therefore for them to be licensed to talk in verse." [7]

In terms of its ability to engage the modern temper, *Murder in the Cathedral* thus falls between the Georgian historical verse drama and Eliot's later contemporary plays. For Eliot's alternative is not, as it is for the Georgians, to turn to naturalistic drama, or even to effect a compromise with it. It is rather to fulfill the sacramental aesthetic implicit in his Canterbury play. This is essential to understand if we are to avoid the misleading conclusions of many critics that Eliot later capitulated to the realistic prose theater and that analysis and judgment of the late plays must accordingly proceed along the lines of the naturalistic aesthetic.[8]

When he writes that in *The Family Reunion* he was "determined to take a theme of contemporary life, with characters of our own time, living in our own world," [9] a practice he continued in the rest of his plays, he is not rejecting a Romantic poetic and its high style for a naturalistic poetic and its low style. He is pursuing the implications of a sacramental poetic, which reconciles poetry and everyday reality, the high and the low styles:

> If the poetic drama is to reconquer its place, it must . . . enter into overt competition with prose drama. As I have said, people are prepared to put up with verse from the lips of personages dressed in the fashion of some distant age; therefore they should be made to hear it from people dressed like ourselves, living in houses and apartments like ours, and using telephones and motor cars and radio sets. . . . What we have to do is to bring

poetry into the world in which the audience lives and to which it returns when it leaves the theatre; not to transport the audience into some imaginary world totally unlike its own, an unreal world in which poetry is tolerated. What I should hope might be achieved, by a generation of dramatists having the benefit of our experience, is that the audience should find, at the moment of awareness that it is hearing poetry, that it is saying to itself: "I could talk in poetry too!" Then we should not be transported into an artificial world; on the contrary, our own sordid, dreary daily world would be suddenly illuminated and transfigured.[10]

This passage from Eliot's definitive theoretic statement of his dramatic aims, particularly the last sentence, is good sacramentalism. It could be interpreted as an analogue of one of those present moments that the poet speaks about in *Four Quartets* where "the impossible union" of time and eternity is perceived and past and future are thus reconciled. As a matter of fact, this is a later version of a similar passage in Eliot's earlier essay, "The Aims of Poetic Drama" (1949), which makes precisely this connection. Despite the repetition, the early passage is worth quoting for the light it throws on Eliot's dramatic aims:

What I should like to do . . . is this: that the people on the stage should seem to the audience so like themselves that they would find themselves thinking: "I could talk in poetry too!" Then, they are not transported into an unaccustomed, artificial world, but their ordinary, sordid, dreary world is suddenly illuminated and transfigured. And if poetry cannot do that for people, then it is merely a superfluous decoration. What poetry should do in the theatre is a kind of humble shadow or analogy of the Incarnation, whereby the human is taken up into the divine.[11]

It will be seen, then, that the sacramental aesthetic which governs the form of *Murder in the Cathedral* (and of *The Rock*, for that matter) also lies behind the form that Eliot's commercial plays about contemporary life assume. In these, as in the earlier play, it transfigures an apparently naturalistic or secular into a sacramental action that is simultaneously itself and other than itself, particular and universal, by figurally integrating into it both a Christian and pre-Christian archetypal action. The difference between *Murder in the Cathedral* and the later plays is essentially quantitative rather than qualitative in character. In the later plays the main action is projected in the contemporary world and is expressed in the everyday language of secular life. The Christian pattern and Greek myth are more closely assimilated into it and therefore less apparent on the surface, though no less present. Thus, whereas in *Murder in the Cathedral* the relative explicitness of the Christian and Greek analogues of the main action forces the abstract pattern into too great a prominence and places the drama in the realm of rhetoric, in the later plays the archetypal nature of the main action comes more and more to be felt dramatically as an underpattern rather than apprehended intellectually (a development that corresponds with Eliot's avowed desire to write for an uneducated audience), and the drama is thus more genuinely poetic. The nature of the multivocal effect that Eliot is trying to achieve in the commercial plays, and, incidentally, the need of a special term to distinguish this kind of poetic drama from both the allegorical mode of, say, Archibald MacLeish's *J. B.* and the symbolic, that is, "angelic," mode of Maurice Maeterlinck's *Pelléas et Mélisande*, are suggested in the definition of poetic drama he arrives at in his essay "John Marston" (1934):

> It is possible that what distinguishes poetic drama from prosaic drama is a kind of doubleness in the action, as if *it took place on two planes at once.* In this it is different from allegory, in which the abstraction is something conceived, not something differently felt, and from symbolism (as in the plays of Maeterlinck) in which the tangible world is deliberately diminished— both symbolism and allegory being operations of the conscious planning mind. In poetic drama a certain apparent irrelevance may be the symptom of this doubleness; or the drama has an underpattern, less manifest than the theatrical one. We sometimes feel, in following the words and behaviour of some of the characters of Dostoevsky, that they are living *at once* on the plane that we know and on some other plane of reality from which we are shut out.[12]

This double pattern that Eliot speaks about may be read, as Melchiori does, in terms of the simultaneous "planes of reality" [13] that E. M. W. Tillyard attributes to Shakespeare's romances in *Shakespeare's Last Plays.*[14] But surely, considering Eliot's Christian orientation, it would be more precise to read the references to the double pattern as a secular aesthetic expression of sacramentalism.

In "East Coker," Eliot writes, "You say I am repeating / Something I have said before. I shall say it again." [15] The quotation applies equally to the verse plays of contemporary life—*The Family Reunion* (1939), *The Cocktail Party* (1949), *The Confidential Clerk* (1953), and *The Elder Statesman* (1959). These constitute dramatic projections in a modern drawing-room setting of a theme Eliot has explored in a variety of ways throughout his career: the redemption of life in time. Despite the surface differences, the central action of each embodies in some measure a reenactment or figure, on the level of ordinary contemporary life, of the Christic pattern of Atonement that reunites man and God and time and eternity. Thus the recurrent theme of these plays broadly determines the sacramental form, which integrates past and present (Greek myth and modern action) and transfigures a naturalistic or psychological into a sacramental, a univocal into a multivocal, drama.

On the surface level, Eliot's plays of contemporary life are, in varying degrees, imitations of everyday secular actions cast in forms that have come to be associated with the realistic modern drama. *The Family Reunion,* for example, which is projected in the framework of Ibsen's problem play, explores the peculiarly modern psyche of a man who has had murderous designs on his wife. *The Cocktail Party,* employing the comedy of manners form, resurrected for the modern theater by Somerset Maugham and brought successfully into the pale of West End by Noel Coward, examines the neurotically trivial attitudes toward love and marriage of the sophisticated upper middle class of modern urban English society. *The Confidential Clerk,* cast in a mold reminiscent of Wilde's *The Importance of Being Earnest,* depicts the farcical search for identity of several young people whose illegitimate births reflect the modern attitude toward the family. And *The Elder Statesman,* which reverts to the form of the problem play, explores the inner life of the apparently successful modern utilitarian man. In each case, Eliot adheres in varying degrees to Ibsen's realistic retrospective method of construction, in which the past is gradually and naturally revealed through conversational reference. Thus he gives the real world of the present its formal due.

Eliot, however, transcends the basic limitation of the naturalistic subject matter and forms—the restriction of significance to the univocal level of social commentary or psychological reality—that he employs in these plays. In each, he covertly schematizes the character groupings and the development of the action in a similar way so that despite the surface differences, all the plays are characterized by a corresponding underpattern, an archetypal image that deepens the surface realism. The characters of these plays fall into three groups. The first two groups, which on the dramatic level constitute the main characters in the action, are the more or less spiritually blind—the ordinary people who "live and partly live" in a world devoid of spiritual significance—and the spiritually aware, those who perceive the imminent irruption of the irrational into their lives and choose to face it whatever the consequences. The third group, whose mysteriousness suggests their possession of a knowledge that transcends that of the main characters, constitutes the agents of the action, their function rendering them remote descendants of the vice figures of the medieval morality plays. In *The Family Reunion,* Amy and the aunts and uncles constitute the spiritually blind group; Harry, Agatha, and, less certainly, Mary, the spiritually aware group; and the Furies, the agents of the action. In *The Cocktail Party,* the first two groups consist of Edward, Lavinia, and Peter, on the one hand, and Celia on the other; and the third consists of the Guardians, Reilly, Julia, and Alex. The schematization of *The Confidential Clerk* is less definite, but it is discernible. Sir Claude, Lady Elizabeth, Lucasta, and B. Kaghan, on the one hand, and Colby, on the other, represent the first two groups; and Eggerson and Mrs. Guzzard, though less explicitly, the third. Finally, in *The Elder Statesman*, Charles and Monica and Michael constitute, in varying degrees, the first group, Lord Claverton-Ferry represents the second, and Gomez and Mrs. Carghill, the third.

To abstract a pattern of action common to all of Eliot's plays is to run the risk not only of oversimplification but also of distorting the strategy behind them, since Eliot's intention is not to present a diagram for intellectual analysis but to elicit "some perception of an order in reality" in terms of the minute particulars of human experience, to elicit, that is, some perception of the archetypal quality of life, the "fringe of indefinite extent, of feeling which we can only detect . . . out of the corner of the eye and can never completely focus." [16] Nevertheless, the risk has to be taken for the sake of the light the archetypal pattern throws on the peculiar form these plays assume.

Broadly, the actions of each, though *The Confidential Clerk* is somewhat different, traces a pattern in which the hero, in a moment of illumination, sloughs off the old, the assumed and therefore unauthentic self for a new, existential self, thereby creating "significant soil" that brings the others, the less perceptive community, to a new awareness in which the terms of existence are no longer the same (the latter effect becoming increasingly prominent with each play). At the outset, the spiritually receptive character, suffering from a psychological malaise and incapable of communicating with the spiritually unaware, attempts to escape his predicament either by denying the past or, what is the same thing, by refusing to acknowledge his real identity, wherein the source of his malaise lies. Nevertheless, he is driven into the "precincts of his last evasions" by the third group, the sinister, or at least mysterious, agents of the action, where, on the edge of despair, he discovers not only the source of his sickness but also the possibility of a cure. At this point he recognizes, like the heroes of Williams' plays, the essential benignity of the dark agents, and acknowledging his past, his true identity, becomes a whole, a new man. Thus, through his suffering he infuses new meaning into the lives of the less perceptive community, whose existence has been, in the terms of

Martin Buber, that of "objects," of "Its" (for Eliot the metaphor is more often that of the actor playing a part in a play) in the mechanistic time world.

This is obviously the recurrent Christian pattern of redemption, which has its ground in the oneness of Adam's fall and the coming of Christ, of original sin and the Incarnation, or, in other words, in the paradox of the Fortunate Fall. As Eliot puts this seminal principle in "East Coker":

> Our only health is the disease
> If we obey the dying nurse
> Whose constant care is not to please
> But to remind of our, and Adam's curse,
> And that, to be restored, our sickness must grow worse.
>
> The whole earth is our hospital
> Endowed by the ruined millionaire,
> Wherein, if we do well, we shall
> Die of the absolute paternal care
> That will not leave us, but prevents us everywhere.[17]

Thus in each of these plays the naturalistic action is, through the agency of the mysterious third group (whose insistent pursuit of the protagonist into awareness of the paradoxically benign nature of his condition may tentatively be related to the "absolute paternal care" that "prevents us everywhere") is transfigured into a sacramental action.

On the level of the immediate action, the psychological process of discovering and acknowledging the true identity is transfigured into a process of discovering and acknowledging sin and the concomitant personal reintegration into a recognition of Incarnation which redeems sin. Thus just as in *Murder in the Cathedral,* murder becomes martyrdom, so in *The Family Reunion,* crime and punishment become sin and expiation; in *The Cocktail Party,* the social gathering becomes the spiritual community; in *The Confidential Clerk,* the search for literal identity becomes the search for spiritual identity; and in *The Elder Statesman,* the progress toward death becomes a progress toward transfiguration. Similarly, the surface forms of these plays assume poetic stature. The problem play forms of *The Family Reunion* and *The Elder Statesman* assume tragic proportions, the West End comedy of manners form of *The Cocktail Party* is transformed into tragicomedy, and the melodramatic farce form of *The Confidential Clerk* becomes high comedy.

The redemptive pattern in these plays also operates on the level of time. The moment of illumination is not only the acknowledgment of sin and the discovery of the redemptive function of the Incarnation. It is also the discovery of intelligible order in the apparent chaos of time or history, of a sacramental pattern in which the past is integrated into the present; this thematic significance, as we shall see, provides the *raison d'être* of Eliot's use of myth in these plays and sharply distinguishes it from other contemporary uses of myth in the drama.

It is impossible in this space to demonstrate the operation of the sacramental aesthetic in all of Eliot's plays of contemporary life. Nevertheless, some suggestion of the strategy that underlies these plays can be given by a relatively detailed analysis of the first of them, *The Family Reunion*, and a briefer examination of the others. *The Family Reunion* is especially useful in this respect, since the lack of satisfactory integration between the various aspects of the form renders Eliot's strategy more apparent than it is in the later plays.

The Family Reunion is ostensibly the story of a neurotic made whole. Harry, Lord Monchensey, returns to Wishwood, his ancestral home, for the first time in eight years of drifting from one watering place to another. He hopes that here he can escape the guilt he feels for the recent death of his wife—whom he thinks he pushed overboard during a trip across the Atlantic—by leaping over the immediate past into his childhood. But his "instinct to return to the point of departure / And start again as if nothing had happened" [18] is futile. As a matter of fact, it is when he returns to his point of departure to encounter his youth that the guilt assumes physical proportions. For he has returned, as he discovers through Dr. Warburton and Agatha, to the point in space and time where the neurosis, the murderous impulse, has its source: to the "cold place" (p. 225) of his youth. As Maud Bodkin observes, it is the place where the "blind, clutching, possessive love of his mother" had driven Harry into an act of resistance against her efforts to impose on him an alien identity, an act which manifested itself first as a blind choice "under a kind of inverted maternal compulsion" of a wife who was his mother's double, and later, when his wife suddenly disappeared, as a belief "that he had committed Orestes' crime—had executed that vengeance upon the mother." [19] But Harry's discovery of the source of his neurosis is precisely what he has needed to regain wholeness. After this psychoanalytic journey, his fixed and therefore destructive passion is released and redirected, "becomes the sustaining force of a better order of individual and social life." [20]

But this psychological interpretation is, of course, not the whole story. For by establishing the action of *The Family Reunion* within a matrix of hidden, though often too overt, references to aspects of the Christian scheme, Eliot transforms the psychological progress into a modern image of the archetypal Christic action. Eliot suggests the Christian interpretation and its archetypal nature by presenting the action as a movement generated by the Furies that resolves two contradictory time planes, the mechanistic or clock time plane of Amy and the quartet of aunts and uncles (the time scheme that underlies naturalistic drama) and the psychological or inverted Bergsonian plane of real duration (the time scheme which underlies at least one kind of "angelic" art).[21]

Amy's mechanistic time world is established at the outset of the action. She dreads the passage of time and especially the end of time; that is, death, the intrusion of an uncontrollable force into the round of her life:

> I do not want the clock to stop in the dark.
> If you want to know why I never leave Wishwood
> That is the reason. I keep Wishwood alive
> To keep the family alive, to keep them together,
> To keep me alive, and I live to keep them.
>
> [p. 227]

In order to keep Wishwood alive, she attempts to ignore the past, the inevitable changes that time wrings in people or, rather, to willfully arrest them by imposing her own design on human events. Thus it is her intention to *produce* a situation in which Harry can assume "command" of Wishwood as if nothing had happened in the interim between his boyhood and the present. When Agatha warns her of the futility of her effort, Amy replies:

> Nothing is changed, Agatha, at Wishwood.
> Everything is kept as it was when he left it,
> . . . .
> Nothing has changed: I have seen to that,
>
> [p. 228]

and goes on to assign the others the roles they must play in her effort to "contrive [Harry's] future happiness" (p. 230). As Miss Anne Ward observes: "The kind of time upon which Amy endeavors to build her life resembles the abstract time of the mathematician or astronomer. According to Bergson, science is able to deal with the material universe by assuming that time does not create anything absolutely new; time, to the physicist, is no more than an inactive medium in which reciprocally external spatial counters are rearranged and juxtaposed. The intellect, geared to the needs of action, tends, when it turns from dealing with dead matter to dealing with its own 'conscious states,' to keep up the 'illusion' through which it makes these conscious states 'share in the reciprocal externality of outer things. . . . [T]his distinctness, and at the same time this solidification, enables us,' [sic] says Bergson, to give our states of consciousness 'fixed names in spite of their instability, and distinct ones in spite of their interpenetration. It enables us to objectify them, to throw them out into the current of social life.' " [22]

Amy's mechanistic concept of time, which denies the influence of the past on the present, thus transforms other human beings into inanimate objects to be used, or, in the metaphor that Eliot employs more frequently in this and the later plays, into actors with assigned roles in a world of make-believe, of appearance.[23]

This is why Wishwood has always been a "cold place." It is a realm of the dead passing as living human beings.

But Agatha knows that Amy's human effort to impose her design on events and an identity on her son is vain. There is no escaping into the safety of the past for Harry:

> . . . Wandering in the tropics
> Or against the painted scene of the Mediterranean,
> Harry must often have remembered Wishwood—
> . . . .
> And thought to creep back through the little door.
> He will find a new Wishwood. Adaptation is hard.
>
> [p. 228]

Agatha, who is referring to the events that have led up to the death of Harry's wife, is aware of a different time plane from Amy's: that of a destructive and uncontrollable spiritual time that is represented in the imagery of flux, of chaos, and of corruption, and has its source in the awareness of sin. In this time world of radical change, the influence of the past on the moral identity of the individual in the present, is the essential characteristic. It resembles Bergson's *durée réelle* in that real time is not a controllable sequence of units of experience but a stream in which past, present, and future intermingle. It is very different, however, in that it is not "creative" but painfully meaningless. It is the time of the fallen world, and this is what is important. To Agatha, Harry's return to the past, to Wishwood, "to meet / The boy who left" (p. 229) will not be, as Amy believes, a happy affair. There he will come face to face with the sin of the house, which has brought chaos to the Monchensey world: "When the loop in time comes . . . / The hidden is revealed, and the spectres show themselves" (p. 229). Yet somehow Harry must descend into this nightmare world of flux and acknowledge its reality if he is to discover a meaningful order in time and in his life. For as Agatha hints, "the future can only be built / Upon the real past" (p. 228).

As Agatha rightly guesses, Harry had, like Amy, hoped he could circumvent his present identity—which is the accumulation of all that had *happened*—by imposing another, earlier identity upon himself. To Mary he says retrospectively:

> All these years I'd been longing to get back
> Because I thought I never should. I thought it was a place
> Where life was substantial and simplified—
> . . . .
> But I thought I might escape from one life to another,
>
> [p. 247]

Unlike Amy, however, Harry is capable of responding to guilt. Despite his conscious efforts, he constantly sees "flickering at the corner of [his] eye" (p. 250), as it were, that he is being pursued by the specters of the past (the pervasive imagery of pursuit, to which I will return, reminds us of its similar use in Charles Williams' *Cranmer of Canterbury*). He is thus at least partially aware that his decision to return to the "point of departure / And start again as if nothing had happened" (p. 249) is his last refuge among human alternatives in the quest for redemption. Ironically, his flight from the specters is one that brings him to the very place where they demand he come to ground, to the past, where he must encounter the real source of his guilt. He has not escaped in coming to Wishwood. He has been driven, rather, into the precincts of his last evasions, where he must make an existential decision about who he is.

Thus on his arrival at Wishwood, it is not peace he finds; it is rather the Furies:

> Can't you see them? *You* don't see them, but I see them,
> And they see me. This is the first time that I have seen them.
> In the Java Straits, in the Sunda Sea,
> In the sweet sickly tropical night, I knew they were coming.
>
> p. 232]

But he does not understand why it is here that they reveal themselves to him for the first time:

Why should they wait until I came back to Wishwood?
There were a thousand places where I might have met them!
Why here? why here?

[p. 232]

Harry's quest for the answer constitutes the main action of *The Family Reunion.*

The process begins with Harry's disillusioning encounter with his mother and his aunts and uncles, whose mechanistic time world, because it is inhabited by counters rather than free human beings, makes them incapable of understanding that his is a problem that goes deeper than morality, that it is more than a matter of "conscience" (p. 236). In this confrontation he reveals his awareness of the reality of the nightmare time world of flux in which past, present, and future interpenetrate each other chaotically, though he is only dimly aware that its roots lie deeper in the past than that cloudless night when he allegedly pushed his wife overboard:

> . . . I am the old house
> With the noxious smell and the sorrow before morning,
> In which all past is present, all degradation
> Is unredeemable. As for what happens—
> Of the past you can only see what is past,
> Not what is always present. That is what matters.

[p. 234]

Suffering from despair, from what he thinks is "the sudden extinction of every alternative, / The unexpected crash of the iron cataract" (p. 249) and the oppression of the Furies, Harry begins, in his encounter with Mary, the painful exploration of his past. In sympathy with him, Mary, who momentarily throws off the identity Amy has imposed on her, perceives, better than she consciously realizes, that his instinct to return is paradoxically the way to discovery:

> But surely, what you say
> Only proves that you expected Wishwood
> To be your real self, to do something for you

> That you can only do for yourself.
> What you need to alter is something inside you
> Which you can change anywhere—here as well as elsewhere.
>
> [pp. 249–250]

Harry curtly dismisses her insight, but in doing so, he betrays his fear of the burden of understanding that Mary's recommendation is, at least partially, what his pursuers demand. This fear becomes clearer in the question he asks, which recalls the opening lines of *The Waste Land*: "Is the spring not an evil time, that excites us with lying voices?" (p. 251). Mary's reply plumbs an even deeper reality:

> The cold spring now is the time
> For the ache in the moving root
> The agony in the dark
>
> [p. 251]

And Harry senses that this is a call for spiritual rebirth: "Spring is an issue of blood / A season of sacrifice" (p. 251). Yet he is still incapable of facing "the ghosts of the dead" (p. 251) who return in the spring.[24]

At this point, as Nathan Scott observes, Mary, "suspecting that Harry's conviction of the painfulness of rebirth may reinforce his reluctance to submit to the process of redemption, responds with the deeper insight": [25]

> Pain is the opposite of joy
> But joy is a kind of pain
> I believe the moment of birth
> Is when we have knowledge of death
> I believe the season of birth
> Is the season of sacrifice
>
> [pp. 251–252]

The trance broken, Harry appears to touch the borders of true understanding when he suddenly cries out:

> . . . You bring me news
> Of a door that opens at the end of a corridor,
> Sunlight and singing; when I had felt sure

That every corridor only led to another,
Or to a blank wall; . . .

[p. 252]

But at this moment, the Furies appear to warn him away from this evasion. What Harry says here is true, as the analogous scene with Agatha—in which Harry, like Lewis Carroll's Alice, does enter the garden that lies beyond the corridor [26]—reveals, but not in the sense that he means it. Instead of responding to the content of Mary's insight, he has responded to Mary physically. As Eliot has said, "This is the first time since his marriage . . . that he has been attracted towards any woman. The attraction glimmers for a moment in his mind, half-consciously as a possible 'way of escape.' " [27] The response is thus another effort to disengage himself from the past, from the Harry who is burdened by the guilt of his wife's death. This is made clear a moment later in his remonstration with the Furies: "When I knew her [his wife], I was not the same person. / I was not any person. Nothing that I did / Has to do with me" (p. 253). But the Furies, "the sleepless hunters" (p. 252), will not let Harry escape the past. He must acknowledge its presence, for as Agatha has hinted, "the future can only be built / Upon the real past." The encounter with Mary thus brings him to the realization that he must "face [the Furies]" (p. 253), though as yet he is hostile to them.

The emergence of the real past into Harry's consciousness begins in his interview with Dr. Warburton, the family physician, who has been called in to diagnose his "strange" behavior. Disturbed by the conversation with Mary, he feels "an overwhelming need for explanation" (p. 259) of his unhappy boyhood at Wishwood, where "The rule of conduct was simply pleasing mother" (p. 258). When the doctor impatiently insists that the immediate concern is with Amy's future, "And not with the past" (p. 259), Harry, echoing Agatha, replies:

How can we be concerned with the past
And not with the future? or with the future
And not with the past?

[p. 259]

and suddenly asks Warburton about his father. The physician's reluctant disclosure triggers Harry's memory and the sordid facts of the family's early history, the intimations of the coldness between wife and husband and the oppressive possessiveness of the mother begin to emerge. This in turn evokes from Harry an obscure presentiment of his identification with his father, which darkly manifests itself a moment later when Sergeant Winchell, who has come to report an accident, asks about Amy:

WINCHELL   . . . How is her Ladyship,
 If I may ask, my Lord?

HARRY   Why do you keep asking
 About her Ladyship? Do you know or don't you?
 I'm not afraid of you.

WINCHELL   I should hope not, my Lord.
 I didn't mean to put myself forward.
 But you see, my Lord, I had good reason for asking. . .

HARRY Well, do you want me to produce her for you?

WINCHELL Oh, no, indeed, my Lord, I'd much rather not. . .

HARRY You mean you think I can't. But I might surprise you;
 I think I might be able to give you a shock.[28]

               [p. 263]

With this intimation of the identity of father and son, of past and present, Harry has come, despite his efforts to the contrary, to the verge of discovering the real source of his anguish and to acknowledging his helplessness before it. Thus when he is again confronted by the family, the world of the mechanistic time mind, he says to them in words that recall the climactic self-evaluation of the Women of Canterbury:

 You go on trying to think of each thing separately,
 Making small things important, so that everything
 May be unimportant, a slight deviation
 From some imaginary course that life ought to take,
 That you call normal. What you call the normal
 Is merely the unreal and the unimportant.

I was like that in a way, so long as I could think
Even of my own life as an isolated ruin,
A casual bit of waste in an orderly universe.
But it begins to seem just part of some huge disaster,
Some monstrous mistake and aberration
Of all men, of the world, which I cannot put in order.[29]

[p. 268]

Harry, in other words, has been driven by the Furies to the edge
of the abyss. His last refuge, the past, it turns out, has revealed
the ultimate horror: the curse on his family, which, of course,
symbolizes the curse on "all men," the Original Sin that since the
Fall has afflicted the human family, and the futility of human
effort in putting the chaos in order. He has arrived, as Stanley
Romaine Hopper says of the existential hero in modern literature,
at that moment in his quest for salvation "just prior to the moment . . . when the groundwork cracks, when the abyss opens,
and 'time, the serpent . . . retrieves the telescope' of indefinite
temporal projection, and 'constricts it to its primal nest of vertigos,
the labyrinth, compressible, of our own egos.' He has reached the
nadir of moral isolation: he is lost. And he knows it." [30]

But Harry's acknowledgment of the past, of sin, and of the
futility of the private will to redeem man is, as we have seen again
and again in this body of drama, paradoxically a positive act. "We
need to recover the sense of religious fear," Eliot has said, echoing
Kierkegaard and other Christian existentialists, "so that it may be
overcome by religious hope." [31] The "extinction of every alternative" and the absolute loss of hope clear the human heart for the
moment of illumination, which reveals the possibility of the redemptive function of the Incarnation. This is the burden of the
climactic scene which finally brings Harry and Agatha together.

Under the pressure of Harry's insistent need for explanation—
"When I know, I know that in some way I shall find / That I
have always known it. And that will be better" (p. 273)—Agatha
leads him over the same ground of the past that he had traversed
in his interview with Warburton, and what were only intuitions
from the dark recesses of his unconscious become conscious knowl-

edge. She tells him of the lovelessness of his parents' marriage, of
the "summer day of unusual heat / For this cold country" (p. 274)
when she and Harry's father fell in love, and of the father's desperate decision to take his wife's life, which Agatha prevented because
of her maternal love for the unborn child. All this confirms his
earlier presentiment of his identity with his father: in desiring the
death of his wife he shares, indeed, has inherited, the father's sin.
But now Harry begins to see things in a new light:

> Everything is true in a different sense,
> A sense that would have seemed meaningless before.
> Everything tends towards reconciliation.
> As the stone falls, as the tree falls. And in the end
> That is the completion which at the beginning
> Would have seemed the ruin.
>
> [p. 275]

And his insight is substantiated by Agatha:

> What we have written is not a story of detection,
> Of crime and punishment, but of sin and expiation.
> It is possible that you have not known what sin
> You shall expiate, or whose, or why. It is certain
> That the knowledge of it must precede the expiation.
> It is possible that the sin may strain and struggle
> In its dark instinctive birth, to come to consciousness
> And so find expurgation. It is possible
> You are the consciousness of your unhappy family,
> Its bird sent flying through the purgatorial flame.
>
> [p. 275]

With this conscious formulation of the significance of the past,
of the sin of his father, on his present moral identity, Harry is
"cured" of his sickness, but it is a cure of the spirit not of the
mind. In spiritual communion with Agatha, he enters the "rose
garden" which Agatha and Harry's father had glimpsed "through
the door" and Harry, in his conversation with Mary, had sensed
beyond "a door that opens at the end of a corridor." This is a
different vision from that in which one gets "what one wanted"

or gets rid of "what can't be got rid of" (p. 275). This is the moment of illumination, the "present moment of pointed light / When you want to burn" (p. 274) that Agatha refers to, "the point of intersection of the timeless with time" when "the past and future / Are conquered and reconciled." It is, in other words, a vision of Incarnation.

Thus Harry's flight from the Furies has taken him first into his past, to the discovery of his true identity in his sin and to the acknowledgment of his inability to make meaningful the world in which past, present, and future flow into each other at random, the fallen world, the

> . . . endless drift
> Of shrieking forms in a circular desert
> Weaving with contagion of putrescent embraces
> On dissolving bone . . .
>
> [p. 277]

and then, at the moment of illumination, back to a present which incorporates past and future, but now in terms of a *sacramental order*. After Agatha has defined their story as one of sin and expiation, he tells her that he feels as if he "had come home" (hence the meaning of the title of the play); that "this is like an end" (p. 275). He has arrived at the point of man's departure, that is, his Fall, and has died to the old, the private, and assumed self. But as Agatha reminds him, his arrival is also "a beginning" (p. 275), for the acknowledgment of sin, of human limitation, brings with it the discovery of Incarnation and the consequent birth of the new, the redeemed self. One recalls at this point the words of Simeon in Auden's *For the Time Being*:

> Before the Positive could manifest Itself specifically, it was necessary that nothing should be left that negation could remove; the emancipation of Time from Space had first to be complete, the Revolution of the Images, in which the memories rose up and cast into subjection the senses by Whom hitherto they had been enslaved. . . .

Before the Infinite could manifest Itself in the finite, it was necessary that man should first have reached that point along his road to Knowledge where, just as it rises from the swamps of Confusion onto the sunny slopes of Objectivity, it forks in opposite directions toward the One and the Many; where, therefore, in order to proceed at all, he must decide which is Real and which only Appearance, yet at the same time cannot escape the knowledge that his choice is arbitrary and subjective. . . .

Before the Unconditional could manifest Itself under the conditions of existence, it was necessary that man should first have reached the ultimate frontier of consciousness, the secular limit of memory beyond which there remained but one thing for him to know, his Original Sin. . . .[32]

The moment in the rose garden, then, is a beginning. It hints at the eternal design in the flux of time, the one in the many, the stillness in motion, but it does not negate the sin:

> . . . I am still befouled,
> But I know there is only one way out of defilement—
> Which leads in the end to reconciliation.
> And I know that I must go.
>
> [p. 279]

As Helen Gardner notes: "The sin remains: it is his birth sin, the 'sin where he begun, which is his sin, though it was done before.' Conceived and brought forth in hatred not in love, he bears the sins of his parents, at once their victim and their perpetuator, for he has been himself incapable of love. . . . He has to learn to love. He must go away into solitude and silence, like the scapegoat, laden with sin, driven out into the wilderness, so that years later, or months, . . . he may find what ways of love are possible for him." [33]

Thus the Furies again appear to recall him to the way of expiation, the *via negativa*, the purgatorial way of St. John of the Cross's *Dark Night of the Soul*, in which the protagonist strips himself of the love of created things in order to redeem the time. But now Harry sees his terrible pursuers differently:

                                              and this time
          You cannot think that I am surprised to see you.
          And you shall not think that I am afraid to see you.
          This time, you are real, this time, you are outside me,
          And just endurable. . . .

                                                                    [p. 278]

Like the heroes of Charles Williams' plays, he comes to perceive
that his malevolent pursuers are paradoxically "bright angels" (p.
281) whom he must follow. In his effort to escape the past, his
whole life, not only the year since his wife's death, "had been a
flight." But now he knows

          That the last apparent refuge, the safe shelter,
          That is where one meets them. That is the way of spectres. . .
          . . . .
                                              And now I know
          That my business is not to run away, but to pursue,
          Not to avoid being found, but to seek.

                                                                    [p. 280]

    It is difficult to determine whether or not Eliot derived his con-
ception of the Furies and the paradoxical imagery of pursuit that
expresses it from Charles Williams' Skeleton in *Cranmer of Canterbury* (1936), or his Third King in *Seed of Adam* (1936), or
even from his analysis of the Skeleton in *Reason and Beauty in
the Poetic Mind* [34] (1933), all of which he must have been familiar
with. What complicates the problem of influence is that the
Aeschylean epigraph to *Sweeney Agonistes* (1926–1927)—"You
don't see them, you don't—but *I* see them: they are hunting me
down, I must move on"—which is repeated by Harry on his arrival at Wishwood, suggests an interpretation of the Furies similar
to that in *The Family Reunion*. At any rate, Williams' and Eliot's
conceptions are virtually the same. Like Williams' paradoxical
figure, Eliot's Furies are divine agents who, from the perspective
of fallen man, appear to be malevolent, but who, from the perspective of spiritual rebirth, are benign guides. Like the Skeleton
in *Cranmer*, for example, the Furies, as Harry reveals, echoing the
lines in "East Coker" where Eliot speaks of "absolute paternal
care," [35] balk the protagonist's private evasions:

> . . . I thought foolishly
> That when I got back to Wishwood, as I had left it,
> Everything would fall into place. But *they* prevent it.
>
> [p. 272]

And they lead him into a full look at the fallen world, the acknowledgment of which is accompanied by a vision of Incarnation. The similarity between Eliot's conception of the Furies and Williams' conception of the Skeleton figures, who are variously referred to as "the Judas that betrays man to God," "Christ's back," "the delator of all things to their truth," "God's true knowledge of all things made," is clearly revealed in a letter Eliot wrote to E. Martin Browne concerning his intention in the scenes depicting Harry's confrontation with Mary and Agatha:

> This is the first time since his marriage . . . that he has been attracted towards any woman. The attraction glimmers for a moment in his mind, half-consciously as a possible "way of escape," and the Furies (for the Furies are *divine* instruments, not simple hell-hounds) come in the nick of time to warn him away from this evasion—though at that moment he misunderstands their function. Now, this attraction towards Mary has stirred him up, but, owing to his mental state, is incapable of developing; therefore he finds a refuge in an ambiguous relation—the attraction, half of a son and half of a lover, to Agatha. . . . And this gives the cue for the second appearance of the Furies, more patently in their role of divine messengers, to let him know clearly that the only way out is purgation and holiness. They become exactly "hounds of heaven." And Agatha understands this clearly, though Harry only understands it yet in flashes.[36]

Like Williams' figures, then, the Furies bridge the gap between Original Sin and Incarnation, between evil and good, or in the temporal terms of the play, between the inverted Bergsonian and the sacramental time worlds. They represent the sacramental principle that operates in the created world, perpetually redeeming time and reordering its "broken structures." As such, they play, along with the references to the various types of time which establish the Christic underpattern of the play, a major role in transmuting the ephemeral contemporary human event into a quest for redemption, or in Eliot's term, in infusing a sense of stillness into movement.

It is true, as Eliot says himself, that the "deepest flaw" in *The Family Reunion* is the "failure of adjustment between the Greek story and the modern situation," [37] that is, the failure to integrate the Furies into the realistic action. But the device itself is dramatically valid. This becomes increasingly clear when one considers that the Guardians in *The Cocktail Party* and the "ghosts" from Lord Claverton's past, and, though less certainly, Eggerson and Mrs. Guzzard in *The Confidential Clerk*, have, as we shall see, virtually the same function as the Furies and are distinguished from them primarily, if not only, by their greater integration into the concrete dramatic situation.

Because *The Family Reunion* ends with Harry's departure from Wishwood, in separation rather than union, to take up the ascetic way of negation—

> To the worship in the desert, the thirst and deprivation,
> A stony sanctuary and a primitive altar,
> The heat of the sun and the icy vigil,
> A care over lives of humble people,
> A lesson of ignorance, of incurable diseases.
>
> [p . 281]

—some critics have concluded that Eliot has established an absolute world—outside of and in opposition to time—toward which it is the business of the protagonist to move. Miss Anne Ward, for example, observes: "Harry's world of concrete duration is intensified until its meaninglessness becomes unendurable. An intellectual and emotional resolution is demanded. There is no possibility of his returning to the superficial stability of Amy's world, in which social relations assume a basis of mathematical time. Harry must cross the frontier into a deeper awareness of time. Eliot's final world, which might also be termed a finalistic world, is rendered necessary by the constitution of his first two worlds. In Harry's assumption of the burden of the guilt of his own past and that of his family he finds the solution which is 'at once the hardest thing, and the only thing possible.' Released for a moment from the

> endless drift
> Of shrieking forms in a circular desert
> Weaving with contagion of putrescent embraces
> On dissolving bone,

Harry stands 'under the judicial sun / Of the final eye.' In that moment, he acknowledges the existence of an absolute realm, beyond time. . . ." [38] Aside from the inappropriateness of the term "resolution," this interpretation is seriously misleading. It makes the world of Eliot's drama Manichaean, a conclusion also arrived at both by William Lynch and Denis Donoghue in their discussions of *The Cocktail Party*.[39] It implies an unredeemed world in which time and eternity, nature and the transcendent, are embodiments of evil and good respectively and therefore radically incompatible and perpetually at war with each other. Furthermore, it conceives man's purpose as a struggle to escape from the bondage of time into eternity. Accordingly—and this is the crux of the matter—this "angelist" theme runs contrary to Eliot's projection of his action in realistic terms and thus obscures the sacramental form of his drama.

A Manichaean interpretation of the world of Eliot's plays travesties his conception of the function of the Incarnation. It is true, of course, that the realm into which the protagonist enters is finalistic or absolute, but not in the sense that Miss Ward and other critics imply. There is for Eliot an Absolute outside of time, the Logos, the "unmoved mover," but He has chosen to fulfill and reveal His purpose in time, to make the Word Flesh. This is the broad function of the Incarnation, which draws past and future into itself in an eternal present. Since man is inextricably part of the time world, he cannot attain direct vision of the Absolute; he must perceive It *in* time. Eliot's final world, then, is absolute in that the meaning of time is already fulfilled in God, having existed from all eternity in His Providence, but it is also and simultaneously tentative in that He fulfills and reveals this meaning in history through the Incarnation and the promise of a second and fully as concrete coming. Eliot's final world, in other words, is that of Incarnation, which integrates the two spheres of existence; it is, as Elizabeth Drew says, "*the point of intersection* between time and the timeless, between stillness and movement, and partakes of the qualities of both the eternal unmoving Logos and the inescapable world of time and movement: 'only through time time is conquered.' " [40]

What Miss Ward fails to perceive in her analysis of *The Family Reunion* is that the whole movement of the play, the painful emergence of the past and its integration into a meaningful, that is, sacramental, present, demands an interpretation of Harry's moment in the "rose garden" as a "liberation" not in the sense of an escape from time but in the sense of a release from chaos, from the patternless and fluid time world of those "who live as if they had each a private wisdom of his own," [41] or as Harry puts it, from "that awful privacy / Of the insane mind" (p. 276). To put it in another way, Harry's "liberation" must be seen as the discovery of sanity and order in the time world, of a harmony in which the radical contradictions of human life—evil and good, change and permanence, motion and stillness—are resolved; in short, in the discovery that the Incarnation, the supreme act of Love, redeems fallen time and absorbs it into the divine economy.

Since Harry's moment of illumination is the moment of decision and thus the determining symbol of the play, it reveals implicitly the nature, both cause and effect, of Harry's pilgrimage. The way of negation, which he chooses, is not for the purpose of escaping from time. The moment has been a "hint" of the harmony grounded in Love, but it cannot be sustained.[42] Thus, though the way of negation appears from a naturalistic point of view inhuman ("Love compels cruelty / To those who do not understand love," p. 279), its purpose is to develop a deeper and more permanent vision of Incarnation, of the meaning of Love, that his knowledge may redeem the past and fructify in the lives of others:

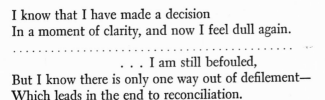

I know that I have made a decision
In a moment of clarity, and now I feel dull again.
. . . .
. . . I am still befouled,
But I know there is only one way out of defilement—
Which leads in the end to reconciliation.

[p. 279]

What Malcolm Ross says about the renunciation of St. Teresa and St. John of the Cross applies equally to the ascetic pilgrimage of Eliot's protagonist: "In St. Teresa, withdrawal is an act of renewal; it is a moment in the rhythm of fulfillment, a coiling up of hidden powers which soon will spring into actualization, into history—just as in St. John of the Cross detachment from the images of the created order is a high strategy to repossess them, as they really are." [43]

One of the chief reasons for the general failure to clearly grasp the sacramentalism of the theme of redemption (and therefore the sacramental form) of *The Family Reunion* is that Eliot fails to resolve the action dramatically, thereby rendering the protagonist an unsympathetic figure. Eliot himself indicates awareness of this when he writes that the audience is "left in a divided frame of mind, not knowing whether to consider the play the tragedy of the mother or the salvation of the son," [44] and elsewhere, that "Harry's career needs to be completed by an *Orestes* or an *Oedipus at Colonus.*" [45] In other words, the dramatic failure is a failure to fully work out the archetypal redemptive pattern which ends in reconciliation, in the repossession of the images of the created order, in this case, the family itself. But even this is a relative matter and should not obscure the theme of sacramental transformation. There is ample evidence that points to it. Just as Harry's departure is a kind of beginning for himself, so, in another sense, it is for the family. With Harry's discovery of direction, Agatha is relieved of the burden of the family's sin and Mary is freed from the role she has been playing in Amy's contrived scenario to assume her own identity and pursue a new life. More significantly, however, the spiritually blind quartet of aunts and uncles have been exposed to, and can no longer escape, the consequences of the operations of the spiritual world. Despite their efforts to prevent it, the irrational has penetrated their mechanistic time world. Though they do not fully understand its implications, they cannot, as the Women of Canterbury cannot, "return to the soft quiet seasons" on the circumference of the Wheel of Being. At the beginning of the play, Harry says that they have never "awakened to the nightmare" (p. 234), to the horror of the incoherent flux of the fallen world, but by the time of Harry's departure they have acknowledged the labyrinth in which they are lost. This is suggested in Amy's and Charles' vague intimations of understanding, but it is most clearly revealed in the progressive awareness of the family in their collective capacity as choric community which culminates in the existential anguish of their final chorus:

> We do not like the maze in the garden, because it too closely resembles the maze in the brain.
> . . . .
> We understand the ordinary business of living,
> We know how to work the machine,
> We can usually avoid accidents,
> We are insured against fire,
> . . . .
> But not against the act of God.
> . . . .
> And what is being done to us?
> And what are we, and what are we doing?
> To each and all of these questions
> There is no conceivable answer.
> We have suffered far more than a personal loss—
> We have lost our way in the dark.[46]

> [pp. 290–291]

After this acknowledgment, the resistance with which the chorus ends—"But we must adjust ourselves to the moment: we must do the right thing" (p. 292)—is itself a positive act. It is something considerably more than indifference to the eternal design operating in time.

Furthermore, it is suggested that Harry will eventually come back to Wishwood, to the world of men ("Until I come again," p. 286 [47]). Whether his return will be actual or in the form of news as is Celia's in *The Cocktail Party* is not important. What is important lies in the fructifying effect his perfected vision will have on the lives of the community. Through his pilgrimage he will have attained, as D. E. S. Maxwell puts it, "the power to nourish 'the life of significant soil.'" [48]

Thus through the agency of the pursuing Furies, Eliot partially at least resolves the opposing mechanistic and inverted Bergsonian schemes into a sacramental time world and establishes thereby an underpattern of redemption which, in turn, assimilates the modern psychological problem into the Christian *schema*. Just as in *Murder in the Cathedral* murder becomes martyrdom, so in *The Family Reunion* "crime and punishment," as Agatha says, becomes "sin and expiation." Harry is a neurotic, but his neurosis has its source in original sin; his moment of illumination brings sanity, but sanity is the awareness of Incarnation—of sacramental order, of permanence in change, in which evil itself is seen as part of the eternal design. In dramatic terms, this act of synthesis, or, in Coleridge's word, of co-adjunction, transmutes the naturalistic surface into a multivocal action, in which the concrete and universal are simultaneously apprehended. Unfortunately, the unnatural "lyrical duets," [49] including the ritual movement at the end of Part II, the communal choruses, and the overt symbolizing render the achievement incomplete.

The sacramental theme of redemption has more far-reaching implications for Eliot's formal experiments in *The Family Reunion*. It is the source of his organic use of the analogous myth of *The Oresteia*. It is also, as it is in *Murder in the Cathedral*, the source of his integral use of the seasonal death-rebirth motif of the primitive fertility religions. For the perception of Incarnation, of the presence of the past, in the history of the individual implies the analogous presence of the past in the history of the human race. Thus, like Dante, in the Siren passage referred to earlier, [50] Eliot can place the modern action within a context of ancient myth without destroying the integrity of the myth, without rendering it merely illustrative. He can integrate the pattern that Orestes enacts in Aeschylus' play into the redemptive figure that Harry traces to give the individual action a historical dimension that universalizes it beyond the bounds of the Christian era. It is as if the Greek myth itself is simultaneously different from and similar to the narrative of the New Testament, a *figura*, in other words, pointing to the Christian action that Eliot is dramatizing. Harry, the modern man, also becomes something of an Everyman, not only within the context of Christian history, but of all time.

Thus the very form of *The Family Reunion* and the later plays (for once the operative principle is isolated, it becomes clear that Euripides' *Alcestis* and his *Ion*, and Sophocles' *Oedipus at Colonus* function similarly, though more integrally, in *The Cocktail Party*, *The Confidential Clerk*, and *The Elder Statesman*, respectively) is seen to be an embodiment of the larger theme of the play.

A comparison of the use to which Eliot puts classical mythology with the very different use to which it is put by the modern French dramatists, Sartre, Anouilh, Cocteau, and Giraudoux, whose more or less humanistic existential view of time and history denies the importance of the past for the sake of commitment to a unique and independent present, illuminates the sacramental concept of time that lies behind the form of Eliot's plays of contemporary life. This comparison is conveniently, if loosely, summarized by Georgio Melchiori, who writes that the French dramatists "deliberately gave a new twist to the ancient myths: keeping even the mythological names, they wanted to emphasize the connection, they wanted their audiences to assume from the very start that their characters were literary creations acquiring little by little new individual personalities. Eliot instead tried to follow the reverse process by starting from characters who were supposed to belong to ordinary life in modern times and making the audience realize that their plight was the same as that of Greek heroes. The result is that while in the first case we have abstract types gradually humanized, in Eliot we have everyday characters dehumanized." [51]

"Dehumanized," as David Jones observes, is certainly not the right word.[52] But if Melchiori means by it that Eliot's modern characters take on a universal significance, the distinction is instructive. In the case of the French dramatists we see that the dramatic process begins with an abstract mythical (literary) image and culminates in a unique image of modern man. Orestes in Sartre's *Les Mouches* and Antigone in Anouilh's play of the same name become existential heroes, individuals committed absolutely to the present, to freedom from universals; the one primarily from divine, the other from political authority. In the end, neither even remotely resembles his classical prototype, which is, of course, the whole point. The Greek myth, in other words, is not intended to remind the audience of a parallel, to convey a sense of the permanence of the human condition. It is deliberately and utterly transformed in the light of the modern predicament. It is also *used* as an object to lend stature to a uniquely modern image of man. Artistically, then, it is reduced to the level of illustrative metaphor.[53]

In Eliot's plays, on the other hand, the dramatic process begins with a realistic image of modern man and ends in an image in which modern and Greek (including the fertility archetype) are seen as significantly analogous, each signifying the other figurally, thus suggesting a universal meaning operating in and through time, that is, "in an image of permanent human nature being subsumed under the divine." [54] From an artistic point of view, the myth as Eliot projects it is not imposed on the modern theme as it is in the French drama; it is an organic part of the reality imitated. It infuses a permanent significance into the modern action, and though it is assimilated into the Christian theology of Incarnation, retains its unique identity. The advance in Aeschylus' trilogy from belief in the concept of a primitive deity of blood vengeance to belief in that of a civilized deity of legal justice which integrates the irrational into its structure rather than rejecting it, and the movement in *The Family Reunion* from belief in a pervasive chaos to belief in a redeemed universe in which evil is assimilated rather than negated (both symbolized by the transformation of the Erinyes into the Eumenides), are simultaneously equivalent and different.

The Greek myth does not lose its identity to become mere literary metaphor. As Ronald Peacock notes: "what [Eliot] attempts to do is to portray a realistic scene—the family in the country house, the barrister with wife, mistress, and social circle—through which an underlying mythical pattern diffuses its meanings to the surface; so that the 'real' becomes, without being negated or displaced, transparent, and through it the myth appears as the immanent meaning. In a drama based on such a view both realistic and mythical forms are authentic; the one is more than a preoccupation with limited aspects of social reality, and the other more than a modern aesthetic device. The symbolism of Eliot's characters is implicit because the personal form contains the meaning. Similarly, the mythical power inheres in the real human situation, since people like Harry and Celia, unlike figures from past myths, begin as ordinary persons leading ordinary lives and remain human even after the assumption of their distinctive functions." [55]

The myth, in other words, renders the modern action a sacramental image that conveys simultaneously the sense of change and permanence, motion and stillness. This achievement, it should be emphasized, results from Eliot's sacramental conception of time.

7

T. S. ELIOT'S PLAYS OF CONTEMPORARY LIFE: THE REDEMPTION OF TIME

> *There are countless places of refuge, there is only one place of salvation: but the possibilities of salvation, again, are as numerous as all the places of refuge.*
>
> Franz Kafka, "Aphorisms"

It should be clear by now to those who are familiar with Eliot's late plays that the form each assumes is fundamentally similar to that of *The Family Reunion*. Detailed analysis of each is therefore unnecessary. What should be pointed out, however, is that in these plays Eliot shifts the dramatic focus progressively from the discovery of vocation by the spiritually perceptive hero to the redemption of time or, more specifically, the less aware community that is subjected by the round of time. This progress tends to verify the integral relationship between the inner theme of redemption and the sacramental dramatic form.

In *The Family Reunion,* which emphasizes the drama of Harry's spiritual pilgrimage, there is only an intimation of the redemptive effect of his conversion on the community: the present negative awareness (anguish) of the aunts and uncles and the suggestion of the development of this awareness in the future when Harry "returns." In *The Cocktail Party,* on the other hand, Celia, the spiritually aware, does return from her pilgrimage (which is similar to the one Harry will undertake), not physically, of course, but in terms of the news of her crucifixion near an ant hill in Kinkanja, where she has been ministering to the disease-stricken natives,[1] and this good news or "gospel" fructifies in the lives of the community.

At the beginning of the play, the Chamberlaynes' cocktail party, the symbol of communal activity, is characterized by schism (Lavinia has left Edward; Edward has decided to break with Celia; and Peter has discarded Lavinia) and public and private deception or what Sartre would call *mauvaise foi.* Each principal presents himself as an invented personality and in turn is confronted as an image contrived in the private mind of another. Everyone thus "uses" the others and, as a result, gradually loses his identity, his particular humanity, and becomes an object (which, along with the analogous imagery of play acting, is, as in *The Family Reunion,* one of the central metaphors of the play). The world of *The Cocktail Party* is the cipher world diagnosed by contemporary existential criticism, the same spiritually dead world that prevails at Wishwood, where the mechanistic view of time (references to which are recurrent, though subdued, in *The Cocktail Party*) transforms existences into manageable essences, particular identities into solidified counters devoid of histories and militantly resistant to the intrusions of unknown dimensions into their vacant lives. When Edward, with at least partial insight, speaks to Reilly in their second interview of the use to which he has been put by Lavinia, he is identifying not only the essential nature of his and his wife's earlier relationship to others, but of Peter's and even Celia's:

I see now why I wanted my wife to come back.
It was because of what she had made me into.
We had not been alone again for fifteen minutes
Before I felt, and still more acutely—
Indeed, acutely, perhaps, for the first time,
The whole oppression, the unreality
Of the role she had always imposed upon me
With the obstinate, unconscious, sub-human strength
That some women have. Without her, it was vacancy.
When I thought she had left me, I began to dissolve,
To cease to exist. That was what she had done to me!
I cannot live with her—that is now intolerable;
I cannot live without her, for she has made me incapable
Of having any existence of my own.[2]

As Eliot puts it in *Notes towards the Definition of Culture* (1948), which, with *The Idea of a Christian Society* (1939), throws much light on the plays of contemporary life and particularly on *The Cocktail Party*:

> It is human, when we do not understand another human being, and cannot ignore him, to exert an unconscious pressure on that person to turn him into something that we *can* understand: many husbands and wives exert this pressure on each other. The effect on the person so influenced is liable to be the repression and distortion, rather than the improvement, of the personality; and no man is good enough to have the right to make another over in his own image.[3]

Following Edward's and Lavinia's choice of the way of ordinary life and Celia's choice of the way of the saint, made under the pressure and guidance of the Guardians, *The Cocktail Party* ends with the Chamberlaynes about to give another party, though this time with the awareness of those who perceive purpose in their lives and community in the life of the social organism. They have each finally accepted their pasts, their real identities, which, in turn, after a moment of isolation, have led them into a collective consciousness of their responsibility in the death of Celia and an

unconscious acknowledgment of the fallen world, of their humanity. When Reilly speaks of Celia's suffering as "part of the design"
(p. 384)—which recalls Becket's "figure of God's purpose"—Edward, seconded by Lavinia, who remembers her unkind treatment
of Celia, says:

> But if this was right—if this was right for Celia—
> There must be something else that is terribly wrong,
> And the rest of us are somehow involved in the wrong.
>
> [p. 385]

Their acknowledgment of the past, of their real identities,
renders them receptive to the redemptive influence of Celia's sacrifice and signals the completion of the design to which Reilly
refers and of which Edward has caught a glimpse. Echoing Agatha
in *The Family Reunion*, Reilly concludes, and the Chamberlaynes
agree, that

> You will have to live with these memories and make them
> Into something new. Only by acceptance
> Of the past will you alter its meaning.
>
> [p. 385]

The new cocktail party, as difficult as it may be to give, is thus
a "new beginning"—references to which reverberate throughout
the closing moments of the play and culminate in the last speech
(Lavinia's): "Oh, I'm glad. It's begun." (p. 387)—but not in the
Greek or Nietzschean sense of mere repetition. It is rather a present
beginning that contains the past, the awareness of sin, and looks to
the future, the awareness of the redemptive function of Celia's
sacrifice. It is the beginning of the new life of dialogue, a rebirth
grounded in an awareness, albeit unconscious, of the still point—
of a figure of the Incarnation operating in their lives—which, like
Celia's more direct awareness, avoids

> . . . the final desolation
> Of solitude in the phantasmal world
> Of imagination, shuffling memories and desires,
>
> [p. 365]

which transcends, in other words, the hellish despair of life in the time world of flux that, as we have seen in *The Family Reunion*, has its source and life in the period between consciousness of sin and the moment of illumination. Recognizing the world of flux that Reilly defines, Celia replies: "That is the hell I have been in." But Reilly, who is aware of the paradoxical benignity as well as the dangers of this stage, corrects her: "It isn't hell, / Till you become incapable of anything else" (p. 365).

Thus, through the "journey," the pilgrimage, that Celia has chosen to take, which is the one Way, the second Way, the "building of the hearth" that the Chamberlaynes have undertaken, can commence fruitfully. The figure of God's purpose, if it is not completed in time, has been intuited and unconsciously acknowledged at the end of the action. Its emergence is reinforced by the structure of the play, which—in beginning with a cocktail party and ending with the news of Celia's crucifixion and the beginning, under its influence, of another cocktail party—suggests Eliot's image of the sacramental relationship between time and eternity: the still point and the turning wheel. When *The Cocktail Party* is seen in the light of this redemptive figure, the frequently voiced criticism represented by Gerald Weales' conclusion that "an ordinary secular audience is likely to share the Chamberlaynes' suspicion that Celia's death is a waste and not a triumph" [4] seems perverse. More perceptive is the view of David Jones:

"The Chamberlaynes are, in fact, accepting their past in this way [by acknowledging their part in the death of Celia], and as a symbol of this acceptance giving just such another cocktail party as they were holding at the beginning of the play. But because their own relationship is altered, the meaning of the party is altered. Celia's death has brought them closer together, as it has tied them to Peter. The life of the spirit is invigorated and the bonds of society are strengthened. Before the party itself begins, a crucifixion has been recalled and a vicarious atonement recognized. The cocktail party can be the secular counterpart of the Communion Service if given in the right spirit. . . . The play is almost a piece of Metaphysical wit in its discovery of analogy in unlikely places." [5]

Weales' and others' criticism of Eliot's dramatic projection of the two ways, on the other hand, is a different matter: "It is true that Sir Henry says of the Chamberlaynes' way, 'It is a good life. Though you will not know how good / Till you come to the end,' but elsewhere he worries at returning the couple 'To the stale food mouldering in the larder, / The stale thoughts mouldering in the minds.' Both ways are presumably honorable ways, even honorable Christian ways, but the tone of the play operates against the assumption that the Chamberlaynes have found anything of value." [6] Yet even this disparity between Eliot's intention and his dramatic projection, which probably receives strength from the dramatist's statement that "the last act . . . only escapes, if indeed it does escape, the accusation of being not a last act but an epilogue," [7] is not as great as it is alleged to be. If we measure the distance, not, as Eliot's critics seem to do, at the point in the play where the Chamberlaynes make their choice of the way of ordinary life (Act II), but at the much later point (Act III) where they encounter the news of Celia's crucifixion, which by activating their acknowledgment of responsibility, fructifies their lives, an extreme judgment is unwarranted. For this *dramatic* awakening is the real new beginning.

In *The Confidential Clerk,* Eliot's modern Christian adaptation of Euripides' tragicomic *Ion,* a primary source of the Greek New Comedy of long-lost relations and mistaken identities,[8] the underpattern of redemption is less schematized and more completely integrated into the surface of the action than in *The Cocktail Party.* The spiritually perceptive character, Colby, is a less heroic figure and as a result his progress ends not in saintly pilgrimage or crucifixion, as Harry's and Celia's do (although B. Kaghan suggests that "He's the sort of fellow who might chuck it all / And go to live on a desert island" [9]), but in discovery of God, the Father, that is, of vocation. Yet the figure of the search for the Father operates in the world of *The Confidential Clerk* in much the same way as the fuller figure of the Christic action does in Eliot's earlier plays: The protagonist's quest for and discovery of his identity, which takes him into his past, redeems the time world, the make-believe world, in which the spiritually blind adjust, as Sir Claude admits, to "What new conditions life will impose on us" (p. 44).[10]

As in *The Cocktail Party*, the characters at the beginning of the action suffer from the peculiarly modern disease of radical alienation. Each wears a public mask, "a prepared face," that hides the essential self and thus isolates him from his fellows and from his authentic self. Sir Claude, under the pressure of his father's desire and an awareness of his artistic limitations, has assumed the character of a man of commerce who believes in "facts" and has hidden his inner love of art, his earlier desire to be a potter, from Lady Elizabeth. ("How strange to have lived with you, all these years, / And now you tell me, you'd have liked to be a potter!", p. 88.) And Lady Elizabeth, under the pressure of Sir Claude's misunderstanding, has assumed the eccentric character of a "cultivated" hostess, and has concealed her earlier desire to "inspire an artist" (p. 89). Lucasta and B. Kaghan, too, under the pressure of Lady Elizabeth's snobbery and their own insecurity—"*You* gave us our parts. And we've shown that we can play them" (p. 100)—play roles in public—the one that of the hard, cynical woman of the world, and the other, of the hearty successful middle-class businessman—and conceal thus a greater sensitivity and seriousness. Accordingly each is divided against and alienated from himself, for eventually the assumed secular mask becomes as real as the inner or spiritual self, and the worlds of both become a kind of make-believe.

This unsatisfactory division between the outer and inner, the material and spiritual, worlds of the characters is epitomized in Sir Claude. Perceiving Colby's abandonment of a musical career as a repetition of his own experience, he recalls his past (in Eliot's plays, always a step in the direction of reconciliation), his early desire to become a potter, and his capitulation to his father's insistance that he become a financier. At first he "loathed this occupation"; but he eventually came to see that despite his passion for the art, he "should never have become a first-rate potter" (p. 40). Thus he began to cultivate a double life, the public life of a man dedicated to commerce and the private life of a man dedicated to the contemplation of art. On the one hand he came "to feel [his] power" in the activity of business and, on the other, to discover a "private door / Into the real world" (p. 41) in the contemplation of his collection of pottery. But this, though he is only dimly aware of it, is an unsatisfactory compromise; for each world is separate from the other and consequently each is not real but make-believe:

> I suppose it takes the place of religion:
> . . . .
> I dare say truly religious people—
> I've never known any—can find some unity.
> Then there are also the men of genius.
> There are others, it seems to me, who have at best to live
> In two worlds—each a kind of make-believe.
> That's you and me. . . .
>
> [p. 42]

Sir Claude attempts to help Colby by suggesting that his new confidential clerk accept, as he had done, "the terms life imposes upon you / Even to the point of accepting . . . make-believe" (p. 42). Colby, however, though he has felt, like Claude, a tempting self-confidence he had never felt before, has been from the beginning uneasy about the new role of identity that the older man is imposing on him: [11]

> . . . Yet at the same time
> It's rather disturbing. I don't mean the work:
> I mean, about myself. As if I was becoming
> A different person. . . .
> . . . .
> I'm not at all sure that I like the other person
> That I feel myself becoming—though he fascinates me.
> And yet from time to time, when I least expect it,
> When my mind is clear and empty, walking in the street
> Or waking in the night, then the former person,
> The person I used to be, returns to take possession:
> And I am again the disappointed organist,

> And for a moment the thing I cannot do,
> The art that I could never excel in,
> Seems the one thing worth doing, the one thing
> That I want to do. I have to fight that person.
>
> [p. 38]

Thus, when Sir Claude offers him a way out, he can only answer:

> . . . At least, I understand *you* better
> In learning to understand the conditions
> Which life has imposed upon you. But. . . something in me
> Rebels against accepting such conditions.
>
> [p. 42]

It is Colby's unwillingness to accept an imposed identity, to live a divided life in two separate worlds of time and eternity, of matter and spirit, that sets the search for his identity in motion and thus transfigures the understanding of the less perceptive characters.

The significance of the inner and outer worlds and the implied third world which reconciles the other two becomes clearer in Act II when Colby and Lucasta, in a scene that recalls the encounter between Harry and Mary in *The Family Reunion* (and, incidentally, reveals, by its evocation of meaning from dramatic voices, the growth of Eliot's command of the sacramental low style since the period of the lyrical duets), achieve something akin to dialogue. Returning to Colby's predicament, Lucasta tells him:

> It's awful for a man to have to give up,
> A career that he's set his heart on, I'm sure:
> But it's only the outer world that you've lost:
> You've still got your inner world—a world that's more real.
> That's why you're different from the rest of us:
> You have your secret garden; to which you can retire
> And lock the gate behind you.
>
> [p. 51]

But this, Colby knows, is the same unreal "real world" behind the private door that Sir Claude distinguishes from the public world on the other side:

> . . . my garden's no less unreal to me
> Than the world outside it. If you have two lives
> Which have nothing whatever to do with each other—
> Well, they're both unreal. But for Eggerson
> His garden is a part of one single world.
>
> [p. 53]

And when Lucasta asks, "But what do you want?" Colby replies,

>   Not to be alone there.
> If I were religious, God would walk in my garden
> And that would make the world outside it real
> And acceptable, I think.
>
> [p. 53]

The garden that Lucasta perceives is the solipsistic "spirituality" of art that compensates for its opposite, the sordidness of life in time, devoid of spirit—Sir Claude's life of commerce, Lucasta's "dirty public square / In a shabby part of London" (p. 52). The two represent the division between eternity and time, spirit and matter. Eggerson's garden, to which he retires not only spiritually but physically as well, and from which he brings real fruit, is, as Denis Donoghue suggests, a variant of the rose garden where Christ walks.[12] It is a single world redeemed by the Incarnation, the truly real world in which the various levels of antinomies in existence are reconciled into the "unity" that, as Sir Claude had suggested earlier, truly religious people are able to discover.

In referring to God's presence in the garden, Colby prefigures the way he is to take in the achievement of that sacramental vision which perceives the unity and reality of the two worlds: it is the way of renunciation, in which the denial of the created world, of parent and lover, leads to the discovery of the Father and the Divine Love that redeems time. But there is another way to sacramental vision, as Colby suggests when Lucasta asks him if anyone else can enter the garden:

> They would just have to come. And I should not see them com-
>   ing.
> I should not hear the opening of the gate.

> They would simply. . . be there suddenly,
> Unexpectedly. Walking down an alley
> I should become aware of someone walking with me.
>
> [p. 54]

This defines the opposite way, that of affirmation, the way of human love between man and woman, parent and child, that finds its ground in the created world.[13]

It is within the framework of these two ways that the action of *The Confidential Clerk* moves. Colby's search for his real identity —which ends in the renunciation first of Lucasta and then of Sir Claude and Lady Elizabeth; the discovery through Mrs. Guzzard, Eliot's counterpart of Euripides' priestess of Apollo, of his real father (at once Herbert Guzzard, also the son of a disappointed musician, and God as revealed in Christ [14]); and the reconciliation of the two worlds (Colby retires into Eggerson's garden)—activates the familiar progress of the less aware. It leads to the removal of their public masks, the acknowledgment of their real identities and need for mutual understanding, and finally to the birth of a new love between husband and wife and children and parents that promises to unify their two worlds of make-believe into a single real world. This effect of Colby's search for identity is clearly suggested at the beginning of Act III when Sir Claude, stunned by the discovery of the shallowness of his understanding of Colby, reveals to his wife his early desire to be a potter, and Lady Elizabeth, in turn, reveals to her husband her early ambition to inspire an artist. Having chosen obedience to the facts, both had disastrously assumed public masks that would hide from each other their ironically complementary wishes. Now each unlocks the gates of his private garden to the other, with the implication that their double lives in two worlds of unreality will become one and real. The culmination of the process comes at the moving close of the play, following Mrs. Guzzard's revelation of Colby's identity, when the members of the family, free from their former "roles" and the obsession to impose identities on others, are united by the bond of love in a truly authentic human community:

LADY ELIZABETH   Between not knowing what other people want of one,
          And not knowing what one should ask of other people,
          One does make mistakes! But I mean to do better.
          Claude, we've got to try to understand our children.

KAGHAN   And we should like to understand *you*. . .
          . . . .
          You know, Claude, both Lucasta and I
          Would like to mean something to you. . . if you'd let us;
          And we'd take the responsibility of meaning it.

                                                      [pp. 134–135]

As in *The Family Reunion* and *The Cocktail Party*, the action
of *The Confidential Clerk* thus ends with the fulfillment of
Agatha's admonition to Amy that "the future can only be built /
Upon the real past" and Sir Harcourt-Reilly's final comment to
the Chamberlaynes that "Only by the acceptance of the past will
you alter its meaning." This is the operative theme below the farcical surface of the play. The discovery and acknowledgment of his
past by each of the characters is a discovery and acknowledgment,
in varying degrees, of sacramental order—of the presentness of the
past—in their personal lives. This results in a new, an authentic,
awareness of community, of the eternal design operating in time.
Like the other plays, then, the end of *The Confidential Clerk* is a
new beginning, a renewal grounded in the recognition of the real
past. And this sacramental theme, as in the other plays, is, in Mark
Schorer's term, "discovered" by the very form of the play, which
is itself an exploration of the past both on the level of personality
(the contemporary characters) and history (the Greek myth of
Ion). What is different in *The Confidential Clerk* is the greater
immediacy of the renewal activated by the protagonist's peripety
and the closer integration of myth and contemporary action, value,
and reality.

The Elder Statesman represents the culmination of the thematic
and formal development of Eliot's plays. In it, the dramatist returns once again to the plot situation, the technique, and the terms
of reference of *The Family Reunion:* like Harry, Lord Claverton,
pursued by the "ghosts" of his past, is driven into the "precincts

of his last evasions," where he discovers his authentic, his sinful, self and is confronted with the necessity of choosing between damnation and salvation. But now it is the *Oedipus at Colonus*, the qualitative significance of which Eliot had found lacking in Harry's career,[15] that provides the structural base of the action. In other words, the redemptive figure, which involves both hero and community, is completed and the sacramental theme thus formally perfected not, as in *The Cocktail Party*, from a distance, but within the immediate action. Furthermore, the distinction between the spiritually perceptive protagonist and the spiritually blind community has become barely visible. The hero, true to the direction that Eliot's sacramentalism has been taking, has become genuinely Everyman. The way of redemption has become the human way of the love of created things.

The human relationships at the beginning of *The Elder Statesman* are patently similar to those of the earlier plays, though the hero is less and the community more perceptive. Lord Claverton, who has striven through his active years—first as a statesman and then as chairman of public companies—to make his public role his real identity, is now confronted in his retirement with the private self from which he has tried to escape. Stripped of "authority's costume," [16] which had, like Amy's mechanistic time world, enhanced his public life and protected him from his past, his private life—"But he's most alive when he's among people / Managing, manoeuvring, cajoling or bullying— / At all of which he's a master." (p. 16)—he has come to see the future as a "nothingness" (p. 19) and himself as an unreal "ghost" (p. 32). All that remains to give him some semblance of identity which will protect him from his emptiness are his children Monica and Michael, whom he has transformed into objects or images of himself (p. 68) without identities of their own.

The harmful effect of Lord Claverton's selfish imposition of his will on others is revealed in the opening moments of the play by the suggestion of futility in the love of Charles and Monica, who represent the community. This scene has been interpreted by David Jones as the achievement of that continuity Colby speaks

about to Lucasta between the private and the public or everyday
worlds that comes when one finds a loved one in his "garden" or
private world. However, the whole tenor of the scene contravenes
such an interpretation.[17] Because of her father's possessiveness, Monica is not free to marry Charles, to consummate that unity which
in *The Confidential Clerk* makes the private and public worlds one
reality. Though she affirms her love for Charles, it is incomplete.
For it exists only in their private world. Its reality cannot extend
into the public world because her father's possessiveness has made
her two persons, as her sudden shift from genuine conversation
with Charles to an evocation of the setting as if in preparation for
the beginning of a scene in a naturalistic drama reveals:

CHARLES   What do the words mean now—*I* and *you*?

MONICA   In our private world—now that we have our private world—
                The meanings are different. Look! We're back in the room
                That we entered only a few minutes ago.
                Here's an armchair, there's a table;
                There's the door. . . and I hear someone coming:
                It's Lambert with the tea. . .

                        (*Enter* LAMBERT *with trolley*)

                                and I shall say, "Lambert
                Please let his lordship know that tea is waiting."
. . . .
                                I'm very glad, Charles,
                That you *can* stay to tea.

                        (*Exit* LAMBERT)

                                —Now we're in the public world.

CHARLES   And your father will come. With his calm possessive air
                And his kindly welcome, which is always a reminder
                That I mustn't stay too long, for you belong to him.

                                                    [PP. 13–14]

    The redemptive pattern that the elder statesman undergoes is
initiated by the appearance of two old acquaintances from his past
(references to which are pervasive in the play). Like Harry in *The
Family Reunion,* Lord Claverton confronts his particular furies

where he least expects to see them. First Mr. Gomez, the former
Fred Culverwell, whose "gift for friendship" (p. 33) Dick Ferry
had corrupted while at Oxford, and then Mrs. Carghill, the former
Maisie Batterson, whose love Dick Ferry had betrayed at the time
he was standing for Parliament, return to confront him with his
early misdeeds and, against his will, to force him painfully and inexorably into his past beyond the successive stages of his respectable public career, to the edge of despair, where, having recognized
his sins, he can no longer evade them by assuming new identities.
Both Gomez and Mrs. Carghill, in their effort to blackmail him
spiritually (they need "to establish contact with someone who can
serve as a link between their divided selves" [18]), dwell on Lord
Claverton's pretenses, his assumption of successive new identities
to negate his guilt, and give impetus to the growing awareness of
his unreality and spiritual alienation. Thus Gomez, distinguishing
his awareness of isolation from Lord Claverton's, tells him:

> . . . Think what that means—
> To take another name.
>
> *(Gets up and helps himself to whisky)*
>
> But of course you know!
> Just enough to think you know more than you do.
> You've changed your name twice—by easy stages,
> And each step was merely a step up the ladder,
> So you weren't aware of becoming a different person:
> But where *I* changed my name, there was no social ladder.
> It was jumping a gap—and you can't jump back again.
> I parted from myself by a sudden effort,
> You, so slowly and sweetly, that you've never woken up
> To the fact that Dick Ferry died long ago.[19]
>
> [p. 29]

And later, Mrs. Carghill replies to Lord Claverton's claim that his
conscience was clear after his betrayal of her:

> At bottom, I believe you're still the same silly Richard
> You always were. You wanted to pose
> As a man of the world. And now you're posing
> As what? I presume, as an elder statesman;

And the difference between being an elder statesman
And posing successfully as an elder statesman
Is practically negligible. And you look the part.
Whatever part you've played, I must say you've always looked it.

[p. 56]

But it is not until his encounter with Michael-Polyneices that
Lord Claverton comes to realize fully the destructive nature of his
evasions, of his self-imposed identity, which has manifested itself
as an assertion of his will over others and resulted in the transformation of his children, particularly Michael, into counters. At
first he is not aware of the irony of Gomez' hints that he is making
Michael into his own image (p. 34). But later when Michael, tired
of being just a "kind of prolongation of [his father's] existence"
(p. 68), expresses his desire to "go far away / To some country"
where he could take "a different name" (p. 68)—become another
person—Lord Claverton begins to see that his son is repeating his
own experience and warns him, "You will find your past failures
waiting there to greet you" (p. 70). And when Mrs. Carghill repeats Gomez' hint—"He's the picture of you, Richard, / As you
were once" (p. 72)—he suddenly realizes his responsibility for the
transformation of his son and that he is lost, that the way of the
public man has disintegrated and he stands blindly in a labyrinth
of his own creation, or, to change the metaphor, that the mask he
has prepared to avoid his real self has been completely torn away
and he is left to confront his "hollow" private self.[20] But Lord
Claverton's acknowledgment of his lostness is paradoxically the
beginning of discovery. When Monica urges her father to escape
from Gomez and Mrs. Carghill, he replies:

What I want to escape from
Is myself, is the past. But what a coward I am,
To talk of escaping! And what a hypocrite!
A few minutes ago I was pleading with Michael
Not to try to escape from his own past failures:
I said I knew from experience. Do I understand the meaning
Of the lesson I would teach? Come, I'll start to learn again.

[p. 79]

Thus in the last act, which takes place in the evening near "the great beech tree" to which he is mysteriously drawn, Lord Claverton at last chooses to face his pursuers: "It is through this meeting that I shall at last escape them" (p. 89). He acknowledges his responsibility for having corrupted Fred Culverwell, Maisie Batterson, and Dick Ferry, "people with good in them" (p. 87), and in so doing sees himself "emerging / From [his] spectral existence into something like reality" (p. 85).

Lord Claverton's acknowledgment of his responsibility, which is the first step toward liberation, is an acknowledgment of his sinful identity (pp. 89–90). And this, as in all Eliot's plays, opens to him the possibility of redemption. But his way of redemption is not the silent and lonely way of negation. It is the way of human love. His admission of guilt takes the form of a confession to Monica, to whom he had formerly addressed himself as an actor because he feared she could not love his real, limited self. It is a final and decisive abandonment of pretenses, of the fraudulent public identity, and a revelation of the private self to another person, an act of love which releases him from the prison of his moral isolation to breathe the free air of community. This meaning is suggested by Monica's prefatory plea to her father: "It is time to break the silence! Let us share your ghosts!" (p. 85), and by her response to her father's revelation of the guilt that has haunted him since the night in the distant past when he ran over an old man on his way back to Oxford and failed to stop: "Poor father! All your life! And no one to share it with; / I never knew how lonely you were / Or why you were lonely" (p. 88). Lord Claverton's choice of the way of human love, the I-Thou relationship with others, is brought into final focus a little later when he says to Monica and Charles:

> I've been freed from the self that pretends to be someone;
> And in becoming no one, I begin to live.
> It is worth while dying, to find out what life is.
>
> [p. 106]

In progressing from the acknowledgment of sin to the discovery of redemptive love, Lord Claverton achieves authentic sacramental vision. This not only saves him, reintegrates his divided life and brings him peace, it also redeems the lives of others. Where, like Amy, he had seen his children as counters, as things to be possessed and utilized, he now sees them as whole human beings, as spiritual creatures that have immense significance in an ordered universe. This vision frees Monica to fulfill her heretofore partial love for Charles. Thus, in the dialogue following Lord Claverton's deliberate exit, which announces that the hour of his death is at hand (and which symbolizes his release of Monica), the lovers achieve the union which in the first scene of the play was incomplete. They achieve an I-Thou relationship. Grounded in Monica's vision of an eternal love, their private and public worlds become, in the terms of *The Confidential Clerk,* a single reality:

MONICA   Yes, he wanted to leave us alone together.
        And yet, Charles, though we've been alone to-day
        Only a few minutes, I've felt all the time. . .

CHARLES   I know what you're going to say!
        We *were* alone together, in some mysterious fashion,
        Even with Michael, and despite those people,
        Because somehow we'd begun to belong together,
        And that awareness. . .

MONICA   Was a shield protecting both of us. . .

CHARLES   So that now we are conscious of a new person
        Who is you and me together.
    . . . .

MONICA   I've loved you from the beginning of the world.
        Before you and I were born, the love was always there
        That brought us together.

                                    [p. 107]

Thus when Monica intuitively realizes that her father lies dead under the great beech tree, it is not sorrow but joy that the lovers experience. For as Charles says, "the dead has poured out a blessing on the living" (p. 108). The play ends, as Denis Donoghue observes, in an "image of communal order" which encompasses "not merely individual felicity but an idea of social harmony." [21]

It is a sacramental image: time and its creatures have been subsumed under the divine.

It is true that at the end of the play Michael has come under the corruptive influence of Gomez and Mrs. Carghill. But the emphasis of the play on the efficacy of love—"love within a family, love that's lived in / But not looked at, love within the light of which / All else is seen, the love within which / All other love finds speech" (p. 72)—which manifests itself in Lord Claverton's assertion that he will never repudiate his son and especially in Monica's insistence that no matter what new identity her brother assumes she will "always pretend that it is the same Michael" (p. 100), suggests that Michael's repetition of his father's experience will be total: will include the final redemption. What Eliot has done here is to define more precisely and dramatically than previously the nature of the redemption that follows upon the sacrifice of the exceptional person. Redemption, that is, is not automatic. Sacrifice creates "significant soil," but the degree of its efficacy depends on the moral decision of the individual.

The inner pattern of *The Elder Statesman* thus recapitulates that of the earlier plays: the progress of the protagonist from sin to love, which is an analogue of the Fall and the Incarnation, redeems the human community. In this play, however, Eliot's voice has become silent and the third voice of poetry has almost wholly taken over. There are no overt symbolic references—no "rose garden," or "crowded desert," or broken spectacles—no verbal reminders of passages from *Four Quartets*, no static incantatory and oracular verse, and no patently mythical character to jar the whole mind into a divided consciousness, part of which is attending to "poetry" and part to a human experience. Nor, on the other hand, is there the taint of prosiness in the verse that damages (though not to the degree that some critics claim) *The Cocktail Party* and *The Confidential Clerk*. *The Elder Statesman* has its limitations (the most severe of which is the thinness of Monica's role, particularly of her unnaturally conventional reception of Lord Claverton's confession, which reduces the emotional impact that the scene demands).[22] But it is the play in which Eliot comes closest to achieving his dramatic ideal: that unity of inner and outer action, of value and reality, that renders the drama a single yet multivocal image, or in his own terms, "an analogy of the Incarnation whereby the human is taken up into the divine."

In the foregoing analysis of the redemptive pattern in the plays following *The Family Reunion*, what has been emphasized is the general functional correspondence of the first two groups of the schema of characters, the spiritually perceptive and the spiritually blind. This correspondence applies equally to the third group, the agents of the redemptive action.

In *The Family Reunion*, the Furies, like the skeleton figures in Charles Williams' plays, pursue the fugitive protagonist into his past, to an acknowledgment of his identity, his fallen nature, and finally to sacramental vision, that is, to the discovery of the Incarnation that redeems sin or chaos. Accordingly, as long as Harry is blind to the meaning of his anguish the Furies are embodiments of evil (Erinyes) that pursue him, but when he achieves illumination, they are transformed into "bright Angels" (Eumenides) whom he follows to his salvation. In *The Cocktail Party*, Eliot somewhat humanizes the agents of the action, Julia, Alex, and Reilly, and integrates them more closely into the action. Their function and significance are, however, essentially similar to the function and significance of the Furies.

Despite their surface frivolity, Julia, Alex, and Reilly are represented at the beginning of the action as mysterious, knowing, and inquisitive beings, who, probing covertly but relentlessly into the lives of the Chamberlayne set, compel them against their wills to come to grips with their pasts and their authentic selves. These "strangers," one of whom is an uninvited guest (suggesting his role as pursuer) prevent at every turn the efforts of their prey to "escape." [23] Because their ubiquity and persistence expose areas of experience better avoided, they seem to the Chamberlayne set, at least beneath the surface of their petulant irritation, mysteriously alarming, almost demonic, agents. Recalling Julia's uncanny knowledge of his affairs and her warning that "you shan't escape"

(p. 302), Edward refers to her as "that dreadful old woman" who "always turns up when she's least wanted," (pp. 303–304) a faint, though palpable allusion to the Furies. And Peter admits to Edward that he is "rather afraid of Julia Shuttlethwaite" (p. 312). To the unidentified guest who takes him farther than he wants to go in his desire to talk about Lavinia's departure, Edward says, "I don't think I want to know who you are" (p. 306), and later, during their private confrontation, Celia says to Edward, "who was that man? I was rather afraid of him; / He has some sort of power" (p. 321).

The implication lurking behind these comments—it is particularly apparent in Edward's and Celia's—is that Reilly, Julia, and Alex are satanic manifestations, and this is borne out by pervasive references to these figures as devils.[24] Thus when Celia's intuition of Reilly's mysterious power is confirmed by Edward's revelation that the uninvited guest is going to bring Lavinia back, she says: "But why should that man want to bring her back— / Unless he is the Devil! I could believe he was." Edward replies that he himself asked the stranger to, and Celia concludes: "Then he *must* be the Devil! He must have bewitched you" (p. 321).[25] After Julia's interruption, when Edward tries to explain how the uninvited guest persuaded him to want his wife back, she exclaims, "That's the Devil's method!" (p. 322). Later, Lavinia characterizes the recent train of events in terms of an infernal machine "that goes on working, / And I cannot stop it; no, it's not like a machine— / Or if it's a machine, someone else is running it. / But who? Somebody is always interfering" (p. 336). A moment later, referring to Julia's mysterious knowledge, she says to Edward, "That woman is the devil" (p. 337).[26]

Consonant with the description of Reilly, Julia, and Alex as devils are the recurrent intimations of and references to a monstrous trap into which the Chamberlayne set feel they are being inexorably driven [27] and their definition of this trap as Hell when they finally begin to face their real selves. Thus Edward, regretting his decision to have his wife back, speaks of his condition, his isolation and lostness, as an imprisonment in a room with no exit, which he equates with Hell (p. 342). He further brings this image of his predicament into relationship with that of the devil, the agent behind his captivity:

> O God, O God, if I could return to yesterday
> Before I thought that I had made a decision.
> What devil left the door on the latch
> For these doubts to enter? . . .
>
> [p. 343]

That Edward is referring, however vaguely, to Julia, Alex, and Reilly, is made eminently clear when we recall that Eliot has focused much stage business around the door of Edward's apartment, through which they frequently and mysteriously pass. At one point in the first scene, Edward asks, "I'd like to know first how you *got* in, Alex" (p. 312). Later, at the end of the scene, as Alex and Peter depart, he says pointedly, "Please *shut the door after you,* so it latches" (p. 318).

This imagery is completely reversed, however, when the Chamberlayne set finally discover their real identities—that they live in a fallen world—and acknowledge the need for and possibility of redemption. They come to see that Reilly, Julia, and Alex are somehow beneficent creatures. They become "Guardians," evoking by an easy association the image not only of Plato's guardians but also and primarily of guardian angels, in turn recalling Harry's "bright angels" in *The Family Reunion.* Celia is the first to see them in this light, since she is the first to perceive her sin, but it is obvious from the tone of the concluding scene ("We don't *want* you to go! p. 387) that both Edward and Lavinia have also come to recognize the mysterious threesome as their guardian angels.

It would be a distortion of *The Confidential Clerk* to claim that the third group of this play, Eggerson and Mrs. Guzzard, are agents that drive the principal characters into an acknowledgment of sin and thus to awareness of the possibility of redemption. In this case, the exceptional person, Colby, clearly initiates his own exploration of his past in search of his identity, and he, as well as the less perceptive characters, sees Eggerson not as a devil but as a model human. Eggerson's function as guardian angel (p. 61) is consistently emphasized over his function as hound of heaven. E. Martin Browne, commenting on Eliot's statement to him that "Eggerson is the only developed Christian in the play" has rightly observed that "to Eliot Eggerson is the catalyst, . . . Everything else becomes soluble in his warmth." [28] But there is another element in his character that is easily overlooked, an authoritativeness that lies just below the surface of his deference. There is, in other words, at least a vague suggestion that he also functions as "pursuer." Like Julia, Alex, and Reilly, he seems to possess mysterious knowledge of the design that is being worked out, and though he is not outwardly coercive in his method, it is difficult to escape the impression that he has had much to do with the final configuration that the principals achieve.

Mrs. Guzzard's function, on the other hand, is a little more clearly in line with that of the Furies and the Guardians. Though she does not appear on stage until the end of the play, she becomes an important character as early as the middle of the second act when Lady Elizabeth recognizes her name as that of the woman with whom her lover had left her child years before. Like the Furies, Mrs. Guzzard is a knowing ghost from the principals' past; and it is finally she who, in bringing them into their pasts where their real selves have their source, also brings them into the present, leads them to authentic self-knowledge. She is, as Grover Smith observes, "a kind of fairy godmother who would like to gratify everyone's wishes," [29] but she is one with a difference. The wishes she grants are those not of the false but of the real self. Thus she says, "We all of us have to adapt ourselves / To the wish that is granted. That can be a painful process" (p. 123). The process is painful as the recognition and facing of reality is painful. But out of it emerges a higher resolution, in this case the awareness of spiritual community.

The agents of the action in *The Elder Statesman* bear a striking similarity to the avenging Furies of *The Family Reunion*. Like them, Gomez and Mrs. Carghill are "ghosts, spectres from [Lord Claverton's] past" (p. 85), in pursuit of their prey. Gomez has

"made a point of following [his] career" (p. 33), and Mrs. Carghill
has "followed [his] progress year by year" (p. 56), and now, near
the end of Lord Claverton's life, they have become visible in the
place where he least expected to find them. Lord Claverton's life
has been a "flight from reality," from the self, the past (p. 79),
but paradoxically his flight has brought him back to the point of
departure. Echoing Harry, he warns Michael that "Those who flee
from their past will always lose the race. / I know this from experience. When you reach your goal . . . / You will find your past
failures waiting there to greet you" (p. 70). The specters, in other
words, despite Lord Claverton's efforts to prevent the revival of
"old memories / Which I should have thought we both preferred
to leave buried" (p. 53), have driven him, as the Furies drive
Harry, to the edge of the abyss, where evasions are no longer possible and a choice must be made. They are thus seen at first simply
as embodiments of evil, as satanic tormentors.

But Lord Claverton's forced confrontation of his past also begins a process whereby the significance of his specters is transfigured. Once he has become conscious of his guilt, neither Monica's nor Charles' reiterated pleas (pp. 79, 85) that he escape from
his ghostly pursuers can persuade him to do so. Rather, he begins
to see that the ghosts are paradoxically the means of his renewal:

>   . . . They've always been with me
> Though it was not till lately that I found the living persons
> Whose ghosts tormented me, to be only human beings,
> Malicious, petty, and I see myself emerging
> From my spectral existence into something like reality.
>
> [p. 85]

The process culminates, as we have seen, when he finally acknowledges his sin, his responsibility for having corrupted the good in
his early friends, renounces flight, and chooses freely to face his
ghosts. This decision to face the specters of his past brings Lord
Claverton into the discovery of love which redeems his life. Thus
the avenging ghosts, which in the beginning symbolized merely
evil, have become something like beneficent agents, if not bright

angels, in Lord Claverton's life. The evil they symbolize has taken on a new meaning: it has been transformed, in Charles Williams' phrase, into an occasion for good. This change is given its definitive expression (and linked with the Furies of *The Family Reunion*) when Lord Claverton retires to the old beech tree to die, an allusion to Oedipus' death and apotheosis in the sacred grove at Colonus, where the Erinyes are worshiped in their capacity as Eumenides or Kindly Ones.

In each of Eliot's plays of contemporary life the transformation of the agents of the action from symbols of the fallen world into symbols of the redeemed world is analogous to the transformation of the Fall into a *felix culpa* by the Incarnation. Ultimately, then, the third group, like the skeleton figures in Charles Williams' plays, are symbols of the sacramental principle that drives the reluctant human protagonist into sacramental vision, into perceiving spiritual significance in time and acknowledging the necessity of commitment.[30]

But the third group in *The Elder Statesman* is, from a dramatic point of view, superior in conception and execution to the parallel groups in the earlier plays. In *The Family Reunion* there is an unsatisfactory discontinuity between the naturalistic surface of the action and the supernatural agents who set it in motion. Aware of this failure, Eliot attempted in *The Cocktail Party* and in *The Confidential Clerk* to humanize the agents, to integrate them more closely into the dramatic action. But this effort was not completely successful. Despite their claims of fallibility, Reilly and his aides still reveal too overtly their supernatural character as, for example, does the stranger figure who invades a "naturalistic" realm in such religious melodramas as Jerome K. Jerome's *The Passing of the Third Floor Back* (1908) and Charles Rann Kennedy's *The Servant in the House* (1907) [31]—which, incidentally, may have had some influence on Eliot's drama, particularly *The Cocktail Party* —thus emphasizing the conspiratorial strategy and reducing the dramatic elements of choice and suspense over the outcome.[32] This becomes particularly clear in *The Cocktail Party* in the embarrassing scene where the guardians break out into incantation and drink libations to the Chamberlaynes and Celia, and in *The Con-*

fidential Clerk in the scene introducing Mrs. Guzzard as *dea ex machina.* In *The Elder Statesman,* however, the third group, like the imagery and the poetic voice, is completely integrated into the human action without loss of their dual significance as satanic pursuers and benign agents. They are not strictly supernatural agents of God as the Furies are in *The Family Reunion,* nor are they agents of God playing roles as devil's advocates as in *The Cocktail Party.* They are, rather, real people seeking revenge against Lord Claverton. Yet because they evoke from the man they pursue a genuine dread and a sense of guilt which lead to his rebirth, a response which is basically Christian, they are also and simultaneously a collective image of the sacramental principle operating in the world. In *The Elder Statesman,* in other words, Eliot achieves the union of reality and value that the sacramental aesthetic ultimately demands. The theology of the Incarnation is not imposed from without by means of patently symbolic figures that break the naturalistic surface. The universal meaning is rather discovered in the action as it unfolds in the world of time.

What has been said about T. S. Eliot's dramatic form applies equally to the verse he developed and perfected in his plays of contemporary life. Beginning in *Murder in the Cathedral* with a "neutral" style, in which rhythm, syntax, diction, and imagery are "committed neither to the present nor to the past," [33] his progress took him through a series of experiments with the recalcitrant idiom of everyday modern life which culminated in *The Elder Statesman* in a low style that conveys simultaneously a precise sense of time, place, and person and of permanent and universal reality.

Between *The Family Reunion* and his last play, Eliot worked out a verse line that is remarkable for its flexibility and precision. It is, as he has described it, "a line of varying length and varying number of syllables, with a caesura and three stresses. The caesura and the stresses may come at different places, almost anywhere in the line; the stresses may be close together or well separated by light syllables; the only rule being that there must be one stress on one side of the caesura and two on the other." [34] The close relationship between the rhythms of this line and those of modern English speech and its ability to imitate the third, the dramatic voice of poetry, has been amply and adequately demonstrated.[35] But an analysis of Eliot's verse which overemphasizes the formal dimension, especially the sound pattern, cannot fully answer the common charge represented by Georgio Melchiori that in the late plays "Eliot . . . has re-discovered prose." [36] The argument in behalf of the "poetry" of Eliot's late dramatic verse requires equal emphasis on the words, including images, as meaning. It is here primarily that such demonstrations of Eliot's "prosaic" verse as Melchiori's juxtaposition of a passage from *The Confidential Clerk* and a prose passage divided into verse lines from Sidney Grundy's *A Pair of Spectacles* can be refuted. Eliot himself has said that the "music" of poetry, by which I take him to mean the poetic under-pattern, "is not something which exists apart from the meaning." [37] A musical poem is, rather, "a poem which has a musical pattern of sound and a musical pattern of secondary meanings of the words which compose it, and . . . these two patterns are indissoluble and one." [38] This is a commonplace of contemporary criticism but it is surprising how little it is adhered to when Eliot's late dramatic verse is considered as verse. What Eliot achieves ultimately is a verse that is capable not only of imitating the rhythms of contemporary speech and distinguishing character realistically, but also of naturally and unobtrusively insinuating into that speech a structure of feeling and meaning that renders it multivocal. And this applies equally to the verse which is pitched at a relatively low emotional level as well as to that which expresses the intensity of illumination.

Thus, for example, at the beginning of *The Elder Statesman*, after Monica has revealed to Charles her father's paradoxical mental state, his "terror of being alone" and his "fear of being exposed to strangers" now that he has divested himself of "authority's costume" and become a private man, Lord Claverton enters with his engagement book and the following dialogue ensues:

MONICA　But what a time || for your engagement book!

　　　You know what the doctors said: || complete relaxation.

　　　And to think about nothing. || Though I know that won't be
　　　easy.

LORD CLAVERTON　That is just what I was doing. ||

MONICA　　　　　　　　　　　　　　　　　　　　Thinking of nothing?

LORD CLAVERTON　Contemplating nothingness.[39]

　　　　　　　　　　　　　　　　　　　　　　[p. 19]

On the surface, the lines of this passage have all the characteristics
—loose rhythms, informal syntax, and colloquial diction—of good
realistic prose dialogue between two distinct individuals. But they
constitute much more. Monica begins the passage in accents that
reveal her as the good-humored, though mildly impatient custodian
of her father's health; but in the third line (which receives a special emphasis from the rhetorical pause at the end of the second
line), her stresses begin to fall insistently on the key words "think,"
"nothing," and the demonstrative "that." Thus when Lord Claverton responds in a half line with stresses squarely on the words that
refer to these ("just," "doing"), the neutral idea of "thinking about
nothing" takes on a faintly ominous tone. This is further emphasized by Monica's question. And in Lord Claverton's definitive
revision of the phrase to "Contemplating nothingness," the recurrent word "nothing" assumes another, a metaphorical dimension that also reverberates backward to enforce the earlier ominous
accents and forward to infuse secondary meaning into his following
observations on the engagement book—which, in contrasting past
and present, define the present and future in terms of insistently
accented negatives:

　　　　　　　　　　　　　. . . Just remember:
. . . .
I could look in the right book, and find out what I was doing
Twenty years ago, to-day, at this hour of the afternoon.
If I've been looking at this engagement book, to-day,

Not over breakfast, but before tea,
It's the empty pages that I've been fingering—
The first empty pages since I entered Parliament.
I used to jot down notes of what I had to say to people:
Now I've no more to say, and no one to say it to.
I've been wondering. . . how many more empty pages?

[p. 19]

This is not merely the conscious uneasiness of a man who foresees a future devoid of activity because his energies have dried up. It has become, through Eliot's skillful deployment of accents, repetitions, and syntactical structures, the unconscious dread of a man without a past, without a real identity, and as the sense of expectation gradually insinuated into the speeches suggests, his terror of the inevitable intrusion of the unknown, or better, of the absurd, to fill the moral vacuum.

The sequence reaches a climax in Lord Claverton's response to Monica's uncomprehending reiteration of her intention to prevent the filling up of the empty pages:

No, || I've not the slightest longing for the life I've left—
Only fear || of the emptiness before me.
If I had the energy || to work myself to death
How gladly would I face death. || But waiting, simply waiting,
With no desire to act, || yet a loathing of inaction.
A fear of the vacuum, || and no desire to fill it.
It's just like sitting || in an empty waiting room
In a railway station || on a branch line,
After the last train, || after all the other passengers
Have left, || and the booking office is closed
And the porters have gone. || What am I waiting for
In a cold and empty room || before an empty grate?
For no one. For nothing.

[p. 20]

In this speech the rhythms, the syntax, and the words and images, the whole linguistic consort, combine to intensify not only the sense of Lord Claverton's emptiness, or better, his self-alienation, but also his moral isolation and consequent dread. The simile, for example, is constructed both verbally and rhythmically as an inexorably progressive stripping away of all possibilities of normal, that is, protective, human contacts, a syntactical movement which activates Monica's earlier dormant metaphor about her father's divestment of authority's costume, to render his predicament, despite his efforts at evasion, that of unaccommodated man. Further, the related words "fear" and "waiting," which are used two and three times, respectively, and in each case receive an inordinate stress, deepens his dreadful anticipation of the intrusion of the unknown into the round of his life. Thus when he returns with accents of finality in the last line to the word with which the whole sequence casually began ("For no one. For nothing"), it assumes the form of a threatening Presence. And this presence physically manifests itself a moment later in the form of Mr. Gomez, one of the pursuing ghosts from Lord Claverton's past. What was at first a word with merely a denotative significance has become an imposing symbol.

But this is not all. For the verse has gradually and subtly built up the intensity and deepened the definition of the idea of "nothing" to the point where it releases in the culminating metaphor of a cold empty room associations that relate it to similar metaphors in modern existential literature and in earlier Christian literature—the Book of Job and Dante's *Inferno*, for example— that make it the inevitable image of Hell (or meaninglessness) in the modern world, and the unconsciously dreaded but expected "no one" the embodiment of negation. This is, of course, Satan or rather the Hound of Heaven, the Christian version of the Greek Furies, who, according to so much of the literature of existentialism, symbolize the Nothingness that drives the inauthentic fugitive into the precincts of his last evasions, where, naked and alone, in fear and trembling, he must come authentically to terms with his pursuer.[40]

Thus through the verse of the low style, Eliot evokes the associations that establish the Christian existential underpattern (the dimensions of which include the Greek myth of Oedipus at the sacred grove of the Eumenides and the humanistic existential interpretation of the myth of the Furies). And not once in the whole sequence has he violated the naturalistic surface, the contemporary idiom, and the third voice to achieve his purpose.

Arguing against the use of poetic diction in behalf of the language of everyday life, Eliot had written in "The Music of Poetry" (1942), which is primarily concerned with poetry in the drama, that "the music of a word is . . . at a point of intersection: it arises from its relation first to the words immediately preceding and following it, and indefinitely to the rest of its context; and from another relation, that of its immediate meaning in that context to all the other meanings which it has had in other contexts." [41] From this it is quite clear that what Eliot means by "music" is not merely the patterns of sound and rhythm but also and even primarily the multivocality established by the intersection of surface meanings and underpattern of associations. It is, in other words, a point of intersection that represents a stylistic analogy of the Incarnation, which, at the point of intersection between time and eternity, transfigures the historical event. Though analysis has required making overt that which is essentially a matter of unconscious association, that is, that "fringe of indefinite extent, of feeling which we can only detect . . . out of the corner of the eye and can never completely focus . . . ," [42] this process of intersection accurately defines the method and the style that both the medieval realists and Eliot employ to discover a universal structure of meaning in the immediate concrete present, to generate, in other words, the "music" of *The Elder Statesman.*

I am not saying that Eliot was consciously modeling his dramatic verse on the Christian low style of the medieval dramatists. Rather, I am suggesting that, given his developed understanding of the Incarnation, which, incidentally but significantly, has its source prior to his conversion in his observations on the historical sense in "Tradition and the Individual Talent" (1919), it was inevitable that he would eventually arrive at a style analogous to the medieval realists, one characterized by a sublime *Humilitas*. This distinction is of crucial importance. For just as Eliot's dramatic verse is not contemporary in the naturalistic sense of the word, so it is not nostalgically historical or "medieval." It is rather contemporary-historical or, more specifically, concrete-universal. At its best, as in the case of the above passage from *The Elder Statesman*, it is a verse that is, in Eliot's words, both a motion and a stillness.

In his review of *The Elder Statesman*, Leslie Paul, after noting Eliot's "typological use of characters," concludes that the play "is . . . not so much about Lord Claverton as about Everyman . . . the structure as well as the versification of the morality plays is to be found in his drama. He is writing moralities in the idiom of our times and in his own idiosyncratic way about eternal values. Like an ancient morality play, *The Elder Statesman* uses a simple and quickly grasped situation presented by uncomplicated characters to speak profound and difficult things about the human spirit. It is the effort to do this which gives to all T. S. Eliot's dramas a timeless and placeless quality." [43] There is some truth in this generalization, but ultimately it obscures rather than throws light on Eliot's achievement because it minimizes the concrete world, the sense of time, place, and person in the drama of contemporary life. *The Elder Statesman* can be about Everyman precisely because it is about Lord Claverton, and the plays in general can have a timeless and placeless quality because they are sacramental imitations of unique and concrete modern events. Though it is not that of the violent city streets of, say, Graham Greene's *Brighton Rock* or of the urban underworld of Albert Camus' *The Fall*, there is no mistaking the modernity of the world of Eliot's late drama as, for example, the existential diagnosis of contemporary human relations clearly shows. Indeed, it is interesting to note in this respect the remarkable parallel between *The Elder Statesman* and Tolstoy's short story "The Death of Ivan Ilych,"

which has been called "a basic scripture for existential thought." [44]
What gives stillness or universality to this motion, this presentness,
is the operation of the sacramental principle, which synthesizes
the presentness into the eternity of the Christian scheme.

8

THE MERCURY THEATRE POETS:
THE COMPOSITION OF
PLACE

> . . , the return to a stylized drama, the return
> to artifice . . . the reminder that the drama had
> its roots in ritual—all these have been of great
> value, have produced the finest poetic drama of
> our century, and will probably continue to do so.
> In spite of this, I feel that the time is now past
> when poetry should dissociate itself entirely from
> the "realist" drama, and while experiment and
> discovery go on, let poets see if it is not possible
> to reconcile the aim of the poet with the needs
> of the popular theatre.
>
> Norman Nicholson,
> "The Poet Needs an Audience"

T. S. Eliot undertook his dramatic experiments with the purpose
of creating a verse drama that was public without capitulating to
the univocal naturalistic aesthetic, and he hoped that his work
would stimulate younger poets to write for the theater in behalf
of this ideal. After the war, in 1945, E. Martin Browne and the
noted actor Robert Speaight,[1] spurred by the popular success of
Murder in the Cathedral and *The Family Reunion* and of the
wartime productions of verse drama throughout England, took over
the Mercury Theatre to produce verse plays, thus opening the way
for young poets to write for the public stage.

Among the new poet-dramatists introduced by Mr. Browne, who, according to Christopher Fry, "has driven more poets to drama than any living man," [2] were Anne Ridler, Norman Nicholson, and Ronald Duncan, whose Mercury Theatre plays achieved a substantial popular success when they were produced during the 1945–1946 season. As was to be expected, the example of Eliot provided the point of departure for their experimental work. His influence is particularly evident in their effort to give universality to the recalcitrant matter of contemporary life by the sacramental assimilation of the past into the present and especially to develop a verse form which at once imitates the rhythms and diction of modern life and conveys poetic significance. But it is misleading to conclude, as some critics do, that these playwrights are slavish imitators of Eliot's matter and manner.[3] Despite the echoes of Eliot, the plays of this group are essentially individual experiments within the broad framework of an emergent Christian aesthetic. And though they are not major achievements, they are intrinsically interesting in form and on occasion even powerful in dramatic impact. They are above all, as comparison with the soft nostalgia of most Georgian verse drama reveals, plays that in varying degrees suggest the poetic potential of the matter and language of contemporary life. Accordingly, they deserve greater notice from the critics of contemporary drama.

This chapter, then, will examine the Mercury Theatre plays, Anne Ridler's *The Shadow Factory*, Norman Nicholson's *The Old Man of the Mountains*, and Ronald Duncan's *This Way to the Tomb*, as further examples of plays of contemporary life that are grounded in the aesthetic of Christian sacramentalism. In one sense these plays represent the culmination of the verse drama movement begun with the production of John Masefield's *The Coming of Christ* at Canterbury in 1928. But in a more important sense, they represent a new beginning. For though these plays realize to a considerable extent the ultimate demands of the sacramental aesthetic concerning time, and thus some measure of contemporaneity without loss of a universal significance, or, on another level, some degree of popularity without doing violence to the

cultivated sensibility, they are nevertheless incomplete achievements, still experimental in essence, and accordingly primarily
valuable, along with T. S. Eliot's late plays, as prototypes which
another generation of Christian poets might refine upon.

Deeply influenced by the thought of Charles Williams,[4] Anne
Ridler, who is primarily a poet, turned to the drama in 1943. At
this time she wrote *Cain,* a short and somewhat discursive verse
play the rhetoric of which recalls that of *Murder in the Cathedral.*
In the play the protagonist figurally reenacts Adam's fall. The
choric angel Michael says to Cain, who conceives of his sin as
predetermined, "Believe that the Fall in you was renewed" [5] and,
lest they dissociate themselves from the magnitude of Adam's and
Cain's sin, to the audience in the Epilogue, "But in each of you
again the Fall is a violence." [6] Though not worked out in the
action, the *felix culpa* theme that plays such a vital part in the
modern Christian drama is also central in Mrs. Ridler's play.
When Cain finally acknowledges that he has sinned by choice and
at the edge of despair asks the angel if he is to suffer damnation,
Michael replies paradoxically:

> No hope is greater than yours: look and take comfort.
> Over the sharp edges of frustration and pain
> You are torn towards God; the mark of your misery
> Is the furrow of His glory engraved in your forehead.
> Nothing else can hurt you. Now begin your journey.[7]

This is underlined in the final chorus of the play, which prophecies
the Incarnation and the Redemption of man and the world.

From the beginning Mrs. Ridler reveals her strategy to be that
of rendering Christian myth sacramentally relevant to the present.
But apparently it was not until her discovery of the techniques of
Eliot's *The Family Reunion* that she came to realize the dramatic-
poetic possibilities (and the problems) of contemporary subject
matter and language: "at present the problem is to discover (as
Eliot has formulated it) how people of the present day would
talk, if they could talk poetry; and we are at least clear about what
has to be done." [8] *The Shadow Factory* (1946), the Mercury

Theatre's second production of the new poets, reflects this influence, though much of the play is written in prose.

Mrs. Ridler's work, significantly subtitled A *Nativity Play*, has, with the exception of a tableau of the Nativity enacted at the structural center by the factory staff, a naturalistic and contemporary surface texture. Spencer Harding, the director, has organized the operations of his electrical appliances factory to achieve a maximum output in production. Reverberating with repeated slogans piped from a loudspeaker system ("THE PIECE-WORK WAY / MEANS BETTER PAY. / KEEP YOUR OUTPUT EVERY DAY."),[9] the plant has an atmosphere reminiscent of the horrible, Utopian efficiency of Aldous Huxley's *Brave New World*. (That Mrs. Ridler has Huxley's novel in mind is suggested when the artist, echoing Huxley's Utopian citizens' oaths "O, Ford!" and "O, Freud!" exclaims at one point, "Freud knows why!" p. 8.) But the director is no nineteenth-century industrialist; he is rather one of the new breed of managers, an enlightened executive, for whom benevolence, particularly in the area of culture, is profitable both to the factory and the workers. Confident of technology and human engineering, this modern version of Dostoevsky's *Grand Inquisitor* sees the world as standing on the threshold of a millennium of comfort and happiness. But for the workers, though they are only vaguely aware of it, the techniques of Progress are leading to their dehumanization, to the disintegration of their identities, and to the reduction of their humanity to the level of animal life. As the Education Officer puts their vague but persistent dissatisfactions, their lives consist of "A decent job, health, sunshine, friends, / And—a black despair at the heart of it all" (p. 24).

The destructive nature of the director's vision is brought home to him when the mural he has commissioned the angry young artist, Timothy Garnish, to paint is unveiled during the Christmas Eve celebration of the opening of the new canteen. In his confidence that all must see the life of the factory as he sees it, the director has asked the artist to paint the "essence of the Works" (p. 13). What he gets from the artist (who has accepted the commission on the condition that the work in progress remain secret until the unveiling) is a scathing satire of himself and the world he is making, an image of the director manipulating, from behind a cloud, his chessboard workers, whose shadows take on animal shapes.[10]

Shaken and humiliated, the director is nevertheless convinced by the parson, whom he had condescendingly invited to present the Crib scene, that he allow the program to continue and the mural to remain for everyone to see. During the Crib scene which follows, he reveals a new understanding and vision when he unexpectedly takes the role of the wise man Melchior and offers the Christ child gold, the symbol of his power. At the end of the play, the reformed director has achieved a more humane relationship with his workers. He invites the artist, who on his return to the factory is surprised to see his work uncovered, to paint another mural, its counterpart, and the artist accepts.

This brief summary of the action clearly suggests that *The Shadow Factory* might be interpreted, however limited such an interpretation might be, as an anti-Utopian problem play written somewhat in the manner of Ibsen's *Doll's House* or Galsworthy's *Strife.* But this does not mean that it has its roots in the naturalistic aesthetic, which is the point that Raymond Williams, one of the few to subject the play to critical scrutiny, makes about it: "Mrs. Ridler's dramatic experiment [can be described as] the versification of naturalist drama, just as Auden's experiments were. . . . Verse drama ought not to be, indeed cannot be, confined to the institution of verse dialogue. What demands dramatic speech at its highest intensity and control is a particular dramatic attitude which we can characterise as poetic. Mrs. Ridler's play might be related to the moralities; but it is nearer Galsworthy than *The Castell of Perseverance,* and not only because of its date." [11] For Williams, apparently, a play must be either naturalistic or poetic; it cannot be simultaneously both. As we shall see, he fails to recognize the operative sacramental strategy behind Mrs. Ridler's form, which transforms the everyday reality of contemporary factory life into an action of universal significance without destroying or circumventing the concreteness. Like T. S. Eliot's plays of contemporary life, the naturalistic surface is transfigured and its key terms—birth, works, vision, God—are charged with poetic (and trenchantly ironic) significance by the covert, or rather unobtrusive, integration of the by now familiar paradoxical archetype of sin and redemption which begins with Adam's pride and fall and culminates in rebirth: in the redemption of the fallen world through Adam's acknowledgment of human limitation and discovery of Christ. The pattern here is characterized, however, by the simplicity of Charles Williams' morality play *House by the Stable* rather than by the intellectual complexity of Eliot's *The Family Reunion*.

Though its full import does not assert itself until later, the first phase of the underpattern, the revelation of Man's pride, is hinted at when two factory hands take advantage of the director's absence from his office to watch the automatic motions of their fellow workers from this central vantage point. Awed by the momentary reversal of their roles, one of them, focusing attention on the director's chair (which emerges later as a key symbol) concludes: "Not bad to sit in a chair like God / And watch it all" (p. 2). This gives point to the director's recurrent references to the factory as "the Works," to himself as "a Works Manager" (p. 5), and to the age as the era in which the "technician / Inherits the earth" (p. 5). To one of his departmental managers he says:

> I tell you, Jennings, the real power,
> The power that's going to possess the future,
> Lies with us—with men like me,
> And men such as you may become:
> Nothing's beyond us.
>
> [p. 5]

In unconsciously assuming the role of a god presiding over his new creation, the factory, the director reenacts Adam's sin of pride. But there is a devastating irony in his words that points to the inevitable fall to come, for his "Nothing's beyond us," which is also a reference to the existential Nothingness, reveals the hollowness of his vision.

With the arrival of the artist, whose genius (as that of the

parson, later) he wishes to enlist in the service of his enterprise—
"Art and industry need each other / In the modern world. . . . /
Ah, business men were quick to see it." (p. 10)—the director's
pride, his appropriation of God's function as creator, is brought
into the open, though his faith in Progress blinds him (the metaphor will become increasingly significant) to it. Perceiving the
horror behind the shadows cast by the workers on the screen near
the director's desk, the artist responds to the director's assured
invitation to admire with a satirical prayer the workers might re-
cite daily at the factory gate:

> O Lord, empty me,
> Pity my complexity,
> Take away my liberty.
> Make me a reflex, take away my complex—
> Make me O make me
> A perfect robot.
>
> [p. 8]

But, with the shadows moving mechanically in the background to
enhance the irony, the director rejects the insight and continues
to brag about his factory and his lordship over it in terms which
recall Eliot's image of the still point and the turning wheel, except
that in the director's metaphors man, not God, is at the center.
The factory, the biggest of several in the company (which he himself has planned) is

> Bigger still in its sphere of influence.
> The single pivot on which depend
> Such huge rotations; the single stone
> Stirring watery circles, vast
> In ratio to the original movement—
> That is the clue to modern power.
>
> [pp. 8–9]

And his office chair is the

>   . . . focal point;
> You get from here a bird's-eye view
> Of the whole process. From this chair

I can control the remotest part
Whenever I choose.

[p. 9]

His boasting culminates in an encomium to the harmony of his machine world ("the vision of the few" p. 10) in visual and auditory imagery and rhythms that ironically evoke the medieval vision of God's creation:

Stand here a moment, watch, and listen.
Watch those drills. This is the music
I like to hear. Rising, falling—
Isn't it the beat of England's heart?
. . . .
So many pairs of hands and eyes
Moved in concert toward one purpose.
Bars and belts in smooth agreement.
Beauty—what is it if not the perfect
Means to an end? . . .

[p. 9]

And after projecting his Huxleyan image of the future brave world in which eugenics and conditioning have brought an ultimate happiness and comfort, he asks the artist—in the metaphor that, as the subtitle suggests, prepares for the introduction of a new dimension into his awareness—to play his part in the fulfillment of the vision by painting "the essence of the Works" (p. 13):

I tell you, it's certain this world is coming,
. . . .
Won't you help us to bring it to birth?
Or, to use a more modern metaphor,
Won't you be the catalyst?

[p. 12]

The artist accepts the commission, warning the director that "I very much doubt / If I shall see what *you* see, / Or whether you'll like my seeing" (p. 15), and thus he too begins a new "work to be in a finished form by December the twenty-fourth when the Canteen will be declared open" [12] (p. 30).

Having ironically established Adam's pride and the expectation of a new birth, Mrs. Ridler develops the remaining phases of the redemptive underpattern in the second and final act of the play, the first two scenes of which are set in the finished canteen on Christmas Eve. As the first scene gets underway, the latent irony of the director's earlier equation of the birth of his mechanistic paradise and the birth of Christ and the New Life emerges in force. Maria, the Director's secretary, who like Eggerson in *The Confidential Clerk,* is the only developed Christian in the play, announces the order of proceedings: "Speech by Director. Unveiling of murals. Formal opening of Canteen. . . . Tea. Tableau at Crib." When Jennings expresses surprise at the crudity of the idea of enacting the Nativity in the canteen, the artist replies: "Surely you know your boss by now? / . . . Christmas Eve—you see the connection?" (p. 31). This connection is charged with greater irony when the director arrives with the parson, whom he has invited to officiate at the tableau. Though he speaks of the social value of religion, it is clear that he has another though unformulated motive for his choice of Christmas Eve as opening day for the canteen and for his decision to include a Nativity scene in the celebration: his desire to mark the triumph of his mechanistic godhead over the God of Christianity. The parson tells him that the Crib which he wishes to transform into a "golden calf" may "set your factory afire" (p. 34); but the director, blinded by his pride, cannot perceive that he is being warned that the Crib may produce a different kind of birth from that which he expects.

Following the parson's partial assignment of the traditional parts of the Nativity, which includes an unsuccessful effort to enlist the director and the artist, and the announcement by the ubiquitous loudspeaker of the "Ceremony of the Opening," the director delivers his triumphant speech prior to the unveiling of the murals. His turgid rhetoric brings into climactic focus his iterated images depicting man as deity and the machine age as a new birth:

> . . . we stand to-day on the threshold of a great enterprise. Our century . . . racked by the pangs of a colossal birth, is about to

achieve its objective. . . . Man is the agent of his fate! . . .
Soon perhaps we shall have solved the mystery of birth, and
learned to prevent the great catastrophe of death itself. . . . Did
I say that ours was an unhappy generation? No, thrice happy,
who are privileged to assist at such a Dawn.

. . . I want it [the canteen] to be worthy of the new ways of
living. And it is for that reason that I have chosen to decorate
its walls with living symbols—the New Age in pictorial form. . . .

Yet, if this new movement is to succeed, you too have your
parts to play. . . . I use no high-sounding metaphors. I do not
demand supernatural powers; I only ask of you that you should
become modern citizens, with all that those words connote: I
only ask that you should assist at this new birth.

[pp. 40–41]

The director then orders the unveiling of the murals. What
meets his eyes in this striking reversal is the artist's rebuttal of his
glowing words: a vision of the frightening reality of the new world
he has been blindly constructing, a world not of life but of death.
A figure, half human, half beast leaning down from a cloud, holds
in one hand a mask that resembles the profile of the director before "a null and empty face, / Empty except for its blind eyes"
(p. 47), and with the other, moves the unindividuated workers,
whose figures cast long animal shadows against a screen, as if they
were counters on a chessboard. "You're just shadows: puppets
worked by your Director-God who pulls the strings" (p. 23),[13]
the artist had said earlier to a group of workers assembled in the
unfinished canteen.

Despite his efforts, there is for the director no evading this new
and unexpected vision of his new world which has staggered and
humiliated him. Employing the metaphor of sight that now comes
to dominate the dialogue, the artist says "I *have* made you see
it, that's evident" (p. 43). And later, shortly before the Nativity,
the director acknowledges the reality of the artist's figures in a
soliloquy:

> . . . Yes, but what remains
> Ineradicable, irretrievable? *Those*. . .

> Ah, must I see them? To see is to admit them there.
> What other choice? Look then, look, and surfeit on the sight.
>
> [p. 49]

In the redemptive pattern, this moment is analogous to Adam's recognition and confession of the sin of pride and his authentic awakening to find himself in a fallen world.

But as in most of these plays, the protagonist's fall is paradoxically a positive achievement in comparison to his earlier blindness and indifference to the spiritual dimension in life. For as the parson says, using the imagery of sight which sharpens the irony of the director's earlier references to his vision:

> It depends on whether you've eyes to see
> Some truth in what he painted. O—
> I know I speak from the opposite camp,
> But can't you even *see* it? Blindness
> Is worst of all. Pursue your ways,
> Impiously set yourself up as God,
> But do for God's sake know you do it.
> . . . .
> So much (for you) depends on whether
> You've still the sight to see it.
>
> [p. 45]

It is not only, as Eliot has said in a striking echo of Kierkegaard, that "the recognition of the reality of Sin is a New Life; and the possibility of damnation is so immense a relief in a world of electoral reform, plebiscites, sex reform and dress reform, that damnation itself is an immediate form of salvation . . . because it at least gives some significance to living." [14] It is also that man's discovery of sin and the fallen world is a tacit discovery of the possibility of the redemptive function of the Incarnation and the need to make a choice between the two. Thus the parson, as spokesman for the Christian Church, urges the uncertain director not only to accept the artist's murals—"As you say, they've now been seen: / The memory can't be hidden with whitewash, / Therefore—accept them" (p. 44)—but also to be courageous enough to commission the artist "to paint / Whatever is good in your factory life; / Make him admit the opposite view" (p. 45) that the factory, like cathedrals which "Are built of a size to shelter gargoyles" (p. 44) is capable of transforming its evil into a paradoxical good. The parson, in other words, is urging the director to choose the world redeemed by Christ, thus preparing for the moment of decision during the Nativity scene that follows.

The director thus arrives at the point in the archetypal journey where Man, stripped of his private resources and finding himself naked and unaccommodated in the labyrinth, becomes receptive to illumination. This is the burden of the director's soliloquy at the end of the first act, which brings the iterative imagery of sight to a climax:

> . . . O, which way, which way to turn?
> Leave them there or destroy them, they'll remain.
> Others in time will forget them, but not I:
> My brain's the wall they're painted on; never
> Never to vanish, the lines are cut for ever.
> Colour-blind—that's shameful.
> What did the voice say? Blindness is worst,
> . . . .
> To leave them there on the wall, postpone action,
> Wait for the Crib? Not for magnanimity,
> . . . .
> In suspension, waiting on the event,
> For once in my life to wait, hiding my wound.
> . . . .
> And I might even wake to find it a dream,
> Or wake to see its meaning.
> I'll not wrestle it further:
> I'll turn with the tide, which way it swings—
> Let the sea flow over,
> Wait for the Crib, see what the moment brings.[15]
>
> [p. 50]

This soliloquy, self-exploratory and uncertain, is the companion piece to the Inquisitor-director's earlier flamboyantly arrogant public speech before the unveiling. Here, too, there is the anticipation of a new birth. But now it is grounded in a new humility begotten by his authentic awareness of the world he has produced.

In the next scene, the enactment of the Nativity play by the factory staff, the director arrives at the end of his journey, which has been a journey to the Crib, and achieves illumination. Prefaced by the parson's prayer that Christ show modern man the continuing efficacy of the Redemption—"*As at this time*—Lord, teach us to know the time; / What happened once for all may happen at all times" (p. 52)—the tableau proceeds through the offerings of the Shepherds (the workers), Balthasar (the Education Officer), whose gift is myrrh (death), and Caspar (the parson), whose gift is incense (the inherited wisdom of the Church) and culminates with the unexpected assumption by the director of the role of Melchior, whose offering is gold (power):

> Child, if I let this go, can I bear to live?
> Power that the babe possessed, the man would retrieve.
> You have taken my certainty, must this too be lost?
>
> (*Coming to the Crib, he falls on his knees.*)
>
> O, lost—for glory and the promptings of love
> Enjoin it: Child, take and teach me to give.
>
> [p. 55]

Thus the Nativity play in the contemporary factory, which, on the surface, the director had included in the program for its social value but actually, as a symbol of the triumph of Man over God, becomes in this ironic reversal an authentic reenactment of the birth of Christ and the beginning of the New Life in the redeemed world. The factory, the symbol of the fallen modern world, is not rejected. It is reconciled with the eternal design, its evil being converted into a paradoxical good. Thus the theme of the eternal presentness of the Incarnation and the sacramental form of the play—in which the past, the Nativity which redeems the fallen world, is integrated into the naturalistic present and transforms it into a symbolic construct—are brought into fusion.

In the climactic unveiling scene, when he is urging the director not only to leave the murals for all to see but also to commission the artist to paint their counterpart, the parson says,

> The Church must turn the world back—
> An endless task, endlessly attempted—
> Only, she works within conditions:
> Since she cannot undo the past,
> Making the best of a bad job
> She works on what she finds. You see?

[P. 44]

Commenting on *The Shadow Factory*, Gerald Weales focuses on "the talk of turning the world back" in this speech as evidence that "Mrs. Ridler's play hints at a nostalgia for an earlier social situation." [16] That the philosophy of the parson's speech is conservative is certainly true, but it does not follow, as Weales supposes, that the play (and "the work of all the Mercury poets, whose ideas and whose verse seems to owe much to T. S. Eliot" [17]) reveals the desire to escape the risks of the present. This point needs emphasis. What we have in this judgment is a representative example of a common misunderstanding (the source of which appears to lie in an essential antipathy to the nature of the experience these plays dramatize) not only of the social ideology but also the aesthetic of the modern Christian poet-dramatists. Weales' interpretation of the parson's speech ignores its structural context and therefore fails to perceive its sacramental significance and, what is worse, obscures both the thematic resolution and the artistic form of the play. Seen in context, as a moment located focally between the unveiling of the murals and the presentation of the Nativity, or, in terms of the underpattern, between the Fall and the Redemption, the speech assumes a significantly different meaning. We see that below its surface lies the parson's (and Mrs. Ridler's) awareness of the analogous figure of the Incarnation—Christ too worked within the framework of "A bad job," the Fall—and the consequent implications for the Church in time. Because the Incarnation absorbs time into eternity, the Church, which, as Christ's body, extends His work through human history, must function in a perpetual present. It "cannot undo the past," the Fall, the establishment of the factory system; it must operate within the conditions of the contemporary world, and, like Christ, transform it into a world in which the evil itself has come to be understood as a good.[18] The parson's assertion that "the Church must turn the world back" has little to do with nostalgia for an earlier society. It is rather a recognition that the function of the contemporary Church is to make the world aware of the identity of the sin of pride and the modern faith in the concept of progress, thereby rendering the fallen industrial society receptive to Christian values and opening up the possibility of its transformation into an agent of good.

Conceptually, the climactic reversal of the Nativity scene is a brilliant achievement. But from a dramatic point of view much of its force is vitiated, as Robert Speaight observes, by the "perilous leap in theatrical logic from the humiliated director of one scene reluctantly learning a hard lesson to the man who is converted by taking part in a Christmas play,"[19] though it should be pointed out that the "conversion," as the director's uncertainty in the last act clearly reveals, is by no means definitive. Mrs. Ridler has partially prepared for the conversion by the logic of the structure and the imagery of sight and birth, and if it were merely a matter of the action, it might have achieved its effect. What makes the conversion hard to accept is the analogous stylistic leap from a sacramental verse that achieves a symbolic dimension without sacrificing the naturalistic surface to liturgical verse reminiscent of those lyrical duets and communal utterances that mar the dramatic continuity of *The Family Reunion:*

> Yes, we have endured.
> Our pleasures monotonous, our loves inadequate,
> Poverty constant, if not extreme;
> We have been starved of more than food; and yet we have endured.

[p. 54]

Again Speaight's commentary is appropriate: "The purpose is defeated because the scene is too close in time and circumstance to what has gone before, and above all . . . because the author has moved from the psychological to the devotional plane."[20]

The last scene of the play presents the effects of the director's reformation on the workers and on the artist himself. Like the director, the artist is an unbeliever, but whereas the former is an optimist, who sees man as the measure of all things and is thus subject to the sin of pride, the artist is a pessimist, a humanistic existentialist perhaps, who sees man as irredeemably limited and is thus subject to the sin of despair. Though his vision is clearer than that of his counterpart, it is inevitably and essentially destructive in function and thus in its own way a form of pride. As George Every observes, it leads "to an isolated superiority that passes judgment upon industrial planning from the outside, without sympathy or pity for the persons involved." [21]

Returning on Twelfth Day to the factory to learn the fate of his mural, the artist finds that the Christmas tree is still standing and in his characteristic manner launches into a biting and partially just attack on the perpetual optimism of the Church: "O this hateful tradition of new beginnings. . . . The Church has no Sons of the Evening: for her it's always cockcrow" (p. 57). But he is astonished first to discover that his murals have not been effaced, then that the employees appear to be more real and the factory more humane, and finally that the director has invited him, if he can "hire or borrow a pair of rose-coloured spectacles for the purpose," to paint "a more flattering picture of factory life . . . to balance this one" (p. 60). Responding to his astonishment, Maria, whose function in the play is that of catalyst, completes his negative half-truths with her fuller vision. Earlier, in a vain effort to answer the artist's pessimistic arguments that there was no human love that did not end in pain, no birth that did not wring tears, she had replied, "The razor-edge between the blind / Paradise and the perceiving hell: / There surely love exists" (p. 25). Now, with the reality of the Nativity manifest, she returns to the same idea. She acknowledges the limitations of man, his capacity for evil, but goes on to reconcile it with good in a higher synthesis grounded in Christian sacramental vision:

> Perhaps we never extend our boundaries,
> But at some point they cease to seem important.
> Instead, we discover a certainty of good,

> Quite impassible, quite inexpressible,
> Offering neither sweetness nor solace—
> No profit for us; and yet, strangely,
> This is joy, this is peace.
>
> [p. 61]

And when a factory hand tells the artist that the workers' vision has undergone a real change and that he must therefore see the image of factory life in a different light, Maria concludes, "Since not to see both ['the good and the bad in it'] / Is Paradise travestied, now we come / To the cold, real world" (p. 62). She says in Charles Williams' words—which no doubt Mrs. Ridler has in mind here—that the way of salvation in the fallen world lies paradoxically in "an increase of knowledge," in the discovery that through the agency of the Incarnation evil becomes itself an occasion of good.[22]

Though the artist insists that Maria's certainty of good may be an illusion, he nevertheless admits that no evil that man can do can destroy the appearance and in the end accepts the director's invitation to paint the second series of murals which, in symbolizing the redeemed world of the factory governed by Christian love, completes the first series, which reveals the fallen world of the factory governed by the concept of progress. These murals thus become a visual analogue of the Fall-Redemption structure of the action of *The Shadow Factory*.

The artist's dramatic function, then, takes on something of the nature of Charles Williams' *Figura Rerum* and T. S. Eliot's Furies. His role in the beginning has been to pursue the protagonist into the agonizing "precincts of his last evasions," into a "boundary-situation," where he becomes authentically aware of his and the world's limitations and must make a choice. After the Inquisitor-director has confronted reality, the artist's function becomes that of guide. The difference between the artist and the *Figura Rerum* and the Furies is that, unlike the latter, he is completely naturalized. He, too, like the director, is "converted." Thus in an important sense, Mrs. Ridler's artist is dramatically more satisfactory; for he establishes the pattern without introducing the note of determinism or conspiracy which mar Williams' *Cranmer* and Eliot's *The Family Reunion* and *The Cocktail Party*. Mrs. Ridler's achievement, in this respect, is thus similar to Eliot's successful naturalization of the Fury figures in *The Elder Statesman*.[23]

Despite the dramatic limitations of *The Shadow Factory*, it is not, as Raymond Williams punningly concludes, "on the dominant naturalistic tradition that Mrs. Ridler is still borne." [24] Williams bases his argument on spot passages which, out of context, appear to resemble the language of the naturalistic aesthetic. Seen in context, within the pattern of action and imagery, any particular passage (with the exception I have noted) assumes and contributes (in varying degrees depending on the emotional intensity) a significance that transcends though it does not violate the naturalistic surface. Mrs. Ridler's strategy, as the above analysis clearly reveals, is similar to that behind the passage of verse analyzed in the previous chapter from Eliot's *The Elder Statesman*, though, to be sure, only rarely is the achievement as striking. It is the strategy by which the language of everyday contemporary life and the rhythms of the human voice are subsumed under the eternal design and transfigured in its universal light. The tradition in which Mrs. Ridler is working is the tradition of sacramentalism which has its dramatic source in the medieval mystery plays and its ultimate source in the Word made Flesh.

Like Anne Ridler, Norman Nicholson, whose *The Old Man of the Mountains* was the first Mercury Theatre production, found his point of departure in the late dramatic theories of T. S. Eliot. The contemporary verse dramatist, he has said, must address himself not to a special audience but "to those who do not particularly want to hear him" [25] and thus should give the concrete and contemporary world its due. He "must be prepared, obviously, to make his words intelligible *at the speed at which the listener receives them,* and he must provide enough of action, plot and character to keep the whole audience entertained and interested even if the deeper significance of his symbolism is missed by some of them, even, perhaps, by most." [26] Nevertheless, Nicholson, who is a native of the Lake District, dissents from Eliot's and Mrs. Ridler's (and, of course, John Millington Synge's) view that in England, unlike Ireland, the naturally poetic speech of rural peoples has been lost and that the verse dramatist must therefore develop a verse form which employs the language of modern urban society:

> It is true that the form of common speech which has so far been accessible on the modern stage has been that of suburban English, and this is certainly not very hopeful material for poetry. It is an oddly DIS-LOCATED speech, its vowels distorted . . . and its natural idiom dug up, carted away, and replaced by concrete paths and wooden gates and whatever mass-produced ornaments are handy. It belongs neither to the country nor to the town. . . . But the life of the suburbs, vast as it is, is still the life of a minority. Out in the provinces, in industrial towns and in the countryside, on the long coasts, in the mountains and islands, and even in the heart of London, are people who still speak with something of the old vitality and splendour. Behind the speech of all country folk lies the imagery of the seasons; behind miners, that of the rock and the depths of the earth; behind sailors, that of the sea.[27]

Considering the neo-Wordsworthian tenor of these comments, it comes as no surprise that in *The Old Man of the Mountains* Nicholson sets his action in the rural Cambrian uplands, where according to him, the people still respond to the permanent forms of nature and thus retain a speech "enriched with natural rhetoric which draws from the imagery and symbols of a commonly-shared experience." [28] On the surface, then, Nicholson's Mercury play appears to have been written under the influence of the poetic realism of the Irish playwrights, particularly Synge. But there is a fundamental formal difference between Synge's and Nicholson's drama of contemporary rural life. Because Synge lacks an ordered universal system of referents which assimilates the imagery of time (nature and human events) into its structure, he cannot achieve an authentically multivocal dramatic form. The best he can do is to infuse a poetic aura, charged though it is with remarkable energy, into his present action.[29] Nicholson, on the other hand, though his native dramatic and poetic gifts are considerably inferior, begins with a Christian sacramental vision of the world which enables him, as we shall see, to infuse the various realistic imageries with symbolic significance.

The Old Man of the Mountains, a dramatization of the Old Testament story of the prophet Elijah's triumph over the Baal worshiper, Ahab, King of Israel, in I Kings xvii–xix, explores the theme of the Ways in imagery suggested by the "still small voice" of the original tale. As in the medieval mystery plays, however, the tale is set, not in the remote Biblical past but in the particular, everyday present in the north of England. In the prologue, the Raven, who is at once the voice of God and choric commentator, says:

> All this has happened before among the hills of Samaria—
> There was Elijah the prophet, and Ahab the ruler,
> There was a greedy and a godless people.
> And what of you? Are you not like them?
> Here in a northwest corner of a northwest island,
> Is not the story of Samaria enacted again?
> The God of Gold, the God of Power,
> Is not that God acknowledged again in your hearts?
> Therefore Elijah the prophet shall speak once more,
> Here in a northwest corner of a northwest island.[30]

Nicholson's mimetic strategy, his plan to fuse the past and the present into an eternal present, bears, in other words, the stamp of the sacramental aesthetic. It will be seen, furthermore, in the examination of the action that the theme itself gives rise to the sacramental form of the play.[31]

The conflict between Squire Ahab and Elijah, the one a materialistic landowner who is intent on squeezing as much profit from the soil as he can (his anachronistic title recalls that of Pilate in *The Second Trial before Pilate* discussed in Chapter 3), and the other an independent farmer who loves the land for its own sake, for the loyalties of the capricious folk of the rural community is established in the opening moments of the play. David, a la-

borer in the pay of the squire, has come to inform the widow Ruth
that he has been ordered to fell the old ash standing near her
cottage and turn it into money. Following a discussion in which
all the tenants except Ruth express their assent to Ahab's systematic exploitation of the land, the squire arrives, first to propose
and then, when Ruth challenges him, to insist, in imagery that
suggests violation, on a concerted community effort to increase
the productivity of the soil. At this point Elijah enters to castigate
Ahab—"You'll answer to the Lord; you have defied His laws, /
And defiled His creation to a muck-heap of money." (p. 21)—and
following the squire's refusal "to listen" (p. 22) and his angry
departure, to reprimand the folk for having succumbed to the
temptation of money and to warn them of the consequences. The
imagery of hearing he employs recalls similar imagery in the
Raven's prologue ("Many times / You are too busy with the buzz-
ing of self / To listen to these voices which are always speaking. /
Listen now. Hold yourself very quiet. . . ," p. 10) and establishes
the central terms of the play's underpattern:

> Oh your ears are blocked with gold like wax,
> For it is all about you in the warning air,
> The Lord God howling His threats across the sky.
> You have ripped from the skull of the fells
> The trees that soothed the dews in their branches
> And stitched the wet soil with their roots. Now
> The sun stares on the bare slope and the rock
> Corrodes into scree by the sockets of the rabbit holes.
> Hark! The wind scraping the crags, the creak of the bracken,
> The cough of the sheep—even the caw of the raven
> Tells of the dry wind and the drought to come.
>
> [pp. 22–23]

When Obadiah, one of the tenants, replies that he "can hear
nothing" (p. 23), Elijah, repeating words spoken off stage by the
Raven, prophecies a long drought in the name of God.[32] But the
new Baal has broken the community's bond with nature. They
thus conclude that he is "an old man / Daft as the jackdaws" (p.
23) and, like Ahab, impatiently depart.

In the ensuing sequence, the old man wrestles with his doubts concerning the reality of the voice he has heard. To Ruth he expresses amazement at his prophecy, taking the Raven's voice as a manifestation of his pride: "Who am I, Lord, who am I / To count myself one of the prophets, to bend and pervert / The sound of the wind to a voice?" (p. 25). But on Ruth's return, the lights dim and the Raven comes into the middle of the stage and, standing behind Elijah, resolves his doubts in words which point up the theme of stillness to which the play will return:

> I could speak the word that would blast away your doubts
> Like dynamite under rock. . .
> The Lord does not choose that way.
> Prodigies are oracles and omens
> Only for the heathen. . . the Lord does not speak in them,
> But in the time of quiet which follows after
> The time when nothing happens,
>
> [p. 26]

Elijah acknowledges the voice "which probes like a needle to the quick of the soul" (p. 26) as that of God, and the Raven gives him food to sustain him through the months of drought to come.[33] And when the lights go up again, Elijah awakes to find that the drought has made a waste land of the country in fulfillment of his prophecy. The landscape has become a projection of the community's soul.

In the following episode, which returns to the dominant mode of homely and immediate comic realism, Elijah returns to Ruth's cottage and both discovers and reveals his miraculous powers. He prophecies that the old woman's flour and milk shall perpetually replenish themselves, and finally in the full realization of the reality of the voice and of his mission, brings her son, Ben, back from death. With his own faith reaffirmed—"Now indeed I know that it was Thy voice. Oh, / There is nothing in the world so deaf as I have been" (p. 32)—and partially acknowledged by Ruth (who here symbolizes the community at large), Elijah turns his thoughts once more to the welfare of the dale.

In Part II of the play, the agon between Elijah and Ahab is renewed. The squire accuses the old man of bringing "down all this
trouble on the dale" [34] (p. 48), but again Elijah blames the drought
on Ahab, whose voice has alienated the people from nature:

> . . . You have turned the hearts of the people
> To bitter brass. They gaze with miser's eyes
> On the God-given landscape; they ravage the harvests,
> Shovelling the gold grain into bellies and money-bags:
> They wrench the trees from the living pores of the earth,
> Till the soil is cracked like scurf—even the rowan,
> That gropes its roots deep in the brain of the rock,
> Sags and droops like a bramble, because the blood
> Is dried in the veins of the men of the dale.
>
> [p. 48]

Obadiah, seeking a resolution of the conflict, argues that the
antagonists represent "two present-day tendencies," Elijah, "the
old agricultural tradition—ready / To work itself to the backbone
for the good of the land, / But unable to see much further than
the end of its nose," and Squire Ahab, the new "enterprise and
initiative," and suggests that a compromise be struck (pp. 48–49).
Elijah, however, arrogantly insists on the exclusive sovereignty of
his God, thus bringing the conflict into focus, and calls on the
community to choose between God and the new Baal, "To decide
and to abide by your decision. Can you longer / Dither between
two gods, like a donkey / Stockstill in doubt between two loads of
hay / That dies in hunger?" (p. 49). Ahab concurs, and it is decided that the people will be convened at dawn on the next day on
Carmel Fell.

Following a stylized Interlude set on the fell, in which Elijah
prays to God that He bring the people back to Him, Part III begins
with the community's response to Elijah's prophecy that " 'All
about me in the air I hear the sound / Of an abundance of rain' "
(p. 54). At the moment of the prophecy, each of the dale folk
had in his own way received a revelation of the coming of rain:
Martha heard it; Rebecca and Obadiah saw it; and Ruth felt it.
But when the rain fails to come, they begin to doubt the authen-

ticity of their vision and the words that Elijah has spoken. Questioned by Ahab, who "did not climb up Carmel . . . / To listen to Elijah" (p. 56), they cannot agree on the nature of their experience, though as Obadiah says, "at the time it was plain as my hand before me" (p. 58), and turn again to Ahab for explanation. Taking advantage of the community's doubts, Ahab, in contrast to Elijah's apparent passivity, proposes to act for their sake as well as his—to build a dam. And though this progressive plan means the inundation of their homes, the community is almost convinced by Ahab's authoritative voice.

When Elijah arrives, the people demand corroboration of the prophecy, each asking him in turn what he saw, or heard, or felt. But Elijah's vision was achieved by the Way of Negation. The voice, he says—a little too aggressively—"spoke to the soul / Without the commerce of the senses" (p. 62), and he goes on to define the nature and quality of his vision, thus also defining the aural metaphor that controls the theme and underpattern of the play:

> I turned and waited for the Lord to speak. Never before
> Was such a stillness in the fells. The air
> Was solid as blue ice. Glaciers of silence
> Smoothed across my eyes. Then the Lord spoke! Oh
> It was not with ears I heard, my ears
> Were plugged still with the silence of the ice. So quiet
> Was the voice that ears could never hear it. So quiet,
> The sound of a mouse nibbling the dry straw
> Would be as a gale in the larches compared to that;
> . . . .
> Yet it entered in my bones and ran along them,
> And cawed like the voice of the raven across the fells— [35]
>
> [p. 62]

This is the "still small voice" of God, which is, although Elijah is not as yet fully aware of it, the source of the hierarchy of voices in the world of the play—nature's (the Beck's), the child's (Ben's), the prophet's (Elijah's), and the Raven's—that speak in opposition to the voice of Ahab. And it can be heard only when the individual, in Eliot's phrase, has learned to sit still, when he has renounced the selfish desire and action that sets up a clamor in the soul and acknowledges the saving element (in this case, the rain) as a gift, a Grace to fallen man.

But the community "can make nowt of this" (p. 63), and ignoring Elijah's plea that they "wait in patience" (p. 64), they once again condemn him as the "troubler" of the dale. "Denied and derided on every side" (as the Raven puts it in the prologue of the play), Elijah begins to doubt for the second time. Thus while playing a game of draughts with Ben, he reveals his uneasiness, his waning ability to sit still, by repeatedly sending the boy to look out toward the sea for a sign of the promised rain. With each negative the boy brings, Elijah's doubt grows increasingly stronger, until, in a speech he addresses to Ben which recalls T. S. Eliot's *Gerontion* (but which unfortunately suffers by the comparison), it becomes despair:

> . . . Stay and watch an old man rave
> Like a thorn tree on the tops with the wind in it,
> And the mad starlings burbling in its boughs.
> And if the trunk should crack and split,
> And dry mouths open in the bark, and every mouth
> Crying: "Hark, at the wind in my leaves. . .
> Brother, it is the voice of God," and every mouth
> Crying: "Hark, at the birds in my branches,
> Brother, they are the hierarchs of the angels of heaven,
> Setting up an aviary in my brain." If such you saw,
> If such you heard, it would not be madder
> Than what you see and hear. . . an old man
> With a swamp in his skull:—One whom the toads
> Croak at mockingly and the yaffle laughs
> Beneath the sun's long sneer at noon. Go, now,
> I will not hide from the derision of the sky,
> I will eye it as an eagle eyes the sun. Go,
> Leap upon the wall. Search the sky for a cloud,
> Tell me there is none and let me shake my fist
> In the defiance of despair.

[p. 71]

Insisting too actively on a sign, Elijah has failed to recognize it in the casual voice of Ben, who, in counterpoint to the old man's agonized doubts, has throughout the scene affirmed as a matter of course (he is more interested in the game than in the prophecy) that the rain will come. The old man has forgotten that the rain is a gift of God and has himself come to see it as his own work. Having become self-conscious, he has lost his ability to hear.

Finally, however, when Ben, echoing Elijah's earlier words to Ruth, tells him that it doesn't matter what he believes or doesn't believe, that "the rain will come" (p. 73), Elijah becomes aware of his pride:

> Boy, can you be right? O Lord, my God,
> Here is faith beyond all that I could reach!
> The prophets again shall learn from the mouths of children.
>
> [p. 73]

As in *A Match for the Devil* (1953) (Mr. Nicholson's adaptation of *Hosea* 1.2, where the sacramental idea that the sublime is revealed through the humble—God through the mouths of babes—is even more fully explored [36]), the roles of the innocent child and experienced man are reversed. Ben sends Elijah to look for the rain, which comes shortly thereafter amidst the rejoicing of the community.

Identifying themselves with Elijah once more, the people turn on Squire Ahab with violence when he enters to complain that the rain might have been stored if there was a dam across the comb. But Elijah, momentarily wiser, prevents them. Bringing Ahab to acknowledge the powerlessness of his "former talk" (p. 79) to bring rain, he goes on to draw the lesson of sacramentalism for the community:

> The children of the world are wise in the ways of the world, and we
> Must not despise their wisdom. Now the people are turned to the Lord,
> Perhaps your plans and projects may be pleasing in his sight.
> The Lord can use the skill and ambition of men,
> Even as He uses the thunder and the clouds. Go, Ahab,
> Consider your plans and offer them to judgment.
>
> [p. 79]

Prior to the revelation received through Ben, Elijah's knowledge of God's ways was partial. He was justified in demanding that the people choose between God and the New Baal, but in insisting that the Way of Negation was the only way, he was dangerously wrongheaded. As George Every observes, Elijah was "tempted to condemn all social engineering in his indignation against Ahab's greed and his violation of the laws of nature." [37] Now he sees, as does the parson in *The Shadow Factory*, that even "machines have their place in the plan," [38] that God's eternal design is worked out in the temporal world. Obadiah, we recall, had suggested compromise. Elijah now proposes sacramental integration.

The same point is made on a more personal (and dramatic) level in the homely comedy of the closing moments of the play. As the people of the dale return one by one to their everyday labors, Elijah, impressed with his high calling, expresses annoyance at their apparent ingratitude. And when one of them mentions his return to the farm from which he has been a long time absent, he is surprised and indignant that such a thought should occur to anyone:

> My farm? Why should I think of it? The birds of the air
> Once spoke to me in prophecy—How they would caw
> And croak in scorn, seeing me bend my mind
> To grubbing for pennies and potatoes.
>
> [p. 82]

At this point, the Raven reenters and, in terms that recall Mary's comic reduction of Gabriel's academic pedagogy in Charles Williams' *House by the Stable*, proceeds to deflate Elijah's angelic pretensions and to reestablish the sacramental validity of life in time:

RAVEN   Elijah, what are you doing here?
        When all the dale is at work, why are you idle?
        Has the Lord sent rain only for the ducks?

ELIJAH (*flummoxed*)   Well. . . I hardly know. I was just saying to
        this lad, mebbe my place was by the beck, like, in case the Lord
        had owt else to say to me.

RAVEN   You will hear as well on the farm that once you loved.

. . . .

  Return and seek a liturgy in your labours.

ELIJAH   Aye, when you come to think about it, the rain's done good,
    and it's a pity not to profit by it.

[p. 82]

Elijah thus finally discovers the validity of the other way, that of
Charles Williams' Affirmation of Images. As the Raven puts it
in the end, "In the preoccupations of day by day / They shall find
grace and a glint of glory, / And blossom yearly like the damsons"
(p. 83).

This extended summary of the action of *The Old Man of the
Mountains*, including the liberal use of quotations of verse and
prose, gives some sense of the immediate, the realistic and contemporary, flavor with which Mr. Nicholson has infused the Biblical archetype. It suggests the play's affinity not to Synge but to
a work such as André Obey's *Noah*, which presents the Biblical
story of the ark as a tale of rural family life in a simple but realistic
vein, thus integrating analogically the immediate family theme
with the ancient theme of the human community, past and present, into an image of an eternal present. Francis Fergusson has
described this play as "a meditation on the allegorical, moral, and
anagogical reality of the Noah story, by means of an imaginative-
histrionic technique like that which Ignatius Loyola in *The Spiritual Exercises* calls 'the composition of place.'" The events, in
other words, are represented and felt in their sensuous and emotional immediacy, their multiple significance being "sought, and
brought home to us, by carefully and patiently building the fiction
of its literal reality." In this way Obey taps "not only the riches
of memories of childhood but as it were the childhood memories
of the race." Unlike the purely realistic dramatist, whose concern
is with the literal level alone, he "envisages the ultimate horizon
of the anagoge; his scene . . . is not only the human world of
history and moral effort, but 'God's world' of the Old Testament.
He offers, not only the realization of *a* change but, by these realis-

tic means, a parable of the end (and the beginning) of the world." [39]

Nicholson is less consistent than Obey in his effort to achieve the sense of immediate reality. Where, for example, the French dramatist presents an unseen God whom Noah addresses as if he were speaking to him over a telephone, Nicholson presents the Raven on stage and though he is never seen by the personae, he speaks a verse that is often highly rhetorical. Furthermore, the English dramatist is more self-conscious, less certain of his ideology, particularly of the resolution of the tension generated by the opposition of the two Ways. Nevertheless, what Fergusson says about Obey's play applies also to *The Old Man of the Mountains* (and perhaps more fully to his later Biblical play, *A Match for the Devil*, where the naturalistic surface is never broken).

By virtue of his conception of a vertical relation between man and God, time and eternity, Nicholson, like Obey, is able to reveal the particular present and the universal simultaneously. *The Old Man* projects not only the unique story of a contemporary northern English village torn between the progressive Squire and the conservative independent farmer, the machine age and the traditional agrarian economy, that is, the various everyday reality that runs the gamut of human emotion, but also the analogous Old Testament myth of Elijah, which, through the use of the imagery of opposing voices addressing the imperfect ears of humanity, establishes a universal reality, the contest for man's soul by Hell and Heaven, Baal and Prophet, bad and good angel, and its resolution by the sacramental principle, which, once Heaven is chosen, transforms Hell itself into an agent of Heaven.[40]

The play is not allegorical in the conventional sense. Its literal level is not merely a vehicle for the expression of a universal, an illustration of an abstract idea. It retains its integrity. In general the appeal, as Fergusson says of Obey's play, is to the "full poetic or histrionic sensibility rather than to the mind." [41] Nicholson has this strategy in mind, no doubt, when he writes (echoing T. S. Eliot) that the natural imitation of the real world need not entail writing down to an audience, for "symbolic meaning (as distinct from allegoric meaning) can often be perceived and understood by the reader or listener without his being aware even that there is a symbolic meaning." [42] *The Old Man of the Mountains* takes its place, then, not, as Raymond Williams claims, in the tradition of naturalistic prose drama,[43] but, like André Obey's *Noah* (and T. S. Eliot's and Mrs. Ridler's plays of contemporary, albeit urban, life) in the tradition of Medieval sacramental realism. What Francis Fergusson says about *Noah* applies equally to *The Old Man:* "We feel behind it, not sentimental contemporary fiction [as in *Green Pastures* and *Our Town*], but a theatrical folk-tradition going back to secular Medieval plays." [44]

This multivocality renders *The Old Man of the Mountains* artistically superior to such a play as Christopher Fry's early mystery *The Boy with a Cart*, which tells the story of St. Cuthman's founding of the church of Steyning in Sussex in terms of a similar homely rural realism without, however, achieving a sense of immediacy and presentness. But in the last analysis, Nicholson's play fails to achieve the dramatic stature of Eliot's and Ridler's plays. This is not only because of the remoteness of the action from the modern temper and the decorative rhetoric ("Now Thy words go bumping round the sky / Like huge empty barrels on the cobbles of the clouds, / Bursting the water-butts and tipping the gullies / On the fells and the woodlands and the dale," p. 77) which, despite Nicholson's view to the contrary, acts as a barrier between the play and the audience, but also, and primarily, because he reverses the strategy of Eliot and Ridler by putting the ancient myth with its patent miracles in the foreground and subordinating the present to it. The sacramental aesthetic demands acknowledgment of the modern consciousness and its synthesis into the religious scheme, as for example, Anne Ridler does in the Nativity scene in *The Shadow Factory*. By asserting the miraculous, Nicholson puts too great a strain on the credulity of the modern secular audience and fails to effect a willing suspension of disbelief on which the contemporary Christian poetic drama must rely to unlock the poetic power of the sacramental action.

Ronald Duncan began his career as a dramatist before World War II with a small volume of plays entitled *The Dull Ass's Hoof* (1940), which includes *The Unburied Dead* (1938), *Pimp, Skunk and Profiteer* (1939) and *Ora Pro Nobis* (1939), the first two of which reveal the influence of Ezra Pound's verse and politics.[45] Only the third is a religious play, a one-act Nativity cast in the form of the mass, the chief interest of which lies in its presentation of a theme that runs through Duncan's plays and provides the main ideological motif of one of his major efforts, *The Death of Satan:* that Christ's efficacy is neutralized by modern man's indifference to sin. (The priest asks, "Lord, how can I ask Thee to forgive their sins, / Since they do not admit any?" [46]) But it was not until *This Way to the Tomb* (1946), the third Mercury Theatre production, that he wrote a Christian verse play of more than ordinary interest.[47]

In this play, Duncan, who has said retrospectively that at the time he wrote the first part he subscribed to the common notion that poetry and contemporary life are incompatible,[48] passes over to a considerable extent the late experiments of T. S. Eliot and the other Mercury poets to return to the rhetorical pattern of the prewar pageants, in which analogous past and present actions are juxtaposed rather than assimilated into a single contemporary episode (and in the first part, to the formal design and rhetoric of *Murder in the Cathedral*). Thus he divides the play into two distinct parts, a "Masque," which is cast in the fourteenth century and tells the story of Antony's quest for the sanctity he has not discovered as Abbot of Ferrata, and an "Anti-Masque," which is projected in the contemporary world, well on its way to becoming a Huxleyan Utopia, and presents the materialistic Astral Group's televised effort to explode the myth of Antony's yearly resurrection. The analogous relationship between the Masque and Anti-Masque is not worked out consistently (and this is one of the serious limitations of the play) but a pattern is discernible. Both parts enact the theme of division, of self-alienation, resulting from the assertion of intellectual pride. In the first part the action focuses on Antony's temptation, that is, on the divisive implications of intellectual pride for the individual, and is presented in the tragic mode; in the second part, the action focuses on the Tempter's decision, that is, on the social implications of intellectual pride, and thus is presented in the satirical mode.

By reintroducing the main characters of the Masque into the Anti-Masque and giving them their original significance, Duncan relates the two parts rhetorically within the framework of the sacramental concept of time. Thus the presenter says:

> To-night we present "This Way to the Tomb."
> It is a Masque with Anti-Masque.
> The former focuses on the past,
> The latter looks at the mere present
> And what the whole reflects is as permanent
> As loose words are, fitted to the hoof of time,[49]

In the Masque, we find the aging Antony with three novices— Marcus, a peasant; Julian, a poet; and Bernard, a scholar—on the island of Zante in search of God, after having renounced his former worldly existence as Abbot of Ferrata. As the play opens, Antony, still afflicted by fear of death and desire for life after three ascetic years, has resolved to isolate himself entirely and to fast until death, hoping that through the private discipline of meditation he will achieve the peace in God, the repose of permanence, for which he has been yearning:

> By fasting with no attachment to life,
> I pray I may lose my fear of death.
> By contemplating the object of my dreams
> I hope to shed my desire.
> By meditating on my intentions
> I hope to achieve my object
> Which is the comfort of His Compassion
> And the simple peace within the tumult of mystery.
> . . . .
> But I do not think either the love of woman or the love of God
> Comes to a man like an unexpected letter.
> Love must be dredged out of our own souls
> > By our own effort.

[p. 23]

Two of the novices, Marcus and Julian, cannot understand Antony's decision. Concerned about what will become of them, they attempt in vain to dissuade him from carrying out his purpose. Only the self-sufficient and strong-willed scholar, Bernard, to whom alone Antony will listen, appears to understand his master's motives. Unlike the others, he exults in Antony's decision, and even encourages him when he begins to doubt the validity of his vow:

ANTONY   Perhaps I should break my vow for their sake.

BERNARD   Many seeds are sown for one to germinate. It would be a pity to turn back for their sake.

ANTONY   Yes, it is even possible to use Mercy to hide our weakness.

[P. 39]

When, as Antony continues his fast on the rock, Marcus and Julian become progressively weaker and Bernard stronger, it becomes clear that the three novices are more than companions of Antony, that they are his attributes—Marcus, his body; Julian, his sensual appetite; and Bernard, his intelligence—and that collectively they represent the essential temptations of the Christian who chooses the way of asceticism in his pilgrimage to God. Antony is thus strong enough to withstand the temptations of the body and the senses but not the temptation of the mind, and this perverts his attitude to the former. Blind to his intellectual pride, he does not realize that he is being tempted by it to violate the way of negation. When Antony, in a moment of despair, admits the futility of human effort to escape temporality—

Only God himself stands outside of Time's circle
And schedule.
                    For time is where there is movement;
It is energy's measurement.
                              And since all life is in Him spent,
God stands outside of Time, alone in still contentment.

I am not alone. Only God can be alone. . . .

[P. 40]

—Bernard, like the Fourth Tempter in *Murder in the Cathedral*, who is also aware of the protagonist's aversion for the life of time, tries to convince his master that he has succeeded in leaping from the movement of time into the stillness of eternity, which, of course, is the temptation to become as God:

> And yet you are alone;
>   for you have rinsed your heart
> Of fear and of desire,
>   and therefore are
>   free of time;
> For by desire and fear we're chained to time,
>   and by time locked within each other's hearts.

[p. 41]

Antony does not admit to having achieved tranquility, but he does conclude that he must "clear this rabble [the things of time] which live within me and consume me" (p. 42). He is tempted by his intellectual pride, in other words, to see time and eternity as discontinuous opposites, evil and good, and the way of negation as an "angelic" process by which the bodily attributes and, by extension, the material world are annihilated rather than a process whereby they are sacramentally renewed.

This becomes clearer in the formal allegorical procession of the tempters (the "rabble"), which finally brings the protagonist to self-knowledge. Antony is first confronted by the various temptations of the body, Gluttony and Lechery, the extremes of which are easily subdued, and Marcus, who, speaking for moderation, warns Antony that "by fasting you feed your mind to gluttony" and entreats him to "revive me, your body's agony" (p. 45). Prompted by Bernard from the shadows, Antony fails to perceive the distinction and rejects Marcus, whose decline is climaxed by his death. Next come the temptations of the senses, Sight and Hearing (Julian), who, on being rejected, hint at Antony's spiritual blindness and deafness, respectively. Finally Antony is confronted by his heart, a beautiful young woman who, when rejected, is transformed before his eyes into an old crone, thus signaling the moment of death, the moment that is to bring the freedom from time for which Antony has been striving:

> At last, I'm out of fear's tight halter
> And desire's short tether,
>   both are broken behind me,
> They cannot retie me, for by my own effort, I am free.

[p. 49]

But it is not, as he expects, Christ who appears in Antony's moment of triumph; it is Bernard, who, echoing the warnings of Marcus and Julian, reveals to him the true nature of his pilgrimage of renunciation:

> And, Antony, have I not always walked
> Before you, beside you and behind you
> As your retinue, your substantial shadow
> For you to lean upon and lead you on?
> Was it not Bernard who made you Abbot
> And did I not lead you from there, to here?
> And have I not stood by you in your fast?
> Why, your whole life's a pilgrimage to me:
> By way of meditation you approached me
> And by privation you have fed me.
> Marcus, the peasant, was your own body and your sight
> And Julian, the poet, your sensual appetite.
> They weakened as you starved, and died.
> But look, Antony, I, Bernard, thrived.
> And stand still, the shadow at your side,
> For, Antony, I am your own Pride.[50]

[p. 50]

With the recognition of his sin of self-sufficiency, Antony cries out in humility to Christ: "For pity's sake lift me into your Mercy, Mercy!" (p. 51).[51] Thus Bernard too falls and Christ appears to Antony. Promising him freedom when he has "renounced all pride / And eaten of humility," Christ directs the repentant abbot to "go back to your body and eat what your poor servants brought to you" (p. 52). Antony then wakes Marcus, thus reaffirming the body he had denied and accepts from the novice the nourishment (bread and milk) he had previously rejected.

The way of negation thus becomes in the end not the annihilation of the things of this world but, as the resurrection of Marcus (which represents the resurrection of Julian and Bernard as well) suggests, their sacramental renewal and union. On the conceptual level, then, the point the Masque appears to make is that man achieves Grace only when he recognizes and acknowledges Christ's redemptive function and thus, in spite of their seductive potential, the essential worth and dignity of his creatural attributes. This is also the point of the contemporary action.

Set in the present and projected as a television program entitled "In Search of Truth and Religious Experience," the Aristophanic (see especially *The Clouds*) or perhaps Brechtian Anti-Masque satirizes the confident scientific utopianism of contemporary life through the agency of a Jonsonian choric figure, to whom we shall return. The particular object of the satire is the Astral Group, a "religious" society resembling a United Nations commission, which journeys from one religious center to another ostensibly in search of faith but actually to expose by means of the latest scientific devices the prevailing myth of each shrine.

As the program opens, the "viewer" is taken to the Island of Zante, where the group has come to debunk the legend

> That Antony comes back to them [the islanders] each eve
> Of his anniversary, if they first
> Put food for his fast and wine for his thirst
> Beside his sepulchre, and there confess
> Their fears, desires and wickedness.
>
> [p. 63]

Led by Father Opine, its high priest, whom the Chorus savagely condemns as a modern charlatan—"Science is his faith to Science he is devout / Cynicism is his psalm, fact his creed, / He follows reason where reason leads" (p. 62)—the Astral Group begins the program with a grotesque ritual in which the novices, after declaring the nine deadly sins (poverty, inefficiency, peculiarity, abnormality, tradition, permanence, disease, the natural state, and love of the spirit) and affirming the article's of faith (Man, Cause,

Fact, and Reason), are initiated "into the new dispensation of Doubt." [52]

Following the ceremony, Father Opine shepherds the group into a circle around the tomb of Antony, which has been wired with photoelectric cells so sensitive that even "A passing shadow will instantaneously break / Their circuit and cause cameras to make / A record of any miracle or fake" (p. 76), and the experiment begins. One by one the representatives of contemporary life, the Mobile Worker, the Man of Culture, the Girl of Leisure, confess their fears as the legend demands, then look into the tomb. What each sees reflected from the ebony surface is his particular hollowness:

> I see a face
> where neither character nor grace
> disturbs the platitude of any feature;
> indeed it's more a mask
> portraying neither saint nor devil
> with little virtue, much less evil.
>
> [p. 79]

But the revelations make no serious impression on Father Opine, who is intent on the recording mechanism. When nothing passes between the beams, he approaches the tomb himself and suddenly has a vague intimation that he has "stood beside this tomb before" (p. 80), which, on his expressing a fear of St. Antony's resurrection, becomes a vision of Bernard, "a young man with an old book / His lips in humble prayer, his eyes with a proud look" (pp. 80–81). Alarmed, he breaks off the investigation, concluding too protestingly that "there's nothing here" (p. 81).

A few moments before midnight, at which hour the saint is supposed to reappear, a mother and a widow (Mary and the Church?) enter to reveal that they too are searching for faith, for a son and husband (Christ) whose martyrdom represents the perpetual crucifixion. In contrast to the Astral Group, however, they genuinely confess their fear that they will not find what they are looking for, their fear, that is, of the finality of death, and at the last stroke of twelve the widow cries out: "For Pity's sake, Christ, . . . lift me into your Mercy" (p. 86). With this decisive act of humility, which, we recall, echoes Antony's in the Masque, an Old Man enters, declaring that he is the resurrected saint.[53]

Confronted by Father Opine, who, though manifestly disturbed, derides his claim, the Old Man says enigmatically: "I am to you what you think I am" (p. 88), and goes on to recall the past and to hint at Father Opine's identity with Bernard: "Do you not recognize me? / You who were always at my side?" (p. 88). But the high priest of science, whose recollection of the past has been dimmed by his creed, fails to recognize his and the Old Man's identity. As a result, the Astral Group, which in a sense are attributes of Father Opine, attack the Old Man as a charlatan. Concluding that "This myth of Antony's resurrection / Is merely insular superstition / Persisting on account of bad transport, / Lack of research and scientific thought" (p. 89), they depart. Though St. Antony has not been acknowledged, their triumph, as their nervous and mechanical exit reveals, has been an empty one.

With the conclusion of the television program and the departure of the Astral Group, which leaves a Post Card Seller, the Chorus, and the Old Man alone by the tomb, the theme suggested by the Old Man's effort to evoke recognition from Father Opine is brought into focus. Despite the evidence of his senses, the Post Card Seller humbly offers his yearly oblation of bread before the empty tomb and thus recalls his previous identity as Marcus and recognizes the Old Man as Antony. Similarly, the choric figure remembers his earlier identity as Julian and recognizes Antony, thereby regaining his old gift of song, which without faith had become (like the artist's talent in *The Shadow Factory*) a negative instrument. Echoing the hint he had expressed before Father Opine, Antony goes on to explain:

I can only be Saint Antony
When my three attributes
Body, desire and intelligence

> Make me complete by each
> Confounding their own separate frailty.
> My body, Marcus, has denied itself
> And thus fed me, recognised me.
> And in Julian, my senses have found their innocence again
> And stopped the fret of small complaint.
>
> [p. 94]

As Antony is lamenting the independence of his intelligence, which "struts in a state of knowing, / Not wise enough for faith" (p. 95), Father Opine returns to the tomb. His intimation of a previous identity too strong to resist, he now expresses anguished doubt in the dispensation of Doubt:

> I am treading an old path with new feet.
> I am standing in footprints already in my mind.
> Is not the test of reason to put it to a fear?
> And it was here the ferret's tooth of fear struck at my bone
> And the draught of alarm blew out my reason.
>
> [p. 95]

Confessing thus his fear that "Faith is the end of reason" (p. 95), he too remembers and accepts his earlier identity as Bernard and —after the Old Man assures him that "Without faith, Bernard, there is no reason" (p. 95)—recognizes and acknowledges Antony.

In recalling their previous identities, the Post Card Seller, the Chorus, and Father Opine perceive that they are reenacting the Fall, which manifests itself in division, and accordingly confound their separate frailties, submit to a higher authority, and achieve reintegration. Antony again becomes a sacramental whole, but now his wholeness is seen in the perspective of the eternal present.

The two parts of the play, in depicting first the past and then the present taking up the past into its structure, achieves a rhetorical unity. In the Masque, the dramatic focus of which falls on Antony's decision, the final sacramental integration becomes a symbol of the Christ figure, who must come to see the things of time and eternity—body, senses, intelligence, on the one hand, and soul, on the other—as co-inherent before he achieves his end.

In the Anti-Masque, which focuses on the choice of the three attributes in their contemporary guise, the final sacramental integration becomes a symbol of the Christian society, which must perpetually renew itself, perpetually forget its self in order to remember its redeemed identity. In one of his last speeches, St. Antony says to Father Opine, who is Bernard once again: "I know who you are; / And you, in recognizing me, prove that our souls / remember by forgetting self in prayer" (p. 96).

Unfortunately, *This Way to the Tomb* has unresolvable thematic difficulties that obscure the pattern outlined in the foregoing analysis. The source of these difficulties lies in Duncan's radical disdain for contemporary life, which manifests itself in the tendency to present the time world, particularly the present, as completely negative, thus cutting across the sacramental theme. This tendency is foreshadowed in the prologue when the presenter refers to the matter of the Anti-Masque as "the mere present," but it is most apparent in the lack of dramatic balance between the two parts of the play. In the second part, Duncan places far too much emphasis on the satire against Father Opine and his Astral Group and too little on the Chorus, whose limitations we do not become aware of until the very end, and the Post Card Seller, who barely exists as a character in the drama. As a result we fail to perceive the parallel between the two parts until the end. When the analogous sacramental resolution does come we feel that it is arbitrary and not dramatically justified and, therefore, that Duncan is not completely sure of his theme.

The play has formal problems as well. Though much of the lyrical verse of the Masque (particularly in some of Antony's introspective speeches written in the canzone form [54]) and the satirical verse of the Anti-Masque (particularly in the speeches of the Chorus written in a couplet form reminiscent of Ben Jonson) is effective, the influence of the "neutral" verse of *Murder in the Cathedral* and of the music hall elements of T. S. Eliot's *Sweeney Agonistes* and W. H. Auden's and Christopher Isherwood's *The Dog Beneath the Skin* is too patent. Lines such as the following from the Masque—

> I've lost the past and feared the present,
> And in the future have foreseen this moment
> Of decision, which I have delayed by prompt postponement.
>
> [p. 28]

—and from the Anti-Masque—

> I am a man of culture
> I travel all alone
> I've lost my destination
> But I'm on the telephone
>   Searching for Faith and Love.
>
> [p. 71]

—reveal, as Raymond Williams has observed, "a kind of debt that jars." [55]

But the primary difficulty lies in Duncan's failure to fulfill the formal demands implied by his sacramental theme, that is, to unify the double action into a single whole and to present it in more realistic terms. Interesting as the relationship between past and present is, it is essentially intellectual and rhetorical rather than dramatic in its effect. The Masque does not escape the stigma of nostalgic remoteness, of "medievalism," and one cannot help but feel that it exists primarily as a norm to measure the decadence of the present action rather than as the first pole of a figural structure. Furthermore, the conventional allegorical mould into which the two actions are cast (though in the first part of the Masque, the action borders on sacramental realism) denies the putative reality of the action and renders them illustrative images. Despite the theatrical effects, it is not so much drama as the modulating voice of Duncan that we encounter in the play.

Duncan seems to have realized the dramatic limitations of the form of *This Way to the Tomb,* for he abandoned the allegorical mode and the strategy of the rhetorical juxtaposition of past and present in his later plays. (It is interesting to note, however, that if *Don Juan* [1953] and its sequel *The Death of Satan* [1954] are considered as a unit, they correspond rather closely to the Masque and Anti-Masque of *This Way to the Tomb.* The first, which is set in the past, presents the story of Don Juan's love for Dona Ana, and the second, which is set in the present, presents Don Juan's return to earth from Hell and his futile effort to evoke recognition from the contemporary counterpart of Dona Ana.[56]) Instead, Duncan projects each as a single and unified whole, achieving a symbolic dimension by integrating a Christian under-pattern into the surface. And though he employs myth (*Don Juan*), legend (*Our Lady's Tumbler*), and fantasy (*The Death of Satan*) rather than contemporary events for his plots, in each case he presents the action realistically, using a verse form modeled after that of Eliot's late plays in which idiom and rhythms are genuinely contemporary and dramatic. But only in *Stratton* (1949), a tragedy of contemporary life, which tells the story of a strong-willed man whose excessive pride destroys everything it encounters and finally causes his fall, does he attempt to fulfill completely the demands of the sacramental aesthetic as it was being worked out by T. S. Eliot. Unfortunately Duncan gives way in this play to his penchant for cluttering the action with complications and un-realized symbols, thus obscuring the Christian underpattern be-yond recognition.

9

CHARLES WILLIAMS AND CHRISTOPHER FRY: THE FIGURE OF THE DANCE

> This theatre I speak of, . . . has to make the
> exploration in its own way. We can do it no
> service by thinking of it as a return to an earlier
> manner, as a sudden reversal to the seventeenth
> century, for example. It will see, I hope, strongly
> with its own eyes, and discover its own tensions.
> It will come about, not as an imposition on the
> twentieth century, but growing naturally from an
> anticipation and a need of the present time, and
> you, the audience, will find it increasingly your
> language, and we, the playwrights, will learn to
> work it more skillfully into shape.
>
> Christopher Fry,
> "Poetry and the Theatre"

The impact of the discovery of poetry (as opposed to rhetoric) in ordinary contemporary life and language in the early 1940's was not limited to new poet-dramatists. It was also felt by older playwrights, a fact that suggests grounds of influence broader than the mere example of Eliot's dramatic experiments: the reemphasis by modern theologians of the reality of the Incarnation and the persuasive criticism of modern culture by Christian critics. Charles Williams, we recall, was moving toward a poetic drama of ordinary contemporary life in his one-act moralities, *House by the Stable* and *Grab and Grace,* and we see a further development in this direction in his last play, *The House of the Octopus* (1945), the setting of which suggests, if it does not name, a Pacific island during World War II. We also see this development in Christopher Fry's *A Sleep of Prisoners* (1951), which, in its World War II setting and in the barer diction and more contemporary ring of its verse, represents a singular if not conclusive departure from his earlier secular and religious Histories.

Charles Williams remained an idiosyncratic dramatist to the end of his career, but in his last full-length play, *The House of the Octopus,*[1] he tacitly acknowledges the dramatic value of contemporaneity and, though to a lesser extent, of naturalism in the Christian poetic drama. Though he continues to employ the familiar symbolic Fury figure, in this case the Flame or *Lingua Coeli* who, as sacramental principle, initiates and resolves the action, he now projects his play in the recognizable present, the period of World War II. And if he does not naturalize the surface action completely, he at least gives it psychological and plot complications that render it more concrete and vitally dramatic than his earlier, more abstract efforts.

Williams achieves this greater dramatic impact in *The House of the Octopus* without minimizing poetic significance. He infuses a sense of universality into the particular action by suggesting the presentness of the past, the pagan persecution of the early Church, which begins with the Crucifixion and the harassing of the Apostles and culminates in the Pentecost, even in the brutal machine-gunning of the recalcitrant fledgling Christian community of natives on a remote Pacific island during World War II by the P'o-l'u soldiers (obviously Japanese), and the survival of one witness. Thus in the prologue, the Flame, in setting the scene, declares:

> Call this a land in the Outer Seas,
> where the ease and joy of our Lord reaches at last;
> as in all the past of his Church, so now here.
> First it was Jerusalem, then Damascus, Rome,
> all the patriarchates; . . .
> . . . .

We are of those who first came into being
when the Holy Ghost measured within the waters
the angle of creation; then in a sudden visibility
we dropped from his rushing flame-scattering wind,
to teach the blessed the speech of heaven and of us.[2]

and at the end of the play in his address to the wounded Torna, who has been chosen to bear witness to the word:

But you, Torna, I will have you
new-called to an old life: wounds
have you, and lie near the grave,
bleeding, lonely, and not even a priest
but the least of our house? Yet I will settle in you
a word, as private as you must, as public as you can,
of the Holy Ghost, heard above Jerusalem; [3]

[pp. 323–324]

Furthermore, Williams deepens the sense of universality by rendering the outer action, the P'o-l'u invasion of the island, a symbol of the spiritual condition of the protagonist. Thus the play presents not only a political invasion but also and simultaneously a process going on in the mind and heart of Anthony, the missionary priest, as he attempts to secure the community from apostasy.

As the play opens, the imminent P'o-l'u invasion convinces the small Christian community that Father Anthony must escape to insure the survival of Christianity in the islands. Anthony, however, is reluctant to leave for fear that the natives will not stand up to the test without his support:

. . . and now I come
to my soul's inward trouble; you are but young
in faith; barely has the tongue of the Holy Ghost
uttered your names to Christ or his white dove
touched you with its wings; is it sure of you? . . .

[p. 260]

Thus at the outset Anthony unconsciously hints at his essential weakness, his feeling that the community needs him more than they need God.

Unconvinced by the arguments of the leaders of the community, Anthony nevertheless agrees to go into hiding. In the meantime, his counterpart, Assantu—a Christian in name only, through whom the priest will come to self-knowledge—has secretly plotted with P'o-l'u agents to hand Anthony over to them, hoping thereby to revive the older cannibalistic rites of the natives. With Anthony's decision to seek safety, Assantu gets the chance to put his plan into action. Aided by his wife, Rais, he strangles Anthony's intended guide and assumes the duty himself. As Act I closes, Alayu, a sensual young girl who has earlier insisted to Anthony that she could not deny her faith, expresses her fear of pain, thus foreshadowing her apostasy before the threats of P'o-l'u.

In Act II, the soldiers of P'o-l'u arrive led by the Prefect, a crude and brutal military man, who offers the Christians the choice of accepting the "infinite nameless Emperor of P'o-l'u" or being fed to the octopuses, which, on one level, symbolize the character of P'o-l'u aggression.[4] Most of the natives, who understand the redemptive function of the Incarnation ("All that goes amiss / cannot at all alter that sweetness of fact," p. 270), withstand the threat. But Alayu breaks down and denies Christ, though this does not save her from being bludgeoned to death by one of the soldiers. Anthony's fears are thus confirmed.

With the arrival of the Marshal, the political agent of P'o-l'u, who in contrast to the Prefect is a sophisticated and witty intellectual—one of the breed of modern Grand Inquisitors that have their source in Dostoevsky—the inner drama of the play begins to take shape. Against the Prefect's violence he recommends, in terms of the central metaphor of the play, the octopus's tentacles, the even crueler policy of "mental and spiritual absorption": "we must creep deep into their mind, / and swallow them there. The cephalopodic process / does not keep its lair only in the ocean" (p. 276). The Marshal understands the essential weakness of the religious mind, its tendency to fall into spiritual pride, in which, according to Williams' usual definition, the faith exists for the individual rather than the individual for the faith, thus transforming him, as the Marshal says, into a "religious [lecher] / fornicating with [his] fancies" (p. 277).[5] He purposes, therefore, to make Anthony, who has been captured, the channel by which he "may come into them [the Christian natives], and embrace them with mental tentacles, / and enlace them into P'o-l'u" (p. 276).

Summoning him, the Marshal tactfully leads the priest into a discussion of the motives of his flight, and by flattering his fatherhood evokes from him an admission of his "soul's inward trouble," the fear that his fledgling parishioners do not have the spiritual strength to uphold the faith at the critical moment:

THE MARSHAL   You were to them the fatherhood in the Faith.
          Losing your fatherhood—I do not say they would lose
          the Faith; but the terrible impersonality of faith
          is hard for young souls.

ANTHONY   That is it! that is it!
          That is what I fear—that they should not be able to bear
          in any crisis the dreadful abstract principles.

                                                  [p. 282]

Having thus confirmed his insight into the weakness of the religious man, the Marshal tempts Anthony into compromise by promising him the opportunity to continue ministering to the natives if he will consent to substitute the name of the P'o-l'u deity for that of the Christian God. Anthony fails to perceive that the proposal is an appeal to his egotism. He succumbs to the temptation that would undermine the Faith, and the tentacles of pride begin to take hold of his soul. The Marshal tells the Prefect:

          I think I may claim the cephalopodic process
          is beginning with some success. Gentleness and sweetness
          are more entangling tentacles, Prefect, than rifles.

                                                  [p. 285]

Seeing the offered peace not only as a means of maintaining his hold on his charges, but also as an opportunity to convert P'o-l'u to Christianity, Anthony now convenes the community to present the Marshal's proposal. When he hears from Siru, one of the native leaders of the community, of Alayu's apostasy—which the

Marshal had cunningly hinted at in their conversation—and murder, he is convinced of the need of his presence and of the rightness of his course of action. In this frame of mind he cannot but see Alayu's apostasy as unforgivable. But Siru's personal Christianity is more understanding than Anthony's strident faith. He insists that despite her apostasy she was a witness:

> Might not, sir, her first baptismal vow
> have swallowed her fault, instead of her fault her vow?
> If God is outside time, is it so certain
> that we know which moments of time count with him,
> and how?
>
> [p. 292]

Anthony, however, blindly rejects Siru's simple insight into the redemptive nature of Christianity as a violation of his fatherhood and despite the community's repeated warning that the god of P'o-l'u is a murderous deity, a man-eater, goes on, in terms that come dangerously close to those of the Marshal, to propose the compromise scheme as a means of converting P'o-l'u to Christianity:

> The Universal Church would well be eased
> with this last miasma of mystical paganry
> dispersed, and the last shire of the world held
> by me for Christ! . . .
>
> [p. 293]

The means of bringing Anthony from this height of pride to authentic self-knowledge is the Flame, who, as Williams explains in his preface, represents "that energy which went to the creation and was at Pentecost (as it were) re-delivered in the manner of its own august covenant to the Christian Church." [6] He is, like the symbolic figures of Williams' earlier plays, the sacramental principle operating in time, who is seen as good or evil according to the vision of the perceiver (Assantu, for example, sees him in his "uncovenanted" shape, that is, as the principle of universal cannibalism). Thus at the climactic point in the agon between

Anthony and the community, when the latter's continued resistance to their priest's demands bends his certainty, the Flame,
who has up to this time merely commented ironically on Anthony's pride, begins to assert his will on the action by forcing the
antagonists to reveal the truth behind their motives. In opposition
to the community's recognition that "the new life must be ours
and not yours; / God is our cause of being, and only God," Anthony is compelled to admit that he wishes himself and not God
to be their father, their center:

> I do not wish you to live from God alone;
> I wish always to be your means of God.
>
> [p. 297]

And when he resists the horrible implications of his secret desire,
the Flame forces Assantu to be his interpreter:

> I wish not to be eaten, but to eat others;
> I wish to grow great and thrive on others;
> And if others will not, I wish them to be compelled.
> I will be a belly to them and they food to my belly.
>
> [p. 298]

Thus Anthony, the priest of Christ, in his unconscious efforts to
possess the native community, has become identified with the
cannibal Assantu. Where Assantu wishes to become a devourer of
human flesh, Anthony wishes to become a devourer of human
souls. On perceiving that he has perverted Christianity into its
opposite, he acknowledges the enormity of his sin. But the lesson
is incomplete, since it has shown him only what Christianity is
not. He has yet to discover the positive principle of *caritas* which
is diametrically opposed to the cannibalism of Assantu and the
absorption of P'o-l'u.

The third act, then, begins with a dream sequence initiated by
the Flame which continues Anthony's enlightenment. In this
"night when souls become themselves, / and dreams become
thoughts, and thoughts acts" (p. 304), the adoring members of
the Christian community converge upon Anthony in the grotesque

shape of an octopus and, wrapping their tentaclelike arms around his body, begin to strangle him. Anthony thus discovers what would be the effect of his desired relation to the community. They too, if they capitulated to Anthony's possessiveness, would become devourers.

When Anthony cries out for help, he is confronted by the spirit of Alayu, who has been sent by the Flame to ask the priest for his forgiveness. Confirming Siru's earlier intuition that "her last scream / was no more than a cry in child-birth, when he [Christ] was born piercingly in her soul, and her very death / her first motherly awaking" (p. 292), she reveals a new awareness of the real nature of Christian love that her earlier sensuality had obscured. Thus when the Flame asks her if she, "who could not bear death / through the falseness of love," could, if Anthony were to be martyred by P'o-l'u, "bear his natural fear" (p. 309) to save him from apostasy, Alayu freely consents (though Williams is careful to make clear that her decision does not come easily). In turn, the priest accepts Alayu's assumption of the burden of his fear, "an equally difficult burden." Anthony thus discovers the essential nature of the virtue of *caritas*, of Exchange or Substitution, which was figured on the Cross, and which carries on the Redemption in the world. As the Flame concludes:

> . . . This is the mind of the Church—
> to discover always the way of the lover and the love.
> The young shall save the old and the old the young,
> the dead the living, and the other living the dead,
>
> [p. 310]

In terms of the central metaphor of the play, the way of Exchange is the way of swallowing *and* being swallowed, of consuming *and* being consumed (p. 111), and thus is opposite to the way of Assantu (and, as Assantu finds, of P'o-l'u), which—as is clearly revealed by his desire to substitute another (Anthony) to his cannibalistic deity to avoid being consumed and to become himself a consumer—is the way of swallowing *or* being swallowed, of consuming *or* being consumed.[7] When Alayu asks what Assantu is

doing as the latter crawls toward Anthony to make the kill, the
Flame replies:

> He thinks—saving himself from being consumed.
> You were blest. You were consumed before you knew.
> Glory to the only God who made us and bade us
> all be food and all eaters of food.
> Is it a wonder Christ gave you your Eucharist?

[p. 313]

When the Marshal enters to receive the decision of the community, Anthony, now freed from the internal tentacles of P'o-l'u,
refuses to compromise, and the invader is forced to abandon his
effort to "absorb" the Christians. Anthony is led away to be fed
to the octopuses in P'o-l'u and the community is brutally machine-
gunned to death. Only Torna survives to become, like the Apostles
after the Crucifixion, witness to Christ. The pentecostal Flame
says to him:

> But you, Torna, I will have you
> new-called to an old life: wounds
> have you, and lie near the grave,
> bleeding, lonely, and not even a priest
> but the least of your house? Yet I will settle in you
> a word, as private as you must, as public as you can,
> of the Holy Ghost, heard above Jerusalem;
> in you fidelity, in you magnanimity and mercy,
> in you justice, in you beatitude. Rise—
> up. . . up. . . up. . .
>
> (*He waves* Torna *to his feet.*)
>
> your wounds shall heal.
> You shall feel no hope; you shall be a hope
> and a witness to us between sea and sea,
> to the Maker of all and the only Taker of flesh.
> . . . .
> Our Lord will not leave himself without a witness,
> and that (in the full fitness of compassion) you.
> Now all begins again; go.
> You are all and you are enough; go.

[pp. 323–324]

Thus the play, like *Seed of Adam* (which the last lines recall), ends with a new beginning that reenacts the new beginning of the Pentecost. Paradoxically, the victory belongs not to P'o-l'u but to the Christians. Anthony, who forgives Alayu's apostasy and in turn is saved from apostasy by Alayu's assumption of his fear, has overcome the tentacles of P'o-l'u and goes to his death in the manner of Christ. In so doing he exemplifies the law of Exchange to which Torna bears witness, thus insuring the continuation of Christianity, which alone is capable of neutralizing the tentacles of external P'o-l'u.

In the "Author's Note" to *The House of the Octopus*, Charles Williams writes: "This play is not meant to have any direct topical relation. The name of P'o-l'u and the title of its Emperor were taken from certain earlier poems published before the outbreak of the Second World War. It is true that they were there referred to the sixth century, but it was unlikely that between the sixth and the twentieth centuries the state of P'o-l'u, within or without, has much changed; and I should regret now an identification with any particular nation or land which would then have been impossible. It is rather a spiritual threat than a mortal dominion." [8] Williams chooses here, and rightly, to emphasize the inner meaning of the action to forestall a purely topical interpretation of the play. But it is important to point out that the outer action does not exist merely for the sake of the inner meaning, that it has an integrity of its own. Though Williams did not conceive of P'o-l'u topically when he first hit upon the symbol in the thirties while working on the Taliessin poems, it is quite clear from his occasional writing that during the war years he had come to see Japan and Nazi Germany as contemporary manifestations of P'o-l'u: "The [Taliessin] poems had also imagined, far beyond the Empire, the antipodes of Empire. Ancient Chinese maps showed, at the point of Java, a harbor named P'o-l'u. It served as the mythical name of the opposite of civilized delight. My small myth imagined there octopuses, and a headless, self-sensational, obscene nightmare of the Divine Emperor walking, phosphorescent, on those waters. Unbelievably, the communiqués—well, they do not print P'o-l'u, but they do print Java. The octopus of an obscene Empire threw out its tentacles. If the Japanese had only attacked the West, one could at least understand. But claiming to defend the East they had also attacked the East. Those tentacles waved, a thousand miles and four years deep, in China. There was, there, a kind of lie in the soul. The myth of the Christian Empire of man's whole structure at least applied to any man. The German myth applied only to Germans, and the Japanese only to Japanese." [9]

And as the foregoing analysis suggests, it is in the particular contemporary action, the invasion by a twentieth-century P'o-l'u of a Pacific island during World War II, that the universal significances—both the idea of the perpetual vitality of the Church and the perpetual threat of spiritual pride or self-sufficiency (internal P'o-l'u) which can only be overcome by the law of Exchange—reside. In *The House of the Octopus*, in other words, Williams achieves an eternally present, a sacramental, action that his warning tends to obscure. By analogically integrating the past into the present and the broad into the specific event (Anthony's development) he creates at once an action which is of the modern world and of all time.

The achievement obviously is not completely satisfactory. The concrete contemporary surface is broken by the dream sequences induced by the Flame and the appearance of the spirit of Alayu; but in comparison with Williams' earlier drama, the play's contemporaneity (which, incidentally, includes a complex expression of the pervasive modern theme of metamorphosis), its subtle characterization (especially that of Anthony and the Marshal) and the essentially dramatic verse, all of which tend to give the universal a local habitation and a name, suggest a development in line with that of the Christian verse drama at large. Despite its difference in tone from, say, *The Family Reunion, The House of the Octopus* is unmistakably similar in its structural strategy to T. S. Eliot's pioneering play.

Christopher Fry's *A Sleep of Prisoners* (1951) remains something of an enigma of the modern verse drama. The few critics who have commented on the play have drawn uneasy and, on the whole, unsatisfactory conclusions about its form and content. Of these, the majority have condemned the play for its thematic obscurity and formal confusion. Even those who, like Gerald Weales and Derek Stanford,[10] have found it to be a positive achievement both in subject and design have failed to clearly reveal why. The cause of this critical *impasse* lies in a failure to diagnose Fry's essential strategy. By regarding *A Sleep of Prisoners* as a departure from the mode of the "secular" seasonal comedies which precede it, the critics have ignored the key which unlocks both its meaning and form and releases the power inhering in them. I am referring to Fry's definition of comedy, which, paradoxically, is more applicable to *Sleep* than to the seasonal comedies with which it is usually associated.

The conventional interpretation of Fry's concept of comedy is that the pattern it traces is a redemption of joy from the *ennui* of life in a world where the "enormous miracle" has been "domesticated."[11] As Monroe K. Spears observes: "The debasement of [the traditional concept of comedy—the 'ridicule of vices and follies, upholding the civilized norm against the individual's wilful departure from it'] into ridicule of virtue and idealism as against cynical 'realism' and worldly materialism seems to be Mr. Fry's specific target. In contrast, he wishes to make custom, convention, common sense, worldly wisdom ridiculous, to redeem joy from these low companions and associate it with the spiritual and idealistic."[12]

Certainly this is in a general way true, but it does not say very much and even obscures or distorts rather than clarifies Fry's particular strategy. What is lacking in the definition is a consideration of Fry's acknowledgment of Charles Williams' sacramental doctrine of the Way of the Affirmation of Images, which ultimately derives from Dante's concept of comedy. This oversight is all the more surprising since in the essay on comedy, Fry presents his central statements about the nature of comedy in terms of his interpretation of something Charles Williams once said to him which he received as an epiphany: ". . . it was shouted from the

tailboard of a moving bus, over the heads of pedestrians and bi-
cyclists outside the Midland Station, Oxford—'When we're dead
we shall have the sensation of having enjoyed life altogether, whatever has happened to us.' The distance between us widened, and
he leaned out into the space so that his voice should reach me:
'Even if we've been murdered, what a pleasure to have been capable of it!'; and, having spoken the words for comedy, away he
went like the revelation which almost came out of the ether.

He was not at all saying that everything is for the best in the
best of all possible worlds.[13] He was saying . . . that there is an
angle of experience where the dark is distilled into light: either
here or hereafter, in or out of time: where our tragic fate finds
itself with perfect pitch, and goes straight to the key which creation was composed in. And comedy senses and reaches out to this
experience. It says, in effect, that, groaning as we may be, we move
in the figure of a dance, and, so moving, we trace the outline of
the mystery." [14] Very broadly, then, Fry's essay is implicitly an
equation of comedy and Williams' *via positiva*, the Way of Affirmation. The world of comedy is thus not merely naturalistic; it
is infused with spirit and therefore meaning. It is, in other words,
a sacramental world. This general identification of Fry's concept
of comedy and Williams' sacramentalism has been noted.[15] But
as Fry's interpretation of Williams' words reveals, there appears
to be more of Williams' thought in the essay than the conception
of the Way of Affirmation. There is also a clear suggestion of the
doctrine of the Incarnation, which by redeeming the fallen world
and transfiguring the horror of evil into a paradoxical good or, in
Fry's words, by distilling the dark into light, establishes the Way
of Affirmation as the way of comedy. Thus comedy, Fry says, "is
an escape, not from Truth but from despair; a narrow escape into
faith." [16] This suggests the paradoxical *felix culpa* pattern which
the protagonists of Williams' plays trace. Like them (consider
Chelmsford or *Cranmer*, for example), the protagonists of comedy,
according to Fry, "have to unmortify themselves: to affirm life
and assimilate death and persevere in joy. Their hearts must be
as determined as the phoenix, what burns must also light and

renew: not by a vulnerable optimism but by a hard-won maturity of delight, by the intuition of comedy, a patience declaring the solvency of good." [17] In suffering evil they discover that "they move in the figure of a dance, and so moving, . . . trace the outline of the mystery"; they catch, that is, a glimpse of the eternal design operating in time, of the Incarnation, which as Cymen says (echoing Eliot's "point of intersection") in Fry's Canterbury Festival play, *Thor with Angels* (1948), renders "our lonely flesh / Welcome to creation." [18]

Further, Fry's conception of human action as a figured dance that traces the outline of the mystery puts him, at least here, squarely in the tradition of figural imitation. For it implies that time and eternity are simultaneous and therefore that the temporal human act is an analogue or incarnation of the eternal design.

Now in the seasonal plays, Fry's idea of comedy turns out to be something quite different. In these, Fry is apparently reluctant to invoke the Incarnation. On the thematic level, the protagonists— Dynamene in *A Phoenix Too Frequent*, Thomas Mendip in *The Lady's Not for Burning*, the Duke in *Venus Observed*, and Richard Gettner in *The Dark Is Light Enough*—trace the comic pattern from contempt for the world and despair to affirmation of a sacramental universe, but the affirmation does not have its source in the discovery of the possibility that the Incarnation redeems time. As a result, the resolution of these plays becomes what Fry wishes to avoid at all costs: "a vulnerable optimism," which sentimentally denies the existence of evil.[19] In Charles Williams' drama, the protagonist is driven by events to the point of self-awareness; by thus acknowledging his inability to make temporal life meaningful, he receives, in the moment of deepest anguish and doubt, the existential intuition of the Incarnation, which redeems the world and renders it purposeful. Thus his joyous affirmation of life is essentially dramatic. For it arises out of an awareness of evil and the accompanying despair. The new vision, that is, *integrates* evil into the world and despair into the affirmation without in the least minimizing their reality. In this way, Williams achieves an aesthetically satisfying dramatic paradox. But in Fry's seasonal comedies the protagonist leaps into affirmation and in the process tacitly, if not directly, denies the existence of evil. He putatively burns in the fires of mortality, but curiously their flame, in Yeats's words, "cannot singe a sleeve."

Nor does Fry fulfill in the seasonal comedies the formal implications of the sacramental view of time suggested in the essay on comedy. Though like Eliot he imitates events which involve more or less ordinary people rather than kings and princes, he apparently feels, along with the Georgian poet-dramatists of the first part of the century, that the contemporary world is essentially unpoetic. Thus Fry relies on the distance of history for the "poetry" of a dramatic action.[20] Nor does he, like Eliot in *Murder in the Cathedral,* render the historical action genuinely symbolic— simultaneously historical and universal—by integrating into it analogous pasts which suggest the relevance of the historical action for the present. At best the action in the seasonal comedies becomes, somewhat in the manner of, say, Arthur Miller's *The Crucible,* a decorative image that illustrates a rationally derived contemporary theme, that of existential alienation, of "man's / Estrangement in a world / Where everything else conforms." [21] The historical image thus has utility but no integrity of its own. Unlike Arthur Miller, however, who never lets the audience forget that his play is about a contemporary issue, Fry too often buries the theme by irrelevancies of action and by the use of language the buoyancy of which cuts across its somberness. Thus in the last analysis, Fry's seasonal comedies tend to be neither contemporary nor historical, but rather to fall into the limbo of fantasy.[22]

A *Sleep of Prisoners,* on the other hand, comes very close to fulfilling the sacramental implications of Fry's essay on comedy. The discovery of the Incarnation lies at the thematic center of this play of contemporary life, and this doctrine, in turn, provides the *raison d'être* of its formal motion. Thus its form and content locate *Sleep* in the category under discussion. It is the failure to perceive the integral relation between the Christic content and form that has led critics to condemn the play as obscure and thus to deny its place among the masterpieces of verse drama in our century.

In *A Sleep of Prisoners*, Fry departs from his usual mode of projecting events in the context of the past. Instead, like T. S. Eliot and the Mercury poets, he presents a contemporary action into which the remote past (the Biblical archetypes) is integrated. This integration is achieved by means of a dream technique in which the contemporary characters identify themselves in their sleep with Biblical figures whose characters and circumstances are analogous to their own. On the surface, this technique might suggest contemporary expressionistic dramatic practice (and it is a measure of Fry's achievement that it does convey contemporaneity); actually, the device has its source, as we shall see, in a much older tradition—the tradition of medieval dramatic realism—which comes to Fry by way of his discovery of the aesthetic implications of the Incarnation.

The contemporary action of *A Sleep of Prisoners* takes place some time during World War II and involves four British enlisted men, Corporal Adams, Private Meadows, Private King, and Private Able, who have been captured and temporarily interned by the enemy in a church behind the lines. With the ambiguous causes and the impersonal violence of modern war as background, the action presents the efforts of these four ordinary soldiers to come to grips with and resolve their difficult situation. Though it involves all four men, the central conflict focuses on Peter Able and David King, whose differing reactions to their plight reflect the essential dilemma of modern man.

The nature of this dilemma is established in the opening moments of the play. Able is in the organ loft ironically playing "Now the day is over." Unable to understand his friend's apparent indifference to their situation, King becomes angry. And when Able, in a mock sermon on the war, includes "the Towzers" (the Germans) as "Dearly beloved brothers / In a general muck-up," [23] and points to King's fury as "An example of the bestial passions that beset mankind" (p. 7), his anger explodes into an irrational, murderous attack on Able, which is frustrated by Corporal Adams and Private Meadows.

The contemporary action, then, defines the basic antinomies that the archetypal dreams will reenact, develop, and resolve. In the moment before his attack, King diagnoses Able's essential weakness:

> Any damn where he makes himself at home.
> The world blows up, there's Pete there in the festering
> Bomb-hole making cups of tea. I've had it
> Week after week till I'm sick. Don't let's mind
> What happens to anybody, don't let's object to anything,
> Let's give the dirty towzers a cigarette,
> There's nothing on earth worth getting warmed up about!
> It doesn't matter who's on top, make yourself at home.
>
> [p. 6]

Able, the passive man, or more inclusively, the "angelist"—King calls Able a "suffering god's body" (p. 14) and refers to him as "Angel-sick" (p. 15) in the Cain and Abel dream sequence—concludes that life in time is "a mystery to me" (p. 7) and seeks reality in a spiritual realm; he is not only incapable of commitment to problems of the present but is also in danger of becoming cynical about them. But in the ensuing assault on Able, King reveals his own weakness: his engagement, his commitment to the present, precludes reflection and leads to blind hatred and violence. As Meadows says after he and Adams have separated the two:

> I see the world in you very well. 'Tisn't
> Your meaning, but you're a clumsy, wall-eyed bulldozer.
> You don't know what you're hitting.
>
> [p. 7]

Ultimately, then, Fry's purpose is to present, through King and Able, not only the familiar conflict between the opposites which confront man in the contemporary world—between the claims of commitment and detachment, action and passivity [24]—but also and simultaneously the conflict between the basic opposites which confront man perennially—between the claims of time and eternity, body and soul, the way of affirmation and the way of negation. This theme is appropriately focused by Corporal Adams, the indecisive man, when as Adam, he cries out after Cain has murdered Abel:

> Pinioned here, when out of my body
> I made them both, the fury and the suffering,
> The fury, the suffering, the two ways
> Which here spreadeagle me.

[p. 18]

When the four prisoners are bedded down for the night, the dream sequence begins. Induced by the church setting and the tensions of the waking action, including its verbal motifs of warfare, these dreams take the form of Biblical analogues of King's murderous attack on Able and progress parallel to the chronological development of the Old Testament, a progress which entails a development in the perception of deity from the wrathful Jehovah to the incarnate God of Love. According to Fry, each prisoner "in his own dream speaks as at heart he is, not as he believes himself to be." [25] Each dream, in other words, is projected from a more fully realized point of view than that possessed by the dreamer in his waking actions.

The first dream is that of Tim Meadows, who becomes God faced with Cain's murder of Abel. It begins with God's confrontation of Adam (Corporal Adams), who rehearses the Fall and reveals the agonizing predicament of man. Without instructions for the future, he is incapable of retracing the elusive way back to Paradise and considers himself a prisoner of time in the fallen world. Thus he is forced to rely on his sons to "reconcile us to our exile" (p. 16), and this leads to the conflict between Cain (David King) and Abel (Peter Able).

In the ensuing agon, Cain defines the human condition from a naturalistic point of view. Man is a self-sufficient animal and his purpose is to survive by avoiding pain and pursuing the pleasures of the senses:

> . . . What you'll do
> Is lose us life altogether.
> Amply the animal is Cain, thank God,
> As he was meant to be: a huskular strapling
> With all his passions about him. . . .

[p. 14]

Abel, on the other hand, sees man's predicament from an idealistic point of view. He scorns Cain's oversimplified hedonism since it reduces man's efforts to "our two-footed prosperity" (p. 15) and the time process to a progressive "ravening" (p. 15). For him, apparently, though Fry is vague here, reality resides elsewhere than in the time world, and thus, as Stanford observes, "there is no point in treating the reality we have to the homage of that serious respect which should properly be reserved for the true one." [26]

When Abel wins the dice game which the antagonists play to determine whom God favors, Cain, sensing a conspiracy against the actualities of mortal life, rejects God and in a fit of rage murders Abel. Thus he fulfills the ultimate demand of his naturalism and reveals the horror implicit in it. For there is no resolution in his act. Instead he has transformed the world into a jungle where man is both hunter and prey. This is the judgment that God pronounces on Cain:

> . . . Cage of the world
> Holds your prowling. Howl, Cain, jackal afraid.
> And nowhere, Cain, nowhere
> Escape the fear of what men fear in you.

[pp. 19–20]

For Meadows, then, David King's doctrine of action has its source in a hedonism which inevitably ends in blind violence and is thus a continuation of Adam's fall in the sense that it denies God and perpetuates killing as the basic pattern of existence in the world. Meadows' dream vision, however, is limited. Despite his sharp insight into King's real self, he fails to perceive the complexity of the problem. For him David-Cain is patently the principle of evil and Peter-Abel the principle of good. He does not see that Abel's flippant passivity hides an evasive angelism. There is partial truth in Cain's complaint that

>   . . . I loved life
> With a good rage you gave me. And how much better
> Did Abel do? He set up his heart
> Against your government of flesh.
>
> [p. 20]

Fry's point of view appears to be that Meadows' dream judgment is primitive, that of an Old Testament civilization in which love has not developed or is denied as a moral-religious category.

Cain's troubled guilt, which manifests itself as a feeling that he himself is now the hunted, leads into David's dream, which re-enacts the act of violence in terms of King David's assassination of his son Absalom through the agency of his subordinate Joab.[27] This time, however, the action is projected from a political rather than a metaphysical perspective.

In the dream, King David (David King), who "keeps the earth" (p. 21), sees the world he has labored to put in order threatened by his enemies. Among them is his son, Absalom (Peter Able), whom he loves but also fears because the young man refuses to see "Hell . . . making straight toward us" (p. 23) preferring to "leapfrog over" the "bent and heavily burdened" "world's back" (p. 22). Against Absalom's callous indifference, David opposes the principle of action, that "Living is Caring" (p. 23), and asserts the necessity of commitment:

>   . . . The indecisions
> Have to be decided. Who's against us
> Reeks to God. . . .
>
> [pp. 23–24]

When David fails to persuade Absalom that action defines human life, he tries to make him a soldier of the good cause by force. But Absalom escapes the nightmare he is being dragged into, which Joab (Corporal Adams), David's obedient strong man, defines as "Humanity's" (p. 25), and flees to the camp of the enemy.

Interpreting this as a betrayal, David tacitly commands Joab to assassinate Absalom by giving him orders to attack the enemy. But when the command is fulfilled, David, like Cain, does not gain the victory, and thus the release, he had hoped for. Instead he is consumed by a deep sense of guilt and he comes to see that the murder he has committed in behalf of order is still an act of sin.

In King's dream, then, the motive behind the act of violence is political expediency. There is some development in the point of view in that the instinctive and brutal hatred of Cain has given over to reason, but the evolution is far from complete. Reason negates the motive of love and puts action on the level of calculation. Thus it fails to satisfy the essential nature of man and to bring a sense of reconciliation with the world.

The third dream, which reenacts the Old Testament story of Abraham and Isaac, is Peter Able's. Of the three, it is the least clearly related to the present action, but an analogy and development is discernible. In the dream Able sees himself as the sacrificial victim, Isaac, and David as the agent of the sacrifice, Abraham. Abraham regards the beauty that the young Isaac sees in the world as a "Lying gentleness, a thin veil over / The long scars from the nails of the warring hearts" (p. 31). He believes sacrifice to be a law of nature and God. God

> Takes evil to inoculate our lives
> Against infectious evil. We'll go on.
> I am history's wish and must come true,
> And I shall hate so long as hate
> Is history, though, God, it drives
> My life away like a beaten dog. . . .
>
> [p. 31]

Despite his love for Isaac and his inability to "forgive necessity" (p. 32), he must sacrifice him for the sake of the world, though Fry does not make it clear how such a sacrifice will benefit mankind.

Isaac, on the other hand, cannot accept Abraham's interpretation of the human condition as an imprisonment in the world's darkness. He asserts the glory of light and claims freedom. But it is clear that his vision is evasive, that behind his claim lies the desire to escape the world as it really is:

> . . . Breath
> And light are cool together now.
> The earth is all transparent, but too deep
> To see down to its bed.

[p. 29]

At the moment Abraham is about to plunge the knife into Isaac's heart in fulfillment of the law of necessity, an angel of God (Corporal Adams) intervenes with "new instructions" (p. 32): the ram caught in the thicket is to be sacrificed in Isaac's place. The purpose of God apparently is to complete both Abraham's and Isaac's half vision—to make Abraham see that man is not the prisoner of necessity but free and to make Isaac see that despite man's freedom from necessity, he is by nature bound to his fellow men. To Abraham's question, "Shall I / Undo the cords?" the angel replies:

> These particular. But never all.
> There's no loosening, since men with men
> Are like the knotted sea. Lift him down
> From the stone to the grass again, and, even so free,
> Yet he will find the angry cities hold him.

[p. 33]

But neither Abraham nor Isaac perceive the full import of this redemption. Abraham is relieved but has nothing more to say; Isaac attributes his salvation to chance.

In projecting a dream God who is so different from the God of Meadows' dream, one who provides man with free will yet demands commitment to this world, Peter Able is moving toward a resolution of the problem of action and suffering. But the development is unconscious. The lesson of the long night is yet incomplete.

The fourth and last dream is that of Corporal Adams, though as it progresses, it "changes to a state of thought entered into by all the sleeping men, as though, sharing their prison life, they shared, for a few moments of the night, their sleeping life also." [28] The dream begins with Adams adrift at sea. Presently he is joined by King and Able and it becomes apparent that the three are prisoners on a forced march. Able is exhausted and on the verge of dropping out. He is indifferent to the threat of execution, seeing death as "a bit of rest" (p. 38). But King and Adams will not allow him the luxury of death:

> . . . Dave and I will be
> Your anchor, boy: keep you from drifting
> Away where you're not wanted yet.
>
> [p. 38]

Suddenly, the three discover that they are in a prison and that somehow they have become the three Biblical characters of the Book of Daniel, Shadrach, Meshach, and Abednego, about to be burned alive in the fiery furnace. Once again each reiterates his fundamental attitude, though with less confidence now.

At this point they perceive that they are being inspected by the commandant of the prison, Nebuchadnezzar, and his aides. Though we do not see these figures, Able's comment on the "bastard language" (p. 42) they speak ("Police on earth. Aggression is the better / Part of Allah." p. 42) suggests Nebuchadnezzar's significance. He is the symbol of the modern state, which transforms human values into meaningless slogans, thus ritualizing human sacrifice and making men unknowing prisoners and victims of dubious causes.

Thus helplessly bound, they begin to feel the flames which "Every damn forest in the world / Has fallen to make" (p. 43)—the purgatorial fires (including those of the atomic bomb) of life in time. They fall in agony and submission to their knees, but in that moment discern through the flames the fourth figure of the Biblical episode (Meadows), to whose identity we will return. On being challenged, he first *"crows like a cock"* then answers

that he is Man under God's command (p. 44). And when one of
the prisoners asks the mysterious figure if they can come through
the flame, he replies: "If you have / the patience and the love"
(p. 44). These are the moral categories of the basic opposites of
the play, which from the point of view of King and Able are incompatible. But as the fourth figure continues to answer the
prisoners' questions, it becomes clearer that they are not.

In a speech which recalls the angel's remarks in the Abraham-
Isaac dream, the Stranger first defines love as commitment to time
and to one's fellow men:

> . . . there's not a skipping soul
> On the loneliest goat-path who is not
> Hugged into this, the human shambles.
> And whatever happens on the farthest pitch,
> To the sand-man in the desert or the island-man in the sea,
> Concerns us very soon. . . .
>
> [p. 45]

King takes this as a justification of his view, since it implies the
necessity of action against evil. But when the figure goes on to
reject King's kind of action, "The cures that never cure" (p. 46)
rehearsed in the dreams, and refers to the patience, the suffering,
of the Biblical heroes Shadrach, Meshach, and Abednego—"Figures of wisdom back in the old sorrows / Hold and wait for ever."
(p. 46)—he comes to see, by the analogy of his own situation, the
necessity of suffering:

> So help me, in
> The stresses of this furnace I can see
> To be strong beyond all actions is the strength
> To have. . . .
>
> [p. 46]

The lesson, however, is incomplete; for this way, he realizes, means
the extinction of his humanity:

> . . . But how do men and forbearance meet?
> A stone forbears when the wheel goes over, but that
> Is death to the flesh.
>
> [p. 46]

Then as the three prisoners discover that the flames are men ("Breath and blood chokes and burns us," p. 44), the fourth figure resolves the dilemma. Man should hate evil deeds, not the men who commit them. For

> No man's in vain. Each man who dies,
> Dies the world with him.
> O forgive us our deaths in all their ways
> Whether of action or of heart
> And make us live in all things living.
>
> [pp. 46–47]

Love of life, then, is the power that "blesses," that releases man from the bondage of the world without separation from it. This love is not Cain's hedonism, nor King David's political expediency, nor Abraham's necessity, all of which are "powers that ruin" (p. 47), modes of the death wish. This love is simultaneously active and passive, since it means one must suffer life's evils and still find life mysteriously good. The resolution, in other words, is an undogmatic version of the Christian paradox grounded in the Incarnation that the fallen world, that evil itself, is transformed into good by genuine sacrifice. When Peter expresses the Kierkegaardian absurdity of such a paradoxical belief—"The blaze of this fire / Is wider than any man's imagination. / It goes beyond any stretch of the heart." (p. 47)—the fourth figure restates the resolution in terms of the advantages of the violent and evil-ridden present:

> The human heart can go to the lengths of God.
> Dark and cold we may be, but this
> Is no winter now. The frozen misery
> Of centuries breaks, cracks, begins to move,
> The thunder is the thunder of the floes,
> The thaw, the flood, the upstart Spring.
> Thank God our time is now when wrong
> Comes up to face us everywhere,
> Never to leave us till we take
> The longest stride of soul men ever took.

> Affairs are now soul size.
> The enterprise
> Is exploration into God,
>
> [p. 48]

Here is the sacramental (which is also the existential) paradox: winter by its very nature is the promise of spring; darkness of light; evil of good; and despair of belief.

Returning once again to King and Able, we see that in viewing action and passion as opposites, they ultimately imply the discontinuity of time and eternity. Both are thus death-centered in that the immersion in a time world devoid of spirit destroys human significance, transforms man into an object, and the effort to achieve spiritual significance by circumventing the time world destroys man's humanity. The fourth figure maintains that the way of salvation lies in the reconciliation of action and passion on the ultimate analogy of the reconciliation of time and eternity; his way thus preserves meaning and manhood. This, of course, is the sacramental resolution which has its source in the Incarnation of Christ. As John Ferguson observes in his analysis of *A Sleep of Prisoners*: "In some sense David stands for the flesh and Peter for the spirit, if we remember that Christianity is an incarnational religion and does not set flesh against the spirit but seeks that both shall be sanctified. Both David and Peter are wrong. David is wrong in that he externalizes evil and refuses to recognize it within himself. Peter is wrong because his failure to commit himself is not constructive and positive, but fundamentally escapist. David lives 'after the flesh,' Peter tries not even to live 'in the flesh'; therefore neither is incarnational. Each is wrong. . . . Each has a lesson to learn. The last sounds of the play, the church-clock and the bugle, indicate the fusion of the two ways." [29]

This brings up and suggests the answer to the question of the identity of the fourth figure. Fry has said, rather coyly, that Meadows in this dream is "human nature with hope." [30] What he ultimately means is that he is God in the person of Christ or, at any rate a *figura Christi*. (The fourth figure in the Biblical episode from the Book of Daniel is traditionally interpreted as a prefiguration of Christ.[31]) This is suggested by his sacramental resolution of the antinomies that torture the main figures in the drama. It is enforced by the traditionally Christic imagery of the cock whose call heralds the coming of morning (and related imagery of the striking hour) which is integrated into the action of this final episode. The figure's first gesture, we recall, is to crow like a cock and immediately thereafter to introduce himself as Man under God's command. Adams refers to him as the "cockeyed son / Of heaven" (p. 45) and King as "the crowing son of heaven" who "Thinks we can make a morning" (p. 47). The suggestion is definitively established at the end of the play when the four prisoners, having awakened and commented on the dream they shared, return to sleep as the morning breaks:

MEADOWS   It began to feel like the end of the world
       With all your bunks giving up their dead.

ADAMS   Well, sleep, I suppose.

DAVID   Yeh. God bless.

PETER   Rest you merry.

MEADOWS   Hope so.

         (They settle down. The church clock strikes. A
         bugle sounds in the distance.)
                                                    [p. 49]

The references to the old Christian song at the moment of reveille (as well as the simultaneous sounding of the church clock and the bugle noted by Ferguson) brings into focus all the symbols of the new sacramental life. We become aware that the long and painful night has been Christmas Eve and that Christ has been reborn in a church behind the German lines.

Like the heroes of Charles Williams' plays, those of *A Sleep of Prisoners* discover the possibility of the Incarnation and suddenly see the tortured and chaotic movements of their agonized experience as the "figure of a dance" which traces "the outline of the mystery." The fires of the world of *Sleep*, unlike those of the seasonal comedies, burn painfully, but now they become the means of renewal. The protagonists, like the fiery phoenix—the most pervasive image of Fry's drama—are reborn in the earthly flames. Thus the play becomes in the words of Fry's interpretation of Charles Williams the imitation of an "angle of experience" where "the dark is distilled into light."

Furthermore, the sacramental resolution in the Nativity accounts for the dream technique that shapes the pluralistic form of the play. Derek Stanford asserts that the "natural comparison of this method is . . . with some of the German Expressionist dramatists, such as Wedekind and Toller." [32] But it becomes obvious from analysis of the play's theme and comparison with the form of other Christian plays of contemporary life that closer at hand is the typological or figural method of medieval mystery drama, which has become the prevailing imitative principle of the contemporary Christian verse drama movement. The action in the present is a reenactment of the archetype of sacrifice that recurs over and over again in Biblical myth and legend and culminates in the sacrifice of Christ. But since the New Testament, which is implicit in the fourth figure of the fiery furnace dream, reveals new understanding of the nature of sacrifice, the first pole of the *figura* in *A Sleep of Prisoners* is the combined stories of Cain and Abel, David and Absalom, Abraham and Isaac, and Shadrach, Meshach, and Abednego; that is, the whole span of history from Cain's crime to the end of Old Testament times. It is this developing movement which, by its analogous relationship to the movement in the German church-prison from the beginning to the end of a night of sleep, illuminates the contemporary action and gives it a symbolic dimension which transfigures its mere presentness into a universal image without destroying its contemporary identity. It is also this movement which makes *A Sleep of Prisoners* Fry's finest achievement.

In his review of the play, Joseph Wood Krutch notes that Fry deliberately avoids giving a local habitation and a name to the dramatic action in order to universalize its meaning.[33] This is not the case at all. The world of *Sleep* is, on the contrary, deliberately particularized. The time is meant to be World War II and the

prisoners British Tommies incarcerated in German territory. This
is clearly indicated by the verbal and visual imagery of modern
warfare that pervades the play and the peculiarly contemporary
British idiom and rhythms of the poetry:

DAVID   How d'you feel now, Pete?

PETER   Beautiful.

DAVID   Why don't
    You do some slaughtering sometimes? Why always
    Leave it to me? Got no blood you can heat
    Up or something?—I didn't hurt you, did I,
    Pete? How d'you feel?

PETER (*almost asleep*)   Um? Fine.

DAVID (*Taking off* PETER's *socks for him*)   The world's got to have
    us. Things go wrong.
    We've got to finish the dirty towzers. It's been
    A festering day, and I'm stinking tired. See you
    Tomorrow.

                                  [p. 9]

    This is true even of the dream sequences. Here, however, the
speech is often distorted in the Joycean manner (though sometimes without the sharp Joycean wit) to give verisimilitude to the
dream situations:

    We could see our own shapes, near enough,
    But not the road. The road kept on dividing
    Every yard or so. Makes it long.
    We expected nothing like it, sir.
    Ill-equipped, naked as the day,
    It was all over and the world was on us
    Before we had time to take cover.

                                  [p. 12]

Like Gerard Manley Hopkins and W. H. Auden, Fry often makes
his characters refer to God as "Sir," a mode of address that suggests the relationship to be one between an enlisted man and a

commanding officer. This is in keeping with the contemporary image Fry is creating and also with the military imagery that carries the burden of the play's meaning.

It is worth reemphasizing that the criticism of drama which claims that the achievement of universal values depends on abstracting characters and situations from the particular is the product of a world view that assumes a division between concrete reality and value and ultimately between time and eternity. Like Eliot, Williams, and the Mercury poets, Fry assumes (in this play at least) a sacramental universe in which the opposites are reconciled and thus expresses the universal *in* the particular, the past *in* the present. This in Fry is a late development. Though all his plays have in some ways a contemporary ring, only in *A Sleep of Prisoners* does he manage to avoid the uncontemporary poetic diction without sacrificing the sense of affirmation of the world which constitutes his basic theme. In this play, then, the aesthetic of the Incarnation clearly provides him with direction.

A Sleep of Prisoners, however, has limitations. Like Duncan's *This Way to the Tomb*, the juxtaposition of past and present results in a rhetorical rather than a poetic structure. Unassimilated into the present action, the past, that is, the Biblical myths, unlike the Christian and Greek myths of Eliot's plays, come dangerously close to becoming illustrative and ornamental metaphors which "heighten" the effect of the contemporary action rather than genuinely poetic images.

The main problem, however, lies in Fry's loose use of point of view in each dream. Though he has said that each character "in his own dream, speaks as at heart he is, not as he believes himself to be," the distinction between the contemporary man and his revelatory Biblical analogue is never quite clear. As a result, the dreams lack the logic of dreaming, the Freudian element of compensation, and thus a sense of verisimilitude. More important, however, the particular point of view of each dream is not sufficiently clear. The first three seem like repetitions of the same theme rather than developments in the understanding of each dreamer. As a result the resolution in the last dream appears to be arbitrary despite Fry's insistence that the play "moves from division to unity." [34]

But these are minor failures of the poet as craftsman, not of the operative aesthetic behind the form, and they do not obscure the levels of the action. As in the plays of the Mercury poets we are able to see how the sacramental principle is capable of infusing poetry into the unpoetic contemporary scene.

10

CHRISTIAN VERSE DRAMA AND THE HUMANISTIC LITERARY IMAGINATION

> A *new humanism* . . . *must remake anthropology. It must discover the rehabilitation and the "dignification" of the creature not in a species of isolation, thus enclosing the creature within itself, but in an opening up of the creature to the universe of the divine and the suprarational. And as a matter of fact such a task implies a work of sanctification of the profane and the temporal. It means the discovery of a more profound and real sense of the dignity of the human person. . . . Such a humanism, which considers man in the integrality of his natural and supernatural being and which sets no* a priori *limits to the descent of the divine into man, could be termed the humanism of the* Incarnation.
>
> Jacques Maritain,
> *The Twilight of Civilization*

It is commonly charged against the Christian drama that it must necessarily be propagandistic. Echoing the view expressed by Henry Arthur Jones over a half century earlier, Nevill Coghill writes: "A Christian play . . . resembles a socialist or other politically governed play; it is *parti pris*, and committed to propaganda. It is a weapon of conversion and makes an assault on the will. In other words, it is something more than, and in a sense something hostile to, a work of art." [1] The Christian drama examined in the previous chapters certainly has its limitations, but that they reside in the desire to propagandize is not clearly justifiable.

Such a charge has validity if by propaganda one means the interpretation of human actions according to a vision of reality. But if this is the case, then every play that is not merely a photographic imitation of concrete reality is propagandistic; for even the so-called theater of the absurd of Samuel Beckett and Eugène Ionesco, to say nothing about the social drama of Arthur Miller, the epic drama of Berthold Brecht, and the existential drama of Albert Camus and Jean-Paul Sartre, is committed to an interpretation of the world, though it may be antithetical to that of Christianity. Obviously such an inclusive definition of propaganda is inadequate. A play is propagandistic, rather, when the image of the action is denied its integrity, its *"Thouness,"* and becomes an "It," when, that is to say, it is *used, like an object, as a means* to promote an idea—any idea—derived from intellectual analysis. If this is a genuine definition, the charge that Christian drama as such is inevitably propagandistic is patently unfair. For it fails to reveal a true understanding of the sacramentalism—which more than anything else attempts to fuse image and value—that underlies the contemporary Christian verse drama movement.

This movement, like any other, has produced, of course, particular propagandistic plays—plays that violate the sacramental aesthetic. But on the whole its development has been toward the achievement of a genuinely poetic dramatic art form. Despite the confusion of purpose among churchmen and amateur religious playwrights catalogued by Gerald Weales in *Religion in Modern British Drama*,[2] it should be apparent from the preceding chapters that the Christian verse drama movement has definitively, if only broadly, established the sacramental aesthetic as its operative principle and thus has acknowledged the integrity of the dramatic image. The ideal drama envisaged by sacramentalism is the imitation of a human action which is at once of the present and of the past and, by analogy, of the future; at once, that is, concrete and universal. It is the projection of a particular and realistic image which reveals the unique condition of man in the twentieth century, without evading the accumulated knowledge of the post-Christian period, and simultaneously reflects the permanent condition of man in the universe. In Eliot's words, it is both a motion and a stillness. The imitated action is not an illustration of a universal; it is rather an enactment or better a discovery of it. It is, in short, an action which appeals to the inclusive histrionic sensibility, not to the intelligence or to the senses only.

It is true that the Christian verse drama falls short of this ideal. Though it has, as I have shown, moved generally in the direction of contemporaneity and realism both in the action and in the verse, no playwright of the group, with the possible exception of T. S. Eliot, has been able fully to achieve that difficult integration of concrete reality and value, of image and significance, which engages the whole man. But this failure does not warrant the charge that this drama is propagandistic. For as we have seen again and again, the artistic fusion of past and present and therefore of concrete and universal is immanent if not actual in these plays. It is usually conceptualized in the form even though it may not be completely objectified in the action. The immediate intention of the poet is obviously the achievement of artistic synthesis, not of religious propaganda.

The source of the Christian dramatists' failure to fuse dramatic image and significance completely lies elsewhere than in their desire to proselytize. The most obvious answer to the problem is that the individual playwrights lack dramatic genius. This is, of course, true, especially of amateurs such as Philip W. Turner and Freda Collins and even of some professionals such as Dorothy Sayers and Christopher Hassall. But when one considers the partial achievements of poets with sensibilities as authentically dramatic as T. S. Eliot, Charles Williams, Christopher Fry, and Ronald Duncan, it becomes evident that an equally significant, if more elusive, source of the failure lies outside the individual dramatist in the society for which he is writing, or, at any rate, in the difficult relationship between the Christian dramatist and the post-Christian modern world, in which God either has been domesticated or has died or has withdrawn.

Unlike Shakespeare, who could assume an audience which thought and felt within the framework of the Christian world order and was aware of the correspondences between man and universe, microcosm and macrocosm, an audience, that is, with its sacramental imagination more or less still intact, the modern Christian poet-dramatist inhabits a world in which the Christian scheme is on the whole either radically denied or accepted in a diluted form as a means of evading the implications of contemporary knowledge, and thus he must address an audience whose imagination is essentially naturalistic. Shakespeare, as T. S. Eliot has observed, was therefore free to employ all his creative energies in representing the human action,[3] whereas the modern Christian dramatist must expend a vast amount of energy in remaking the Christian myth within the confines of his form, an activity that invariably manifests itself in the more or less overt assertion of theology in the work, thus tipping the balance between image and significance in favor of the latter. This is not to say that Shakespeare arrived at the unconscious use of myth or underpattern immediately, without first going through the stage of self-consciousness. In the early Henry VI plays and in *Richard III*, for example, the morality pattern clearly obtrudes at the expense of the human image. But for Shakespeare the failure, one suspects, is primarily a matter of learning his craft. By the time of *Hamlet* and the great tragedies, that pattern has become the soul of an organic and concrete world and rarely reveals its structure. Better off than a Goethe, who, according to Eliot, unlike the Elizabethans, had to impose a philosophy on his drama and thus render his form "a means," [4] or than a Yeats, who had to create his own private myth and thus deny the public function of drama, the contemporary Christian poet-dramatist does not, however, have the advantages of a Shakespeare. His problem is not merely a matter of craft but also and in a sense primarily a matter of audience.

Another way of putting the problem is that the contemporary situation compels the Christian dramatist to project his image of the human predicament from the self-conscious point of view of his commitment. Despite Eliot's desire for "a literature which should be unconsciously, rather than deliberately and defiantly Christian" [5]—a desire, incidentally, that reveals his deep awareness of the pressure to be self-conscious—the disintegration of the Christian tradition has imposed an undesired certainty on the Christian dramatist's art. As George Every observes: "There are particular difficulties in the creation of good modern Christian art. . . . It is not easy to hold orthodox doctrine in a world which is secularized and unbelieving, without throwing a contentious emphasis on those elements in the orthodox faith which the modern world rejects, or diluting orthodoxy with humanism in an effort to make it intelligible again." [6]

This deliberateness or defiance tends to minimize the sense of genuine search and discovery in the dramatic action. Again the contrast with Shakespeare is instructive. The Elizabethan dramatist was not a prophet nor did he have to assume the persona of a prophet or a perfect Christian. His traditional world afforded him the opportunity to be a man writing for other men. Thus he was capable of *exploration* and of projecting sin and damnation or redemption as a felt experience. When the Shakespearean protagonist arrives at the point of decision, it is a real and painful, an existential choice that he must make. On the other hand, because the contemporary Christian dramatist must adopt the role of certainty, must underscore the value of his Christianity, he finds it difficult to render the dark element psychologically and aesthetically attractive without giving the impression of being academic. Thus, for example, when the protagonist, whether it is Becket in *Murder in the Cathedral* or the director in *The Shadow Factory*, reaches the point of decision, the choice is often not quite real enough. In the case of Shakespeare, there is rarely anything in the action which suggests the arbitrary and reveals the dramatist's hand. We thus feel the genuineness and respond accordingly. The modern Christian dramatist, however, despite his effort to naturalize the pattern of sin and redemption, tends to reveal himself in the action, to intellectualize the concrete experience.

Although the failure of the contemporary Christian verse dramatists to integrate completely the two realms of existence and essence is generally apparent in the foregoing analyses of the plays, it will be useful to classify the formal techniques that contribute to the overall impression. Such a classification not only serves to define the limitations of this body of drama specifically and to suggest their focal source, but also to summarize the essential development of the movement.

The techniques in question fall under three broad though ultimately related categories: (1) the image of the action; (2) the chorus and other links with the audience; and (3) the dramatic verse. These may appear to be arbitrary, but actually they represent the three focal areas of the drama with which the Christian dramatist has been most concerned in his effort to achieve multivocality.

In the first category, the image of the action, the earliest technique is that of the figural juxtaposition of past and present actions in order to suggest a sense of the presentness of the past and thus to give a symbolic dimension to the contemporary image of ordinary life. This is the technique of the early pageants *The Rock* and *Judgement at Chelmsford*. The integrity of both images, however, is only conceptual. For the overt presentation of the historical or mythical action focuses attention on the analogy. As a result the structural pattern—the common pattern which defines the dramatic action—becomes more important than the images.

It was in part the realization that the technique of juxtaposition was essentially a rhetorical rather than a poetic formal device that led to the rediscovery of the figural method of imitation whereby the older past is integrated into a historical action by verbal references as in the cases of *Murder in the Cathedral* and *The Zeal of Thy House*. By this method the double action of the earlier technique of juxtaposition becomes a unified dramatic whole and the structural pattern more a part of the action. But because the analogy of the two pasts points to the present, that is, implies the relevance of the action to the contemporary world, the pattern still overshadows the image of the action.

At this point in the development of the figural method of imitation, the Christian dramatist begins to perceive the real implications of the Christian concept of time for the drama. He sees that the idea of an eternal present ultimately means that the past inheres in the present and thus demands the integration of the past—which in the case of T. S. Eliot includes Greek myth and Christian narrative—into a concrete image of ordinary contemporary life. Thus what begins as a uniquely contemporary and particular human action comes, theoretically at least, in the course of the plot to assume simultaneously a universal significance. But even in these late plays—with the exception perhaps of Eliot's *The Elder Statesman*—the structural pattern lies too close to the surface of the action. This can be seen, for example, in *The Family Reunion*, where the Greek myth of Orestes threatens to overwhelm the contemporary drawing room action; in *The Shadow Factory*, where, despite Mrs. Ridler's effort to naturalize the Nativity, the birth asserts itself overtly to focalize the structure of the contemporary action; and in the *House of the Octopus* and *The Old Man of the Mountains*, where the miraculous intrudes on the naturalistic contemporary action to define its significance. In each case the dramatist seems to force the pattern because he is not sure that his audience will discover it in the action. As a result of his self-consciousness the action becomes something less than an incarnation of the pattern, an image which is more intellectually apprehended than wholly experienced.

This self-consciousness also underlies the various uses to which the chorus and other links with the audience are put. The theoretical function of these choric devices is to dissolve the naturalistic time mind of the contemporary audience and to reactivate its sacramental imagination. But in the earliest phase of the movement, the chorus tends to become simply the author's means of directly assaulting or satirizing the modern audience's naturalistic perception and its materialistic values. Thus in *The Rock*, the voice of the Temporal Church, which conceptually is supposed to point to the sacramental structure of the action—to the analogous relation of past and present—often becomes, as Eliot himself has admitted, sheer harangue. Even when the chorus in this early stage is not browbeating the audience but participating in the action, it is still to the sacramental structure rather than to the human action that it points. When, for example, the choric Sees in Williams' *Judgement at Chelmsford* explain the related concepts of Exchange and Romantic Love to the protagonist, one feels that these speeches are not so much a part of the action as they are a means of defining it. They represent the authorial voice restating the Christian myth and clarifying its significance in order to teach the audience how to see the action. Only when the chorus becomes an integral participant in the events of the play, as in *Murder in the Cathedral,* does its function become dramatic. But being generalized, "a type of the common man," the chorus, even in this case, tends to emphasize the pattern of its development at the expense of the concrete particulars of the action.[7]

A more subtle and generally later development of the chorus is that initiated by Charles Williams and adopted by T. S. Eliot and the other Christian dramatists whereby the passive choric group becomes an ambiguous agent of the action. As both antagonist and omniscient commentator, who forces the protagonist into acknowledging his guilt and thus into discovering the possibility of a Redemption which transforms evil into good, chaos into order, he indirectly distinguishes for the audience the sacramental from the naturalistic action. But this figure—whether the Skeleton of *Cranmer of Canterbury,* the Furies of *The Family Reunion* or Mephistopheles of *The Devil to Pay,* on the one hand, or Harcourt-Reilly of *The Cocktail Party* or the Verger of *The Missing Bridegroom,* on the other—inevitably gives in some degree the impression that he is a supernatural agent and his activity a conspiratorial stratagem. Thus, however imposing an artistic device the figure may be, his function necessarily forces the *felix culpa* pattern into prominence. Only when the figure is completely naturalized, as in the cases of the artist in Anne Ridler's *The Shadow Factory* and Mr. Gomez and Mrs. Carghill in Eliot's *The Elder Statesman,* does the pattern he symbolizes come to inhere in the human action.

Finally, the main limitation of the Christian verse drama has been its reluctance to break fully from the tradition of the *Stiltrennung,* the axiom that the imitation of religious experience requires the use of the high style, a special poetic language and metric commensurate with the elevation of the subject matter. This limitation is ultimately the result of a failure to perceive fully what the medieval realist knew instinctively: that the Incarnation demands the use of the third voice of poetry, which means that the verse should be not only dramatic, the verbal gesture of encounter, but that it should also represent the idiom and rhythms of the present and an imagery drawn from the whole range of contemporary experience.

From the beginning the poets of the Christian verse drama movement reacted against the archaic Biblical and Shakespearean diction and syntax of the sentimental and romantic religious drama of the first decades of the century, but this early achievement did not get much beyond a pruning of the pious archaic personal pronouns and syntactical inversions. The verse remained essentially traditional and rhetorical rather than dramatic, its metric imitating the Elizabethan blank verse line and its imagery drawn from the Shakespearean reservoir established and conventionalized by the Romantic and Victorian poets. Not until T. S. Eliot turned to the drama did the verse assume a distinctly contemporary ring. In the dramatic dialogue (as opposed to the choral passages) of *Murder in the Cathedral* there appears a genuine suggestion of the rhythm, syntax, and imagery of the modern world. But because Eliot was imitating a historical event, he was reluctant to render the verse in completely realistic and contemporary terms. The style, as he has said, "had to be neutral, committed neither to the present nor to the past." In practice, furthermore, the suggestion of contemporaneity is minimized by a more emphatic suggestion of the past in the medieval alliterative technique, in the rhyming, and above all, in the elevated diction. Despite, then, the intimation of real contemporary speech, the neutral style is closer to the high than to the low and, to the extent that it is, it tends to detract from the immediacy of the action.

The rendering of the verse dialogue in the neutral style is generally as far as most of the Christian verse dramatists have been willing to go in the direction of contemporaneity and concreteness. Unsure of the ability of a modern audience to perceive multivocality in a verse in the low style, they have been reluctant to take the risk of misinterpretation, of being taken as naturalistic dramatists. This, apparently, is even true of some dramatists who have had the sense and courage to cast their actions in the present. Thus, for example, Norman Nicholson in *The Old Man of the Mountains*, Charles Williams in *The House of the Octopus* and Christopher Fry in *A Sleep of Prisoners* have failed to fulfill in their verse the demands implicit in the sacramental aesthetic (though Fry does come close). Despite its real advance over the verse of the early Christian drama, and in the cases of Williams and Fry over that of their earlier work, the verse in these plays lacks the concrete immediacy and the dramatic gestures of the totally committed contemporary voice. It is still in the neutral style.

Even in the later stage, when T. S. Eliot and, under his influence, Anne Ridler and Ronald Duncan go beyond the neutral style, self-consciousness inhibits the full realization of a dramatic verse that mirrors the language of contemporary conversation. This is evident, for example, in the choral verse and "lyrical duets" of Eliot's *The Family Reunion*, the rhapsodic rhetoric of Duncan's Don Juan plays, and in the liturgical chants of Anne Ridler's *The Shadow Factory*, which in each case break the otherwise naturalistic texture of the action. It is as if the poet distrusts the medium he has developed, as if he is unsure that he has not reduced poetry to versified prose.

Only T. S. Eliot in *The Elder Statesman* takes the risk—it is a measure of his greatness—of carrying the implications for verse of the sacramental aesthetic to their logical conclusion and thus achieves a consistently low style, a *sermo remissus* which, on the analogy of the Incarnation, is characterized by a sublime *humilitas* and which conveys the voices of unique contemporary men who are also and simultaneously Men in a universal setting.

In summarizing the achievement of the Christian verse drama movement, one can say that it has been much more successful in realizing the implications of sacramentalism for content than for

form. From the beginning the drama reveals in its themes a conscious recognition that the Incarnation demands a vision of life
in which time is the authentic vehicle of divine disclosure. Torn
between the claims of time and eternity, body and soul, evil and
good, the Christian hero, whether he is a historical or contemporary figure, discovers in his anguish that the way of salvation
necessitates an existential immersion in time, an authentic acknowledgment of the present life of concreteness, which in turn
transfigures the irregular fallen world of temporality into a paradoxical order and thus bestows dignity and worth on its things
and events. In some of these plays the conflict is presented in terms
of the abstractions of good and evil (good standing for eternity
and evil for the fallen world of time), but more often it is projected
in the ascetic terms *de contemptu mundi* and the modern fragmented world diagnosed by contemporary existential thought. In
either case the resolution involves sacramental synthesis.

But the corresponding realization of the humanism of the Incarnation in the form of a fully concrete and particular action has
been a slower process. Malcolm Ross has said that a "sacramental
re-entry into the experience, the knowledge, the sensibility, of our
time can scarcely be effected by any effort, however fervent, to
restore a Christian idiom appropriate to another and vastly different cultural movement." [8] However, one detects behind the variety
of experimental work a reluctance to commit the action to a finite
form and concrete contemporary idiom for fear of returning to
precisely what the Christian dramatists wished to avoid, the uni-
vocality of naturalism. But as hesitant as this experimental work
has been, it is clear that the movement has proceeded in the direction of sacramental realism and contemporaneity. The integrated sacramental form has been established to the extent that
it has at least become a norm for professional poet-dramatists. No
serious Christian dramatist writing for the commercial theater can
now return to the earlier mode of juxtaposition without considering the late achievements of T. S. Eliot, Charles Williams, and
the Mercury poets. Nor can those who write specifically for the
church, whether in the form of the Nativity or the history, return

to the pious religiosity, to the "paper Gothic," [9] of the turn of the century religious drama.

It is true, as Gerald Weales says, that a great many bad religious plays have been written (and continue to be written) in England since the revival of religious drama.[10] But this is not an unnatural phenomenon, nor does it imply that Christianity and dramatic art are incompatible. More plays of low than of high quality are written during the life span of any dramatic movement. Like all forms of art, the drama requires natural genius as well as a viable aesthetic, and thus far—it has been a relatively short period—only a few Christian dramatists of considerable talent have emerged. What needs clarification and emphasis, however, is that the movement which began with the initiation of the Canterbury Festival in 1928 has not only created an atmosphere in England which makes the writing of religious verse plays both for the church and commercial theater possible but also, and more important, has, in returning to the main stream of the English dramatic tradition, pointed the way to the creation of public poetic drama that is relevant to contemporary life in an age in which it has been said that public poetic drama is dead. For the time being the momentum which reached its climax in the 1950's has partially subsided. Nevertheless there is still considerable interest in the possibility of creating significant Christian verse plays. When the new cycle of creative activity is begun by a new generation of Christian poets, their task will have been rendered easier.

Despite the limitations, then, the achievement of the Christian verse drama movement remains impressive. This is clearly revealed in a number of the plays examined and also in the general development of the movement. In comparison with the form of the slice of life drama of contemporary English playwrights like John Osborne and Shelagh Delaney, on the one hand, and on the other, the anti-drama of the theater of the Absurd—the latest manifestations of the naturalistic and angelic imaginations—the developed form of the Christian drama is more genuinely dramatic and poetic. Perhaps none of the Christian poets has written plays which generate the theatrical excitement of *Look Back in Anger* and *A*

Taste of Honey or of *The Birthday Party;* but if the drama at its best is something more than a representation of an image of raw adolescent life or of the hallucinatory life of a particular subconscious, that is, more than the apotheosis of the novel, they have produced a new drama that also reminds us of the great dramatic tradition of the West, which begins with the Greeks and ends with the Elizabethans.

Contemporary criticism has on the whole failed to take cognizance of the significant implications of the rediscovery of the sacramental aesthetic. Oriented by secular humanistic aesthetic principles, this criticism (particularly that of the drama, which despite the impact of the New Criticism, still evaluates dramatic works according to the norms of the first decades of the century) tends to dismiss Christian art as irrelevant to the issues that confront modern man. F. R. Leavis, for instance, one of the few important contemporary critics to comment on other Christian poets than T. S. Eliot, writes of George Every's assertion of Charles Williams' significant status: "Charles Williams is ostensibly inspired by Christian doctrine, but if you approach as a literary critic, unstiffened by the determination to 'discriminate Christianly,' or if you approach merely with ordinary sensitiveness and good sense, you can hardly fail to see that Williams' preoccupation with the 'horror of evil' is evidence of an arrest at the schoolboy (and -girl) stage rather than of spiritual maturity, and that his dealings in 'myth,' mystery, the occult, and the supernatural belong essentially to the ethos of the thriller. To pass off his writings as spiritually edifying is to promote the opposite of spiritual health." [11] Though Leavis is apparently speaking about Williams' poetry and novels, what he says clearly applies to the drama as well. It is a criticism which indicates little understanding of the Christian doctrine that inspired Williams' art. And one cannot help feel from the rather impatient tone and sweeping generalities of the passage that Leavis' critical assumptions preclude genuine understanding.

The humanistic bias against Christian art, of which the passage by Mr. Leavis is an example, has its source, no doubt, in the effort to protect art against Puritan intolerance, or, what is in this case much the same thing, to defend against the pressures of the Christian ascetic tradition the essential subject matter of art: the life of man in the concrete world of time. There was, of course, real justification for this bias in the past. But it has been rendered anachronistic by the sacramental aesthetic, which, as we have seen, is not only capable of, but also insists on, embracing the chaotic and painfully problematic temporal plane. Indeed, it is one of the most curious ironies of our confused time that the humanist imagination which refuses to acknowledge Christian art because of its alleged contempt for time is itself becoming, in the form of the solipsistic angelic imagination—the imagination of Marcel Proust, of Virginia Woolf, of Guillaume Apollinaire, of Eugène Ionesco, to name but a few—the greatest antagonist of time and, as such, a far more serious threat to art, at least the art that imitates the life of man in time, than the Christian or rather sacramental imagination. As Nathan Scott has significantly observed, ". . . we are confronting . . . a major phenomenon of contemporary cultural life, a sharply reversive movement: for, whereas the [contemporary] literary imagination often wants very much to escape from time altogether and to find a timeless eternity, the theological imagination, on the other hand—to the perplexed astonishment, one imagines, of an old-fashioned secularism, relying on its conventional critiques of 'other-worldliness'—begins to regard the eternity of the traditional Christian view as largely misconceived, if not chimerical." [12] The Christian verse dramatists with which this book has been concerned have not committed themselves to a view of time as radical as that held by the theologians—Oscar Cullman, Rudolph Bultmann, Paul Tillich, Dietrich Bonhoeffer, among others—to whom Scott refers. But there is little question that both in theory and practice they have, minimally, acknowledged the dignity and worth of life in time.

APPENDIX:

The Canterbury Festivals

Under the direction of Dean Bell, the first official Canterbury Festival was given in 1929 and included productions of *Everyman* before the West Door of the Cathedral and Marlowe's *Dr. Faustus* in the Chapter House by Nugent Moncks and his Maddermarket Players. In 1930, after Dean Bell was appointed Bishop of the diocese of Chichester, the Friends of Canterbury Cathedral assumed at his request responsibility for the festival. The same year saw the production of Shakespeare's *Henry IV*, Part 2, and *Henry V* by the Ben Greet Company. The festivals of 1931 and 1932 were makeshift affairs, but in 1933 Tennyson's *Becket*, arranged according to the demands of the Chapter House and produced by Eileen Thorndyke, met the artistic standards set by Dean Bell and established the importance of the festival. In 1934, the Friends, encouraged by Bishop Bell, turned once more to a living poet—Laurence Binyon—for their annual festival production. His contribution, *The Young King* (written earlier in 1924 but completely revised for the Canterbury Festival), which is based on the life of Henry II's rebellious son, takes up where Tennyson's *Becket* leaves off and thus established the subsequent practice of presenting plays dealing with the history of the Cathedral. It was not, however, until the Friends of Canterbury Cathedral, again on the suggestion of Bishop Bell (who in 1934 had seen the pageant play *The Rock* in London and had recognized the potential drama in the work of the new playwright), commissioned T. S. Eliot to write a religious verse play for the 1935 season that the Canterbury Festival became an occasion for the presentation of original contemporary Christian verse drama.

The following, kindly provided by the late Mrs. E. M. Thoseby, Steward of the Friends of Canterbury Cathedral, is a list of the major Canterbury Festival productions since 1928.

1928　　*The Coming of Christ,* John Masefield

1929　　*Everyman* and Christopher Marlowe's *Tragical History of Dr. Faustus*
　　　　　　Producer: Nugent Moncks

1930　　*Henry IV,* Part 2, and *Henry V,* William Shakespeare
　　　　　　Producer: Sir Philip Ben Greet

1931　　———

1932　　*Becket,* Alfred Tennyson
　　　　　　Producer: Eileen Thorndyke

1933　　*Becket,* Alfred Tennyson
　　　　　　Producer: Eileen Thorndyke

1934　　*The Young King,* Laurence Binyon
　　　　　　Producer: Eileen Thorndyke

1935　　*Murder in the Cathedral,* T. S. Eliot
　　　　　　Producer: E. Martin Browne
　　　　　　Becket: Robert Speaight

1936　　*Thomas Cranmer of Canterbury,* Charles Williams
　　　　　　Producer: E. Martin Browne
　　　　　　Cranmer: Robert Speaight

1937   *The Zeal of Thy House,* Dorothy Sayers
         Producer: Harcourt Williams, assisted by Frank Napier
         William of Sens: Harcourt Williams

1938   *Christ's Comet,* Christopher Hassall
         Producer: Michael MacOwen
         Artaban: Robert Speaight
         Melchior and Angel of the Tree: Christopher Casson

1939   *The Devil to Pay,* Dorothy Sayers
         Producer: Harcourt Williams
         Faustus: Harcourt Williams
         Mephistopheles: Frank Napier
         Christopher Wagner: Philip Hollingworth
         Music for songs and closing Chorus: Gerald Knight

THE WAR YEARS: No productions

1947   *Peasants' Priest,* Laurie Lee
         Producer: E. Martin Browne
         John Ball: Bernard Giles
         Songs by Gerald Knight

1948   *Thor with Angels,* Christopher Fry
         Producer: Christopher Fry
         Cymen: Michael Golden
         Clodesueda: Barbara Cavan

1949   *The Zeal of Thy House,* Dorothy Sayers   (repeat)
         Producer: Christopher Hassall
         William of Sens: Michael Goodliffe

1950   ———

1951   *The Makers of Violence,* Robert Gittings
         Producer: John Allen
         Archbishop Alphege: John Byron

1952   *The Drama of Our Festival Years:* Excerpts

1953   *His Eminence of England,* Hugh Ross Williamson
         Reginald Pole: Robert Speaight

1954   *The Man from Tuscany,* Cathedral Choristers—Festival Hall,
         London

1955   ———

1956   Drama and Poetry Recital: Sybil Thorndike and Lewis Casson

1957   ———

1958 *Christ's Comet,* Christopher Hassall   (repeat)
         Producer: E. Martin Browne

1959 ⸺

1960 *Everyman* (amateur production)

1961 ⸺

1962 A *Durable Fire,* Patric Dickinson

1963 *Noye's Fludde* (opera), Benjamin Britten

1964 *Murder in the Cathedral,* T. S. Eliot (amateur production)

1965 *The Boy from the Catacombs* (opera), Alan Rideout

1966 *Sons of Adam,* Philip Lamb (amateur production)

NOTES

CHAPTER 1

1 Lionel Trilling, *Matthew Arnold* (New York, 1955), p. 107.
2 T. S. Eliot, "The Waste Land," *The Complete Poems and Plays, 1909–1950* (New York, 1952), p. 38.
3 W. B. Yeats, "The Second Coming," *The Collected Poems of W. B. Yeats* (New York, 1956), pp. 184–185.
4 I am indebted to Nathan Scott's essay "The Broken Center: A Definition of the Crisis of Values in Modern Literature," *Chicago Review*, XIII, 2 (Summer, 1959), 182–202 (reprinted in *Symbolism in Religion and Literature*, ed. Rollo May [New York, 1961], pp. 178–200 and in *A Casebook on Existentialism*, ed. William V. Spanos [New York, 1966], pp. 162–183), not only for the lead that took me to Mannheim's book but also for his insights into what he calls, by way of Erich Kahler's *The Tower and the Abyss* (New York, 1957), "the existential experience" of contemporary literature.

5 For a general acknowledgment of T. S. Eliot's debt to Mannheim's thought, see Eliot's "Preface," *Notes towards the Definition of Culture* (New York, 1949), pp. 7 and 35 ff. See also Chapter 2 of this book.
6 Karl Mannheim, *Diagnosis of Our Time: Wartime Essays of a Sociologist* (London, 1943), pp. 134 ff.
7 For a discussion similar to that of Mannheim and Buber and other existentialists (but of more immediate interest to the subject of this book) on the difficulty of dialogue in contemporary life, see also Allen Tate, "The Man of Letters in the Modern World," *The Forlorn Demon: Didactic and Critical Essays* (Chicago, 1953), pp. 3–17.
8 Scott, "The Broken Center," p. 188.
9 Tate, *The Forlorn Demon*, pp. 37–38.
10 See William F. Lynch, S.J., *Christ and Apollo: The Dimensions of the Literary Imagination* (New York, 1960), p. 130. Father Lynch's respective terms for these species of perception are the "univocal" (which crushes the concrete reality and diversity out of being in its pursuit of sameness) and the "equivocal" (which negates sameness by perceiving only difference in being).
11 Jacques Maritain, "The Cartesian Heritage," *The Dream of Descartes*, tr. Mabelle L. Andison (New York, 1944), pp. 179–186.
12 The counterpart in the French theater of the symbolist poet is Alfred Jarry (1873–1907), whose notorious play *Ubu Roi* (1896) was, in part, a fulfillment of Mallarmé's demand for a theater that would be wholly un-French in its irrationality, with a story "freed of place, time, known characters"; for "the century, or our country that exalts it, has dissolved the myths by thought." Stéphane Mallarmé, "Richard Wagner, Rêverie d'un poète français," *Oeuvres* (Bibliothèque de la Pléiade, Paris, 1945), pp. 544–545, quoted in Martin Esslin, *The Theatre of the Absurd* (Garden City, 1961), p. 255.
13 See Edmund Wilson, *Axel's Castle* (New York, 1931); and Frank Kermode, *Romantic Image* (London, 1957).
14 Eugène Ionesco, "The Bald Soprano," *Four Plays*, tr. Donald M. Allen (New York, 1958), pp. 38, 40.
15 T. S. Eliot, "Tradition and the Individual Talent," *Selected Essays* (New York, 1950), p. 4.
16 W. B. Yeats, "The Cutting of an Agate," *Essays and Introductions* (New York, 1961), pp. 283–285.
17 Yeats's desire to achieve a sacramental drama can be seen in his successive efforts to integrate the primordial images of the Irish imagination within a mythic framework: first, in the plays that attempt to organize the traditional folk tales and legends within a loose occult system; later, in the transitional plays that organize the heroic Cuchulain matter (collected by Lady Gregory in *Cuchulain of Muirthemne*, 1902), within the embryonic tragic messianism out of which the system of *A Vision* emerged; and, finally, in those that organize various matters within the inclusive cyclic theology of *A Vision*, the work, as Herbert Howarth has pointed out in *The Irish Writers: Literature and Nationalism, 1880–1940* (New York, 1959), p. 221, that Yeats considered a sacred book, though not for Ireland.

CHAPTER 2

1 Laurence Irving, *The Canterbury Adventure: An Account of the Inception and Growth of the Friends of Canterbury Cathedral, 1928–1959* (Canterbury, no date), pp. 1–9. See Appendix for the history of the Canterbury Festival.
2 George Kennedy Bell, Lord Bishop of Chichester, "Speech on the Church and

Religious Drama," *The Chronicle of Convocation: Being a Record of the Proceedings of the Convocation of Canterbury, Session of January* 14, 15, *and* 16, 1958 (London, 1958), p. 83.

3 John Synge, "Preface," *The Playboy of the Western World,* in *The Complete Works* (New York, 1935), p. 4.

4 W. B. Yeats, *The Irish Dramatic Movement,* in *The Collected Works of William Butler Yeats* (Stratford-on-Avon, 1908), IV, 137.

5 T. S. Eliot, *Religious Drama: Mediaeval and Modern* (New York, 1954), unpaginated.

6 T. S. Eliot, *The Use of Poetry and the Use of Criticism: Studies in the Relation of Criticism to Poetry in England* (Cambridge, Mass., 1933), pp. 152–153.

7 *Ibid.,* p. 154.

8 Gordon Bottomley, "Poetry Seeks a New Home," *Theatre Arts Monthly,* XIII, 12 (December, 1929), 926. See also his "Poetry and the Contemporary Theatre," *Essays and Studies by Members of the English Association,* XIX, ed. D. Nichol Smith (Oxford, 1934), p. 140; and "Notes," *Scenes and Plays* (New York, 1929), p. 121.

9 Eliot, *Religious Drama.*

10 *Ibid.*

11 *Ibid.*

12 Henry Arthur Jones, "Religion and the Stage," reprinted from *Nineteenth Century Review,* XVII (January-June, 1885) in *The Renascence of the English Drama* (London, 1895), pp. 26–55.

13 *Ibid.,* pp. 39–40.

14 *Ibid.,* pp. 46–47.

15 Gerald Weales, *Religion in Modern English Drama* (Philadelphia, 1961), indicates the vastness of this diffuse and, on the whole, artistically worthless body of "religious" drama.

16 T. S. Eliot, "Ulysses, Order, and Myth," reprinted from *Dial* (1923) in *Forms of Modern Fiction,* ed. William Van O'Connor (Bloomington, 1959), pp. 123–124. See also T. S. Eliot, "Yeats," *On Poetry and Poets* (London, 1957), p. 260. For an even earlier statement of the need of a common system of referents see T. S. Eliot, "The Possibilities of a Poetic Drama," *The Sacred Wood: Essays on Poetry and Criticism* (New York, 1920), pp. 63–64.

17 Oscar Cullman, *Christ and Time: The Primitive Christian Conception of Time and History,* tr. Floyd V. Filson (London, 1962), p. 55.

18 *Ibid.,* pp. 51–60.

19 *Ibid.,* p. 55.

20 Nathan A. Scott, "Mimesis and Time in Modern Literature," *The Scope of Grace,* ed. Philip J. Hefner (Philadelphia, 1964), pp. 22–23.

21 Arthur Michael Ramsey, D.D., *An Era of Anglican Theology from Gore to Temple: The Development of Anglican Theology Between* Lux Mundi *and the Second World War,* 1889–1939 (New York, 1960), *passim.*

22 Scott, "Mimesis and Time," p. 21

23 William Temple, *Nature, Man and God: Being the Gifford Lectures Delivered in the University of Glasgow in the Academical Years* 1932–1933 *and* 1933–1934 (London, 1940), p. 431. It is interesting to notice that Archbishop Temple's pervasive use of the analogy of a work of art to arrive at the nature of the Creation has its literary counterpart in Dorothy Sayers' use of the Creation to arrive at the nature of a work of art. See Dorothy Sayers, *The Mind of the Maker* (New York, 1956).

24 Temple, *Nature, Man and God,* p. 448.

25 Scott, "Mimesis and Time," p. 21.

26 Malcolm MacKenzie Ross, *Poetry and Dogma: The Transfiguration of Eucharistic Symbols in Seventeenth Century English Poetry* (New Brunswick,

1954), pp. 9–10. The following discussion is indebted for much of its specific content to Professor Ross's chapters on the Christian aesthetic, "The Firmament of Symbol," pp. 3–27, and "History and Poetry," pp. 88–112; and Erich Auerbach, "Figura," *Scenes from the Drama of European Literature: Six Essays*, tr. Ralph Mannheim (New York, 1959), pp. 11–76. See also Nathan Scott, "Prolegomenon to a Christian Poetic," *Modern Literature and the Religious Frontier* (New York, 1958), pp. 46–65; and Charles Moorman, *Arthurian Triptych: Mythic Materials in Charles Williams, C. S. Lewis, and T. S. Eliot* (Berkeley, 1960).

27 The doctrine of the Trinity, of course, contains the Incarnation, but it is the latter from which the basic principles of the Christian aesthetic are derived. It could be said that, in a sense, the doctrine of the Three-Personed God, hierarchical yet coequal and coeternal, exists for the Incarnation; that is, to make it possible.

28 Ross, *Poetry and Dogma*, p. 10.

29 Erich Auerbach, *Mimesis: The Representation of Reality in Western Literature*, tr. Willard Trask (Garden City, 1957), p. 63.

30 *Ibid.*, pp. 131–132.

31 Ross, *Poetry and Dogma*, pp. 10–11.

32 *Ibid.*, p. 98.

33 Auerbach, "Figura," pp. 53–54.

34 *Ibid.*, p. 69.

35 *Ibid.*, pp. 59–60.

36 Hans Meyerhoff, *Time in Literature* (Berkeley, 1955), p. 111.

37 Auerbach, *Mimesis*, p. 136.

38 It is significant that Allen Tate relies heavily on Charles Williams' *The Figure of Beatrice: A Study in Dante* (New York, 1961) in his essay on Dante and that his definition of the "symbolic imagination" is essentially the same as the sacramental vision that characterizes Williams' literary theory and art.

39 Ross, *Poetry and Dogma*, p. 18.

40 Denis Donoghue, *The Third Voice: Modern British and American Verse Drama* (Princeton, 1959), p. 37. Of Yeats's earlier plays, particularly *The Shadowy Waters*, Mr. Donoghue has pointed out that their lack of solidity brings them "dangerously close to what Allen Tate has called the 'angelic fallacy.'" See also T. S. Eliot's "Yeats," *On Poetry and Poets*, in which he diagnoses this play in a similar way (p. 256), and Nathan Scott, "Prolegomenon to a Christian Poetic," *Modern Literature and the Religious Frontier* (New York, 1958), in which he writes that "Notwithstanding their frequent invocation of the dogma that 'existence precedes essence,' . . . it is, paradoxically, in [many existentialist writers] that the solipsistic idealism of the Cartesian age finally reaches a kind of dead end in the general declaration for absurdity . . ." (p. 59).

41 Francis Fergusson, "Myth and the Literary Scruple," *The Human Image in Dramatic Literature* (Garden City, 1957), pp. 163–164.

42 *Ibid.*, p. 164.

43 *Ibid.*, p. 172.

44 Ross, *Poetry and Dogma*, p. 88.

45 Fergusson, *The Human Image*, p. 174.

46 Weales, *Religion*, p. 107. Besides commissioning Masefield and founding the Friends of Canterbury Cathedral and the Canterbury Festival, he implemented the founding of the Religious Drama Society (1929), and also created a Religious Drama post in the Diocese of Chichester (1930), appointing E. Martin Browne as director. But that his function was essentially a formal one is indicated by the fact that although he was president of the Religious Drama Society from 1929, he attended his first General Meeting in 1954.

47 Karl Mannheim, "Towards a New Social Philosophy: A Challenge to Christian Thinkers by a Sociologist," *Diagnosis of Our Time: Wartime Essays of a Sociologist* (London, 1943), p. 100. According to the English theologian A. R. Vidler, Fellow and Dean of King's College, Cambridge, and editor of the controversial collection of essays *Soundings: Essays Concerning Christian Understanding*, "The Moot was thought up by the theologian J. H. Oldham. . . . It was the best group I have been a member of, and the most high-powered. In the Moot there were T. S. Eliot, Karl Mannheim, Middleton Murray—people like that. The Moot used to meet for long weekends three or four times a year. . . . The papers read there were circulated among the members. A very few of them found their way into print." Ved Mehta, "The New Theologian, II–The Ekklesia," *The New Yorker* (November 20, 1965), 64. Mannheim's chapter "Towards a New Social Philosophy: A Challenge to Christian Thinkers by a Sociologist" from *Diagnosis*, was without doubt one of the papers that got into print.

48 George Kennedy Bell, Lord Bishop of Chichester, "Sermon on *The Coming of Christ*" preached at Wittersham Parish Church on December 13, 1953. Compare this statement with Eliot's in *Religious Drama*: "It is not so much that the Christian Faith needs the drama [for its evangelizing possibilities] but that the drama needs the Christian Faith."

49 Bell, "Speech on the Church and Religious Drama," p. 83.

50 T. S. Eliot, *Selected Essays* (New York, 1950), p. 4. (My italics.)

51 See also Moorman, *Arthurian Triptych*, p. 130.

52 T. S. Eliot, *Four Quartets*, in *The Complete Poems and Plays, 1909–1950* (New York, 1952), p. 129.

53 T. S. Eliot, *The Rock: A Pageant Play* (London, 1934), p. 50.

54 Eliot, *Four Quartets*, pp. 118–119.

55 *Ibid.*, pp. 123–124.

56 "Introduction" to Charles Williams, *The Image of the City and Other Essays*, ed. Anne Ridler (London, 1958), p. xxxviii. The quotation within the quotation is from Coventry Patmore, *The Rod, the Root, and the Flower*, ed. Derek Patmore (London, 1950).

57 Williams, "Natural Goodness," *The Image of the City*, p. 78.

58 *Ibid.*, pp. 76–77.

59 Williams, "Sensuality and Substance," *The Image of the City*, p. 69.

60 Charles Williams, *Reason and Beauty in the Poetic Mind* (Oxford, 1933), p. 55. Williams attributes this definition to S. T. Coleridge, who in "The Statesman's Manual," *The Complete Works of Samuel Taylor Coleridge*, ed. W. G. T. Shedd (New York, 1860), I, 437–438, writes, "a symbol . . . is characterized by a translucence of the special in the individual, or of the general in the special, or of the universal in the general; above all by the translucence of the eternal through and in the temporal. It always partakes of the reality which it renders intelligible; and while it enunciates the whole, abides itself as a living part in that unity of which it is the representative." But it is obvious that Williams cites Coleridge as an authority, not as the source of the definition.

61 Williams, *Reason and Beauty*, p. 54. See C. S. Lewis, *The Allegory of Love: A Study in Medieval Tradition* (London, 1936), pp. 45–48, for a similar distinction between symbolism (or sacramentalism, as Mr. Lewis prefers to call it) and allegory.

62 It is interesting to note that Williams' interpretation of the status of Beatrice in *The New Life* and the *Divine Comedy* is similar to Erich Auerbach's. Williams writes: "It seems extraordinary that learned men should have discussed whether Beatrice was Theology, and thought that their affirmative

answer meant that Beatrice was not a woman. She is, of course, Theology because she is a woman. She is a given fact which has in two categories of experience two different names. But the fact itself is identical everywhere." *Reason and Beauty*, pp. 54–55. Auerbach writes: "The romantic realism of the nineteenth century overemphasized the human Beatrice. . . . Since then a reaction has set in; the new tendency is to do away with her entirely, to dissolve her in an assortment of increasingly subtle theological concepts. But actually there is no reality in such a choice. For Dante the literal meaning or historical reality of a figure stands in no contradiction to its profounder meaning, but precisely 'figures' it; the historical reality is not annulled, but confirmed and fulfilled by the deeper meaning. The Beatrice of the *Vita Nuova* is an earthly person; she really appeared to Dante. . . ." "Figura," p. 73. Similarly, in the *Comedy* "she is no *intellectus separatus*, no angel, but a blessed human being who will rise again in the flesh at the Last Judgement. Actually there is no dogmatic concept that would wholly describe her. . . ." "Figura," p. 74.

63 Williams, *Reason and Beauty*, p. 55.
64 *Ibid.*, p. 62.
65 Williams, "The Index of the Body," *The Image of the City*, pp. 80–87. By "index" Williams does not mean merely references to the whole but rather a list that contains in little the material that is treated at greater length in the text: "To treat the body as an index is to assume that, as in an index the verbal element—the *word* given—is the same as in the whole text, so in the physical structure of the greater index the element—the *quality* given —is the same as in the whole structure" (p. 82).
66 Moorman, *Arthurian Triptych*, p. 52.
67 S. L. Bethell, *The Cultural Revolution of the Seventeenth Century* (London, 1951). See also Theodore Spencer, *Shakespeare and the Nature of Man* (New York, 1949); E. M. W. Tillyard, *The Elizabethan World Picture*; and Patrick Crutwell, *The Shakespearean Moment and Its Place in the Poetry of the Seventeenth Century* (New York, 1960).
68 Williams, *The Image of the City*, p. 82.
69 Charles Williams, *The Descent of the Dove: The History of the Holy Spirit in the Church* (New York, 1956), pp. 69–70.
70 Charles Williams, *All Hallows' Eve* (London, 1945), pp. 167–168.
71 *The Book of the Blessed Dionysus Concerning the Divine Names*, vii, lect. 4, quoted in Raymond Preston, *"Four Quartets" Rehearsed: A Commentary on T. S. Eliot's Cycle of Poems* (New York, 1946), p. 16.
72 John Burnet's translation, quoted in Preston, *"Four Quartets" Rehearsed*, p. viii.
73 Williams, *The Descent of the Dove*, pp. 57–58.
74 Eliot, *Four Quartets*, p. 134.
75 *Ibid.*, p. 136.
76 Dorothy L. Sayers, "Towards a Christian Aesthetic," *Unpopular Opinions: Twenty-one Essays* (London, 1946), p. 39. Also printed in *Our Culture: Its Christian Roots and Present Crisis*, ed. V. A. Demant (London, 1947), pp. 50–69. See also *The Mind of the Maker*, in which Miss Sayers expands the subject matter of this essay into a full-length book. Besides Williams and Eliot, the sources of Miss Sayers' triple analogy include St. Augustine, St. Thomas Aquinas, Dante, Nicholas Berdyaev, and perhaps William Temple.
77 Sayers, "Towards a Christian Aesthetic," p. 37.
78 *Ibid.*, pp. 37–38.
79 *Ibid.*, p. 42.

CHAPTER 3

1 T. S. Eliot, "Poetry and Drama," *On Poetry and Poets* (London, 1957), p. 79. See also similar remarks on *The Rock* in "The Three Voices of Poetry," *On Poetry and Poets*, p. 91.

2 T. S. Eliot, *Religious Drama: Mediaeval and Modern* (New York, 1954), unpaginated.

3 Theodore Spencer, "Man's Spiritual Situation as Reflected in Modern Drama," *Spiritual Problems in Contemporary Literature*, ed. Stanley Romaine Hopper (New York, 1957), p. 53.

4 Gordon Bottomley, *Gruach*, in *Gruach and Britain's Daughter* (Boston, 1921), pp. 13–14.

5 W. B. Yeats, *The Shadowy Waters*, in *The Collected Plays of W. B. Yeats* (London, 1953), p. 167. See also Denis Donoghue, *The Third Voice: Modern British and American Verse Drama* (Princeton, 1959), p. 37.

6 Malcolm MacKenzie Ross, *Poetry and Dogma: The Transfiguration of Eucharistic Symbols in Seventeenth Century English Poetry* (New Brunswick, 1954), p. 89.

7 I derive this date from A. P. Rossiter, *English Drama from Early Times to the Elizabethans: Its Background, Origins and Developments* (London, 1950). Rossiter attributes the "masterly sketch of Pilate" to "the York realist, a rugged and tumultuous alliterator" whose "work is not earlier than 1400" (p. 67).

8 *The Second Trial Before Pilate: The Scourging and Condemnation* in *The York Cycle of Mystery Plays*, ed. and tr. J. S. Purvis (New York, 1957), pp. 259–260. For the original version, see *York Mystery Plays*, ed. Lucy Toulmin Smith (Oxford, 1885), pp. 320–321.

9 Terence Vale, "Lest One Good Custom," *Christian Drama*, I, 5 (February, 1948), 11. Vale's article reviews the twenty-fifth anniversary of Clay's pageant. His criticism of its flamboyance and its aura of pastness reflects the new approach to religious drama. But his interpretation of the new movement to achieve a truly timeless mode of experience as one leading toward a highly "stylized, conventionalized, and abstract" drama analogous to the Byzantine mosaics of San Appollinaire is misleading. Though it does reflect a tendency of the Christian drama movement, it does not recognize the operation, even in the early plays, of the sacramental aesthetic. His argument assumes the separation of time and eternity that sacramentalism reconciles and thus is a manifestation of the angelic imagination.

10 Gordon Bottomley, *The Acts of Saint Peter: A Cathedral Festival Play* (London, 1933), pp. 34–35. Further page references will be incorporated in the text in parentheses.

11 E. Martin Browne, in a review of *Poet and Painter, Being the Correspondence of Gordon Bottomley and Paul Nash, 1910–1946*, ed. Colleer Abbott and Anthony Bertram (London, 1955), *Drama*, 37 (Summer, 1955), 6–7.

12 Laurence Housman, *Little Plays of St. Francis: A Dramatic Cycle from the Life and Legend of St. Francis of Assisi* (New York, no date), p. 19.

13 T. S. Eliot, "Prefatory Note," *The Rock: A Pageant Play* (London, 1934), p. 5.

14 Derek Verschoyle, "Review of *The Rock*," *The Spectator*, 152 (June 1, 1934), 851.

15 T. S. Eliot, reply to a letter, *The Spectator* 152 (June 8, 1934), 887.

16 Denis Donoghue, for example, does not even mention the play in *The Third Voice: Modern British and American Verse Drama*. D. E. Jones, *The Plays of T. S. Eliot* (London, 1960), concludes, "*Sweeney Agonistes* and the choruses of *The Rock* were . . . only fragmentary essays in verse drama and hardly went beyond the problem of a suitable dramatic speech" (p. 48).

17 T. S. Eliot, "The Possibility of a Poetic Drama," *The Sacred Wood: Essays on Poetry and Criticism* (London, 1920), p. 70. See also T. S. Eliot, *The Use of Poetry and the Use of Criticism: Studies in the Relation of Criticism to Poetry in England* (Cambridge, Mass., 1933), pp. 152–154.

18 It is possible that Eliot's and his colleagues' portrayal of the modern workmen was influenced by the modern shepherds of John Masefield's *The Coming of Christ* (New York, 1928), whom they closely resemble. More generally, the workmen in T. S. Eliot's *The Rock* are reminiscent of the shepherds of the mystery tradition epitomized by the anonymous medieval *Second Shepherds' Play*.

19 Eliot, *The Rock*, p. 14. Further page references will be incorporated in the text in parentheses.

20 The idea expressed in Ethelbert's speech is the Cockney equivalent of the definition of the Incarnation given in the opening Chorus of Part II.

21 Giorgio Melchiori, *The Tightrope Walkers: Studies of Mannerism in Modern English Literature* (London, 1956), p. 127.

22 Verschoyle, "Review of *The Rock*," p. 851.

23 Eliot's adherence to the implications of the sacramental concept of time concerning knowledge is also seen in his incorporation of anthropological knowledge in the Chorus' account of the Creation and the development of the religious spirit in history that begins Part II of *The Rock*. It is also seen in his dealing with the problems of capitalism and unemployment and with those of communism and totalitarianism.

24 E. Martin Browne, "The Dramatic Verse of T. S. Eliot," *T. S. Eliot: A Symposium*, ed. Richard March and Tambimuttu (Chicago, 1949), pp. 197–198.

25 Charles Williams, "Prefatory Note," *Judgement at Chelmsford*, first edition (London, 1939), p. 3. The play, under the direction of Miss Phyllis Potter, Director of Religious Drama in the Diocese of Chelmsford, was to have been presented at the New Scala Theatre in London from September 23 to October 7, 1939, but the outbreak of war prevented production.

26 E. Martin Browne, "*Judgement at Chelmsford*," *Christian Drama* I, 4 (November, 1947), 2.

27 Charles Williams, *Judgement at Chelmsford*, in *Collected Plays*, ed. John Heath-Stubbs (London, 1963), p. 76. All future page references will be incorporated in the text in parentheses.

28 The influence of Dante's view of Virgil's Rome is obvious here. For an explication of Dante's figural interpretation of Augustan Rome see Erich Auerbach, *Mimesis: The Representation of Reality in Western Literature*, tr. Willard Trask (Garden City, 1957), pp. 170 ff.

29 John Heath-Stubbs, *Charles Williams: Writers and Their Work: 63*, ed. Bonamy Dobrée (London, 1955), p. 34.

30 The moment in which Constantius sees in Helena the New City, sees that their "two hearts / making a future from this quality of greatness / *shall strew time with a fresh order of perfection*, / a holy wisdom, sprung from Colchester and Rome, / redeemed flesh blazing with primordial glory— / Love our first child, and our second child / the tiaraed Augustus, woman and man in Victory" (pp. 135–136, my italics).

31 I have changed the order of Williams' syntax in order to retain the striking metaphor.

32 My italics.

33 This theme, which Williams expresses by the formula "All luck is good," is central to the poet's work—indeed, as I intend to show, to the drama of the Canterbury movement. Anne Ridler interprets the doctrine as follows: "Just as the Fall in each of us happens when we see good as evil, so the highest activity of love must be to transform even what we call evil into good. The

apparent co-existence of good and evil (in the world, in one person) is a
contradiction, an antinomy, which is the prime cause of conflicts in man's
soul." "Introduction," *The Image of the City and Other Essays* (London,
1958), p. xxxiii. Behind the transformation, of course, is the paradox of the
Fortunate Fall *(felix culpa)*, in which Adam's sin is seen as a positive event
in that it occasions the sacrifice of Christ and thus, through the manifestation of God's love, the salvation of man.

34 Eliot, *On Poetry and Poets*, p. 91.

35 Charles Williams, "Religious Drama," *The Image of the City and Other Essays*,
p. 58.

36 *Ibid.*, pp. 58–59.

37 My italics.

38 Job 1.7: "And the LORD said unto Satan, Whence comest thou? Then Satan
answered the LORD, and said, From going to and fro in the earth, and from
walking up and down in it." Williams exploits the suggestion in the Old
Testament story that Satan is God's agent, who brings man into encounter
with evil in order to generate existential commitment to the life of faith:
"But put forth thine hand now, and touch all that he hath, and he will
curse thee to thy face. And the LORD said unto Satan, Behold, all that he
hath is in thy power; only upon himself put not forth thine hand. So Satan
went forth from the presence of the LORD." Job 1.11–12. Further quotations
from the Bible in this book derive from the King James version unless otherwise noted.

39 Francis Fergusson, *The Idea of a Theater, a Study of Ten Plays: The Art of
Drama in Changing Perspective* (Princeton, 1949), p. 18. Fergusson derives
these terms from Kenneth Burke.

40 Anne Ridler, "Introduction," *Seed of Adam and Other Plays*, by Charles Williams (London, 1948), p. vi.

41 *Ibid.*

42 Since *Judgement* follows *Thomas Cranmer of Canterbury* in Williams' canon,
I postpone discussion of the dramatic verse of this period (which is different
from that of the *Cranmer* period) until Chapter 5, where the Nativity-
Morality *The House by the Stable* and its sequel *Grab and Grace*, to which
the verse of *Judgement at Chelmsford* is related, are discussed.

CHAPTER 4

1 Denis Donoghue, *The Third Voice: Modern British and American Verse Drama*
(Princeton, 1959), p. 76.

2 David E. Jones, *The Plays of T. S. Eliot* (London, 1960), p. 81.

3 Francis Fergusson, *The Idea of a Theater, a Study of Ten Plays: The Art of
Drama in Changing Perspective* (Princeton, 1949), pp. 211–212.

4 Jones, *Plays of T. S. Eliot*, p. 63.

5 Donoghue, *The Third Voice*, p. 85.

6 T. S. Eliot, *Murder in the Cathedral*, in *The Complete Poems and Plays, 1909–
1950* (New York, 1952), p. 184. Further page references will be incorporated
in the text in parentheses. See also p. 185, where Thomas' concluding contrast of the dead past with the present leads directly into the second temptation, which is oriented in the present.

7 T. S. Eliot, *Four Quartets*, in *The Complete Poems and Plays, 1909–1950* (New
York, 1952), p. 136.

8 William F. Lynch, "Theology and the Imagination: I," *Thought*, XXIX, 112
(March, 1954), 72. The analogy between Thomas' descent into time and

Christ's assumption of flesh is enforced by the parallel between their temptations. Lynch continues in the same passage, "His [Christ's] assumption of
finitude is complete and absolute. . . . And this decision, this assumption
of the path through the body, is made absolute and irrevocable in the scene
of the desert temptation where Christ tempted to the way of magic and
tricks and *the direct use of glory and the infinite* chooses the human way."
(My italics.)

9 Denis Donoghue's comment about the tempters is characteristic of the criticism
that fails to perceive the four tempters on the level of time: "The nature of
the Archbishop's character and of his past life is filled out by [the tempta-
tions]; his present spiritual condition is clarified, both to himself and to his
audience, by the fourth Tempter. These, then, are the functions of agents
whose presence in the play seems at first sight a rather trite association of
Thomas with the tempted Christ" (*The Third Voice*, p. 86). Seen on the
level of time, however, these encounters establish the figural dimension of
the play.

10 Louis L. Martz, "The Wheel and the Point: Aspects of Imagery and Theme in
Eliot's Later Poetry," *T. S. Eliot, a Selected Critique*, ed. Leonard Unger
(New York, 1948), p. 461.

11 Eliot, *Four Quartets*, p. 136.

12 Martz, "The Wheel and the Point," p. 458.

13 My italics.

14 See Chapter 2, pp. 27–34.

15 Here the analogy between Thomas and Christ is enforced by the reference to
Peter's denial of "his master."

16 Matthew xxi.8–9: "And a very great multitude spread their garments in the
way; and others cut down branches from the trees, and strawed them in
the way. And the multitudes that went before, and that followed, cried,
saying, Hosanna to the Son of David: Blessed is he that cometh in the name
of the Lord; Hosanna in the highest."

17 Erich Auerbach, "Figura," *Scenes from the Drama of European Literature: Six
Essays* (New York, 1959), pp. 63–64. See also Auerbach, *Mimesis: The
Representation of Reality in Western Literature* (Garden City, 1957), p. 13.

18 Auerbach, *Mimesis*, pp. 170 ff.

19 Malcolm MacKenzie Ross, *Poetry and Dogma: The Transfiguration of Eucharistic Symbols in Seventeenth Century English Poetry* (New Brunswick,
1954), p. 247.

20 Jones, *Plays of T. S. Eliot*, p. 75.

21 T. S. Eliot, "The Metaphysical Poets," *Selected Essays* (New York, 1950), p.
247.

22 Eliot, *Four Quartets*, p. 136.

23 Patricia M. Adair, "Mr. Eliot's *Murder in the Cathedral*," *Cambridge Journal*,
IV, 2 (November, 1950), 89.

24 Ronald Peacock, *The Poet in the Theater* (New York, 1946), p. 7.

25 See also pp. 211–212, where Thomas says to the Priests who are trying to defend him from the Knights:

You think me reckless, desperate and mad.
You argue by results, as this world does,
To settle if an act be good or bad.
You defer to the fact.

26 Hugh Kenner, *The Invisible Poet: T. S. Eliot* (New York, 1959), pp. 281–282.

27 Denis de Rougemont, "Religion and the Mission of the Artist," *Spiritual Problems in Contemporary Literature*, ed. Stanley Romaine Hopper (New York,
1957): "I define it [the nature of the work of art] as a *calculated trap for*

meditation, we see that the understanding of its nature is tied up with that of its end: a trap is made in order to capture something. In the work of art, nature and aim, essence and end, are inseparable. It is a question of a single and identical function, which is, to signify something by sensible means" (p. 177).

28 Fergusson, *Idea of a Theatre*, p. 217.

29 D. E. S. Maxwell, *The Poetry of T. S. Eliot* (London, 1952), p. 183.

30 Kenner, *Invisible Poet*, p. 283.

31 Janet Adam Smith, "Review of *Thomas Cranmer of Canterbury*," quoting the Canterbury Festival brochure, in the *London Times Literary Supplement* (June 20, 1936), 512.

32 Charles Williams, *Thomas Cranmer of Canterbury*, in *Collected Plays*, ed. John Heath-Stubbs (London, 1963), pp. 3–4. Further page references will be incorporated in the text in parentheses.

33 The allusion is to Walton's famous statement, in *The Life of Dr. John Donne*, about Donne's intellectual pride (he was "diverted by leaving that [study of law] and embracing the worst voluptuousness, a hydroptic immoderate desire of humane learning and languages"). The anachronism is another indication of the freedoms with time that sacramentalism allows the Christian dramatist to take.

34 Everywhere in Williams' work, the "webbed light of the glory" is a symbol of the integrated orders of being, the "co-inherence," which is grounded in the Incarnation.

35 Charles Williams, *He Came Down from Heaven and the Forgiveness of Sins* (London, 1950), pp. 20–21.

36 *Ibid.*, pp. 58–60.

37 As Alice M. Hadfield points out in her critical biography *An Introduction to Charles Williams* (London, 1959), p. 126, Williams began editing (for Oxford University Press) Kierkegaard's *Philosophical Fragments*, the first work by the Danish philosopher to be published in England, in 1935. This was the year that *Cranmer* was commissioned by the Friends of Canterbury Cathedral. Kierkegaard's work was published in May, 1936; *Cranmer* was produced in the summer of the same year. Thus Williams' reading of Kierkegaard, which, as Miss Hadfield notes, was enthusiastic, was simultaneous with the composition of the play.

38 David Roberts, *Existentialism and Religious Belief*, ed. Roger Hazelton (New York, 1959), p. 67. The following discussion of the Kierkegaardian progress is greatly indebted to Roberts' excellent commentary on the thought of Kierkegaard, which constitutes Chapters II, III, and IV of his book.

39 *Ibid.*, p. 67. Three further extracts from Roberts' exposition of Kierkegaard's ideas will serve to reveal the striking similarity between Cranmer's progress and that of the Christian as Kierkegaard sees it: (1) ". . . the trouble with metaphysics is that it cannot find a point of union between the Eternal and existence because it abstracts from existence; while the trouble with the aesthetic approach is that it also cannot find a point of union because it immerses itself in pure temporalism" (p. 72); (2) "A genuine remedy [for the human condition] requires a union of the temporal and the eternal which might be characterized as 'finding everlasting significance in the present moment'" (p. 67). This "point where Eternity touches Time" (p. 74) is, for Kierkegaard, the Incarnation: (3) ". . . Christianity has rightly diagnosed the problem of history when it seeks salvation, not by escape from temporality, in an Eternal meaning which by entering history, transforms it" (p. 75).

40 Martin Heidegger, *Being and Time*, tr. John Macquarrie and Edward Robinson (New York, 1962), pp. 296–299.

41 Stanley Romaine Hopper, *The Crisis of Faith* (Nashville, 1944), p. 126.

42 See Charles Williams' *Reason and Beauty in the Poetic Mind* (Oxford, 1933), pp. 48–49, for an interesting passage that throws light on the origins and meaning of Williams' recurrent choric figure. The ultimate mythic source of the Skeleton image is, no doubt, the figure of Satan in The Book of Job. As for the metaphor of the Skeleton as "Christ's back," Williams' source is the pervasive Biblical motif that man cannot perceive God directly but must come to Him through the mediation of experience, as, for example, in I Corinthians XIII.12: "For now we see through a glass, darkly." More specifically, Williams is alluding to Exodus XXXIII.20–23: "And he said, Thou canst not see my face: for there shall no man see me, and live. . . . And I will take away mine hand and thou shalt see my back parts: but my face shall not be seen." It is likely that Williams hit on the metaphor by way of John Milton's *The Christian Doctrine*, where both Exodus XXXIII.20–23, and I Corinthians XIII.12 are quoted together as evidence that knowledge of God "must be understood with reference to the imperfect comprehension of man." *Complete Poems and Major Prose*, ed. Merritt Y. Hughes (New York, 1957), p. 905. I am indebted to my student Jeremiah Lyons for referring me to the passage from Milton.

43 Dorothy Sayers, *The Devil to Pay* (New York, 1939), pp. 138–139. See also Sayers, *The Mind of the Maker* (New York, 1956), pp. 98–107, which not only reveals Charles Williams' influence but also provides a gloss to this passage.

44 Smith, "Review of *Thomas Cranmer of Canterbury*," *Criterion*, XVI, 62 (October, 1936), 141.

45 *Ibid.*

46 Anne Ridler, "Introduction," *Seed of Adam and Other Plays*, by Charles Williams (London, 1948), p. vii.

47 *Judgement at Chelmsford*, which follows *Cranmer*, is an advance in this respect.

48 "Introduction," *The Image of the City and Other Essays*, by Charles Williams (London, 1958), p. lxix.

49 Bonamy Dobrée, "Poetic Drama in England Today," *Southern Review*, IV (1938–1939), 595.

50 Williams had written several plays of minor importance prior to 1936 (*The Masque of the Manuscript*, 1927; *A Myth of Shakespeare*, 1928; *The Masque of Perusal*, 1929; *The Masque of the Termination of Copyright*, 1930; *The Witch, The Chaste Wanton*, and *The Rite of Passion*, collected in *Three Plays*, 1931). Between these and *Cranmer* a significant development occurred in his verse. The early plays, as Anne Ridler notes in her introduction to *Seed of Adam* (p. v) and in her introduction to *The Image of the City* (p. lxiii), are written in blank verse after the model of Lascelles Abercrombie. From 1931 to 1935, Williams, under the influence of Eliot's free line in *The Rock* and particularly of Hopkins' alliterative verse, was experimenting with a new verse form in his Arthurian poems in an effort to bring the power of sound back into harmony with intellect. The result was the poetry of *Cranmer*.

51 Gervase of Canterbury, "History of the Burning and Repair of the Church of Canterbury," *A Documentary History of Art*, I, ed. Elizabeth G. Holt (Garden City, 1957), pp. 52–62.

52 *Ibid.*, p. 54.

53 See Chapter 2, pp. 48–50.

54 Sayers, "Preface," *The Devil to Pay* (New York, 1939), p. 5.

55 The closeness of Miss Sayers' adherence to the character of William and to the significance of the action as it is suggested by Gervase is revealed by the following passage from the chronicle: "Amongst the other workmen there

had come a certain William of Sens, a man active and ready, and as a workman most skillful both in wood and stone. Him, therefore, they retained, on account of his lively genius and good reputation, and dismissed the others. And to him and to the providence of God was the execution of the work committed" (p. 55).

56 Dorothy Sayers, *The Zeal of Thy House* (London, 1937), p. 64. Further page references will be incorporated in the text in parentheses.

57 Dorothy Sayers, *The Mind of the Maker* (New York, 1956). "It is the Energy that is the creator in the sense in which the common man understands the word, because it brings about an expression in temporal form of the eternal and immutable Idea . . . it is something distinct from the Idea itself, though it is the only thing that can make the Idea known to itself or to others, and yet is . . . essentially identical with the Idea—'consubstantial with the Father' " (pp. 49–50). The third member of the Trinity, the Holy Ghost—Creative Power (the means by which the Christ-Creative Activity is communicated to others and which produces a corresponding response in them)—does not, indeed, by its nature cannot, play a concrete role in the analogy.

58 The sustained allusion to the myth of Prometheus is an example, similar to Eliot's allusions to the myths of the corn god, of the way the sacramental aesthetic integrates pre-Christian matter.

59 Gerald Weales, *Religion in Modern English Drama* (Philadelphia, 1961), p. 176.

60 *Ibid.*, pp. 164–165.

61 George R. Kernodle, "England's Religious-Drama Movement," *College English*, I, 5 (February, 1940), 422.

62 Miss Sayers defines the quality of Beddoes' art as consisting of "a brilliant Energy, accompanied by an impressive Power, but disintegrated by lack of reference to a strong Idea" (*The Mind of the Maker*, p. 149). She concludes that "in everything but that absence of Idea, purpose, integrating wholeness, Beddoes had the quality of a great poet" (p. 150).

63 T. S. Eliot, "Poetry and Drama," *On Poetry and Poets* (London, 1957), p. 73.

CHAPTER 5

1 John Masefield, *The Coming of Christ* (New York, 1928), p. 27. Further page references will be incorporated in the text in parentheses.

2 Erich Auerbach, *Mimesis: The Representation of Reality in Western Literature* (Garden City, 1957), p. 137.

3 C. Townsend, "Review of Masefield's *The Coming of Christ*," *The Spectator*, 140, 5214 (June 2, 1928), 824.

4 A. M. Buckton, *Eager Heart*, in *The Story of Christmas*, ed. R. J. Campbell (New York, 1934), pp. 210–211.

5 *Ibid.*, pp. 229–230.

6 Gerald Weales, *Religion in Modern English Drama* (Philadelphia, 1961), p. 137.

7 *Ibid.*, p. 139.

8 Masefield's treatment of the shepherds is still far superior to that of Housman in *Bethlehem*. Housman's shepherds speak a highly self-conscious rural dialect, and nothing distinguishes them as modern men: "You come wi' me, lad! come along o' me! / We'll all be off to Bethlehem, and see / What they be doing there!" Laurence Housman, *Bethlehem: A Nativity Play* (New York, 1902), p. 21.

9 See also the chorus of the Host of Heaven, p. 19, and especially the Sword's final speech, p. 56.

10 This is suggested by the *London Times* reviewer, who, in speaking of the colloquy of the shepherds, the only scene in which the characters imitate the human voice, writes, "This scene emphasizes the severe limitation imposed by the vastness of the theatre. Voices were apt to soar upward instead of outward." LX, 22 (May 31, 1928), 611.

11 Gerald Weales, *Religion in Modern English Drama*, pp. 139–140.

12 There are two versions of *Christ's Comet*, the first published in 1938 and the second in 1958 on the occasion of the twentieth anniversary of the Canterbury Festival. In the following discussion I use the second version (except where noted) because it is the more accessible and represents the definitive text. Hassall's alterations are slight (their function being to reduce the musical aspect of the play), and they do not greatly affect the theme and general design.

13 Christopher Hassall, *Christ's Comet: The Story of a Thirty Years' Journey Which Began and Ended on the Same Day*, 2d ed. (London, 1958), p. xi. Further page references will be incorporated in the text in parentheses.

14 In the preface to the 1938 edition of *Christ's Comet*, 1st ed. (London, 1938), p. xi, Hassall acknowledges the American's work as the source of the plot of his play, but he says that he did not know the book at first hand.

15 This motif is expressed in Artaban's soliloquy following the departure of the three kings:

There are two Distances,
One is of Place, the other of Sympathy.

. . . .
It now wants fewer footsteps to complete
My journey, than to walk twice round my palace.
Beyond that hill, and down the other side—
But in my heart, three chafing seas, a desert,
And countless snow-peaks of division.

[P. 44]

16 Christopher Hassall, "Notes on the Verse Drama," *The Masque*, 6 (London, 1948), 22.

17 *Ibid.*, p. 23.

18 Christopher Hassall, "Preface," *Christ's Comet*, 1st ed., p. 9.

19 Hassall, "Notes on the Verse Drama," p. 19.

20 Hassall's defense of blank verse against Eliot's charge that it is contrary to the idiom of contemporary speech ("Notes on the Verse Drama," pp. 25–26) is, I think, part of his general attraction to the kind of robust rhetoric he finds in the Elizabethan drama. He does not want to give up the periodic cadences in the iambic line.

21 Laurence Housman, *Bethlehem: A Nativity Play* (New York, 1902), p. 69.

22 Charles Williams, "Synopsis," *Seed of Adam*, in *Collected Plays*, ed. John Heath-Stubbs (London, 1963), p. 173. Further page references are incorporated in the text in parentheses.

23 Williams has reversed the traditional identities of these two magi, since it is Melchior whose gift to the Christ child is gold.

24 Christopher Edward Fullman, "The Mind and Art of Charles Williams: A Study of His Poetry, Plays and Novels," unpublished Ph.D. thesis, University of Wisconsin, 1954, p. 425.

25 Running through this passage is the dramatic suggestion of Joseph's quite human fear that Mary has had an affair with another man. The sequence, then, is in the "realistic" tradition of the medieval drama that sees Joseph generally as a cuckolded husband. Unfortunately, Williams thins out the realism by presenting the scene as a verbal encounter rather than as a concrete image.

The degree to which the abstractness mars the drama can be seen by comparing Williams' scene with W. H. Auden's "The Temptation of St. Joseph" in *For the Time Being*, in which the poet also employs the medieval tradition as a means of projecting the condition of existential decision.

26 See Chapter 4, pp. 114–115.

27 Adam's conquest of Rome merely emphasizes the alienation of man from the web of co-inherence. When the Third King sees Adam-Augustus, this "new Adam" he has been seeking, he says, "Why, father! the old Adam, after all" (p. 17). Williams keeps the image of Christ, the real "new Adam," ironically present throughout the encounter.

28 The Third King is Balthasar, whose gift is myrrh, one of the uses of which was the embalming of the dead. Mother Myrrh is therefore appropriately named.

29 The reference is to Ezekiel's vision of God, Ezekiel 1.22.

30 See David Roberts, *Existentialism and Religious Belief* (New York, 1959), p. 67. See also Søren Kierkegaard, "Dread as a Saving Experience by Means of Faith," *The Concept of Dread*, tr. Walter Lowrie (Princeton, N.J., 1944), pp. 239–245, and Martin Heidegger, *Being and Time*, tr. John Macquarrie and Edward Robinson (New York, 1962), pp. 296–299.

31 Matthew XVI.25.

32 Alice Mary Hadfield, *An Introduction to Charles Williams* (London, 1959), p. 133.

33 Anne Ridler, "Introduction," *Seed of Adam and Other Plays*, by Charles Williams (London, 1948), p. vii.

34 This is not so much a matter of colloquial diction as it is of the tone generated by a sophisticated use of language, particularly of commonplaces and specialized vocabulary:

> Father Adam, you were always a fool,
> and it seems at the top of your Roman school
> no better; will you arrest the itch
> with your great hands? will your bands pitch
> their javelins against the diabetes of the damned?
> The belly is empty in hell though the mouth is crammed:
> a momentous place!
>
> [p. 166]

35 The other branch had its base at Canterbury and was directed by E. Martin Browne. Both toured wartime England under the auspices of the Religious Drama Society, founded in 1929.

36 The wide appeal of this group is attested to by the numerous productions before varied audiences that these plays received. As Anne Ridler notes, the Pilgrim Players gave performances of *The House by the Stable*, the best of the group, "in halls, air-raid shelters, garages, churches, schools, and theatres in many parts of the country" during the war. It was also "given by E. Martin Browne in a tour of north-western Europe in May 1945, and it has been broadcast (December, 1945)." "Introduction," *Seed of Adam and Other Plays*, by Charles Williams, pp. ix–x.

37 Charles Williams, *The Death of Good Fortune*, in *Collected Plays*, p. 179. Further page references will be incorporated in the text in parentheses.

38 Charles Williams, *The House by the Stable*, in *Collected Plays*, p. 211. Further page references will be incorporated in the text in parentheses.

39 R. H. Ward, who notes the recurrence in Williams' work, particularly in *Seed of Adam* and *The House by the Stable*, of "a male force of evil (a false good, or 'magical' good) accompanied by a female counterpart or 'medium' through whom the force knows and acts," refers to this archetype as "a kind of spiritual gangster with his moll" to convey, apparently, the sense of

contemporaneity it suggests. "Imagination Breaks Through," *Christian Drama*, I, ix (April, 1949), 3–5. However, in his effort to establish the abstract character of Williams' drama, a view based on his erroneous belief that Williams lacks *caritas*, Ward overlooks the movement toward greater concreteness in the projection of this archetype.

40 In *Grab and Grace*, it is the lively child, Grace, who deflates Gabriel's angelism. To Gabriel's pontifical, first-person-plural advice to Man concerning the fate of Pride—

> I do not advise perpetual prison here,
> not trusting Pride—nor, sir, to be frank,
> thinking you would have much chance against her.
> We have seen——

—Grace interposes, "Gabriel! Come off your grand angelic / passion for instruction. This is Man's affair" (p. 240).

41 Anne Ridler, "Introduction," *Seed of Adam and Other Plays*, p. vi.

42 Walter J. Burghardt, "On Early Christian Exegesis," reprinted from *Theological Studies*, XI (1950) in William F. Lynch, S.J., "Supplement IV," *Christ and Apollo: The Dimensions of the Literary Imagination* (New York, 1960). Williams mentions the history and defines the method in *The Descent of the Dove: A History of the Holy Spirit in the Church* (New York, 1956), p. 38.

43 Dorothy Sayers, "Preface," *He That Should Come*, in *Four Sacred Plays* (London, 1957), p. 215.

44 *Ibid.*, p. 218.

45 Ward has written other religious plays in a more conventional mode: *The Prodigal Son* (1944), *Faust in Hell* (1944), *The Wise and Foolish Virgins* (1949).

46 See R. H. Ward, "Elements of Religious Drama, Part I," *Christian Drama*, I, 2 (April, 1947), 2–5; "Elements of Religious Drama, Part II," *Christian Drama*, I, 3 (July, 1947), 3–9; "Elements of Religious Drama, Part III," *Christian Drama*, I, 4 (November, 1947), 5–9; and "The Nature of Religious Drama," *London Quarterly and Holborn Review*, 179 (1954), 251–256.

47 R. H. Ward, *Holy Family* (Ilkley, Yorkshire, 1943), p. xii, quoted in Weales, *Religion*, p. 256.

48 Ward, *Holy Family* (London, 1952), pp. 5–6.

49 In his "Introduction" to Williams' *The Descent of the Dove*, Auden implicitly acknowledges an intellectual debt to Williams' thought, particularly to the doctrine of exchange or substitution, and the corollary doctrines of coinherence and the Way of the Affirmation of Images. Auden employs Williams' terms several times in *For the Time Being* in his attempt to define the modern predicament and the way out, though they are, of course, assimilated into his own thought.

50 W. H. Auden, *For the Time Being: A Christmas Oratorio*, in *The Collected Poetry* (New York, 1945), pp. 410–411.

51 Amos Wilder, *Modern Poetry and the Christian Tradition: A Study in the Relation of Christianity to Culture* (New York, 1952), pp. 202–203. For an excellent formal analysis of Auden's oratorio, see Edward Callan, "Auden and Kierkegaard: The Artistic Framework of *For the Time Being*," *Christian Scholar*, XLVIII, 3 (Fall, 1965), 211–223.

52 Auden, *Collected Poetry*, pp. 453–454.

53 The first three of these Histories are Canterbury Festival plays.

CHAPTER 6

1 T. S. Eliot, *Four Quartets*, in *The Complete Poems and Plays, 1909–1950* (New York, 1952), p. 144.
2 Joseph Wood Krutch, "The Tragic Fallacy," in *The Modern Temper: A Study and a Confession* (New York, 1956), pp. 79–97.
3 W. H. Auden, *For the Time Being: A Christmas Oratorio*, in *The Collected Poetry* (New York, 1945), pp. 452–453. By "recurrence" (in the last paragraph) Auden means, I think, that poetry is not restricted to the heroic ages but is perpetually relevant, because all history and thus all human events are relevant *sub specie aeternitatis*.
4 Erich Auerbach, *Mimesis: The Representation of Reality in Western Literature* (Garden City, 1957), pp. 131–136.
5 Shakespeare's dramatic verse, it is true, has affinities with the classical high style, but this is not because he adheres to the *Stiltrennung*. The elevated verse is not artificially imposed on the characters; it is, on the whole, the natural language of a world view that is essentially dynamic and poetic. This can be seen in the increasingly close integration of poetic diction and speech idioms and rhythms in his plays.
6 T. S. Eliot, "Poetry and Drama," in *On Poetry and Poets* (London, 1957), p. 80.
7 *Ibid.*, p. 79.
8 See, for example, Sean Lucy, *T. S. Eliot and the Idea of Tradition* (London, 1960), pp. 165–182, 191; Giorgio Melchiori, *The Tightrope Walkers: Studies of Mannerism in Modern English Literature* (London, 1956), pp. 104–149, 249–256; John Peter, "Sin and Soda," *Scrutiny*, XVII, i (1950), 65; Kenneth Tynan, "Prose and the Playwright," *Atlantic Monthly*, 194, 6 (December, 1954), 76; Philip Rahv, "T. S. Eliot: The Poet as Playwright," in *The Myth and the Powerhouse: Essays on Literature and Ideas* (New York, 1965), p. 190.
9 Eliot, *On Poetry and Poets*, p. 82.
10 *Ibid.*, pp. 81–82.
11 T. S. Eliot, "The Aims of Poetic Drama," *Adam International Review*, 200 (November, 1949), 12.
12 T. S. Eliot, "John Marston," in *Essays on Elizabethan Drama* (New York, 1956), p. 173. My italics. Eliot reiterates this "ideal towards which poetic drama should strive" in "Poetry and Drama," p. 87.
13 Melchiori, *The Tightrope Walkers*, p. 140.
14 E. M. W. Tillyard, *Shakespeare's Last Plays* (London, 1958), pp. 59 ff.
15 Eliot, *Four Quartets*, p. 127.
16 Eliot, *On Poetry and Poets*, p. 86.
17 Eliot, *Four Quartets*, pp. 127–128.
18 T. S. Eliot, *The Family Reunion*, in *The Complete Poems and Plays, 1909–1950*, p. 249. Further page references will be incorporated in the text in parentheses.
19 Maud Bodkin, *The Quest for Salvation in an Ancient and a Modern Play* (London, 1941), p. 33.
20 *Ibid.*, p. 46.
21 I am indebted for much of the material on the time-worlds of *The Family Reunion* to Anne Ward's article, "Speculations on Eliot's Time-World: An Analysis of *The Family Reunion* in Relation to Hulme and Bergson," *American Literature*, XXI (1949), 18–34. It will be seen, however, that I am in radical disagreement with her on the fundamental issue of the final concept of time that is worked out in the play.

22 Anne Ward, "Speculations on Eliot's Time-World," pp. 23–24. The quotation from Bergson is from *Time and Free Will: An Essay on the Immediate Data of Consciousness* (New York, 1910), p. 231. For an interesting analogy of this analysis of the psycho-social implications of mechanistic time, see Martin Heidegger's analysis of Everyday-Being-towards-the-end, which manifests itself as an effort to evade death, to negate its personal sting, by rendering it a public phenomenon, in which "what gets reached as it were, by death, is the 'they' [*das Man*]," in *Being and Time* (New York, 1962), pp. 296–299.

23 See Helen L. Gardner, *The Art of T. S. Eliot* (New York, 1950), pp. 142–143, and Hugh Kenner, *The Invisible Poet: T. S. Eliot* (New York, 1959), pp. 328–331, on Eliot's use of the metaphor of play-acting.

24 See Mircea Eliade, *Cosmos and History: The Myth of the Eternal Return*, tr. Willard R. Trask (New York, 1959), p. 62.

25 Nathan A. Scott, Jr., *Rehearsals of Discomposure: Alienation and Reconciliation in Modern Literature: Franz Kafka, Ignazio Silone, D. H. Lawrence, T. S. Eliot* (New York, 1952), p. 232. This discovery is exactly that which transfigures Lord Claverton in *The Elder Statesman*, and thus should serve as a corrective to interpretations of this scene, such as Grover Smith's, which categorically delimits Mary's insight, claiming simply that she "regards herself and Wishwood as supplying the solution" to Harry's problem. Grover Smith, Jr., *T. S. Eliot's Poetry and Plays: A Study in Sources and Meaning* (Chicago, 1956), p. 207.

26 See Louis L. Martz, "The Wheel and the Point: Aspects of Imagery and Theme in Eliot's Later Poetry," *T. S. Eliot, a Selected Critique*, ed. Leonard Unger (New York, 1948), p. 167. See also Kafka's parable of the law in *The Trial*.

27 Letter to E. Martin Browne, quoted in F. O. Matthiessen, *The Achievement of T. S. Eliot: An Essay on the Nature of Poetry* (New York, 1959), p. 167.

28 Amy catches a glimpse of Harry's identity with his father shortly after: "You looked like your father / When you said that" (p. 266).

29 This is only one of several allusions to *Hamlet* scattered throughout the play that serve to establish another underpattern operating analogously to the pattern of the *Oresteia*. See Matthiessen, *Achievement of T. S. Eliot*, pp. 168–169. Particularly interesting are the numerous references (some of which are made by the Ghost) that remind Hamlet of the past he is trying to forget. See *Hamlet, The Complete Works of Shakespeare*, ed. Hardin Craig (Chicago, 1951), I.ii.143; I.v.91; III.iv.110.

30 Stanley Romaine Hopper, "The Problem of Moral Isolation in Contemporary Literature," *Spiritual Problems in Contemporary Literature*, ed. Stanley Romaine Hopper (New York, 1957), pp. 161–162. The quotations are from an early draft of Hart Crane's poem "Cape Hatteras." Though Professor Hopper does not refer specifically to Eliot's plays in this brilliant essay, his interpretation of modern literature in terms of the redemptive quest of the Prodigal, of the archetype of alienation and return, illuminates the essentially existential theme of *The Family Reunion*. I cannot, however, completely agree with him that Eliot is reluctant "to take more than a backward half-look at this Mystery [of sin]," preferring rather to escape "into a theology which, though containing it formally, avoids meeting it actually" (pp. 168–169). *The Family Reunion* bears witness to the dubiousness of this view.

31 T. S. Eliot, *The Idea of a Christian Society* (New York, 1940), p. 63.

32 W. H. Auden, *For the Time Being: A Christmas Oratorio*, pp. 449–450.

33 Gardner, *Art of T. S. Eliot*, p. 154.

34 Charles Williams, *Reason and Beauty in the Poetic Mind* (Oxford, 1933), pp. 48–49.

35 See above, p. 194.
36 Quoted in Matthiessen, *Achievement of T. S. Eliot*, p. 167.
37 Eliot, *On Poetry and Poets*, p. 84.
38 Anne Ward, "Speculations on Eliot's Time-World," p. 30.
39 William F. Lynch, S.J., *Christ and Apollo: The Dimensions of the Literary Imagination* (New York, 1960), pp. 167–168, 176. See also Lynch, "Confusion in Our Theater," *Thought*, XXVI, 102 (Autumn, 1951), 351, and Denis Donoghue, *The Third Voice: Modern British and American Verse Drama* (Princeton, 1959), pp. 126–128.
40 Elizabeth Drew, *T. S. Eliot: The Design of His Poetry* (New York, 1949), p. 148.
41 From the first epigraph, from Heraclitus, of *Four Quartets*: "Although the Word (logos) is common to all, most men live as if they had each a private wisdom of his own." Translated by Elizabeth Drew, *T. S. Eliot*, p. 147.
42 Drew, *T. S. Eliot*, p. 149.
43 Malcolm MacKenzie Ross, *Poetry and Dogma: The Transfiguration of Eucharistic Symbols in Seventeenth Century English Poetry* (New Brunswick, 1954), p. 235.
44 Eliot, *On Poetry and Poets*, p. 84.
45 Letter to E. Martin Browne, quoted in Matthiessen, *Achievement of T. S. Eliot*, p. 168.
46 This development of the family's awareness has also been noted by D. E. S. Maxwell, *The Poetry of T. S. Eliot* (London, 1952), pp. 194–196.
47 See also *The Family Reunion*, p. 287, where the idea is repeated several times.
48 D. E. S. Maxwell, *The Poetry of T. S. Eliot*, p. 200. The inner quote is from *Four Quartets*, p. 137.
49 Eliot, *On Poetry and Poets*, p. 82.
50 See above, pp. 32–34.
51 Melchiori, *The Tightrope Walkers*, p. 136.
52 David E. Jones, *The Plays of T. S. Eliot* (London, 1960), p. 88.
53 Archibald MacLeish's use of the myth of Job in his verse drama *J. B.* (1956) is similarly arbitrary and artificial. The story of the Biblical Job is not integrated into the action. It is used; it is a "poetic" prop without an identity of its own and thus violates the true function of an image. This is made quite clear when, at the end of the play, after it has served MacLeish's ornamental purpose, the myth is brusquely (and undramatically) discarded as meaningless for the modern humanistic existentialist J. B. There can be no other alternative but to abandon the myth, considering that the message —which is always prominent in plays which employ myth in this way— repudiates the Absolute and thus the belief that the past (Job) is contained in the present (J. B.) for something like existential commitment to the present self in the face of overwhelming reasons to the contrary. Form and content are at odds, as they are not in Eliot. And since little respect is paid to the image of Job in the first place, it is that which goes in the end.
54 Jones, *Plays of T. S. Eliot*, p. 88. I am indebted to Jones' discussion of Eliot's use of myth, particularly to his development of Melchiori's contrast between Eliot and the French dramatists.
55 Ronald Peacock, "Public and Private Problems in Modern Drama," *Tulane Drama Review*, III, 3 (March, 1959), 71.

CHAPTER 7

1 Celia's "return" through the agency of Heracles-Reilly is one manifestation of the motif of the return of the dead in Euripides' *Alcestis*. The other is the return of Lavinia, who has "died" to her husband, Admetus-Edward.

2 T. S. Eliot, *The Cocktail Party*, in *The Complete Poems and Plays, 1909–1950* (New York, 1952), pp. 348–349. Further page references will be incorporated in the text in parentheses. In her interview with Reilly, Celia says of her relationship with Edward:

> And then I found we were only strangers
> And that there had been neither giving nor taking
> But that we had merely made use of each other
> Each for his purpose. That's horrible. Can we only love
> Something created by our own imagination?
>
> [p. 362]

See also p. 327.

To Peter, Lavinia says at the end:

> . . . You were saying just now
> That you never knew Celia. We none of us did.
> What you've been living on is an image of Celia
> Which you made for yourself, to meet your own needs.

And this Peter acknowledges a moment later:

> You know, all the time that you've been talking,
> One thought has been going round and round in my head—
> That I've only been interested in myself:
> And that isn't good enough for Celia.
>
> [p. 382]

3 T. S. Eliot, *Notes towards the Definition of Culture* (New York, 1949), pp. 64–65. In this essay, Eliot employs the marriage relationship defined above as an analogy of the relationship between cultures. The word "something" or its equivalent, which is opposed to "someone," recurs throughout the play.

4 Gerald Weales, *Religion in Modern English Drama* (Philadelphia, 1961), p. 198.

5 David E. Jones, *The Plays of T. S. Eliot* (London, 1960), p. 142.

6 Weales, *Religion*, pp. 198–199. See also William F. Lynch, S.J., "Theology and the Imagination, I," *Thought*, XXIX, 112 (March, 1954), 66, 67, 84; Denis Donoghue, *The Third Voice: Modern British and American Verse Drama* (Princeton, 1959), pp. 126–128; Nathan A. Scott, Jr., "T. S. Eliot's *The Cocktail Party*: Of Redemption and Vocation," *Religion in Life*, XX, 2 (Spring, 1951), 285; and Lionel Trilling, "Wordsworth and the Iron Time," *Kenyon Review*, XII, 3 (Summer, 1950), 493–494.

7 T. S. Eliot, "Poetry and Drama," *On Poetry and Poets* (London, 1957), p. 85.

8 For Eliot's general debt to Euripides and to the New Comedy, see Jones, *Plays of T. S. Eliot*, pp. 155–159. Grover Smith, Jr., *T. S. Eliot's Poetry and Plays: A Study in Sources and Meaning* (Chicago, 1956), pp. 237–247, claims that Eliot is indebted more to A. W. Verrall's interpretation of Euripides' *Ion* in *Euripides the Rationalist: a Study of the History of Art and Religion* (Cambridge, England, 1895), than to the *Ion* itself in that the true identity of Colby is, like that of Verrall's Ion, other than that given by the priestess of Apollo (Mrs. Guzzard) at the end of the play. But since this interpretation does not, as Smith admits, affect the significance of Eliot's play and, more important, since Colby has said, and the whole play

insists, that one cannot "build [his] life upon a deception" it is not only inconsequential but misleading.

9 T. S. Eliot, *The Confidential Clerk* (London, 1954), p. 65. Further page references will be incorporated in the text in parentheses.

10 Cf. *The Confidential Clerk*, pp. 37, 43.

11 The theme of the imposition of identity, which plays a key part in *The Family Reunion* and *The Cocktail Party*, culminates at the end of the play when Kaghan says to Claude: "You know, Claude, I think we all made the same mistake— / All except [Eggerson]. . . . / We wanted Colby to be something he wasn't" (p. 134).

12 Donoghue, *The Third Voice*, p. 152.

13 Jones, *Plays of T. S. Eliot*, p. 164.

14 *Ibid.*, p. 166. In answer to Mrs. Guzzard's question, Colby describes the father he would like to have as one "whom I could get to know / Only by report, by documents" (p. 125), that is, as David E. Jones observes, by the Gospels.

15 F. O. Matthiessen, *The Achievement of T. S. Eliot: An Essay on the Nature of Poetry* (New York, 1959), p. 168.

16 T. S. Eliot, *The Elder Statesman* (London, 1959), p. 16. See also pp. 34, 35, 56, 83–84. Further page references will be incorporated in the text in parentheses.

17 Jones, *Plays of T. S. Eliot*, p. 196. Furthermore, it minimizes the significance of Lord Claverton's peripety and of the last moments of the play, which, in revealing Charles' and Monica's new love for each other, recall the earlier scene and define the thinness of their earlier relationship.

18 *Ibid.*, p. 185.

19 See also Gomez' summation of Lord Claverton's career, which recalls the "prepared face" motif of "The Love Song of J. Alfred Prufrock," *Complete Poems and Plays*, p. 35.

20 Maisie's friend Effie had warned her that "that man is hollow" (p. 51).

21 Donoghue, *The Third Voice*, p. 166.

22 See the *London Times* (August 26, 1958), 11.

23 Though the metaphor of flight and pursuit is not verbalized as it is in Eliot's *The Family Reunion*, the pervasive references to the metaphor of "escape" render the entire action of the first part of the play an image of pursuit.

24 William Arrowsmith also makes much of the Chamberlaynes' description of Reilly and Julia as devils in his analysis of *The Cocktail Party*. For him, the meaning of these references can be found in another proverb: "*to play the devil for God's sake.* This is what Reilly and Julia are doing; Reilly . . . tempts Edward in the matter of Lavinia's return and the Christian meaning of Edward's reply is: Get thee behind me, Satan. Eliot (and Reilly) . . . would say that this reply of Edward's is possible only because we still have a culture which is to some extent Christian; but so much has gone out of our conscious Christianity that the reply has to be elicited in a negative way: the way of the devil which is also the way of the world" (p. 418). Although his emphasis on the conspiratorial strategy is justified, Arrowsmith fails to perceive the genuine theological principle that lies behind the creation of these characters: that in the fallen world, the good can only be known by an increase of knowledge, that is, by the acknowledgment not the evasion of evil. "English Verse Drama (II): *The Cocktail Party*," *Hudson Review*, III, 3 (Autumn, 1950), 411–430.

25 The reference is emphasized at this point when Edward's exclamation, "What the devil's that?" evoked by a pop coming from the kitchen, is followed by Julia's re-entrance with a tray and glasses.

26 See also pp. 343, 352.

27 See pp. 319, 339, 341, 346.

28 Quoted by Burke Wilkinson, "A Most Serious Comedy by Eliot," *New York Times* (February 7, 1954), sect. 2, p. 1.
29 Grover Smith, Jr., *T. S. Eliot's Poetry and Plays*, p. 123.
30 This meaning is emphasized in Eliot's *The Cocktail Party* by the parallel, pointed out by Robert B. Heilman in *"Alcestis* and *The Cocktail Party," Comparative Literature*, V (1953), between Reilly and his mythic counterpart Heracles: "It is difficult to resist the conclusion that [Eliot] found in [Heracles] the suggestion for the thematic basis of his own play—the dualism of world and spirit, and the interpretation of world by spirit. For Heracles, as the son of Alcmena and Zeus, is half human, half divine; and in Reilly there is an ambiguity which makes a limited naturalistic view of him seem continually inadequate" (p. 114). See also Arrowsmith, "English Verse Drama (II), p. 413, for his discussion of the imagery of sight in terms of the proverb: "In the kingdom of the blind the one-eyed man is King."
31 For a brief history of this genre, see Weales, "Sentimental Supernaturalism," in *Religion in Modern English Drama*, pp. 38–50.
32 See also Anne Ridler, *The Missing Bridegroom*, in *Henry Bly and Other Plays* (London, 1950), written under the influence of T. S. Eliot. In this one act verse play the mysterious Verger performs a function in the action that is similar to that of the Guardians in Eliot's *The Cocktail Party*.
33 Eliot, *On Poetry and Poets*, p. 80.
34 *Ibid.*, p. 82.
35 See especially Donoghue, *The Third Voice.*
36 Giorgio Melchiori, *The Tightrope Walkers: Studies of Mannerism in Modern English Literature* (London, 1956), p. 253.
37 Eliot, "The Music of Poetry," in *On Poetry and Poets*, p. 29.
38 *Ibid.*, p. 33.
39 I have marked the accents and caesuras in this passage for the reader's convenience.
40 This is broadly the pattern traced by the protagonist of Tolstoy's "The Death of Ivan Ilych," of Kafka's *The Trial*, of Sartre's *The Flies*, of Camus' *The Fall*, and Greene's *The Power and the Glory*, to name but a few works by obvious existential writers. For the humanistic existential analysis of the flight from death or Nothingness, see Martin Heidegger, *Being and Time*, tr. John Macquarrie and Edward Robinson (New York, 1962), pp. 296–299. Its Christian existential counterpart is discoverable throughout the work of Kierkegaard, but see especially "Dread as a Saving Experience by Means of Faith," *The Concept of Dread* (Princeton, 1944), pp. 139–145. See also William Barrett, *Irrational Man: A Study in Existential Philosophy* (New York, 1962), pp. 275–280, in which the author uses the Furies to define the existential diagnosis of modern man's flight from the irrational and to present the existential insistence on authenticity.
41 Eliot, *On Poetry and Poets*, pp. 32–33.
42 *Ibid.*, p. 86.
43 Leslie Paul and Christopher Salmon, "Two Views of Mr. Eliot's New Play," *Listener*, LI (September 4, 1958), 341. This passage gains significance by the fact that it is quoted by Jones, *Plays of T. S. Eliot*, p. 209, to summarize his concluding definition of Eliot's drama.
44 William Barrett, "Existentialism as a Symptom of Man's Contemporary Crisis," in *Spiritual Problems in Contemporary Literature*, ed. Stanley Romaine Hopper (New York, 1957), p. 143.

CHAPTER 8

1 Robert Speaight is also the author of several books on the theater: *Drama since 1939* (London, 1947); *William Poel and the Elizabethan Revival* (Cambridge, Mass., 1954); *Nature in Shakespearean Tragedy* (New York, 1962); *Christian Theatre* (New York, 1960).

2 Christopher Fry, "Headpiece," *Christian Drama*, II, 1 (June, 1951), unpaginated.

3 Gerald Weales, *Religion in Modern English Drama* (Philadelphia, 1961), pp. 241–242; William Arrowsmith, "Notes on English Verse Drama: Christopher Fry I," *Hudson Review*, III, 2 (Summer, 1950), 205.

4 A former student of Williams' during his Oxford period, Mrs. Ridler has written one of the best critical introductions to his thought and poetry in her "Introduction" to Charles Williams' *The Image of the City and Other Essays* (London, 1958), and a valuable seminal essay on his drama in her "Introduction" to *Seed of Adam and Other Plays*, by Charles Williams (London, 1948).

5 Anne Ridler, *Cain* (London, 1943), p. 31.

6 *Ibid.*, p. 31.

7 *Ibid.*, p. 30.

8 Anne Ridler, "A Question of Speech," in *T. S. Eliot: A Study of His Writings by Several Hands*, ed. B. Rajan (London, 1948), p. 114.

9 Anne Ridler, *The Shadow Factory: A Nativity Play* (London, 1946), p. 15. Further references will be incorporated in the text in parentheses.

10 The image bears a striking resemblance to the ubiquitous caricature of Bernard Shaw which shows him manipulating his puppet-characters from above a cloud. The artist's earlier reference to the workers as "puppets worked by your Director-God who pulls the strings" (p. 23) suggests that Mrs. Ridler may be alluding to the caricature and thereby satirizing, unfairly perhaps, Shaw's Utopian creative evolution.

11 Raymond Williams, *Drama from Ibsen to Eliot* (New York, 1953), p. 259.

12 The reference to the artist's "work," the at least partial creativity of which is an ironic comment on the Director's Works, recurs throughout the play. See pp. 15, 16, and 28, for example.

13 The artist again refers to his patron as "your benevolent Director-God" (*ibid.*, p. 25).

14 T. S. Eliot, "Baudelaire," in *Selected Essays* (New York, 1950), pp. 378–379.

15 The idea is expressed in T. S. Eliot's "Ash Wednesday," *The Complete Poems and Plays, 1909–1950* (New York, 1952), p. 67: "Suffer us not to mock ourselves with falsehood / Teach us to care and not to care / Teach us to sit still." See also Eliot's "East Coker," p. 126: "I said to my soul, be still, and wait without hope"; and the numerous references to "waiting" in the choruses of T. S. Eliot's *Murder in the Cathedral*. Mrs. Ridler emphasizes the idea at the beginning of the Nativity scene that follows by giving the parson an introductory prayer which alludes to Eliot's lines: ". . . teach us to wait on thee and be still" (p. 52).

16 Weales, *Religion*, p. 229.

17 *Ibid.*

18 Mrs. Ridler's awareness of the Redemption as a paradoxical transformation of evil into a good is clearly revealed in her "Introduction" to Williams' *Image of the City*, where she observes that this function of the Redemption is "Williams' grand theme" (p. xxxiii).

19 Speaight, *Drama since 1939*, p. 43.

20 *Ibid.*

21 George Every, *Poetry and Personal Responsibility: An Interim Report on Con-temporary Literature* (London, 1949), p. 88.
22 Charles Williams, *He Came Down from Heaven and The Forgiveness of Sins* (London, 1950), pp. 20–21, 58–60.
23 In *The Mask*, a short verse play which is a modernized adaptation of the Somerset folk song "Shooting of Her Dear," Mrs. Ridler employs the figure, as his name "The Prompter" suggests, much more clearly in the manner of Williams. In *The Missing Bridegroom*, the play most clearly revealing the influence of Eliot's drawing-room comedy of contemporary life, she models the figure (the Verger) somewhat after Eliot's Sir Henry Harcourt-Reilly. Both these plays appear in Anne Ridler's *Henry Bly and Other Plays* (London, 1950).
24 Raymond Williams, *Drama from Ibsen to Eliot*, p. 260.
25 Norman Nicholson, "The Poet Needs an Audience," *Orpheus: A Symposium of the Arts*, I, ed. John Lehmann (London, 1948), p. 149.
26 *Ibid.*, pp. 148–149.
27 *Ibid.*, p. 153. Eliot and Mrs. Ridler express the opposite view in "Poetry and Drama," in *On Poets and Poetry* (London, 1959), p. 77, and "A Question of Speech," p. 113, respectively.
28 Nicholson, "The Poet Needs an Audience," p. 154. See also his "The Abandoned Muse," *Theatre Arts*, XXXII, 5 (Fall, 1948), 70.
29 For a similar criticism of Synge's representation of reality, see Ronald Peacock's chapter on Synge in *The Poet in the Theatre* (New York, 1946). See also Herbert Howarth, *The Irish Writers: Literature and Nationalism, 1880–1940* (New York, 1959), for his chapter on Synge.
30 Norman Nicholson, *The Old Man of the Mountains: A Play in Three Acts* (4th impression, London, 1955), p. 12. Further references to the play will be incorporated in the text in parentheses. The play was first published in 1946 and later slightly revised by the author.
31 Although not Christian in the strict sense, Norman Nicholson's second play, *Prophesy to the Wind: A Play in Four Scenes and a Prologue* (London, 1950), nevertheless makes use of the sacramental concept of time in two ways: formally, by introducing John, a man from the atomic-age civilization which has destroyed itself, into the primitive rural community emerging from the ashes; and thematically, by resolving the problem of whether this future world should develop or renounce the scientific knowledge John brings with him. The resolution of this problem hinges on the community's attitude toward the child about to be born to John and Freya, the daughter of Hallbjorn, the leader of the new society. Hallbjorn, who fears John's knowledge, has him put to death and discovers thereby that the potential for destruction lies not in scientific knowledge but in man, and discovers, as Elijah did, that evading knowledge of nature cannot save the world. Thus in the end Hallbjorn acknowledges the child, who—by carrying in his being past and present (or rather, present and future) scientific knowledge and the awareness of the lethal power it unlocks—becomes a symbol of the sacra-mental affirmation of the world.
32 See I Kings, XVII.1.
33 *Ibid.*, XVII.4: "I have commanded the ravens to feed thee there [by the brook Cherith]."
34 *Ibid.*, XVIII.17: "And it came to pass, when Ahab saw Elijah, that Ahab said unto him, Art thou he that troubleth Israel?"
35 *Ibid.*, XIX.11–13. In the Biblical story, it is Elijah who receives the partial visions that Nicholson gives to Ruth, Martha, Obadiah, and Rebecca. These and Elijah's hearing of the "still small voice" of the Lord come after the

fulfillment of the prophecy, when Elijah is in flight from Jezebel, Ahab's wife, who has threatened him with death.

36 In this delightful comedy, the boy David, who embodies the *via positiva*, deflates the prophet Amos, who preaches the *via negativa*. David reveals to Hosea, whose wife, Gomer, has returned to her earlier trade as temple prostitute, that his business is not—as Amos advises—to withdraw from the love of the things of this world in the face of God's wrath, but to go to the temple and through forgiveness to regain his wife. Nicholson's immediate texts, which give this play its symbolic dimension, are Genesis III.15 ("And I will put enmity between thee and the woman, and between thy seed and her seed; it shall bruise thy head, and thou shalt bruise his heel") and Romans XVI.20 ("And the God of peace shall bruise Satan under your feet shortly"). Ultimately, however, the text of this play and Nicholson's *The Old Man of the Mountains* is the idea expressed in Matthew XI.25: "At that time Jesus answered and said, I thank thee, O Father, Lord of heaven and earth, because thou hast hid these things from the wise and prudent, and has revealed them unto babes." (See also Luke X.21 and I Corinthians 1.26 ff.) The idea expressed in these passages falls, of course, in the theological category, but it serves equally as the aesthetic principle that underlies Nicholson's drama of humble folk life. For a discussion of the relationship between the sacramental concept of a sublime humility and its aesthetic implications in the medieval drama, see Erich Auerbach, *Mimesis: The Representation of Reality in Western Literature*, tr. Willard Trask (New York, 1957), pp. 131 ff.

37 Every, *Poetry and Personal Responsibility*, p. 88.

38 *Ibid.*

39 Francis Fergusson, *The Idea of a Theatre, A Study of Ten Plays: The Art of Drama in Changing Perspective* (Princeton, 1949), pp. 205–208. See also William F. Lynch, S.J., *Christ and Apollo: The Dimensions of the Literary Imagination* (New York, 1960), pp. 53–61, for further observations on the artistic implications of St. Ignatius' *Spiritual Exercises*.

40 The sacramental theme is also worked out in terms of the imagery of nature. In the beginning, when the people are in Ahab's camp, nature is described as a dying or dead organism, a waste land, a slave. In the end, however, when they have acknowledged Elijah as a man of God, nature assumes the attributes of a living organism, a chorus of praise, a mother; and man's relationship to it becomes a liturgy.

41 Fergusson, *Idea of a Theatre*, p. 205.

42 Nicholson, "The Poet Needs an Audience," p. 149.

43 Raymond Williams, *Drama from Ibsen to Eliot*, pp. 257–258.

44 Fergusson, *Idea of a Theatre*, pp. 209–210.

45 The title *The Dull Ass's Hoof* derives from Ben Jonson's "An Ode: To Him self": "And since our Dainty age, / Cannot indure reproofe, / Make not thy selfe a Page / To that strumpet the Stage, / But sing high and aloofe, / Safe from the wolves black jaw, and the dull Asses hoofe." Duncan has shown a continuing admiration for Ben Jonson's peculiarly robust and detached, yet harshly satiric verse, which has served as one of the models for his own. He also dedicates *This Way to the Tomb: A Masque and Anti-Masque* (London, 1946), to the Elizabethan master of the masque form.

46 Ronald Duncan, *The Dull Ass's Hoof* (London, 1940), p. 90.

47 Duncan's *This Way to the Tomb* was the most commercially successful of the Mercury Theatre productions discussed in this chapter. By the end of 1946, it had had over three hundred performances in London; it has also been presented for a special season at the Studio des Champs-Elysées in Paris. Speaight, *Drama since 1939*, p. 39.

48 Ronald Duncan, "The Language of Theatre To-day," *Drama*, N.S., 50 (Autumn, 1958), 25–27.
49 Duncan, *This Way to the Tomb*, p. 11. Further references to the play will be incorporated in the text in parentheses.
50 The rhythms and syntax suggest that Bernard attributes sight to Marcus. This, however, contradicts the foregoing representation of the allegorical figure of Sight, who is clearly related to the sensual appetite. Duncan is often guilty of this kind of looseness.
51 This motif is echoed in *Our Lady's Tumbler* (London, 1951), Duncan's dramatization of the familiar twelfth century French tale of the tumbler and the Virgin Mary, when Brother Andrew, broken by his efforts before the statue, cries out, "Sweet Lady, I can never reach thee / Unless thou reach down to lift me" (p. 56). Duncan's re-employment of central verbal motifs in subsequent plays is characteristic. For example, the refrain "Oh proud heart take pity on that part of me / Which lies in you as your own lost heart," that recurs throughout the masque to measure Antony's pride (sung offstage by a soprano voice, it signifies the voice of Christ), reappears in Duncan's *Don Juan* (London, 1954), although in a different context. But it is in his *The Death of Satan: A Comedy* (London, 1955), which employs several motifs first used in *Don Juan*, that the device is most fully and creatively exploited.
52 Speaight, *Drama since 1939*, p. 41.
53 *Ibid.* Though not in the stage directions, the matter concerning the timing of the saint's entry is given on the authority of Robert Speaight, who acted the part of Antony in the Mercury Theatre production.
54 E. Martin Browne, in "The Poet and the Stage," *The Penguin New Writing*, 31, ed. John Lehmann (London, 1947), has pointed out the remarkable dramatic effectiveness of this unlikely verse form: "If the actor allows the form to mould his reading, he finds its tortuousness matches and thus enhances the thought-process of the old man seeking to know himself" (p. 90). Duncan also employs the canzone form in *Our Lady's Tumbler*.
55 Raymond Williams, *Drama from Ibsen to Eliot*, p. 260.
56 The device of introducing a figure from the past into the contemporary scene to symbolize the presentness of the past is also used by Norman Nicholson in *Prophesy to the Wind*.

CHAPTER 9

1 The play was commissioned by the United Council for Missionary Education in 1945.
2 Charles Williams, *The House of the Octopus*, in *Collected Plays*, ed. John Heath-Stubbs (London, 1963), p. 249. Further page references to the play will be incorporated in the text in parentheses.
3 See Acts 2.
4 It is quite possible that Williams derived the symbol of the octopus from the device on the Japanese flag.
5 Elsewhere, Williams calls this state "Gomorrah." It is best exemplified by Wentworth in Williams' novel, *Descent into Hell* (London, 1945). W. H. Auden has a similar definition of artistic and, by extension, spiritual narcissism. In *For the Time Being: A Christmas Oratorio*, in *The Collected Poetry* (New York, 1945), which clearly shows Williams' influence, he writes: "Because in Him the Flesh is united to the Word without trans-

formation, Imagination is redeemed from promiscuous fornication with her own images" (p. 452).

6 Williams, "Author's Note to the First Edition," *The House of the Octopus*, p. 246.

7 Dorothy L. Sayers, "Review of *The House of the Octopus*," *International Review of Missions*, 34 (1945), 431. Earlier in the dream scene Assantu has prayed, "O to consume and not to be consumed" (p. 88).

8 Williams, *Collected Plays*, p. 246. The poems to which Williams refers are those of his unfinished Arthurian cycle collected in *Taliessin Through Logres and The Region of the Summer Stars* (London, 1954). In these, P'o-l'u lies at the feet of the Empire (which he represents as a human body) and symbolizes Hell (the self-sufficiency that undermines the co-inherence).

9 Charles Williams, "Notes on the Way," *Time and Tide*, 23, 9 (February 28, 1942), 171. See Christopher Edward Fullman, "The Mind and Art of Charles Williams: A Study of His Poetry, Plays and Novels" (unpublished Ph.D. thesis, University of Wisconsin, 1954), pp. 386–387. Fullman notes Williams' equation of Japan and Germany with P'o-l'u, but following the lead of Williams' preface, he makes nothing of it in his interpretation of the form of *House of the Octopus*.

10 Gerald Weales, *Religion in Modern English Drama* (Philadelphia, 1961), pp. 215–217; Derek Stanford, *Christopher Fry: An Appreciation*, 2d ed. (London, 1952), pp. 204–216.

11 Christopher Fry, "A Playwright Speaks," *Listener*, XLII (February 23, 1950), 331.

12 Monroe K. Spears, "Christopher Fry and the Redemption of Joy," *Poetry*, LXXVIII, 1 (April, 1951), 29–30.

13 This suggests that Fry is acquainted with Williams' distinction between Pope's formula and the Christian existential precept that evil is a paradoxical good (*felix culpa*), which Williams makes in *Reason and Beauty in the Poetic Mind* (Oxford, 1933), pp. 48–49.

14 Christopher Fry, "Comedy," reprinted from *Adelphi*, XXVII, 27 (November, 1950), in *Tulane Drama Review*, IV, 3 (March, 1960), 77. In a letter to Christopher Fullman (July 24, 1952) included in his unpublished dissertation, Fry revealed that his acquaintance with Williams began at Oxford in 1940.

15 Weales, *Religion*, p. 207. See also Giorgio Melchiori, *The Tightrope Walkers: Studies of Mannerism in Modern English Literature* (London, 1956), where he notes that "Eliot's influence reached Fry filtered through Williams' dramatic experiments" (p. 153).

16 Fry, "Comedy," p. 77.

17 *Ibid.*, p. 78.

18 Christopher Fry, *Thor, with Angels* (London, 1950), pp. 52, 53, 54.

19 Monroe K. Spears, "Christopher Fry and the Redemption of Joy," p. 30.

20 *Venus Observed: A Play* (New York, 1950), it is true, takes place in the present, but the setting is tonally remote from the ordinary and suggestive of a bygone, perhaps the Edwardian, period.

21 Fry, *Venus Observed*, p. 53.

22 See Raymond Williams, *Drama from Ibsen to Eliot* (London, 1953), p. 263.

23 Christopher Fry, *A Sleep of Prisoners* (New York, 1951), p. 7. Further references to the text will be incorporated in parentheses.

24 The contemporary relevance of this conflict is clearly suggested by Joseph Wood Krutch in *The Modern Temper: A Study and a Confession* (New York, 1956). The two alternatives of modern man, he asserts, are (1) the animal pursuit of survival, which ultimately entails the negation of value, and (2) the pursuit of the inner life, which ultimately ends in the extinction of the

human species. This is, as Krutch observes in the 1956 preface, the diagnosis of existentialism (pp. xi–xiii). It is within the framework of this dilemma of modern man that Fry shapes the contemporary action of *A Sleep of Prisoners*.

25 Fry, "Dedicatory Letter to Robert Gittings," *A Sleep of Prisoners* (London, 1952). Unpaginated.

26 Stanford, *Christopher Fry*, p. 212.

27 It is interesting to note that in the case of each of the first three dreams there is a blood relationship between the antagonists, which suggests the Christian principle that we are all members of a corporate body, and thus magnifies the horror of the act of violence.

28 Fry, "Dedicatory Letter to Robert Gittings," *A Sleep of Prisoners*.

29 John Ferguson, "Christopher Fry's *A Sleep of Prisoners*," *English*, X (Summer, 1954), 46.

30 Christopher Fry, "Drama in a House of Worship," *New York Times* (October 14, 1951), sect. 2, p. 3.

31 See Daniel III.24: "Then King Nebuchadnezzar the king was astonished, and arose up in haste, and spake, and said unto his counselors, Did not we cast three men bound into the midst of the fire? They answered and said unto the king, True, O King. He answered and said, Lo, I see four men loose, walking in the midst of the fire, and they have no hurt; and the form of the fourth is like a Son of the God."

32 Stanford, *Christopher Fry*, p. 207.

33 Joseph Wood Krutch, "Review of *A Sleep of Prisoners*," *The Nation*, CLXXII (November 3, 1951), 381.

34 Fry, "Drama in a House of Worship," p. 3.

CHAPTER 10

1 Nevill Coghill, "Hyaena and Bone," *Christian Drama*, I, 5 (February, 1948), 6; Henry Arthur Jones, "Religion and the Stage," *The Renascence of the English Drama* (London, 1885).

2 Gerald Weales, *Religion in Modern English Drama* (Philadelphia, 1961), pp. 266–272.

3 T. S. Eliot, "The Possibility of a Poetic Drama," in *The Sacred Wood: Essays on Poetry and Criticism* (London, 1920), pp. 63–64.

4 *Ibid.*, p. 66.

5 T. S. Eliot, "Religion and Literature," in *Selected Essays* (New York, 1950), p. 346.

6 George Every, *Christian Discrimination* (London, 1940), p. 21.

7 A less satisfactory variation is that used by Ronald Duncan in *This Way to the Tomb: A Masque and Anti-Masque* (London, 1946), where the choric figure harangues the audience but is revealed in the end to have his own serious limitations.

8 Malcolm MacKenzie Ross, *Poetry and Dogma: The Transfiguration of Eucharistic Symbols in Seventeenth Century English Poetry* (New Brunswick, 1954), p. 249.

9 *Ibid.*

10 Weales, *Religion*, p. 272.

11 F. R. Leavis, "The Logic of Christian Discrimination," *The Common Pursuit* (London, 1952), p. 253.

12 Nathan A. Scott, "Mimesis and Time in Modern Literature," in *The Scope of Grace*, ed. Philip J. Hefner (Philadelphia, 1964), pp. 29–30.

SELECTED
BIBLIOGRAPHY

I PRIMARY SOURCES: *Plays*

Anonymous. *The Second Trial Before Pilate: The Scourging and Condemnation,*
in *The York Cycle of Mystery Plays: A Complete Version,* ed. and tr. J. S.
Purvis. New York: Macmillan, 1957.
Auden, W. H. *For the Time Being: A Christmas Oratorio,* in *The Collected Poetry.*
New York: Random House, 1945, pp. 403–466.
Auden, W. H., and Christopher Isherwood. *The Ascent of F6.* London: Faber and
Faber, 1946.
———. *The Dog Beneath the Skin, or Where Is Francis?* New York: Random
House, 1935.
Binyon, Laurence. *The Young King.* London: Macmillan, 1935.
Bottomley, Gordon. *The Acts of Saint Peter: A Cathedral Festival Play.* London:
Constable, 1933.

Bottomley, Gordon. *Choric Plays and a Comedy*. London: Constable, 1939.
———. *Gruach and Britain's Daughter*. Boston: Small, Maynard & Co., 1921.
———. *Kate Kennedy*. London: Constable, 1945.
———. *King Lear's Wife and Other Plays*. Boston: Small, Maynard & Co., 1915.
———. *Lyric Plays*. New York: Macmillan, 1932.
———. *Poems and Plays*. With an Introduction by Claude Colleer Abbott. London: The Bodley Head, 1953.
———. *Scenes and Plays*. New York: Macmillan, 1929.
Buckton, A. M. *Eager Heart*, in *The Story of Christmas*, ed. R. J. Campbell. New York: Macmillan, 1934.
Duncan, Ronald. *The Death of Satan: A Comedy*. London: Faber and Faber, 1955.
———. *Don Juan*. London: Faber and Faber, 1954.
———. *The Dull Ass's Hoof* (containing *Ora Pro Nobis, Pimp, Skunk and Profiteer*, and *The Unburied Dead*). London: Fortune Press, 1940.
———. *Our Lady's Tumbler*. London: Faber and Faber, 1951.
———. *The Rape of Lucretia*. London: Faber and Faber, 1953.
———. *Stratton*. London: Faber and Faber, 1950.
———. *This Way to the Tomb: A Masque and Anti-Masque*. London: Faber and Faber, 1946.
Eliot, T. S. *The Complete Poems and Plays, 1909–1950*. New York: Harcourt, Brace, 1952.
———. *The Confidential Clerk*. London: Faber and Faber, 1954.
———. *The Elder Statesman*. London: Faber and Faber, 1959.
———. *The Rock: A Pageant Play*. London: Faber and Faber, 1934.
Fry, Christopher. *The Boy with a Cart: Cuthman, Saint of Sussex*. New York: Oxford University Press, 1950.
———. *Curtmantle*. London: Oxford University Press, 1961.
———. *The Dark Is Light Enough: A Winter Comedy*. New York: Oxford University Press, 1954.
———. *The Firstborn: A Play in Three Acts*. London: Oxford University Press, 1950.
———. *The Lady's Not for Burning*. London: Oxford University Press, 1950.
———. *A Phoenix Too Frequent: A Comedy*. London: Oxford University Press, 1951.
———. *A Sleep of Prisoners*. New York: Oxford University Press, 1951.
———. *Thor, with Angels*. London: Oxford University Press, 1950.
———. *Venus Observed: A Play*. New York: Oxford University Press, 1950.
Gittings, Robert. *The Makers of Violence*. London: Heinemann, 1951.
———. *Man's Estate*, in *Two Saint's Plays*, by Leo Lehman and Robert Gittings. London: Heinemann, 1954.
———. *Parson Herrick's Parishioners*, in *Out of This Wood*. London: Heinemann, 1955.
Hassall, Christopher. *Christ's Comet: The Story of a Thirty Years' Journey That Began and Ended on the Same Day*, 1st ed. New York: Harcourt, Brace, 1938.
———. *Christ's Comet: The Story of a Thirty Years' Journey That Began and Ended on the Same Day*, 2d ed. London: Heinemann, 1958.
———. *Devil's Dyke with Compliment and Satire*. London: Heinemann, 1936.
———. *Out of the Whirlwind: A Play for Westminster Abbey*. London: Heinemann, 1953.
———. *Song of Simeon: A Nativity Masque for Mimers, Soloists, Mixed Chorus, and Orchestra*. London: Oxford University Press, 1960.
Heath-Stubbs, John. *Helen in Egypt and Other Plays*. London: Oxford University Press, 1958.
Housman, Laurence. *Bethlehem: A Nativity Play*. New York: Macmillan, 1902.

————. *Little Plays of St. Francis: A Dramatic Cycle from the Life and Legend of St. Francis of Assisi.* New York: Jonathan Cape and Harrison Smith (no date).

Ionesco, Eugène. *Four Plays,* tr. Donald M. Allen. New York: Grove Press, 1955.

Jarry, Alfred. *Ubu Roi: Drama in 5 Acts,* tr. Barbara Wright. New York: New Directions, 1961.

Kaye-Smith, Sheila. *Saints in Sussex* (containing *The Child Born at the Plough* and *The Shepherd of Lattenden*). New York: Dutton, 1927.

Lamb, Philip. *Go Down Moses.* London: published for the Religious Drama Society by the Society for Promoting Christian Knowledge, 1954.

————. *Sons of Adam.* London: The Sheldon Press, 1944.

Lee, Laurie. *Peasants' Priest.* Canterbury: H. J. Goulden, 1952.

MacLeish, Archibald. *J. B.: A Play in Verse.* Cambridge, Massachusetts: Riverside Press, 1961.

Masefield, John. *Collected Plays.* New York: Macmillan, 1918.

————. *The Coming of Christ.* New York: Macmillan, 1928.

————. *Easter.* London: Heinemann, 1929.

————. *The Trial of Jesus.* New York: Macmillan, 1925.

Nicholson, Norman. *A Match for the Devil.* London: Faber and Faber, 1955.

————. *The Old Man of the Mountains: A Play in Three Acts,* 4th impression. London: Faber and Faber, 1955.

————. *Prophesy to the Wind: A Play in Four Scenes and a Prologue.* London: Faber and Faber, 1950.

Obey, André. *Noah,* tr. Arthur Wilmurt. New York: Samuel French, 1934.

Ridler, Anne. *Cain: A Play in Two Acts.* London: Nicholson and Watson, 1943.

————. *Henry Bly and Other Plays (The Mark; The Missing Bridegroom).* London: Faber and Faber, 1950.

————. *The Shadow Factory: A Nativity Play.* London: Faber and Faber, 1946.

————. *The Trial of Thomas Cranmer.* London: Faber and Faber, 1956.

Sayers, Dorothy. *The Devil to Pay: A Stage Play.* New York: Harcourt, Brace, 1937.

————. *The Emperor Constantine.* New York: Harper, 1951.

————. *Four Sacred Plays* (containing *The Devil to Pay; The Zeal of Thy House; The Just Vengeance; He That Should Come*), 2d ed. London: Victor Gollancz, 1957.

————. *The Man Born to Be King: A Play-Cycle on the Life of Our Lord and Saviour Jesus Christ.* London: Victor Gollancz, 1943.

————. *The Mocking of Christ,* in *Catholic Tales and Christian Songs.* Oxford: B. H. Blackwell, 1918.

————. *The Zeal of Thy House.* London: Victor Gollancz, 1937.

Smith, Lucy Toulmin, ed. *York Plays: The Plays Performed by the Crafts or Mysteries of York on the Day of Corpus Christi.* Oxford: Clarendon Press, 1885.

Synge, John M. *The Complete Works of John M. Synge.* New York: Random House, 1935.

Turner, Phillip W. *Christ in the Concrete City.* London: Published for the Religious Drama Society by the Society for Promoting Christian Knowledge, 1956.

Ward, R. H. *The Destiny of Man.* Ilkley, Yorkshire: Published for "The Theatre of Persons" by the Adelphi Players, 1943.

————. *Faust in Hell.* London: Published for "The Theatre of Persons" by the Adelphi Players, 1945.

————. *The Figure on the Cross.* London: Published for the Religious Drama Society by the Society for Promoting Christian Knowledge, 1952.

————. *Holy Family.* Ilkley, Yorkshire: Published for "The Theatre of Persons" by the Adelphi Players, 1943.

Ward, R. H. *The Prodigal Son*. London: Published for the Religious Drama Society by the Society for Promoting Christian Knowledge, 1952.
——. *The Wanderer*. London: Society for Promoting Christian Knowledge, 1962
——. *The Wise and the Foolish Virgins*. London: The Religious Drama Society, 1949.
Williams, Charles. *Collected Plays* (containing *Thomas Cranmer of Canterbury; Judgement at Chelmsford; Seed of Adam; The Death of Good Fortune; The House by the Stable; Grab and Grace, or It's the Second Step; The House of the Octopus; Terror of Light;* and *The Three Temptations*), ed. John Heath-Stubbs. London: Oxford University Press, 1963.
Williamson, Hugh Ross. *His Eminence of England*. London: Heinemann, 1953. (Prose).
Yeats, W. B. *The Collected Plays of W. B. Yeats*. London: Macmillan, 1953.

II PRIMARY SOURCES: *Commentary and Other*

Bottomley, Gordon. "Poetry and the Contemporary Theatre," *Essays and Studies by Members of the English Association*, XIX, ed. D. Nichol Smith. Oxford: Clarendon Press, 1934, pp. 137–147.
——. "Poetry Seeks a New Home," *Theatre Arts Monthly*, XIII, 12 (December, 1929), 920–926.
Duncan, Ronald. "The Language of Theatre To-day," *Drama*, N.S., 50 (Autumn, 1958), 25–27.
Eliot, T. S. *After Strange Gods: A Primer of Modern Heresy*. New York: Harcourt, Brace, 1934.
——. "The Aims of Poetic Drama," *Adam International Review*, 200 (November, 1949), 10–16.
——. *Essays on Elizabethan Drama*. New York: Harvest Books, 1956.
——. *The Idea of a Christian Society*. New York: Harcourt, Brace, 1940.
——. "Introduction," *Shakespeare and the Popular Dramatic Tradition*, by S. L. Bethell. London: Staples Press, 1948.
——. Letter to the Editor on *The Rock*, *The Spectator*, 152, 5528 (June 8, 1937), 887.
——. "The Need for Poetic Drama," *Listener*, XVI, 411 (November 25, 1936), 994–995.
——. *Notes towards the Definition of Culture*. New York: Harcourt, Brace, 1949.
——. *On Poetry and Poets*. London: Faber and Faber, 1957.
——. *Religious Drama: Mediaeval and Modern*. New York: House of Books, 1954. Unpaginated.
——. *The Sacred Wood: Essays on Poetry and Criticism*. London: Methuen, 1920.
——. *Selected Essays*, enl. ed. New York: Harcourt, Brace, 1950.
——. "Ulysses, Order, and Myth," *Forms of Modern Fiction*, ed. William Van O'Connor. Bloomington: Indiana University Press, 1959, pp. 120–124.
——. *The Use of Poetry and the Use of Criticism: Studies in the Relation of Criticism to Poetry in England*. Cambridge, Massachusetts: Harvard University Press, 1933.
Fry, Christopher. *An Experience of Critics*. London: Perpetua, 1952.
——. "Comedy," *Tulane Drama Review*, IV, 3 (March, 1960), 77–79.
——. "Comments on John Gielgud's Production of *The Lady's Not for Burning*," *World Review*, N. S., 4 (June, 1959), 21.
——. "Dedicatory Letter to Robert Gittings," *A Sleep of Prisoners*. London: Oxford University Press, 1952.

———. "Drama in a House of Worship," *New York Times* (October 14, 1951), sect. 2, p. 3.
———. "Headpiece," *Christian Drama*, II, 1 (June, 1951), unpaginated.
———. "A Playwright Speaks," *Listener*, XLII (February 23, 1950), 331–332.
———. "Poetry and the Theatre," *Adam International Review*, XIX, 16, 214–215 (1951), 2–10.
Hassall, Christopher. "Notes on the Verse Drama," *The Masque*, 6. London: The Curtain Press, 1948.
Nicholson, Norman. "The Abandoned Muse," *Theatre Arts*, XXXII, 5 (Fall, 1948), 70.
———. *Man and Literature*. London: SCM Press, 1943.
———. "Modern Verse-Drama and the Folk Tradition," *Critical Quarterly*, II, 2 (Summer, 1960), 166–170.
———. "The Poet Needs an Audience," *Orpheus: A Symposium of the Arts*, I, ed. John Lehmann. London: John Lehmann, 1948, pp. 147–154.
———. "T. S. Eliot," *Writers of To-day*, ed. Denys Val Baker. London: Sidgwick & Jackson, 1946.
Ridler, Anne. "Introduction," *Seed of Adam and Other Plays*, by Charles Williams. London: Oxford University Press, 1948, pp. i–x.
———. "A Question of Speech," *T. S. Eliot: A Study of His Writing by Several Hands*, ed. B. Rajan. London, 1948, pp. 107–118.
———. "The Passion in Drama," *Drama*, 27 (Summer, 1955), 7–10.
Sayers, Dorothy L. *Further Papers on Dante*. New York: Harper, 1957.
———. *Introductory Papers on Dante*. London: Methuen, 1954.
———. *The Mind of the Maker*. New York: Meridian Books, 1956.
———. *The Poetry of Search and the Poetry of Statement and Other Posthumous Essays on Literature, Religion and Language*. London: Victor Gollancz, 1963.
———. "Review of *The House of the Octopus*," *International Review of Missions*, 34 (1945), 430–432.
———. "Towards a Christian Aesthetic," *Unpopular Opinions: Twenty-one Essays*. London: Victor Gollancz, 1946, pp. 29–43.
Ward, R. H. "Elements of Religious Drama, I," *Christian Drama*, I, 2 (April, 1947), 2–5.
———. "Elements of Religious Drama, II," *Christian Drama*, I, 3 (July, 1947), 3–9.
———. "Elements of Religious Drama, III," *Christian Drama*, I, 4 (November, 1947), 5–9.
———. "Imagination Breaks Through," *Christian Drama*, I, 9 (April, 1949), 3–5.
———. "The Nature of Religious Drama," *London Quarterly and Holborn Review*, 179 (1954), 251–256.
———. "Plays in Churches, I," *Christian Drama*, I, 6 (June, 1948), 6–8.
Williams, Charles. *All Hallows' Eve*. London: Faber and Faber, 1945.
———. *Arthurian Torso: Containing the Posthumous Fragment of The Figure of Arthur by Charles Williams and a Commentary on the Arthurian Poems of Charles Williams*, ed. C. S. Lewis. London: Oxford University Press, 1948.
———. "Boars of Vau," *Time and Tide*, 24, 3 (January 16, 1943), 50–52.
———. *Descent into Hell*. London: Faber and Faber, 1949.
———. *The Descent of the Dove: A History of the Holy Spirit in the Church*, introd. W. H. Auden. New York: Meridian Books, 1956.
———. *The Figure of Beatrice: A Study in Dante*. London: Faber and Faber, 1943.
———. *He Came Down from Heaven and The Forgiveness of Sins*. London: Faber and Faber, 1950.
———. *The Image of the City and Other Essays*, ed. Anne Ridler. London: Oxford University Press, 1958.
———. "Notes on the Way," *Time and Tide*, 22, 37 (September 13, 1941), 769.

Williams, Charles. "Notes on the Way," *Time and Tide*, 23, 9 (February 28, 1942), 170–171.
———. "Prefatory Note," *Judgement at Chelmsford*. London: Oxford University Press, 1933, p. 3.
———. *Poetry at Present*. Oxford: Clarendon Press, 1931.
———. *Reason and Beauty in the Poetic Mind*. Oxford: Clarendon Press, 1933.
———. *Taliessen Through Logres and The Region of the Summer Stars*. London: Oxford University Press, 1954.
Williamson, Hugh Ross. "What Is Christian Drama?" *Christian Drama*, I, 13 (July, 1950), 2–4.

III SECONDARY SOURCES: *Books*

Andreach, Robert J. *Studies in Structure: The Stages of the Spiritual Life of Four Modern Authors* [Gerard Manley Hopkins, James Joyce, T. S. Eliot, Hart Crane]. London: Burns and Oates, 1964.
Auerbach, Erich. *Mimesis: The Representation of Reality in Western Literature*, tr. Willard Trask. Garden City, New York: Anchor Books, 1957.
Bainbridge-Bell, Kathleen, and June Ottaway. *A Brief Historical Sketch of the Religious Drama Society of Great Britain*. London: The Religious Drama Society of Great Britain (no date).
———, and Jessie Powell. *A Catalogue of Selected Plays*. London: The Religious Drama Society of Great Britain, 1951.
Baxter, Kay M. *Contemporary Theatre and the Christian Faith*. Nashville: Abingdon Press, 1964.
Berdyaev, Nicolas. *The Meaning of the Creative Act*, tr. Donald A. Lowrie. New York: Harper, 1955.
Bergson, Henri. *Time and Free Will: An Essay on the Immediate Data of Consciousness*, tr. F. L. Pogson. New York: Macmillan, 1910.
Bethell, S. L. *The Cultural Revolution of the Seventeenth Century*. London: Dennis Dobson, 1951.
———. *Essays on Literary Criticism and the English Tradition*. London: Dennis Dobson, 1948.
———. *Shakespeare and the Popular Dramatic Tradition*, introd. T. S. Eliot. Westminster: King and Staples, 1944.
———. *The Winter's Tale: A Study*. London: Staples Press (no date).
Bodkin, Maud. *The Quest for Salvation in an Ancient and a Modern Play*. London: Oxford University Press, 1941.
Bradbrook, M. C. *T. S. Eliot, Writers and Their Works: 8*, rev. ed., gen. ed. Bonamy Dobrée. London: Published for the British Council and the National Book League by Longmans, Green, 1960.
Braybrook, Neville, ed. *T. S. Eliot: A Symposium for His Seventieth Birthday*. New York: Farrar, Straus and Cudahy, 1958.
Bryant, Joseph Allen, Jr. *Hippolyta's View: Some Christian Aspects of Shakespeare's Plays*. Lexington: University of Kentucky Press, 1961.
Buber, Martin. *Between Man and Man*, tr. Ronald Gregor Smith. London: Routledge & Kegan Paul, 1949.
———. *I and Thou*, 2d ed., tr. Ronald Gregor Smith. New York: Charles Scribner's Sons, 1958.
Coleridge, Samuel T. *The Complete Works of Samuel Taylor Coleridge*, ed. W. G. T. Shedd. 7 vols. New York: Harper and Brothers, 1860.
Crutwell, Patrick. *The Shakespearean Moment and Its Place in the Poetry of the Seventeenth Century*. New York: Modern Library Paperbacks, 1960.

Cullman, Oscar. *Christ and Time: The Primitive Christian Conception of Time and History*, 2d ed., tr. Floyd V. Filson. London: Student Christian Movement Press, 1962.

Demant, V. A., ed. *Our Culture: Its Christian Roots and Present Crisis.* London: Society for Promoting Christian Knowledge, 1947.

Donoghue, Denis.. *The Third Voice: Modern British and American Verse Drama.* Princeton, New Jersey: Princeton University Press, 1959.

Drew, Elizabeth. *T. S. Eliot: The Design of His Poetry.* New York: Charles Scribner's Sons, 1949.

Driver, Tom F. *The Sense of History in Greek and Shakespearean Drama.* New York: Columbia University Press, 1960.

Eastman, Fred. *Christ in the Drama.* New York: Macmillan, 1947.

Ellis-Fermor, Una. *The Irish Dramatic Movement*, 2d ed. London: Methuen, 1954.

Esslin, Martin. *The Theatre of the Absurd.* Garden City: Anchor Books, 1961.

Every, George, S. S. M. *Christian Discrimination.* London: Sheldon Press, 1940.

——. *Poetry and Personal Responsibility: An Interim Report on Contemporary Literature. Viewpoints: Contemporary Issues of Thought and Life, 14.* London: Student Christian Movement Press, 1949.

Fergusson, Francis. *The Idea of a Theatre, a Study of Ten Plays: The Art of Drama in Changing Perspective.* Princeton, New Jersey: Princeton University Press, 1949.

Frank, Joseph. *The Widening Gyre: Crisis and Mastery in Modern Literature.* New Brunswick, New Jersey: Rutgers University Press, 1963.

Fullman, Christopher Edward. "The Mind and Art of Charles Williams: A Study of His Poetry, Plays and Novels." Unpublished Ph.D. thesis, University of Wisconsin, 1954.

Gardner, Helen L. *The Art of T. S. Eliot.* New York: Dutton, 1950.

George, A. G. *T. S. Eliot: His Mind and Art.* New York: Asia Publishing House, 1962.

Hadfield, Alice Mary. *An Introduction to Charles Williams.* London: Robert Hale, 1959.

Heath-Stubbs, John. *Charles Williams, Writers and Their Work: 63*, gen. ed. Bonamy Dobrée. London: Published for the British Council and the National Book League by Longmans, Green, 1955.

Heidegger, Martin. *Being and Time*, tr. John Macquarrie and Edward Robinson. New York: Harper, 1962.

Heller, Erich. *The Disinherited Mind.* Cambridge: Bowes and Bowes, 1952.

——. *The Hazard of Modern Poetry.* Cambridge: Bowes and Bowes, 1953.

Hopper, Stanley Romaine. *The Crisis of Faith.* Nashville, Tennessee: Abingdon-Cokesbury Press, 1944.

——, ed. *Spiritual Problems in Contemporary Literature.* New York: Harper Torchbooks, 1957.

Howarth, Herbert. *The Irish Writers: Literature and Nationalism, 1880–1940.* New York: Hill and Wang, 1959.

——. *Notes on Some Figures Behind T. S. Eliot.* Boston: Houghton Mifflin, 1964.

Hulme, T. E. *Further Speculations*, ed. Sam Hynes. Lincoln: University of Nebraska Press, 1962.

——. *Speculations: Essays on Humanism and the Philosophy of Art*, ed. Herbert Read. New York: Harcourt, Brace, 1924.

Irving, Laurence. *The Canterbury Adventure: An Account of the Inception and Growth of the Friends of Canterbury Cathedral, 1928–1959.* Canterbury: The Friends of Canterbury Cathedral, printed by J. A. Jennings, 1959.

Jarrett-Kerr, Martin. *Studies in Literature and Belief.* London: Rockliff, 1954.

Jones, David E. *The Plays of T. S. Eliot*. London: Routledge & Kegan Paul, 1960.

Jones, Henry Arthur. *The Renascence of the English Drama: Essays, Lectures, and Fragments, Relating to the Modern English Stage, Written and Delivered in the Years 1883–1894*. London: Macmillan, 1895.

Kahler, Erich. *The Tower and the Abyss*. New York: George Braziller, 1957.

Kenner, Hugh. *The Invisible Poet: T. S. Eliot*. New York: McDowell, Obolensky, 1959.

Kermode, Frank. *Romantic Image*. London: Routledge & Kegan Paul, 1957.

Kierkegaard, Søren. *The Concept of Dread*, tr. Walter Lowrie. Princeton, New Jersey: Princeton University Press, 1944.

———. *Either/Or: A Fragment of Life*, Vol. I, tr. David and Lillian Swenson. Princeton, New Jersey: Princeton University Press, 1946.

———. *Either/Or*, Vol. II, tr. Walter Lowrie. Princeton, New Jersey: Princeton University Press, 1946.

———. *Fear and Trembling: A Dialectical Lyric*, tr. Walter Lowrie. Princeton, New Jersey: Princeton University Press, 1941.

———. *Philosophical Fragments: Or, A Fragment of Philosophy*, tr. David F. Swenson. Princeton, New Jersey: Princeton University Press, 1941.

———. *The Sickness unto Death*, tr. Walter Lowrie. Princeton, New Jersey: Princeton University Press, 1941.

Kitto, H. D. F. *Form and Meaning in Drama: A Study of Six Greek Plays and of "Hamlet."* New York: Barnes and Noble, 1950.

Krutch, Joseph Wood. *The Modern Temper: A Study and a Confession*. New York: Harvest Books, 1956.

Lewis, C. S. *The Allegory of Love: A Study in Medieval Tradition*. London: Oxford University Press, 1936.

———. ed. *Essays Presented to Charles Williams*. London: Oxford University Press, 1947.

Lewis, Wyndham. *Time and Western Man*. Boston: Beacon Press, 1957.

Lucy, Sean. *T. S. Eliot and the Idea of Tradition*. London: Cohen & West, 1960.

Lynch, William F., S.J. *Christ and Apollo: The Dimensions of the Literary Imagination*. New York: Sheed and Ward, 1960.

Mannheim, Karl. *Diagnosis of Our Time: Wartime Essays of a Sociologist*. London: Kegan Paul, Trench, Trubner, 1943.

March, Richard, and Tambimuttu, ed. *T. S. Eliot, a Symposium*. Chicago: Henry Regnery, 1949.

Maritain, Jacques. *The Dream of Descartes*, tr. Mabelle L. Andison. New York: Philosophical Library, 1944.

———. *The Twilight of Civilization*, tr. Lionel Landry. New York: Sheed and Ward, 1943.

Matthiessen, F. O. *The Achievement of T. S. Eliot: An Essay on the Nature of Poetry*, 3d ed. New York: Oxford University Press, 1959.

Maxwell, D. E. S. *The Poetry of T. S. Eliot*. London: Routledge & Kegan Paul, 1952.

May, Rollo, ed. *Symbolism in Religion and Literature*. New York: George Braziller, 1961.

Melchiori, Giorgio. *The Tightrope Walkers: Studies of Mannerism in Modern English Literature*. London: Routledge & Kegan Paul, 1956.

Meyerhoff, Hans. *Time in Literature*. Berkeley: University of California Press, 1955.

Moorman, Charles. *Arthurian Triptych: Mythic Materials in Charles Williams, C. S. Lewis, and T. S. Eliot*. Berkeley: University of California Press, 1960.

———. *The Precincts of Felicity: The Augustinian City of the Oxford Christians*. Gainesville: University of Florida Press, 1966.

Nicholson, Marjorie Hope. *The Breaking of the Circle: Studies in the Effect of the "New Science" upon Seventeenth Century Poetry.* Evanston, Illinois: Northwestern University Press, 1950.

Nott, Kathleen. *The Emperor's Clothes.* Bloomington: Indiana University Press, 1958.

Peacock, Ronald. *The Art of the Drama.* London: Routledge & Kegan Paul, 1957.

———. *The Poet in the Theatre.* New York: Harcourt, Brace, 1946.

Poulet, Georges. *Studies in Human Time,* tr. Elliott Coleman. New York: Harper Torchbooks, 1959.

Preston, Raymond. *"Four Quartets" Rehearsed: A Commentary on T. S. Eliot's Cycle of Poems.* New York: Sheed and Ward, 1946.

Prior, Moody E. *The Language of Tragedy.* New York: Columbia University Press, 1947.

Rahv, Philip. *The Myth and the Powerhouse: Essays on Literature and Ideas.* New York: Farrar, Straus and Giroux, 1965.

Rajan, B., ed. *T. S. Eliot: A Study of His Writings by Several Hands.* London: Dennis Dobson, 1948.

Ramsey, Arthur Michael, D.D. *An Era of Anglican Theology from Gore to Temple: The Development of Anglican Theology Between Lux Mundi and the Second World War, 1889–1939.* New York: Charles Scribner's Sons, 1960.

Roberts, David. *Existentialism and Religious Belief,* ed. Roger Hazelton. New York: Oxford University Press, 1959.

Ross, Malcolm MacKenzie. *Poetry and Dogma: The Transfiguration of Eucharistic Symbols in Seventeenth Century English Poetry.* New Brunswick, New Jersey: Rutgers University Press, 1954.

Rossiter, A. P. *English Drama from Early Times to the Elizabethans: Its Background, Origins and Developments.* London: Hutchinson, 1950.

Scott, Nathan A., Jr. *The Broken Center: Studies in the Theological Horizon of Modern Literature.* New Haven: Yale University Press, 1966.

———. ed. *The Climate of Faith in Modern Literature.* New York: Seabury Press, 1964.

———. *Modern Literature and the Religious Frontier.* New York: Harper, 1958.

———, ed. *The New Orpheus: Essays Toward a Christian Poetic.* New York: Sheed and Ward, 1964.

———. *Rehearsals of Discomposure: Alienation and Reconciliation in Modern Literature: Franz Kafka, Ignazio Silone, D. H. Lawrence, T. S. Eliot.* New York: King's Crown Press, 1952.

———. *The Tragic Vision and the Christian Faith.* New York: Association Press, 1957.

Shideler, Mary McDermott. *Charles Williams: A Critical Essay.* Grand Rapids: William B. Eerdmans, 1966.

———. *The Theology of Romantic Love: A Study in the Writings of Charles Williams.* New York: Harper, 1962.

Smalley, Beryl. *The Study of the Bible in the Middle Ages.* New York: Philosophical Library, 1952.

Smidt, Kristian. *Poetry and Belief in the Work of T. S. Eliot,* 2d ed. New York: Humanities Press, 1961.

Smith, Carol H. *T. S. Eliot's Dramatic Theory and Practice.* Princeton, New Jersey: Princeton University Press, 1963.

Smith, Grover, Jr. *T. S. Eliot's Poetry and Plays: A Study in Sources and Meaning.* Chicago: University of Chicago Press, 1956.

Spanos, William V., ed. *A Casebook on Existentialism.* New York: Thomas Y. Crowell, 1966.

Speaight, Robert. *Christian Theatre.* New York: Hawthorn Books, 1960.

Speaight, Robert. *Drama since 1939*. London: Published for the British Council by
    Longmans, Green, 1947.
_____. *Nature in Shakespearean Tragedy*. London: Hollis and Carter, 1955.
_____. *Thomas Becket*. London: Longmans, Green, 1938.
_____. *William Poel and the Elizabethan Revival*. Cambridge, Massachusetts:
    Harvard University Press, 1954.
Spencer, Theodore. *Shakespeare and the Nature of Man*. New York: Macmillan,
    1949.
Stanford, Derek. *Christopher Fry, Writers and Their Work: 54*, rev. ed., gen. ed.
    Bonamy Dobrée. London: Published for The British Council and the Na-
    tional Book League by Longmans, Green, 1955.
_____. *Christopher Fry: An Appreciation*, 2d ed. London: Peter Neville, 1952.
Steiner, George. *The Death of Tragedy*. New York: Knopf, 1961.
Styan, J. L. *The Elements of Drama*. Cambridge: Cambridge University Press,
    1960.
Tate, Allen. *The Forlorn Demon: Didactic and Critical Essays*. Chicago: Henry
    Regnery, 1953.
_____. *The Man of Letters in the Modern World: Selected Essays, 1928–1955*.
    New York: Meridian Books, 1955.
Temple, William. *Nature, Man and God: Being the Gifford Lectures Delivered in
    the University of Glasgow in the Academical Years 1932–1933 and 1933–
    1934*. London: Macmillan, 1940.
Teselle, Sallie McFague. *Literature and the Christian Life*. New Haven: Yale Uni-
    versity Press, 1966.
Thouless, Priscilla. *Modern Poetic Drama*. Oxford: Basil Blackwell, 1934.
Tillyard, E. M. W. *The Elizabethan World Picture*. London: Chatto and Windus,
    1956.
_____. *Shakespeare's Last Plays*. London: Chatto and Windus, 1958.
Trilling, Lionel. *Matthew Arnold*. New York: Meridian Books, 1955.
Turnell, Martin. *Modern Literature and Christian Faith*. London: Darton, Long-
    man & Todd, 1961.
Unger, Leonard, ed. *T. S. Eliot, a Selected Critique*. New York: Rinehart, 1948.
_____. *The Man in the Name: Essays on the Experience of Poetry*. Minneapolis:
    University of Minnesota Press, 1956.
Weales, Gerald. *Religion in Modern English Drama*. Philadelphia: University of
    Pennsylvania Press, 1961.
Whale, J. S. *Christian Doctrine: Eight Lectures Delivered in the University of
    Cambridge to Undergraduates of All Faculties*. Cambridge: Cambridge Uni-
    versity Press, 1941.
Wheelwright, Phillip. *Metaphor and Reality*. Bloomington: Indiana University
    Press, 1962
Wilder, Amos. *Modern Poetry and the Christian Tradition: A Study in the Re-
    lation of Christianity to Culture*. New York: Charles Scribner's Sons, 1952.
_____. *The Spiritual Aspects of the New Poetry*. New York: Harper, 1940.
_____. *Theology and Modern Literature*. Cambridge, Massachusetts: Harvard
    University Press, 1958.
Willey, Basil. *The Seventeenth Century Background: Studies in the Thought of
    the Age in Relation to Poetry and Religion*. London: Chatto and Windus,
    1949.
Williams, Raymond. *Drama from Ibsen to Eliot*. New York: Oxford University
    Press, 1953.
Wilson, Edmund. *Axel's Castle: A Study in the Imaginative Literature of 1870 to
    1930*. New York: Charles Scribner's Sons, 1931.
Yeats, W. B. *The Collected Poems of W. B. Yeats*. New York: Macmillan, 1956.
_____. *Essays and Introductions*. New York: Macmillan, 1961.

—————. *The Irish Dramatic Movement,* in Vol. IV of *The Collected Works of William Butler Yeats,* 8 vols. Stratford-on-Avon: Shakespeare Head Press, 1908, pp. 79–232.

IV SECONDARY SOURCES: *Articles*

Adair, Patricia M. "Mr. Eliot's *Murder in the Cathedral,*" *Cambridge Journal,* IV, 2 (November, 1950), 83–95.

Adler, Jacob H. "Shakespeare and Christopher Fry," *Educational Theatre Journal,* XI (May, 1959), 85–98.

Alexander, John. "Christopher Fry and Religious Comedy," *Meanjin,* XV (Autumn, 1956), 77–81.

Arrowsmith, William. "English Verse Drama (II): *The Cocktail Party,*" *Hudson Review,* III, 3 (Autumn, 1950), 411–430.

—————. "Menander and Milk Wood," *Hudson Review,* VII, 2 (Summer, 1954), 291–296.

—————. "Notes on English Verse Drama: Christopher Fry, I," *Hudson Review,* III, 2 (Summer, 1950), 203–216.

—————. "Transfiguration in Eliot and Euripides," *Sewanee Review,* LXIII (1955), 421–442. Reprinted in *English Stage Comedy,* ed. W. K. Wimsatt, Jr., *English Institute Essays 1954.* New York: Columbia University Press, 1955, pp. 148–172.

Auden, W. H. "The Christian Tragic Hero: Contrasting Captain Ahab's Doom and Its Classic Greek Prototype," *New York Times Book Review* (December 16, 1945), 1, 21.

—————. "Introduction," *The Descent of the Dove: The History of the Holy Spirit in the Church,* by Charles Williams. New York: Meridian Books, 1956, pp. v–xii.

Auerbach, Erich. "Figura," tr. Ralph Manheim, *Scenes from the Drama of European Literature: Six Essays.* New York: Meridian Books, 1959, pp. 11–98.

Bain, Donald. "The Cocktail Party," *Nine,* II, 1 (January, 1950), 16–22.

Barrett, William. "Existentialism as a Symptom of Man's Contemporary Crisis," *Spiritual Problems in Contemporary Literature,* ed. Stanley Romaine Hopper. New York: Harper Torchbooks, 1957, 139–152.

Battenhouse, Roy. "Eliot's *The Family Reunion* as Christian Prophecy," *Christendom,* X, 3 (Summer, 1945), 307–321.

Baxter, Kay M. "On Being Too Highbrow," *Christian Drama,* I, 10 (July, 1949), 1–5.

—————. "A Visit to Sheffield," *Christian Drama,* II, 5 (Autumn, 1952), 9–11.

Belgion, Montgomery. "Review of *Seed of Adam and Other Plays,*" *Theology,* LII, 343 (January, 1949), 74–75.

—————. "The Theatre Today and Its Relation to Christian Thinking," *London Quarterly and Holborn Review* (July, 1960), 191–195.

Bell, George Kennedy, Lord Bishop of Chichester. Sermon Given at the Royal Academy of Dramatic Art Jubilee Service at S. Martin's in the Fields, June 25, 1954, reprinted in *Christian Drama,* II, 11 (Autumn, 1954), 16–19.

—————. "Sermon on *The Coming of Christ,*" preached at Wittersham Parish Church on Sunday, 13th December, 1953.

—————. Speech at the Annual General Meeting of the Religious Drama Society in November, 1954, reprinted in *Christian Drama,* II, 12 (Spring, 1955), 15–16.

—————. "Speech on the Church and Religious Drama," *The Chronicle of Convocation: Being a Record of the Proceedings of the Convocation of Canter-*

bury, *Session of January 14, 15, and 16, 1958.* London: Society for Promoting Christian Knowledge, 1958, pp. 81–87.

Bentley, Eric. "Yeats as a Playwright," *Kenyon Review*, X, 2 (Spring, 1948), 196–208.

Bethell, S. L. "Shakespeare's Theology," *Christian Drama*, I, 8 (January, 1949), 7–11

Blackmur, R. P. "T. S. Eliot: From *Ash Wednesday* to *Murder in the Cathedral*," *Form and Value in Modern Poetry*. Garden City, New York: Anchor Books, 1957, pp. 121–151.

Brooks, Cleanth. "Metaphor and the Function of Criticism," *Spiritual Problems in Contemporary Literature*, ed. Stanley Romaine Hopper. New York: Harper Torchbooks, 1957, pp. 127–138.

Browne, E. Martin. "The Church and Drama," *Church Quarterly Review*, CXIII (October, 1931), 66–70.

——. "The Church as Theatre," *Theatre Arts Monthly*, XV, 19 (October, 1931), 850–854.

——. "The Dramatic Verse of T. S. Eliot," *T. S. Eliot: A Symposium*, ed. Richard March and Tambimuttu. Chicago: Henry Regnery, 1949, pp. 196–207.

——. "From T. S. Eliot to Christopher Fry," *Adam International Review*, XIX, 16, 214–215 (1951), 14–16.

——. "From *The Rock* to *The Confidential Clerk*," *T. S. Eliot: A Symposium for His Seventieth Birthday*, ed. Neville Braybrooke. New York: Farrar, Straus and Cudahy, 1958, pp. 57–69.

——. "Judgement at Chelmsford," *Christian Drama*, I, 4 (November, 1947), 1–5.

——. "The Poet and the Stage," *The Penguin New Writing*, 31, ed. John Lehmann. London: Penguin Books, 1947, pp. 81–92.

——. "Poetry in the English Theatre," *Proceedings: Royal Institute of Great Britain*, XXXIV (1952), 287–293.

——. "Review of *Poet and Painter, Being the Correspondence of Gordon Bottomley and Paul Nash*," *Drama*, 37 (Summer, 1957), 6–7.

——. "*The Rock*: Ecclesiastical Revue," *Theatre Arts*, XVIII (1934), 927–928.

——. "Theatre Aims of T. S. Eliot," *New York Times* (January 15, 1950), sect. 2, p. 3.

Burghardt, Walter J., S.J. "On Early Christian Exegesis," *Theological Studies*, XI (1950), reprinted in William F. Lynch, S.J., "Supplement IV," *Christ and Apollo: The Dimensions of the Literary Imagination*. New York: Sheed and Ward, 1960.

Callan, Edward. "Auden and Kierkegaard: The Artistic Framework of *For the Time Being*," *Christian Scholar*, XLVIII, 3 (Fall, 1965), 211–223.

Coghill, Nevill. "Hyaena and Bone," *Christian Drama*, I, 5 (February, 1948), 5–8.

——. "The Trial of Thomas Cranmer," *Drama*, N.S., 42 (Autumn, 1956), 44–45.

Cornell, Corbin S. "Creation's Lonely Flesh: T. S. Eliot and Christopher Fry on the Life of the Senses," *Modern Drama*, VI, 2 (September, 1963), 141–149.

Cunliffe-Jones, Hubert. "Religious Drama and the Nonconformist Conscience," *Christian Drama*, I, 8 (January, 1949), 2–6.

Davey, F. N. "The Christian Religion and Drama," *Christian Drama*, I, 3 (July, 1947), 1–3.

——. "Question and Answer," *Christian Drama*, I, 11 (December, 1949), 1–3.

——. "Review of *The Cocktail Party*," *Christian Drama*, I, 7 (March, 1950), 8–9.

Dobrée, Bonamy. "Poetic Drama in England Today," *Southern Review*, IV (1938–1939), 581–599.

——. "Some London Plays," *Sewanee Review*, LXIII (Spring, 1955), 270–280.

Donoghue, Denis. "Christopher Fry's Theatre of Words," *Essays in Criticism,* IX (January, 1959), 37–49.

Eastman, Fred. "Religious Drama in England," *Christian Century,* 46, 2 (October 2, 1929), 1212–1214.

Every, George, S. S. M. "Charles Williams—I. The Accuser," *Theology,* LI, 333 (March, 1948), 95–100.

——. "Charles Williams—II. The City and the Substitution," *Theology,* LI, 334 (April, 1948), 145–150.

——. "The Way of Rejections," *T. S. Eliot: A Symposium,* ed. Richard March and Tambimuttu. Chicago: Henry Regnery, 1949.

Ferguson, John. "A Sleep of Prisoners," *English,* X (Summer, 1954), 42–47.

——. "*The Boy with a Cart,*" *Modern Drama,* VIII, 3 (December, 1965), 284–292.

Fergusson, Francis. "Myth and the Literary Scruple," *The Human Image in Dramatic Literature.* Garden City, New York: Anchor Books, 1957, pp. 161–175.

——. "T. S. Eliot's Poetry and Drama," *The Human Image in Dramatic Literature.* Garden City, New York: Anchor Books, 1957, pp. 98–104.

——. "Three Allegorists: Brecht, Wilder, and Eliot," *The Human Image in Dramatic Literature.* Garden City, New York: Anchor Books, 1957, pp. 41–71.

Gardner, Helen L. "*Four Quartets:* A Commentary," *T. S. Eliot: A Study of His Writings by Several Hands,* ed. B. Rajan. London: Dennis Dobson, 1947, pp. 57–77.

Gervase of Canterbury. "History of the Burning and Repair of the Church of Canterbury," *A Documentary History of Art,* I, ed. Elizabeth G. Holt. Garden City, New York: Anchor Books, 1957, pp. 51–62.

Heath-Stubbs, John. "Introduction," *Collected Plays of Charles Williams.* London: Oxford University Press, 1963, pp. v–xiii.

Heilman, Robert B. "*Alcestis* and *The Cocktail Party,*" *Comparative Literature,* V (1953), 105–116.

Hopper, Stanley Romaine. "The Problem of Moral Isolation in Contemporary Literature," *Spiritual Problems in Contemporary Literature.* New York: Harper Torchbooks, 1957, pp. 153–170.

James, G. Ingli. "The Autonomy of the Work of Art: Modern Criticism and the Christian Tradition," *Sewanee Review,* LXX, 2 (Spring, 1962), 296–318.

Jenkins, Daniel. "The Theologian and the Artist," *Christian Drama,* I, 14 (October, 1950), 4–8.

Johns, Eric. "Poet's Playhouse," *Theatre World,* XLIV (February, 1948), 28–31.

Kernodle, George R. "England's Religious-Drama Movement," *College English,* I, 5 (February, 1940), 414–426.

——. "Patterns of Belief in Contemporary Drama," *Spiritual Problems in Contemporary Literature,* ed. Stanley Romaine Hopper. New York: Harper Torchbooks, 1957, pp. 187–206.

Kornbluth, Martin L. "A Twentieth-Century Everyman," *College English,* 21, 1 (October, 1959), 26–29.

Krutch, Joseph Wood. "Review of *A Sleep of Prisoners,*" *The Nation,* CLXXII (November 3, 1951), 381.

Lambert, J. W. "The Verse Drama," *Theatre Programme,* ed. J. C. Trewin. London: Frederick Muller, 1954, pp. 51–72.

Leavis, F. R. "The Logic of Christian Discrimination," *The Common Pursuit.* London: Chatto & Windus, 1952, pp. 248–254.

Lecky, Eleazer. "Mystery in the Plays of Christopher Fry," *Tulane Drama Review,* IV, 3 (March, 1960), 80–87.

Lynch, William F., S.J. "Adventure in Order," *Thought*, XXVI, 100 (Spring, 1951), 33–49.
———. "Confusion in Our Theatre," *Thought*, XXVI, 102 (Autumn, 1951), 342–360.
———. "Theology and the Imagination, I," *Thought*, XXIX, 112 (March, 1954), 51–86.
———. "Theology and the Imagination, II," *Thought*, XXIX, 115 (December, 1954), 529–555.
Marshall, Norman. "The Plays of John Masefield," *The Bookman*, LXXIX, 471 (December, 1940), 164–165.
Martz, Louis L. "The Saint as Tragic Hero: *Saint Joan* and *Murder in the Cathedral*," *Tragic Themes in Western Literature*, ed. Cleanth Brooks. New Haven: Yale University Press, 1955, pp. 150–178.
———. "The Wheel and the Point: Aspects of Imagery and Theme in Eliot's Later Poetry," *T. S. Eliot, a Selected Critique*, ed. Leonard Unger. New York: Rinehart, 1948, 444–462.
Maura, Sister M. "Christopher Fry: An Angle of Experience," *Renascence*, VIII, 1 (Autumn, 1955), 3–11, 36.
McCall, John P., ed. "Supplement IV: Medieval Exegesis: Some Documents for the Literary Critic," *Christ and Apollo: The Dimensions of the Literary Imagination*, by William Lynch, S.J. New York: Sheed and Ward, 1960, 229–267.
McCulloch, Joseph. "Religious Drama," *Christian Drama*, II, 5 (Autumn, 1952), 1–9.
Mehta, Ved. "The New Theologian, II–The Ekklesia," *The New Yorker* (November 20, 1965), 60–144.
Mueller, W. R. "*Murder in the Cathedral*: An Imitation of Christ," *Religion in Life* (Summer, 1958), 414–426.
Palmer, Richard E. "Existentialism in T. S. Eliot's *The Family Reunion*," *Modern Drama*, V, 2 (September, 1962), 174–186.
Paul, Leslie, and Christopher Salmon. "Two Views of Mr. Eliot's New Play" [*The Elder Statesman*], *Listener*, LI (September 4, 1958), 340–341.
Peacock, Ronald. "Public and Private Problems in Modern Drama," *Tulane Drama Review*, III, 3 (March, 1959), 58–72.
Peter, John. "*The Family Reunion*," *Scrutiny*, XVI, 3 (September, 1949), 219–230.
Pottle, Frederick A. "Drama of Action," *Yale Review*, XXV, 2 (December, 1935), 426–430.
Prior, Moody E. "Poetic Drama: An Analysis and a Suggestion," *English Institute Essays, 1949*, ed. Alan Downer. New York: Columbia University Press, 1950, pp. 3–32.
Remington, Douglas. "Spirit or Goblin," *Christian Drama*, I, 10 (July, 1949), 6–8.
"Review of *The Coming of Christ*," *London Times*, LX, 22 (May 31, 1928), 611.
Robbins, Rossell Hope. "A Possible Analogue for *The Cocktail Party*," *English Studies*, XXXIV (1953), 165–167.
Robins, Carina. "The Trial of Thomas Cranmer," *Christian Drama*, III (Autumn, 1956), 24–25.
Ross, Malcolm MacKenzie. "The Theatre and Social Confusion," *University of Toronto Quarterly*, V, 2 (January, 1936), 197–215.
Rougemont, Denis de. "Conference on Art at the Oecumenical Institute," *Christian Drama*, I, 14 (October, 1950), 9–13.
———. "Religion and the Mission of the Artist," *Spiritual Problems in Contemporary Literature*, ed. Stanley Romaine Hopper. New York: Harper Torchbooks, 1957, pp. 173–186.
Scott, Nathan A., Jr. "The Bias of Comedy and the Narrow Escape into Faith," *Christian Scholar*, XLIV, 1 (Spring, 1961), 9–39.

————. "The Broken Center: A Definition of the Crisis of Values in Modern Literature," *Chicago Review*, XIII, 2 (Summer, 1959), 182–202.

————. "Mimesis and Time in Modern Literature," *The Scope of Grace*, ed. Philip J. Hefner. Philadelphia: Fortress Press, 1964, pp. 3–40.

————. "The Realism of Erich Auerbach," *The Christian Scholar*, XXXVII, 4 (December, 1954), 538–547.

————. "T. S. Eliot's *The Cocktail Party*: Of Redemption and Vocation," *Religion in Life*, XX, 2 (Spring, 1951), 274–285.

Shear, Bernice, and Eugene Prater. "Christopher Fry: A Bibliography," *Tulane Drama Review*, IV, 3 (March, 1960), 88–98.

Sinclair, Margaret. "Evangelism by Drama," *International Review of Missions*, XXXVI (April, 1947), 287–289.

Smith, Janet Adam. "Review of *Thomas Cranmer of Canterbury*," *Criterion*, XVI, lxii (October, 1936), 140–143.

Spanos, William V. "Abraham, Sisyphus, and the Furies: Some Introductory Notes on Existentialism," *A Casebook on Existentialism*, ed. William V. Spanos. New York: Thomas Y. Crowell, 1966, pp. 1–13.

————. "Charles Williams' *Judgement at Chelmsford*: A Study in the Aesthetic of Sacramental Time," *Christian Scholar*, XLV, 2 (Summer, 1962), 107–117.

————. "Charles Williams' *Seed of Adam*: The Existential Flight from Death," *Christian Scholar*, XLIX, 2 (Summer, 1966), 105–118.

————. "Christian Drama and the Contemporary Religious Consciousness," *Christian Scholar*, XLVI, 4 (Winter, 1963), 317–323.

————. "Christopher Fry's *A Sleep of Prisoners*: The Choreography of Comedy," *Modern Drama*, VIII, 1 (May, 1965), 58–72.

————. "*Murder in the Cathedral*: The *Figura* as Mimetic Principle," *Drama Survey*, III, 2 (Fall, 1963), 206–223.

————. "T. S. Eliot's *The Family Reunion*: The Strategy of Sacramental Transfiguration," *Drama Survey*, IV, 1 (Spring, 1965), 3–27.

Spears, Monroe K. "Christopher Fry and the Redemption of Joy," *Poetry*, LXXVIII, 1 (April, 1951), 28–43.

Spencer, Theodore. "Man's Spiritual Situation as Reflected in Modern Drama," *Spiritual Problems in Contemporary Literature*, ed. Stanley Romaine Hopper. New York: Harper Torchbooks, 1957, pp. 45–58.

Spender, Stephen. "Review of Duncan's *Death of Satan* and Nicholson's *Match for the Devil*," *London Magazine*, 2, 12 (December, 1955), 77–82.

Stamm, Rudolph. "Christopher Fry and the Revolt Against Realism in Modern Drama," *Anglia*, LXXII, 1 (1954), 78–109.

Stanford, Derek. "God in the Drama of Christopher Fry," *London Quarterly and Holborn Review* (April, 1957), 124–130.

Stanley-Wrench, Margaret. "But Why Verse . . . ?" *Christian Drama*, II, 10 (Summer, 1954), 11–15.

Townsend, C. "Review of Masefield's *The Coming of Christ*," *The Spectator*, 140, 5214 (June 2, 1928), 824–825.

Trilling, Lionel. "Wordsworth and the Iron Time," *Kenyon Review*, XII, 3 (Summer, 1950), 477–497.

Vale, Terence. "Lest One Good Custom," *Christian Drama*, I, 5 (February, 1948), 10–12.

Verschoyle, Derek. "Review of *The Rock*," *The Spectator*, 152 (June 1, 1934), 851.

Versinger, Georgette. "Etudes Critiques: Charles Williams," *Etudes Anglaises*, XVIII, 3 (July–September, 1965), 285–295.

Ward, Anne. "Speculations on Eliot's Time-World: An Analysis of *The Family Reunion* in Relation to Hulme and Bergson," *American Literature*, XXI (1949), 18–34.

Weisstein, Ulrich. "*The Cocktail Party:* An Attempt at Interpretation on Mythological Grounds," *Western Review,* XVI, 3 (Spring, 1952), 232–241.
Wilkinson, Burke. "A Most Serious Comedy by Eliot," *New York Times* (February, 7, 1954), sect. 2, p. 1.
Zabel, M. D. "Poetry for the Theatre," *Poetry: A Magazine of Verse,* XLV, iii (December, 1934), 152–158.

INDEX